*This is dedicated
with love and thanksgiving for His
Unmerited Awe-Inspiring Love, Glory,
Mercy, Truth, and Faithfulness
to our
Father God,
LORD Jesus Christ,
and the Holy Spirit,
Who never fails us nor forsakes us.*

KNOWING GOD IN YOUR HEART – ISBN AND SCRIPTURE CREDIT PAGE

ISBN 978-1-935529-99-6
Copyright © 2011 by Barbara S. Waddell
Printed in the United States of America

No part of this publication may be reproduced, stored in a retrieval system, or transmitted in any form by any means ~ electronic, mechanical, digital photocopy, recording, or any other without the prior permission of the author.

All rights reserved solely by the author. The author guarantees all contents are original and do not infringe upon the legal rights of any other person or work. You may use brief quotations from this book in reviews, presentations, articles and books not to exceed 500 words. No part of this book may be reproduced in any form without the permission of the author. Resources are offered for free download on www.knowinggodinyourheart.com.

Scripture quotations taken from the *New American Standard Bible®*, Copyright © 1960, 1962, 1963, 1968, 1971, 1972, 1973,1975, 1977, 1995 by The Lockman Foundation Used by permission. (www.Lockman.org).

Scripture quotations taken from the *New King James Version,* Copyright © 1982 by Thomas Nelson, Inc. Used by permission. All rights reserved.

Scripture quotations taken from the *Holy Bible, New International Bible®*, Copyright © 1973, 1978, 1984 Biblica. Used by permission of Zondervan. All rights reserved.

Scripture quotations taken from the *Amplified® Bible* Copyright © 1954, 1958, 1962, 1964, 1965, 1987 by The Lockman Foundation. Used by permission. (www.Lockman.org).

Scripture quotations taken from *The Message*. Copyright © 1993, 1994, 1995, 1996, 2000, 2001, 2002. Used by permission of NavPress Publishing Group.

Scripture quotations taken from the *Jewish New Testament.* © 1989 by Dr. David H. Stern, P.O. Box 615, Clarksville, MD 21029, (410) 764-6144. Used with permission.

KNOWING GOD IN YOUR HEART

IN THREE SERIES

The WAY ~ Lessons I-III
INTIMACY WITH CHRIST
RIGHT THOUGHTS AND ATTITUDES
SPIRITUAL WARFARE

The TRUTH ~ Lessons IV-VI
TAKING AUTHORITY
GOD'S CONQUERING LASERS
AGAPAŌ LOVE TRIUMPHS

The LIFE ~ Lessons VII-IX
PREMIER PRAISE
GOD'S PEERLESS NAMES
CHRIST THE PANORAMA OF HEAVEN

Resources and Tools for Personal Growth

Barbara S. Waddell

KNOWING GOD IN YOUR HEART

SERIES AND TABLE OF CONTENTS

In The Beginning . . .
With Thanksgiving
Welcome — *Explaining the Unique Lesson Setup*

SERIES I ~ THE WAY

I ~ INTIMACY WITH CHRIST
Scriptural Meditation — *Be Still and Know That I AM God*
II ~ RIGHT THOUGHTS AND ATTITUDES
Scriptural Meditation — *Putting On The Inner Armor Of God*
Scriptural Meditation — *Putting On The Armor Of God*
III ~ SPIRITUAL WARFARE
Scriptural Tool — *Moses ~ The High Price of a Hot Temper*
Scriptural Tool — *Testing The Spirits*

SERIES II ~ THE TRUTH

IV - TAKING AUTHORITY
Scriptural Overcoming — *Strongholds*
Scriptural Awareness — *The Devices Of Satan*
V ~ GOD'S CONQUERING LASERS
Scriptural Prayer Guide — *Praying The Word For Areas of Influence*
VI ~ AGAPAŌ LOVE TRIUMPHS
Scriptural Meditation — *Imitating Christ In Our Prayers*

SERIES III ~ THE LIFE

VII ~ PREMIER PRAISE
Scriptural Study — *Pursue God's Names*
VIII ~ GOD'S PEERLESS NAMES
Scriptural Study — *Proclaim God's Names*
IX ~ CHRIST THE PANORAMA OF HEAVEN
Poster Page — *HE IS COMING WITH CLOUDS OF GLORY*
Testimony — *Eternal Father Strong To Save*
Biography
Endorsements

    Life Application Questions, Scripture Sequences, Endnotes, resources and tools are included to encourage growth in Christ ~ growth by applying His Word through an intimate fellowship with the LORD Jesus our Savior.
    Group study leaders for Victorious Life Application will find suggestions for lessons and Life Application Question answers in the Leader Answer Key Guide on the website. Resources and tools may be freely downloaded from the website at www.knowinggodinyourheart.com

IN THE BEGINNING . . . I WISH I HAD KNOWN

*"Now that I am older and gray . . . give me the time to tell this new generation
(and their children too) about all Your mighty miracles." Psalm 71:18*

If only we had known God's Victorious Life Applications . . . known that in the beginning was the Word, and the Word was with God, and the Word was God. In Him is life and His life is the Light of men and His Light shines into darkness so we can be set free [John 1:1-5,12; 3:16-17].

His instructions are vital to know what we are to do in life's circumstances. His precious Word both directs and instructs us how to walk in His peace, wisdom, knowledge, understanding, grace, unmerited love and most of all can bless us beyond our comprehension. We need the Light of His Word to shine in our lives so we can walk victoriously with Christ in God.

Oh, how I wish we had known that we needed His Light of understanding in our lives during our early marriage. It was Christmas Eve and an excited 3-year old Diane had said her prayers and was tucked into bed with a kiss. Infant David devoured his bottle as we kissed him and Mama and Papa (Gene's mother and father) goodnight. With excitement we approached the boxes containing Diane's unassembled refrigerator, oven and sink.

Papa had offered to help us but we thanked him and told him we could manage. (I remember thinking, 'there is nothing to it ~ all we need to do is do it!') However, our confidence waned as we began to read the incomprehensible overwhelming instructions. Joy departed ~ *apprehension entered!*

After we assembled the refrigerator we were dismayed to see that the door fit upside down and opened inward! We struggled against suspicion and anger as we looked at the picture, reread the unfamiliar words then reassembled it. Frustrated, and blaming each other, we found mistakes that made us highly aware of each other's inabilities *due to our different interpretations* of the instructions ~ *disunity entered!*

Unsure of how to proceed, we realized we still had to assemble the oven and sink. We read the instructions and things went a little smoother so we gained confidence. But the oven wobbled no matter what we tried. Exhausted, on the defensive and battling tears, we glared at each other . . . *Merry Christmas!*

Diane often said, "Papa fix it!" Defeated, angry and embarrassed, her words rang in our ears and we began to hope that Papa *would fix it* . . . and before Diane awakened!

Thankfully, Papa no longer ignored our 'animated' accusations and arose from the bed to help us. This time we joyfully let him. Right away Papa pointed out that *instructions are useless if we do not follow them and use the required tools.* Papa put on his coat, hat and boots and went out into the blowing snow to get the proper tools from his car trunk. He soon returned then patiently walked us through the instructions, step by step.

Facing our inadequacies, we turned from the *folly* of *accusing one another* and fled to the *wisdom* of our earthly father. We welcomed Papa's enabling power (his wisdom and tools) and overcame the desire to be wise in our own eyes. He taught us the importance of reading instructions, following directions and then showed us how he used the tools that empowered him to accomplish the task. How we wished we had sought his help in the beginning!

Little Diane awakened to find the gifts she had hoped for beside the tree. Two month old David awoke and eagerly devoured his bottle. They were not disappointed that Christmas morning and neither were we as we watched Diane's excitement.

A Christian's walk parallels our traumatic time that Christmas Eve when we were handicapped by self-sufficiency, lack of knowledge, wrong attitudes, etc. Our experience with Papa, our earthly father, gave us a clear illustration of the importance of turning from our wisdom and folly to seeking our Father's Wisdom and Power ~ *God's gift to believers.*

Christ, Who is the Power of God and the Wisdom of God [1Cor. 1:24], triumphed over flesh through His Death, Resurrection and Ascension. The LORD Jesus was and remains the Supreme Sacrifice required by our Heavenly Father that provides for the Spirit of Christ to indwell, instruct and enable us. He sent the Holy Spirit to empower and mold our character into His likeness *when* we invite the Holy Spirit to open God's Word to our hearts and understanding. He wants to guide us and speak to us through His Word which teaches us how to use His authority, power and resources so we can become His overcomers.

Knowing God In Your Heart was written to share insight into God's instructions and the LORD's tools that He gave us to empower us to be victorious and improve our lives. Many of us may be walking in defeat simply because we have not learned about God's conditions, promises, principles, plans, purposes and provisions that help us be Christ-like. We may have sat under cultural messages and did not learn basic truths that protect, strengthen and teach us about His Word, His Name and His Blood, along with the importance of putting on His armor daily and with having a living relationship with our Father God, the Lord Jesus Christ and the Holy Spirit.

Have we been taught about Heaven and Hell? ~ that we need conviction and repentance because we are sinners saved by grace? ~ that we need to ask Jesus to be the LORD of our lives? ~ have we been taught to Honor God? ~ learned the importance of praise and thanksgiving? ~ learned the meaning of the word "Hallelujah"? ~ learned about God's Peerless Names that He Himself established which memorialize and reveal His faithfulness and power? ~ have we learned about His nature, character and the authority He entrusted to us?

It is so easy to 'blow it'! *How well I know!* That is why it is important for us to recognize and identify wrong thoughts and attitudes and know what to do about them. Because Satan attacks us day and night (remember, he cannot touch God so he attacks God's children), we need to know how to identify his tactics and ultimate goal of keeping us from spending eternity with God. Yielding to his attacks keeps us from a victorious *walk with* and *witness of Christ.* We need God's Word for *Victory in Jesus!*

Let us turn from the 'folly' of doing things 'our way' and follow instructions from the Holy Spirit. He will lead us and teach us what scripture says about loving the LORD, walking in His Light and serving Him with all of our heart. The following study is humbly shared from lessons learned, many times the hard way, many times from anointed authors or speakers, and many times during scriptural meditation that brought insight, conviction and joy.

My prayer is that the Lord blesses you as much as I have been blessed preparing this and that you are enriched studying His Word, His promises, Who He is, and what He has done for us.

May our LORD keep you in the palm of His Loving Protecting Hand,   Barbara Waddell

WITH THANKSGIVING

Knowing God In Your Heart evolved over the years from a seminar presented to the Ohio Concerned Women for America. Afterward many asked for Scripture references and examples given during the seminar. Due to the requests, a summary manual entitled *Being About Our Father's Business* was written. Later, it was enlarged to *Prevailing Prayer* then again it was enlarged to *Christ Calls Us To Prevail In Prayer*. The *New American Standard Bible Reference Edition (NASB)* was used for all three.

Knowing God In Your Heart began many years later at the urging of Pastor Robert Messner, who asked me to enlarge and magnify *Christ Calls Us To Prevail In Prayer,* by using more examples to enhance understanding plus include helpful resources. He further requested that I use the *New International Version of the Holy Bible* (NIV) in the rewrite as our Church, The Chapel in Akron, Ohio, elected to use the NIV corporately. As a result, Scriptures are from the NASB or NIV versions unless otherwise noted.

Soon after I began, a debilitating illness prevented me from writing for many years. Thankfully, through many prayers, doctors and therapy, The Lord brought forth His healing hand. Praise God for Pastor Messner's and Pastor Lynn Warner's encouragement, Lynnae Seeley's wise input from the very beginning of the teachings within, and for Judy Wilfong, who not only pushed to have the book made available as a Bible Study, but organized the pilot group of mature Christians to critique it as it was written, lesson by lesson. She sacrificially edited this book and wrote the Lesson Questions and the *Leader Answer Key Guide*, which are free to download (along with resources and tools) at www.knowinggodinyourheart.com.

Shelagh McAlpine was my mentor who encouraged and called me "friend." In 2004, Shelagh returned the proof of this Bible Study that was sent to her in England to insure that the references to her, Lydia, and the experiences she shared were acceptable and accurate. I treasure the note Shelagh wrote back:

> "The corrections you made were just fine. I expect you have published your manuscript by now and it is a blessing to those that want to get to "know" God at the "place of prayer."...
> Well done! The Manual is full of good practical/spiritual teachings."

The teachings and lifestyles of Shelagh, Tryna Bahl, Joy Dawson (Shelagh's longtime prayer partners), Adrienne "Laddie" Bowman, Wendy Beckett, Dr. John Hash, Shirley Dobson, Evelyn Christenson, Vonette Bright, Lynne Dugan, Geneva Chervenic, Art McMahon, Danna Testa, Ron Glosser, Herb Pyles, Jan Garrard, Florence Littauer, Betty Southard, Gerry Wakeland, Jim and Angel DeGrado, Brenda Jossee, Penny Wrobel, Joyce Arnold, Joan Foor *and many others,* blessed and inspired many things shared within. Praise God for their faithful walk that glorified Him and encouraged us to press on "hidden with Christ in God."

Completing this is a challenging journey. I cannot thank the Lord enough for His insights, guidance, and protection. Deepest thanks to my forever husband, David E. "Gene" Waddell who encouraged and supported this endeavor. I wish I could thank each one who has been personally involved over the years. Sadly, there are too many to name individually. The Lord knows who they are and I pray that His blessings will always be upon them.

May the Lord be glorified as this belongs to Him, Barbara Waddell

Welcome To Knowing God In Your Heart

Victorious Life Applications

Understanding the setup For This Overview of God's Instructions

Dear Reader,

THERE ARE THREE LESSONS in each of *THE THREE SERIES:* THE WAY ~ THE TRUTH ~ THE LIFE. They may be read at any time for personal growth, a group Bible Review or Study.

EACH LESSON IS UNIQUE IN ITS PRESENTATION. IT HAS ITS OWN PAGE NUMBERING due to cross-referencing. At the end of each lesson are Life Application Review Questions, Scripture Sequences, Endnotes and resources. Below is an example of how the lessons are setup:

- Lesson 1 ~ *INTIMACY WITH CHRIST*: pages 1-19 from the beginning through to the Endnotes.
- Scriptures: [bracketed] on the pages are for reference (if quickened to look up a topic).
- Life Application Discussions are on pages 14-15.
- All Scriptures [bracketed] are listed on pages 16-17 in the Scripture Sequences at the end.
- Endnotes on pages 18-19 at the end. It is helpful to bookmark endnote pages for easy reference.
- Lesson Resources: follow or precede each Lesson and are un-numbered.

PLEASE READ "IN THE BEGINNING . . . I WISH I HAD KNOWN" as it gives a personal lesson learned from our first big Christmas preparation and illustrates why we need to learn to follow instructions and use specific and necessary tools in both the physical and spiritual realms of our lives.

IT IS IMPORTANT AND ENLIGHTENING TO READ A.W. TOZER'S POWERFUL ENDNOTE[1] in *INTIMACY WITH CHRIST*, referenced on Page 3 (see page 18). It explains why many have not been taught God's principles. Instead they were taught what *man's* interpretation said the body of Christ should do. It demonstrates our need to return to God's Word and apply its teachings to live the Victorious Life Christ provided for us.

THERE ARE MANY WAYS TO GET THE MOST OUT OF THIS PRESENTATION. Some read it devotionally for personal growth, some discuss it as a Book Review, some study in a group Bible Study. It is helpful to underline, highlight, make notes on the page and/or Life Application pages. Some mark Question numbers next to the answer (good idea), some use a notebook or do both. The best way to get the most out of *KNOWING GOD IN YOUR HEART,* personally or in a group, is to ask the LORD to lead you and decide how you will be comfortable reading/studying it. Never feel pressured ~ TRUST GOD!

KNOWING GOD IN YOUR HEART is shared to learn God's basic instructions, principles, conditions, provisions, character and nature. It shows how to apply His Word to our lives and relationships.

The Life Application Leader Answer Key Guide, Suggestions for Leaders, Discussion Page answers and resources may be freely downloaded from the website: www.knowinggodinyourheart.com

ALWAYS PRAY BEFORE BEGINNING.
INVITE THE HOLY SPIRIT TO BE YOUR TEACHER.
ASK THE HOLY SPIRIT TO OPEN THE EYES OF YOUR HEART, SPIRIT AND MIND.

May the LORD bless you and eternally keep you in the palm of His Hands, Barbara Waddell

KNOWING GOD IN YOUR HEART

THE WAY
Series I

Lessons I - III

INTIMACY WITH CHRIST

RIGHT THOUGHTS AND ATTITUDES

SPIRITUAL WARFARE

Lesson I

Intimacy With Christ

*"Truly my soul finds rest in God; my salvation comes from Him.
Truly He is my Rock and my Salvation;
He is my fortress, I will never be shaken."*

Psalm 62:1

MY HIDING PLACE

Thou art my hiding place and my shield;

I wait for Thy Word.

Depart from me, evil doers,

That I may observe the commandments of my God.

Sustain me according to Thy Word

that I may live;

And do not let me be ashamed of my hope.

Uphold me that I may be safe,

That I may have regard for Thy statutes continually.

Psalm 119:14-17

INTIMACY WITH CHRIST

"Be still and know that I am God . . ." Psalm 46:10 KJV

K*NOWING **G**OD IS FOUNDATIONAL TO HONORING **G**OD IN OUR HEARTS AND LIVES.* Meditating in the Word saturates our minds with His eternal Truth and focuses our spirit to pray, praise, worship, glorify and walk as Christ would have us walk. It becomes manna to our spirits when we listen to God in our heart with childlike faith.

It seems like yesterday that I was sitting on the patio enjoying the beauty around me, pondering the wondrous security of God's love and the freedom that came from knowing Him. Abruptly my thoughts were changed to the stark realization that freedom *demands* responsibility. Freedom *in* God demands responsibility *to* God! Was I flippant about His sacrificial love? Did I understand that God loved me, even bask in His love, *yet not know Him like I should?*

***W**HILE PONDERING MY RELATIONSHIP WITH **G**OD,* going back to when I was a little girl, I could not remember a time when I did not talk or pray to Father God with childlike faith in His love and goodness. Yet, did I know that I was *responsible* to God? Did I know Him in my heart the way He wanted me to? Looking back upon my younger years I remembered our many moves (eight times in Florida and once to Michigan during WWII). Mother said throughout the moves that Sunday School, Church and Church youth activities were a magnet for me. During public school days, starting with elementary school just before we fought in World War II, we were taught to honor God and Country. The teacher read the Bible to us, we prayed The LORD's Prayer and pledged allegiance to our flag. When I was twelve years old and a junior high student, I accepted Christ as my Savior and was taught to love, trust, and honor God. In junior high we daily honored God and Country.

***I**N HIGH SCHOOL WE CONTINUED THE ESTABLISHED PATTERN* taking turns and reading our own selection from the Bible. We pledged the flag and prayed *THE LORD'S PRAYER*. Our Jewish classmates read from the Old Testament and no one thought anything of it. During the Korean War a new dimension was added to our godly routine. The bugle played over the PA system at noon and called the entire campus to stop, wherever we were and whatever we were doing, to pray silently for our forces for one minute.

Later, working in Washington, D.C., I continued my walk with God. I sang in the choir, taught Sunday School, and actively participated in our church's Young Professional Group. As a result I bonded with new Christian friends who introduced me to Washington's sophistication. I continued church activities and "good works" to the point of becoming prideful in them. It is painful to remember that one morning while walking to Church I told God how pleased He must be with me because *I* did so much for Him at church, Gray Ladies (Red Cross), the Veteran's Hospital, etc.

SOON AFTERWARD MY ACTIONS GRIEVED THE LORD. Although begging for His forgiveness, it was hard to forgive myself when convicted that God had not been honored as He deserved. Although I had grieved the Holy Spirit, God in His mercy, grace and compassion worked things out for good. Praise God, He promised that once we are His, He will *never* let us go! [John 10:27-30] Confusion can come from not knowing the LORD or rebellion toward God. Submission to God's guidance is paramount to overcoming our flesh and the enemy.

Although many years ago, it seems like yesterday that I cried out to God with intense physical and spiritual hunger to have meaning and purpose in my life. I needed to know Him spiritually and intimately, to honor Him, and walk in His True Light! *We are called to know God.* We are required to honor God in our hearts and lives. We are commanded to walk in His principles, character, attributes, conditions, and to obey His still small voice. Christians are prevented from enjoying intimacy with God due to laziness, apathy, misinterpretation, wrong priorities ~ misunderstanding Who God is!

IT WAS BEWILDERING TO HEAR CONTRADICTORY TEACHINGS from well known leaders that watered down what I had been taught and believed about God. I needed direction on how to sift through the new "reasonable" teachings that did not sit right in my heart. I earnestly prayed to God for understanding. Providentially, a few days later, I found an old copy of *Keys to The Deeper Life* by A.W. Tozer at a garage sale. Praise God, He used it in a mighty way to answer many of my questions. It introduced me to Christ's way to live a balanced Christian life (an ongoing process).

Reverend Tozer's book taught me to rely upon Scripture, not man's interpretation, to find the truth, power, strength and guidance needed to overcome my difficulties. Reverend Tozer wrote about the pitfalls of *Fundmentalism* and the way that an unofficial hierarchy had decided what Christians were to believe. Not the Scriptures, he said, but what the scribe thought the Scriptures meant, became the Christian creed. He said that Christian colleges, seminaries, Bible Institutes, Bible Conferences, popular Bible expositors had all joined to promote the cult of *textualism* . . . that the system of extreme dispensationalism was devised, which relieved the Christian of repentance, obedience and cross-carrying in any other than the most formal sense . . . Whole sections of the New Testament were taken from the church and disposed of after a rigid system of "dividing the truth" . . . All this resulted in a religious mentality opposed to the true faith of Christ. A kind of cold mist settled over Fundamentalism. Below, the terrain was familiar; it was New Testament Christianity, to be sure. The basic doctrines of the Bible were there, but the climate was just not favorable to the sweet truths of the Spirit . . . The whole mood was different from that of the Early Church, and of the great souls who suffered, sang, and worshiped in the centuries past. The doctrines were sound, but something vital was missing. The tree of correct doctrine was never allowed to blossom. The voice of the turtle [dove] was rarely heard in the land; instead, the parrot sat on his artificial perch and dutifully repeated what he had been taught and the whole emotional tone was somber and dull. Faith, a mighty, vitalizing doctrine in the mouths of the apostles, became in the mouths of the scribes, another thing altogether, and power went from it. (See Endnote[1])

REVEREND TOZER UNDERSCORED THE IMPORTANCE AND NEED to acquire biblical knowledge through reading the Word and scriptural meditation [John 17:3], learning God's principles, and daily walking in the fullness of the LORD. Reading His book devotionally freed me. What a wonderful influence for God's hungry child who needed to learn more about the One Who will not let us go! [John 10:28]

A vital spiritual dimension evolved a few years later when we were shown a scriptural way to learn to know God and His ways at the 1981 Lydia Conference in Blackstone, Virginia. The speaker, Reverend Campbell McAlpine, taught us how to meditate in the Word. Then he instructed us to pray and ask God to give us a book in the Bible to meditate on. He said that we would be blessed if we transcribed it, word by word, and wrote down the thoughts that the verses inspired. He also said it would help us internalize Christ's truth to change our lives (and it did).

DURING PRAYER THE LORD PROMPTED "JOSHUA" TO MY HEART. Upon arriving home I took a spiral notebook and divided it into three sections. Two inches from the left side a line was drawn down, and another line two inches from the right side, leaving a space in the middle. On the left side the date, comments, and Scripture references were written down. In the center each verse was transcribed, word by word, and prayed over for God to speak to my heart about what had been read and pondered. On the right side, in the third column, my personal interpretation was recorded.

STARTING WITH JOSHUA 1, THE VERSES WERE WRITTEN DOWN IN CONTEXT, followed by prayer asking God to make them relevant to me. After transcribing verses one and two, I wrote underneath the verses, in brackets [ ], my personal paraphrase . . . "[upon dying to self, by serving others, the LORD will say to me, arise, cross into a new ministry ~ cross into God's promise to me.]" On the left side was written "Joshua needed a commission and fresh word from God to proceed" along with some Scripture references I had looked up that also were applicable. After praying over the verse/s, my insights were written down (when received) in the right column. There I wrote "by being anonymous in serving others, the LORD will give me a new ministry, new territory, new responsibilities and use me to complete a promise made to another just as Joshua was used to complete a promise made to another." It is good to date and save notebooks. My Joshua notebook was dated twenty-eight years earlier. Notebooks record insights and direction, and bring back memorable times alone with God.

Scriptural meditation gave me direction, confirmation, conviction, and strengthened me in incredible ways [Ps. 119:130]. Memorization had always been difficult for me. It was easier to retain Scripture when recording it, pondering it, then asking the Holy Spirit to make it real. God's Holy Spirit took it from my head and planted understanding in my heart to glorify Him. Praise God!

SCRIPTURAL MEDITATION IS ESSENTIAL TO KNOWING GOD. Meditation gives us an understanding of God's ways. The Holy Spirit uses meditation to teach us the LORD's *culture* ~ His humor, justice, mercy, grace and love that endures forever. Scriptural meditation prepares our hearts to praise, worship, imitate Christ in our prayers, glorify Christ and walk as Christ would have us walk.

MARTYN LLOYD-JONES WROTE, "They (New Testament believers) always spent their time in worship and adoration and in the glorification of Christ. It seems to me that this is the note that we must recapture, *and that there is no real hope for revival and true awakening until we come back to this.*"[2]

It was marvelous how His love shined the Light of His Word into my heart with precious insights for worship and prayer and even taught me how to "be still and know that *I AM* God" [Ps. 46:10]. I hungered to share Christ ~ to glorify Him ~ to see revival ~ to enjoy a true awakening.

From that day forward Scripture was alive. It was vital to talk about God and share the inspirations learned during meditation to the exclusion of all else. It was important to seek the company of godly people who knew His exciting reality and majesty. His Word thrilled my heart as never before! Biblical truths were grasped joyfully with great anticipation. The Holy Spirit led me through the Scripture references from Joshua 1 to Jeremiah 1 then to Isaiah 55. The referenced New Testament verses truly helped me understand, for the first time, that the LORD Jesus Christ was in operation throughout *both* the Old and New Testaments!

AS A BELIEVER IT IS IMPORTANT TO HONOR THE POWER OF GOD'S WORD, whether thought or spoken, and the need to recognize our accountability, to devote ourselves to prayer and the *ministry* of God's Word [Acts 6:4]. It was wonderful to grasp what the miracle at the Cross accomplished. This sinner, saved by Grace, yearned to spend more time learning to respond to my Redeemer's incredible love and mercy [1 Pet. 3-5a], to share Christ, see Christ glorified, see revival and to enjoy a true awakening.

LEARNING GOD'S PRINCIPLES AND CONDITIONS enables us to pray Christ-like prayers ~ effectual fervent prayers ~ and empowers us to be the conquering instruments that Christ calls us to be!

As His child, I hoped to know God in a real way ~ a powerful way! [Eph. 1:18-23]

As His believer, I wanted to know how to respond to His Holiness, His Word, His requirements, His justice, His perfect love [2 Cor. 7:1; Ps. 105:42, 44; John 3:16, 17].

As His worshiper, I wanted to know my Risen Savior ~ Who, in His amazing grace, loves me and is my friend [John 15:15].

It became vital to know God as my resource, and to be empowered to walk in His will, as I sought to fulfill His strategies in my everyday battles. I continued to study Scripture by writing it down, word by word in notebooks, and praying to God to show me how to apply His truth in a practical way that would meet my needs. His Word strengthened and helped me *submit* to His revealed Truth. He proved that the "unfolding of His Word gives Light. His Word gives understanding to the simple" [Ps. 119:130]. His unfolded Word truly helped this child set my mind inwardly upon Him. My revealed critical spirit left, as joy literally entered my life.

KNOWING GOD AND HIS WAYS ARE PARAMOUNT AND FOUNDATIONAL to honoring God and overcoming our flesh and the enemy. We are called to be overcomers and to honor God by seeking His heart and submitting to Him [Ps. 14:2] through scriptural meditation and prayer. Overcomers are to obey His still small voice and live in the perspective of His revealed Word [1 Sam. 15:22; 1 Kings 19:12-13; John 10:11-16]. Overcomers are to seek Him to learn how He would have us pray and proclaim His Word of Righteousness into all areas of concern.

ANOTHER TRUTH THAT TAUGHT ME HOW TO THINK UPON GOD was learned in *EXPERIENCING THE DEPTHS OF JESUS CHRIST,* which was written around the end of the seventeenth century, by saintly Madame Jeanne Guyon. What she wrote was so precious that it is included for your enjoyment and blessing.

>Madam Guyon shared:
>>You begin by setting aside a time to be with the Lord. When you do come to Him, come quietly. Turn your heart to the presence of God . . . You turn to Him by faith. By faith you believe you have come into the presence of God. Next, while you are before the Lord, begin to read some portion of Scripture. As you read, pause. The pause should be quite gentle. You have paused so that you may set your mind on the Spirit. You have set your mind inwardly ~ on Christ. (You should always remember that you are not doing this to gain some understanding of what you have read; you are reading to turn your mind from outward things to the deep parts of your being. You are not there to learn or to read . . . but to experience the presence of your Lord!)
>>
>>While you are before the Lord, hold your heart in His presence. How? This you also do by faith . . . Now, waiting before Him, turn all your attention toward your spirit. Do not allow your mind to wander. If your mind begins to wander, just turn your attention back again to the inward parts of your being. You will be free from wandering ~ free from any outward distractions ~ and you will be brought near to God.[3]
>>
>>(. . . The Lord is found only within your spirit, in the recesses of your being, in the Holy of Holies; this is where He dwells. The Lord once promised to come and make His home within you [John 14:23]. He promised to be there to meet those who worship Him who does His will. The Lord will meet you in your spirit. It was St. Augustine who once said that he had lost much time in the beginning of his Christian experience by trying to find the Lord outwardly rather than by turning inwardly.) Once your heart has been turned inwardly to the Lord, you will have an impression of His presence. You will be able to notice His presence more acutely because your outer senses have now become very calm and quiet. Your attention is no longer on outward things or on the surface thoughts of your mind; instead, sweetly and silently, your mind becomes occupied with what you have read and by the touch of His presence.[4]

HIS PRESENCE BECAME REAL WHEN MEDITATING IN HIS WORD. Streams of conviction and repentance were followed by forgiveness and His sweet cleansing. I learned to pray His Truth, His scriptural promises, into my life and called that *internalizing* His Word into my heart. Then prayed His Scripture out for others, concerns, or circumstances, and called it *externalizing* His Word.

Looking up Scripture references was like a magnet that the Holy Spirit used to teach me, draw me, and develop a deeper dependence on Christ. Learning God's biblical principles followed by prayer helped me develop a solid foundation for my daily walk. Over and over again, our LORD proved that His Word, which cannot be broken, *is alive, active,* and *will not return void!* [Isa. 55:11]

WHEN REVERENTLY PONDERING HIS NAME, LORD (YHWH),[5] the Holy Spirit revealed that an Awesome Absolute Omnipotent God was my Master, yet intimate friend. That was simply amazing!

OSWALD CHAMBERS WROTE IN *MY UTMOST FOR HIS HIGHEST:*

> Friendship is rare on earth. It means identity in thought and heart and spirit. The whole discipline of life is to enable us to enter into this closest relationship with Jesus Christ . . . Fruit bearing is always mentioned as the manifestation of an intimate union with Jesus Christ [John 15:1-4].[6]

THE REALITY OF ALL THAT HE IS, IS FAR TOO COMPLEX for our finite minds to comprehend. Yet, we are called to have an intimate relationship with Him and to seek His guidance. We are instructed to seek His face [Ps. 105:4] and to seek the LORD while He may be found [Isa. 55:6]. We cannot glorify our Father, or have victory in the LORD Jesus Christ, unless we know *Who* the Word is, *What* His Name represents, *Why* and *Whom* we should obey, *Where* His Spirit leads, *How* to pray with His authority, and *When* His perfect time arrives.

MANY OF US WHO GREW UP IN AMERICA WHEN I DID believed that being an American was synonymous with being a Christian. But, we did not know THE CHRIST, Whom we are called to know and represent. Although Jesus was asked to come into my heart when I was three years old, gradually Jesus was overpowered by Easter clothes, Easter baskets, egg hunts, Christmas trees, Santa Claus, plays about the manger birth, gifts, and so forth! Many no longer understood His glorious distinction, much less His *entitlement* to His people [Titus 2:13, 14].

I knew Father God's Son was Jesus, that He died on a cross because *God* loved me, and Jesus had existed long ago. Although baptized, I did not understand Jesus was a *living* God, what His sacrifice did and does for me, what His eternal *unconditional* love represents or what it means to honor God by truly believing Him *and in Him!* My love and prayers were limited to Father God in Heaven.

PRAISE GOD! EVENTUALLY THE LORD OF HISTORY BECAME REAL! My love for Christ Jesus blossomed and deepened. It was convicting to grasp just a tiny facet of the honor due to Him and the submission that His ownership required from me. No longer could I take His grace and mercy lightly. *He is GOD!* GOD of the universe! GOD, Whose very Being, requires our reverent fear, submission, accountability, and honor. *Our Almighty God* loves us unconditionally and wants us to honor Him and live to glorify Him. *He even wants us to be His friend!*

MARTYN LLOYD-JONES WROTE IN SAVED IN ETERNITY:
> The essential proof (of salvation) is that the supreme object and ambition of the Christian's life is to live to the glory of God . . . Christianity is not something light and superficial that just does certain things to you, and gives you pleasant feelings. It is something that brings you into a relationship with God. You begin to fix your gaze upon Him with reverence and godly fear, you do not drop lightly into His presence.[7]

Christ, he (Paul) says, is the power of God, and the wisdom of God, and nowhere is the wisdom of God so gloriously and magnificently displayed as in this Christian gospel.[8]

AWARENESS OF HIS POWER, WISDOM, AND MAJESTY GREW when searching Scripture and learning that He is much more than the God of our salvation and deliverance. The LORD Jesus, GOD in the *flesh,* is the Creator of the Cosmos! He walked this earth in human frailty, yet, He walked in the authority of three separate personalities: *LORD, Jesus,* and *the Messiah.* It is amazing to think about.

It was awe-inspiring and revolutionary to learn that His Names represented much more than a first, middle, or last name.

Each Name represented one of His victoriously unique personalities!
Each Name represented a different attribute, event, role, or function!
Each Name enlarges our ability to praise Him, thank Him,
 . . . *and call upon His Unique Names.*

I HAD NOT THOUGHT ABOUT, NOR COMPREHENDED, what "LORD *of lords,* or KING *of kings"* meant to me personally, spiritually, or practically. I did not understand that *"to believe in"* literally meant "to trust in, to cleave to, to adhere to [like glue!]" [Phil 1:29 AMP] Did I believe in the LORD Jesus Christ like that? No, but I wanted to. Did I honor and glorify God? No, but I wanted to learn how. Meditations initiated a quest to better understand and learn about His character, attributes, nature, and worthiness. Thanks to the godly influence of others, and the Holy Spirit's leading, I began to study His peerless Old Testament Names, *His Hallowed Names* that revealed His nature, character, and attributes. His Names will be further examined in other Lessons.

HIS NAME IS THE EXACT REPRESENTATION OF GOD'S AUTHORITY, CHARACTER AND NATURE [Heb. 1:3]. It was humbling and exciting to learn that each of His Names represented much more than His identity. Hallelujah!

One morning I was thinking about Jesus' Name and knelt at the fireplace hearth and began to sing unto my beloved LORD "Isn't He?"[9] I sang slowly, reverently, worshipfully, prayerfully, joyfully, on and on, with delighted abandonment. I revered the pure, majestic, sweet sound of His Hebrew Name, *YESHUA.* His beauty was being deeply engraved on my heart and my mind became one with my spirit. It was natural to sing to Jesus that I loved Him and appreciated what His Triumph on the Cross did for me. The sweetness of His love unfolded when I spoke His Hallowed Name, "YESHUA," then followed with praises to "YESHUA" (pronounced Yay-shoo-'ah in Hebrew). Although feeling unworthy, I understood that I was protected in His stronghold of praise and wondered if the love being experienced was similar to being "Hidden with Christ in

God?" [Col. 3:3] I yearned to know more about Jesus, to be like Him, to reflect His nature, to have Him be my priority and to honor Him in all things.

HIS NAMES, ALONG WITH SCRIPTURE VERSES, popped into my thoughts and enlarged my vocabulary and helped me express my thanksgiving and love to Him. Reverently, tearfully, singing about His holiness, omnipotence and sovereignty while glorying over His absolute power, triumph and love, I began singing His Old Testament Names and in the eye of my mind I envisioned in front of me a beautiful Crimson curtain with scintillating threads. As I sang "El Shad-dai, Al-might-y God," a thread came out of the curtain, went behind me, and pulled me closer to the Crimson curtain. Every time I sang another one of His Hallowed Names another thread came out of the curtain and pulled me closer, and closer, until I was part of the Crimson Curtain! I had begun singing "Ye-shu-a, Ye-shu-a, Ye-shu-a, Ye-shu-a … and my song (still to the tune of "Isn't He?") had evolved while I kneeled in front of the fireplace to singing "Yes, You Are . . . Yes, You Are" *Isn't He?*

HIS WONDERFUL SENSE OF HUMOR AND PLAY ON WORDS MADE ME GIGGLE that He would take the beautiful song "Isn't He?" that always blessed me, and use the same melody with words that worshiped *"Ye-shu-ah, Ye-shu-ah"* into *"Yes You Are, Yes You Are!"* Isn't He *Wonderful?*

It was a profoundly moving time. I knew, that I knew, that I was beloved of the LORD and that verbally acknowledging Jesus' Names that identified His various attributes, interventions, and character, in both the Old Testament and the New Testament, had pleased my Heavenly Father.

The Word of God was sung to the WORD of God [1 Cor. 2:12, 13]. His Precious Blood was shed at Golgotha for me, *for us!* The veil of the temple was rent in two for me, *for us!* What love!

AFTERWARD, WITH THE EXQUISITE MELODY OF "ISN'T HE?" *still ringing in my heart* I went to my little office and recorded the above precious moments in my journal. "Be still and know that *I AM* God" [Ps. 46:10] echoed in my thoughts as I recorded the above blessing. A further blessing took place when the following verses flowed unto the paper and I sang them to the tune of "Isn't He?" Beautiful . . .

Beautiful VEIL of CHRIST, Crimson Blood ~ Sacrificed,
Thread of God, Spun to give, Victory, ~ In Trinity Unity.
Your Word, Your Name, Your Blood, All Three ~ Spoken, Sang, Brings Victory.
Your BANNER flies over us ~ Oh Most High, In You we trust;
Eternally, We worship Thee. Eternally, we worship Thee. Eternally, we worship Thee . . .

PERSONAL, INTIMATE, VERBAL WORSHIP deepened my awareness of *Christ's ALL* and my nothingness. Commitment and faith grew by hearing His words of truth spoken out loud [Rom. 10:17]. Freely, intimately, the knowledge came that "With Thee is the fountain of life; in Thy Light we see light" [Ps. 36:9]. His love called for a response to His Righteousness. Enveloped in the warmth of His love, I *knew* that I was covered by His triumphant blood and sheltered in Christ in God [Col. 3:3].

My notebooks bulged with insights of His character. A growing confidence and new found faith in Christ developed in my heart. The largest diamond in the world cut into trillions or more facets could not reflect all that there is to learn about the Father, Son, and the Holy Spirit [John 21:25]. It was awesome to understand some of His ways and to learn about His nature and fervency when He took authority over evil, walked, talked, and prayed on earth. It challenged my complacency and concerns about little things. My attitude and prayers changed when I endeavored to look at things from the LORD's perspective so I could imitate Christ in my prayers. God is a Holy, Sovereign, and Jealous God. Yet, amazingly, He really loves us and wants us to be His friend.

DURING ONE MEDITATION THE NAME LORD JUMPED OUT AT ME. His Name, Yahweh, was a thread clearly interwoven throughout the Bible. Disciples were *emphatic* that Jesus Christ was LORD! Wondering what it meant that they repeatedly declared Jesus was LORD, and *why* they *stressed* His Lordship, initiated an ongoing study about His Old and New Testament title: LORD ~ *YAHWEH*.

> **CHARLES C. RYRIE** confirmed the meaning of Christ as LORD:
> LORD (KURIOS)
> C. "Christ as Kurios". . . Thus the essence of the Christian faith was to acknowledge Jesus of Nazareth as the *Yahweh* of the Old Testament.[10]

LORD, ALL CAPITAL LETTERS IN THE OLD TESTAMENT (many translations), was a wonderful introduction to the fullness of Jesus Christ's attributes of love, faithfulness, justice, sovereignty, jealousy, justice, etc. One without the other gives incomplete understanding of our LORD Jesus Christ's Sovereign, Absolute, Eternal role throughout history. As a result, LORD is capitalized throughout to represent Jesus as YAHWEH.

> **KEVIN J. CONNER WROTE IN *THE TABERNACLE OF DAVID*:**
> . . . it would be profitable to refer to important principles used in interpreting Scripture, for it is through the discovery and use of these that the truth is to be found . . . it is the glory of God to conceal a thing, but the honour of kings is to search out a matter [Prov. 25:2]. It should be remembered that the Early Church had no New Testament . . . Their "New Testament" was to be found in the "Old Testament" . . .

Hence, because the New Testament Canon of Scripture had not been written or completed in Early Church history, the Apostles continually appealed to the Old Testament writings for everything that God was doing in their midst.

Kevin Connor also wrote:
> The New is in the Old contained, The Old is in the New explained,
> The New is in the Old concealed, The Old is in the New revealed,
> The New is in the Old enfolded, The Old is in the New unfolded.[11]

JESUS IS THE ONE THAT THE EARLY CHURCH RECOGNIZED AS THE LORD OF THE OLD TESTAMENT AND THE PROMISED MESSIAH OF THE NEW TESTAMENT [Acts 2:36]. The Spirit of Christ was and is God's eternal creative empowerment. *It's mind boggling!* [John 1; Gen. 1]

Studying Abraham's intervention for Sodom and Gomorrah taught me about mercy, grace, and perseverance in intercession. Our LORD never told Abraham to stop interceding, limited his requests, or even scolded him for his persistence [Gen. 19:1-19]. Do we stop before He releases us?

IT WAS HEART-WARMING TO LEARN OF THE LORD'S HUMOR when reading that Sarah had laughed to herself behind a curtain about the LORD's promise. The LORD gently reminded her that she had ridiculed His promise, yet she *denied to His face* that she had laughed! Amazingly, in His mercy and grace our LORD simply stated the truth, "No, but you did laugh." Our LORD did not punish Sarah nor take away her beauty ~ she was chosen a *second time* for a king's harem [Gen. 12:15; 20:2]. Nor did the LORD deny her the "promised child" she no longer believed was possible. The LORD even named the baby "Isaac" ~ which means laughter! [Gen. 21:6, 7] Can't you envision the LORD smiling and sense the warmth of His humor?

Learning of His unconditional love and humor relaxed me. Seeing His humor taught me to be comfortable with Him and to openly, intimately, and transparently talk to the LORD without feeling unworthy or threatened.

STUDYING ABOUT THE SHEPHERD BOY, DAVID, showed that our Heavenly Father does not look upon outward qualifications, but He *looks upon the heart.* God's servant Samuel had anointed David as *King* of Israel, however, David's motivation was to know God, not self-realization or glory!

After Samuel anointed David as King of Israel, his *earthly* father sent him back to the wilderness *to be king of a pasture!* His reign waited for His Heavenly Father's lessons to be learned *along with* God's perfect timing. David's *qualification* for kingship came through *testings* among sheep, dung, nature, fleas, deprivations, loneliness, and threats from beasts of prey. David's tenure in the wilderness developed a *reverent friendship* with God, *opened his heart* to the knowledge of God, proved God's ways are faithful and *taught* him God's perfect timing is flawless. Ultimately the wilderness *prepared* David to be king of Israel [1Sam. 16, 17].

THE WORSHIP THAT DAVID LEARNED AND PRACTICED during his wilderness tenure was unto his LORD. David trusted and maintained a reverent fear of the LORD. He worshiped his King God. The LORD not only prepared David's heart to worship and glorify his Heavenly King, but his intimate wilderness worship opened the door for him to become King Saul's musician and armor bearer. Unmistakably, it paved a *highway* to David's kingship over Israel.

Due to David's youth, his father sent him back to the pasture where he watched his brothers march off to battle the Philistines. Eventually his earthly father sent him to the front line with a care package for his brothers. He heard the Philistines mock God's people then heard Goliath mock the *character* of his LORD Sabaoth, the LORD of Hosts! David's righteous indignation amazed his brothers. God's wilderness strengthening and pasture training prevailed! David asked to fight Goliath. King Saul granted him authority and offered David his armor, which David turned down.

DAVID WENT INTO THE BATTLE ARMED BY THE LORD OF HOSTS! Unlike Saul, he was not dismayed by the negative circumstances. David knew that God's ways are not man's ways and that His thoughts are higher. He *chose* to trust in God's ways and won! The LORD did not fail him nor forsake him [1 Sam. 17]. David knew Whom he represented and that he was armored by the authority of the LORD of Hosts. David was fearless! He triumphed by using the weapons he was familiar with, the Name of Yahweh Sabaoth, LORD of Hosts, his slingshot, and five smooth stones. David was blessed by God. The Holy Spirit gave him focus, authority, and empowered him as he faced Goliath and killed him. David's humble, uncomplicated belief in God enabled him to be obedient, trusting, fervent, and single-minded as a worshiper who did not fear gigantic obstacles ~ including what a giant could do! David heard the call to prevail *and he did!*

FACETS OF GOD'S UNFATHOMABLE CHARACTER settled into my heart and enhanced my prayer life. God is our Source, Strength, Song, the Eternal Rock ~ Who loves us enough to teach us His ways. We need teachable, transparent, forgiving, obedient child-like faith, with expectant hearts, if we want to know God and understand His Word. Most of all, we need to ask the Holy Spirit to guide us [Luke 11:13] in order to understand His Word and ask for His empowerment to overcome.

"Come, let us reason together" [Isa. 1:18] became a basic scriptural blueprint that enabled me to lay my concerns at His feet and subsequently taught me to replace selfish prayers with *Christ-centered prayers*. The disciples and believers recognized that Jesus walked in God's anointing. The anointing from God, previously upon one person at a time, is now available to believers through Christ's triumph at Calvary. What wonders the Spirit of Christ has wrought!

Truly, we have been called To Honor God and To Know God. They are parallel themes that call us to learn about His character, principles, and conditions. Many believers do not understand that we must have clean hands and a pure heart, be still before God, and submit to God, before we can learn how to prevail against the Adversary. Submission, transparency and genuine oneness with God will glorify the LORD and give us the righteous balance that we need to prevail over the enemy.

Recognizing the role of the Spirit of Truth will turn us from apathy and mere survival cries, to victorious living when we know and walk in God's practical and righteous Holy Word [1 John 4:6; 5:3-8], recognize His prompting, and submit to Him [James 4:7].

Let us pray that we will follow David's example and become the LORD's worshiping, prevailing pray-*ers* (people of prayer ~ intercessors) who are available to receive the Holy Spirit's illumination and strategies that enable us to overcome our difficulties. Let us lay aside all of our preconceived ideas and allow His Word to grow in our hearts and guide us.

We can barely touch the surface of God's awesome multifaceted personality.

It is important to remember when we seek to know more of God that we can never learn all that there is to learn about our FATHER GOD and the LORD JESUS our MESSIAH. Yet, we are charged to learn all that we can of God and His Word.

> WE ARE CHARGED . . . *to believe in, rely upon, trust in, and depend upon the LORD.*
> WE ARE CHARGED . . . *to prevail over the LORD's enemy and ours.*
> WE ARE CHARGED . . . *to Know God in Our Heart and to remember . . .*

"May He be our hiding place and shield as we wait for His Word ...
"May we be sustained according to His Word that we might live"
[Ps. 119:114, 116]

God's Word is Our Plumb Line ~ His Plumb Line to Heaven!

LIFE APPLICATION

1. What prevents intimacy with God? (P. 2)

2. How did Rev. McAlpine teach the author to meditate in the Word? (P. 3)

3. A. Why is scriptural meditation essential to knowing God? B. What does scriptural meditation prepare our heart for? (P. 4)
we understand God's way
B praise, worship, imitate Christ

4. A. How did the New Testament believers spend their time? B. What do we need to recapture and why? (P. 4)
worship & adoration, glorification of Christ

5. What is paramount and foundational to honoring God and overcoming our flesh and the enemy? (P. 5)
Knowing Him & His expectations for us

6. We are called to be overcomers by doing what? (P. 5)
seeking His heart & knowing His heart

7. According to Madam Guyon, how does scriptural meditation help your mind turn inwardly to Christ? (P. 6)
Turning totally focused on Him 4

8. A. What did Oswald Chambers say about friendship? B. And the whole discipline of life? (PP. 6, 7)
it is rare, it is for us to enter into the closest relationship of Christ

9. According to Martyn Lloyd-Jones, what is the essential proof of salvation? (P. 7)
to live to the glory of God

10. What did Ryrie write about the essence of Christian faith regarding the LORD Christ Jesus? (P. 10)
to recognize JC as the Yahweh of the OT

11. What does LORD in all capital letters represent to the author? (P. 10)
it emphasizes Jesus as Lord

12. A. During the Early Church history, what did the Apostles use to support what God was doing in their midst? B. How did the Early Church view Jesus? (PP. 10-11)
the OT *He was the OT Messiah*

13. How did David's qualifications for kingship come? (PP. 11, 12)
    came through testing & experience

14. What did David use to defeat Goliath beside stones and a slingshot? (P. 12)
    boldness, God's blessing, trust in God's ways → face Goliath

15. A. What did David's qualities and belief in God enable him to do? B. What are some of the things we need to be if we want to know God and understand His Word? C. What do we need most of all? (P. 12)
    trusting, humble, obedient, single minded, we need child-like hearts to come to God

16. What must believers understand and do before we learn to prevail against the adversary? (P. 13) *have clean hands & pure hearts to know G*

17. What are believers charged to do? (P. 13) *believe in, rely upon & trust, prevail over enemies, to know G in our hearts & remember He is our "plumb line"*

INTIMACY WITH CHRIST~ BE STILL SCRIPTURE SEQUENCES

Page 2
John 10:28 [Once we are His, He will never let us go]

Page 3
John 17:3 [Those with eternal life know the True God and Jesus Christ whom the Father hast sent]
John 10:28 [Once we are His, He will never let us go]

Page 4
Ps. 119:130 [The unfolding of Thy words gives light ~ it gives understanding to the simple]
Ps. 46:10 [Be still and know that I AM God; I will be exalted among the nations, I will be exalted in the earth]

Page 5
Acts 6:4 [. . . and will give attention to prayer and the ministry of the word.]
1 Pet. 3-5a [In His great mercy, He has given us new birth into a living hope through the resurrection of Jesus Christ from the dead ~ an inheritance that can never perish, spoil or fade, who through faith are shielded by God's power until the coming of the salvation ~ ready to be revealed in the last time.]
Eph. 1:18-23 [I pray also that the eyes of your heart may be enlightened in order that you may know the hope to which He has called you.]
2 Cor. 7:1 [Perfect holiness in the fear of the LORD]
Ps. 105:42, 44 [God remembered His promises; they fell heir to what others had toiled for]
John 3:16, 17 [God gave His Son to save the world, not to condemn it, but to set it free]
John 15:15 [Jesus told His disciples "I have called you friends."]
Ps. 119:130 [The unfolding of His Word gives Light]
Ps. 14:2 [The LORD looks down from heaven on the sons of men to see if they understand and seek God.]
1 Sam. 15:22 [. . . as much as obeying the voice of the LORD? To obey is better than sacrifice]
1 Kings 11-13 [. . . After the fire came a gentle whisper, When Elijah heard it, he pulled his cloak over his face
John 10:11-16 ["I am the Good Shepherd . . . and My sheep know Me . . . they too will listen to My voice."]

Page 6
John 14:23 ["If anyone loves Me, he will obey my teaching, My Father will love him, and We will come to him and make Our home with him."]
Isa. 55:11 ["My word from My mouth will not return to Me empty, but will accomplish what I desire and achieve the purpose for which I sent it."]

Page 7
John 15:1-4 [Jesus is the Vine. We remain "in Him" to bear fruit]
Ps. 105:4 [Look unto the LORD and His strength; seek His face always.]
Isa. 55:6 [Seek the LORD while He may be found]
Titus 2:13, 14 [Jesus redeemed us, purified us to be His possession; that we may be eager to do what is good]

Page 8
Phil. 1:29 AMP [. . . to believe in . . . (to trust in, to cleave to, to adhere to (like glue!)]
Heb. 1:3 [He is the radiance of His glory, the exact representation of His nature, and upholds all things by the word of His power.]

Page 9
Col. 3:3 [For you died, and your life is now hidden with Christ in God]
1 Cor. 2:12, 13 [We received the Spirit from God to understand what God has freely given us which we speak, not in words taught by human wisdom, but in words taught by the Spirit]

Page 9 (continued)
Ps. 46:10   [Be still and know that I AM God; I will be exalted among the nations, I will be exalted in the earth]

Page 10
Rom. 10:17   [Faith comes by hearing the Word of Christ]
Ps. 36:9   [For with You is the fountain of life; in your light we see light]
Col. 3:3   [For you died, and your life is now hidden with Christ in God]
John 21:25   [Jesus did more than can be recorded in all of the books in the world]
Prov. 25:2   [It's to God's glory to conceal; but the honor of kings is to search out a matter]

Page 11
Acts 2:36   [Peter testifies at Pentecost that God made Jesus both LORD and Christ]
Gen. 1; John 1   [The Spirit of Christ was and is God's eternal creative empowerment.]
Gen. 1:1-19   [And God said . . . and God saw that it was good.]
Gen. 12:15   [Sarah was taken for the Pharaoh's harem]
Gen. 20:2   [Abimelech king of Gerar sent and took Sarah.]
Gen. 21:6, 7   [Isaac was promised, Isaac was born]
1 Sam. 16   [The Spirit of the LORD came mightily upon David from that day forward]

Page 12
1 Sam. 16, 17   [The Spirit of the LORD came mightily upon David from that day forward]
1 Sam. 17   [David kills Goliath in the Name of the LORD of Hosts (Yahweh Sabaoth), he trusts God and is not forsaken]
Luke 11:13   ["If you then, though you are evil, know how to give good gifts to your children, how much more will your Father in heaven give the Holy Spirit to those who ask?"]

Page 13
Isa. 1:18   [Come now, let us reason together . . .]
1 John 4:6   [We are from God, and whoever knows God listens to us. This is how we recognize the Spirit of Truth and the spirit of falsehood.]
1 John 5:3-10   [This is love for God: to obey His commands . . . who overcomes the world? Only he who believes that Jesus is the son of God . . . Who came by blood and water . . . there are three that testify: the Spirit, the water, and the blood and the three are in agreement . . . Anyone who believes in the Son of God has this testimony in his heart.]
James 4:7   [Submit yourselves, then, to God. Resist the devil, and he will flee from you.]
Ps. 119:114   [Thou art our hiding place and our shield as we wait for Your Word]
Ps. 119:116   [Sustain us according to Thy Word that we might live, let us not be ashamed of our hope.]

MEDITATION: **BE STILL AND KNOW THAT I AM GOD**

Page 1
Ps. 46:10   [Be still and know that I am God]
Hab. 2:20   [The LORD is in His holy temple; let all the earth be silent before Him]
Ps. 62:1   [My soul finds rest in God alone; my salvation comes from Him]
2 Cor. 7:1   [Perfect holiness in the fear of the LORD]
2 Chron. 16:9   [He is strong in behalf of those whose heart is perfect toward Him]
1Thess. 5:21-24 [His cleansing; examine everything; He is faithful and brings all things to pass]
John 15:7   [Abide in Me and My Words abide in you ~ ask and it shall be done unto you]

INTIMACY WITH CHRIST ENDNOTES

1. A. W. Tozer, *Keys to the Deeper Life*, From the series in Christian Life, by Sunday Magazine, Inc., (Grand Rapids: Zondervan Publishing, 1957).

P.12 A generation ago, as a reaction from Higher Criticism and its offspring, Modernism, there arose in Protestantism a powerful movement in defense of the historic Christian faith. This, for obvious reasons, came to be known as Fundamentalism . . . its purpose was to stay "the rising tide of negation: in Christian theology and to restate and defend the basic doctrines of New Testament Christianity. This much is history."

P.13 What is generally overlooked is that Fundamentalism, as it spread throughout the various denominations and non-denominational groups, fell victim to its own virtues. The Word died in the hands of its friends. Verbal inspiration, for instance (a doctrine which I have always held and do now hold), soon became afflicted with *rigor mortis* . . . the scribe captured the minds of the faithful.

In large areas the religious imagination withered. An unofficial hierarchy decided what Christians were to believe. Not the Scriptures, but what the scribe thought the Scriptures meant became the Christian creed. Christian colleges, seminaries, Bible Institutes, Bible Conferences, popular Bible expositors all joined to promote the cult of textualism.

The system of extreme dispensationalism which was devised relieved the Christian of repentance, obedience and cross-carrying in any other than the most formal sense. Whole sections of the New Testament were taken from the church and disposed of after a rigid system of "dividing the truth."

P.14 All this resulted in a religious mentality inimical to the true faith of Christ. A kind of cold mist settled over the Fundamentalism. Below, the terrain was familiar. This was New Testament Christianity, to be sure. The basic doctrines of the Bible were there, but the climate was just not favorable to the sweet truths of the Spirit.

The whole mood was different from that of the Early Church and of the great souls who suffered and sang and worshiped in the centuries past. The doctrines were sound but something vital was missing. The tree of correct doctrine was never allowed to blossom. The voice of the turtle [dove] was rarely heard in the land; instead, the parrot sat on his artificial perch and dutifully repeated what he had been taught and the whole emotional tone was somber and dull.

Faith, a mighty, vitalizing doctrine in the mouths of the apostles, became in the mouth of the scribe another thing altogether and power went from it.

As the letter triumphed, the Spirit withdrew and textualism ruled supreme. It was the time of the believer's Babylonian captivity. In the interest of accuracy it should be said that this was a general condition only. Certainly there were some even in those low times whose longing hearts were better theologians than their teachers were. These pressed on to a fullness and power unknown to the rest. But they were not many and the odds were too great; they could not dispel the mist that hung over the land. The error of textualism is not doctrinal.

P.15 It is far more subtle than that and much more difficult to discover, but its effects are just as deadly. Not its theological beliefs are at fault, but its assumptions. It assumes, for instance, that if we have the word for a thing we have the thing itself. If it is in the Bible, it is in us. If we have the doctrine, we have the experience. If something was true of Paul it is of necessity true of us because we accept Paul's epistles as divinely inspired. The Bible tells us how to be saved, but *textualism* goes on to make it *tell us that we are saved,* something which in the very nature of things it cannot do. Assurance of individual salvation is thus no more than a logical conclusion drawn from doctrinal premises, and the resultant experience wholly mental. (Emphasis added.)

2. Martyn Lloyd-Jones, *Saved In Eternity*, (Weschester, IL: Crossway Books [division of Good News Publishers], 1988).

   P.69 "They (New Testament Believers) always spent their time in worship and adoration and in the glorification of Him. It seems to me that this is the note that we must recapture, *and that there is no real hope for revival and true awakening until we come back to this*. And the way we do that is to study the Scriptures, to spend our time in reading and meditating upon them and then in humbling ourselves in worship and in adoration before such a marvelous truth . . . apart from anything else, the real cure for most of our subjective ills is ultimately to be so enraptured by the beauty and the glory of Christ that we will forget ourselves and will not have time to think about ourselves at all.

   "Now that is a good bit of psychology."

3. Madame Jeanne Guyon, *Experiencing the Depths of Jesus Christ* (about 1685) (*One of the greatest Christian writings of all time*), Library of Spiritual Classics ~ Volume 2, SeedSowers, (Auburn, ME: Christian Books Publishing House), p.10.

4. Ibid. P.11

5. *MASTER STUDY BIBLE*, New American Standard, Encyclopedia Concordance, (Nashville, TN: Holman Bible Publishers).

   Principles of Translation ~ The Proper Name of God in the Old Testament: In the Scriptures, the name of God is most significant and understandably so. It is inconceivable to think of spiritual matters without a proper designation for the Supreme Deity. Thus the most common name for the Deity is God, a translation of the original Elohim. One of the titles for God is Lord, a translation of Adonai. There is yet another name which is particularly assigned to God as His special or proper name, that is, the four letters YHWH (Exod. 3:14 and Isa. 42:8). This name has not been pronounced by the Jews because of reverence for the great sacredness of the divine name. Therefore, it has been consistently translated LORD. The only exception to this translation of YHWH is when is occurs in immediate proximity to the word Lord, that is, Adonai. In that case it is regularly translated GOD in order to avoid confusion.

   It is known that for many years YHWH has been transliterated as Yahweh, however no complete certainty attaches to this pronunciation.

6. Oswald Chambers, *My Utmost For His Highest*, (Westwood, NJ: Barbour and Company), p. 5, Intimate With Jesus ~ January 7th (John 14:9).

7. Martyn Lloyd-Jones, *Saved In Eternity*, (Westchester, IL: Crossway Books [Division of Good News Publishers]), p. 46.

8. Ibid. P.48

9. John Wimber, *The Best of Praise Vol. 2*, MARANATHA! MUSIC, Distributed by WORD, Inc., p. 30.

10. Charles C. Ryrie, *Basic Theology*, (Wheaton, IL: Victor Books, 1988), p. 49.

11. Kevin J. Conner, *The Tabernacle of David*, (Portland, OR: Conner Publications, 1976), p.1, *Chapter One* ~ THE USE OF THE OLD TESTAMENT IN THE NEW TESTAMENT.

BE STILL AND KNOW THAT I AM GOD
Psalm 46:10

Be Still and Know that I Am GOD!
    Allow Me time to make Myself known to you!
        Cease Striving . . . . . Know that I Am GOD!
            Let Go . . . . . Know that I Am GOD!
                Relax . . . . . Know I AM GOD!

SEEK GOD IN SILENCE . . . . .

Put aside concerns, fears; Worship GOD in silence. [Hab.2:20]
My soul, be thou silent unto God, for my expectation is from Him. [Psa.62:1]
Perfect holiness in the fear of the LORD [2Co.7:1]
"For the eyes of the LORD run to and fro throughout the whole earth,
to show Himself strong in behalf of them whose heart is perfect toward Him." [2Ch.16:9]

SEEK HIS CLEANSING . . . . .

Examine everything carefully; hold fast to that which is good;
abstain from every form of evil.
May the GOD of Peace Himself sanctify you entirely;
May your spirit, soul and body be preserved complete without blame
at the coming of our LORD JESUS CHRIST.
Faithful is He Who calls you; He will also bring it to pass. [1Th.5:21-24]

SEEK HIS PRESENCE . . . . .

"If ye abide in Me, and My Words abide in you,
Ask whatever ye will and it shall be done unto you." [Joh.15:7]
He who dwells in the shelter of the MOST HIGH,
Will abide in the shadow of the ALMIGHTY. [Psa.91:1]

SEEK HIS THOUGHTS . . . . .

"As the heavens are higher than the earth,
so are My thoughts higher than yours." [Isa. 60:9]
"Call unto Me, and I will answer thee,
and will show thee great things, and difficult, which thou knowest not." [Jer.33:3]
"I, The LORD, have spoken it and will do it . . .
I will let the house of Israel ask me to do for them . . .
I will increase their men like a flock." [Eze.36:36]
"If I go away, the Comforter will come unto you. He shall glorify Me,
for He shall take of Mine, and shall declare it unto you." [Joh.16:7, 14]

SEEK HIS ONENESS . . . . .

"I pray that they will all be one ~ even as Thou, Father, are in Me and I in Thee,
That they may be one ~ I in them and Thou in Me.
I have made thy Name known to them ~
That Your love may be in them ~ and I in them."
John 17

Lesson II

RIGHT THOUGHTS AND ATTITUDES

or

CHRIST'S ARMOR WITHIN ~ CHRIST'S ARMOR WITHOUT

*And whatever you do, whether in word or deed,
do it all in the name of the Lord Jesus,
giving thanks to God the Father through Him.*

Colossians 3:10

CHRIST WITHIN ~ CHRIST WITHOUT

COLOSSIANS THREE MEDITATION

If I have been elevated (raised up) with God's Anointed One, my beloved Christ, do I keep seeking the things above as instructed? Seek His heart? Do I get God's understanding through His Anointed One? Do I understand Christ's illumination of Sovereign Authority and Power? Christ is the One Who shatters the contender! The One Who sits at the Most High Place ~ next to Him Who Sits On The Throne. Precious Abba Father, forgive me. Change my selfish heart.

Do I set my mind on the things above? God's interests? His attributes? His character? His timing? His demonstrations and examples of love? Do I Know my LORD's framework? His standards as my example? Do I live by and in His Grace He so freely gave? Do I walk in forgiveness at all times? Sadly, Father, not like I should! Not like I want to. O, LORD, forgive me.

Is my flesh dead to self? Have I stopped seeking recognition and appreciation? Do my thoughts reflect Christ crucified? Are my thoughts, interests, and priorities truly "hidden with Christ in God," hidden with God's Anointed One, hidden *in* Him? Have I let the very GOD of all creation take me, through Christ's anointing and authority, to the right hand of Your Presence to be truly hidden, unseen by anyone, except Elohim, my true Father? Abba Father, I sadly confess that I fall short; my flesh is so abrasive. Oh, LORD, forgive my selfishness and create a clean heart in me.

When Christ, the Anointed One, has control of me, and is revealed in my life, then I will walk without fear. I'll be empowered by the Highest Everlasting Authority to be the overcomer that His victory provides. Precious LORD, You are my Stronghold, my Enabler, my Rock, my Refuge, please change me so that I will not have to sadly admit to You, *"No, but . . . !"*

LORD, I pray to be . . .

RAISED UP . . . with the Holy One!
RAISED UP . . . with Christ, my Seal!
RAISED UP . . . with the Giver of Peace!
RAISED UP . . . with the Savior of Mankind!
RAISED UP . . . with the Blessed One, Your Ordained!
RAISED UP . . . with the Liberator, the Divinely Anointed One!
RAISED UP . . . with the Anointed Consecrated One ~ Messiah, our Messianic Prince!
RAISED UP . . . with the Hallowed One, Your wisdom, and the Enabler of Your Power!
RAISED UP . . . with Christ's Authority to tread on scorpions and serpents to Your glory!
RAISED UP . . . TO WALK IN YOUR GLORIOUS AND HOLY PRESENCE!

RAISED UP . . . TO EXPRESS ADORATION TO YOU . . . to be empowered by Your anointing that You give Your children, even this child. Empowered to seek things from above through the Righteous blood of Christ. LORD, I yearn to see You, Eternal Sovereign Christ, our King, as revealed through the WORD . . . You are Yahweh of Ancient of Days.

LORD, Thank You, Praise You ~ I love You, adore You, help me to reflect Your love.

RIGHT THOUGHTS AND ATTITUDES

CHRIST'S ARMOR AND WITHOUT

*"Let your attitude toward one another be governed by
your being in union with the Messiah Yeshua."*
[Phil. 2:5   Jewish New Testament]

***A**BATTLE RAGES FOR OUR SOULS AND STARTS IN OUR MINDS.* We need to take a stand against the enemy by becoming aware of how Christ would have us think and how we can acquire right thoughts and right attitudes. Doing so will prepare us to be ready for God's purposes and plans for our lives. Thoughts and attitudes determine the effectiveness of our lives and prayers.

This lesson explores where wrong thoughts and attitudes originate, tells how to resist them by testing the spirits behind them, and enlightens you on how to protect yourself with God's armor and through the power of the blood of the Lamb. It will also give you biblical steps to help resist wrong thoughts and attitudes that might withhold God's blessings and answers to your prayers.

Wrong thoughts instigate wrong attitudes and for that reason they are referred to in similar fashion in some of the following areas.

***R**IGHT AFTER SEVERAL INTERNATIONAL CRASHES,* I was on an airplane and listening to the flight attendant's passionate instructions to her passengers. I was amazed at how she paralleled my current study in Colossians on right thoughts and attitudes. She talked about the importance of having a right attitude at all times in order to be prepared for a crisis. She said that carelessness causes vulnerability and that it is vital to our personal safety to listen keenly and follow instructions. She added it was important to avoid unnecessary obstacles, that carry-ons should be safely stowed away, and warned that daydreaming at the wrong time, and even wrong posture, can create a potentially dangerous situation. She continued that ignorance, presumption, misunderstanding, willfully doing your own thing, even fear, can turn a successful rescue plan into a disaster. If one person fails to follow instructions, it may not be critical, however, if several do not follow instructions, it can cause confusion, disorder, and invite disaster. Lastly, she stressed that it was essential to have faith in who is leading you because they know how to protect you.

I REFLECTED THAT HER PHYSICAL INSTRUCTIONS PARALLELED PAUL'S TEACHINGS that a believer should listen keenly to God's commands and follow His rescue plan ~ His instructions. The flight attendant's emotional conversation about a person's flight safety in the event of a crisis, paralleled Paul's instructions for our safety (Salvation), and our need to be prepared daily (armed for battle). The safety pamphlet that she held up (the Bible) illustrated the airplane's safety features (God's instructions for a godly life, His plans, purposes and protection).

PAUL'S INSTRUCTIONS CONTINUED TO PARALLEL THE FLIGHT ATTENDANT when she talked about the importance of wearing a seat belt at all times (belt of Truth), and she pointed out that the aisle's floor light (God's Light) will guide us toward escape routes (conviction, repentance, forgiveness, restoration, etc.). If there is trouble in the operating system (unrighteous thought or attitude that is a stronghold), an oxygen mask (God's Holy Spirit) drops down to revive us. Our respect (fear of the LORD) in following instructions (the Bible) is our shield (Faith) and refuge (Peace). She later shared with us that she hoped that seasoned travelers (believers/intercessors) had listened so they would be ready and prepared (follow God's instructions) for any event. When she talked about the importance of having a right attitude in all situations, I was reminded Paul taught us that our attitude should be the same as Christ Jesus [Phil. 2:5].

COLOSSIANS 3 UNDERSCORES WHAT OUR CHRISTIAN GOALS SHOULD BE and how we need to continually practice having our mind, our thoughts, renewed by putting on the new self so that we are continually "renewed in fuller and fuller knowledge, closer and closer to the image of our Creator" [Col. 3:10 JNT]. We are so blessed that Christ, the wisdom and power of God ~ *God's true knowledge* ~ wants to direct us, protect us, and rescue us from the disastrous actions and attitudes that easily invade our hearts that cause an inward crash (sin). We need Christ to be all, and in all, that we think, say, and do ~ without discrimination ~ to have Christ's all for our all! [Col. 3:11]

GOD WANTS US TO CHOOSE CHRIST-LIKE THOUGHTS to put in our hearts for our protective *"inner armor"* to help guard against fleshly suggestions, wrong attitudes, presumptions, and affections. Although it is hard to do some of the time, it is important to continually check our thoughts before we speak.

We need to train ourselves to listen keenly to God's Word, study His ways, and seek Christ's thoughts to replace our own. We need to guard our hearts against the things here on earth (threatening, presumptive, unforgiving negative thoughts) that evolve into disobedience and ultimately produces wrong attitudes that grieve the Holy Spirit.

Many times, a wrong attitude (major obstruction) had prevented me from communicating Christ to others. Self-righteousness and a critical spirit had made me a poor witness. I deeply repented, then confessed my need and desire to have Christ's attitude inside my heart, as well as God's armor outside *(outer armor)*. I began searching Scripture for instructions that would teach me how to train my thoughts and attitudes to be in union with Christ's thoughts, attitudes, strength through humility, and love, so that I could better look out for the interest of others[1] [Phil. 2:1-11; Col. 3:2].

(Please understand that I am sharing what Scripture teaches, not what I have achieved. It is an ongoing battle. Praise God, Jesus came into this world not to judge it, but to set it free! [John 3:17] When I blow it, it is a blessing and comfort after confessing my sin/s to remember that *only* Christ was perfect, and He came to set us free. What awesome mercy and grace!)

THE BATTLE RAGES IN OUR MINDS. Peter said for us to be self-controlled and alert. Our enemy, the devil, prowls around like a roaring lion looking for someone to devour [1 Pet. 5:8]. The enemy likes to take us captive to wrong thoughts, attitudes, imaginings, unforgiveness, and even presumptions that he subtly plants. Accepting wrong thoughts gives the devil legal grounds to attack us. The obstructive, distracting, fleshly thoughts of anger, self-righteousness, bitterness, slander, faultfinding, lies, filthy language from our lips, and so forth [Col. 3:8], can be triumphed over by repenting and appropriating the mind of Christ and asking to be renewed in the knowledge of our Creator [Col. 3:10].

Paul exhorted us to take Christ's attitude, nature, and character for our new self, which is our *inner armor*. We need to raise our humble hearts into God's presence and put on (put in) our heart Christ's anointed attitude, and His Word, to fill our thoughts to be prepared to prevail *through Christ* in our daily battles. We are to follow the LORD "with the spirit of our mind renewed to that which is good, acceptable, and the perfect will of God" [Rom. 12:2], without distinction [Col. 3:11].

OUR THOUGHTS CONSTANTLY CHOOSE between the examples of Christ, our flesh, and the enemy's influence ~ there is no gray area! *He takes things that we know are wrong and makes them appear to be right.* To give in to the enemy's thoughts and suggestions *enslaves* us to his control and opens us up to unrighteousness. The resulting obstructions, distractions, and sin inevitably cause casualties to God's plan for our lives ~ or His plan for others!

Let us rejoice that Christ provided our rescue from the enemy's captivity over our thoughts and attitudes to His captivity. The fruit of the Spirit is to replace our sinful nature. Let us put on, *"put in"* our hearts, the fruit of the Holy Spirit which is love, joy, peace, patience, kindness, goodness, faithfulness, gentleness and self-control [Gal. 5:22, 23], plus His compassion, humility, and forgiveness.

AN AREA OF CONCERN FOR ALL CHRISTIANS IS UNFORGIVENESS which starts in our thoughts, evolves in our attitudes and ultimately our actions. We are to forgive others as we have been forgiven by Christ [Col. 3:12, 13]. Christ said from the Cross, "Father, forgive them, they know not what they do" [Luke 23:34]. Jesus demonstrated His patience, love, and forgiveness for others during His anguish on the Cross. We, too, are to forgive in the darkest of moments. God's children are instructed to forgive and not discriminate or show preference. It is not an option, but a command [John 20:23].

THE JEWISH NEW TESTAMENT **translated Colossians 3:11, 15:**

> The new self allows no room for discriminating between Gentile and Jew, circumcised and uncircumcised, foreigner, savage, slave, free man; on the contrary, in all, the Messiah is everything . . . let the shalom (peace) which comes from the Messiah be your heart's decision maker, for this is why you were called to be part of a single Body.[2]

Christ, Messiah in Hebrew, means "anointed, consecrated, set apart, i.e., the One Who by His Holy Spirit and power indwells believers and molds their character in conformity to His likeness."[3]

THE HOLY SPIRIT'S POWER INDWELLS BELIEVERS TO MOLD OUR CHARACTER into Christ's likeness. We are exhorted to "put in" our new self, Christ's attitude (our inner armor), renewed to a true knowledge, according to the image of the One Who created us. Pondering God's armor, in relation to right and wrong attitudes, I envisioned how a soldier would suffer when putting on heavy cold metal armor (bitterness, anger, unforgiveness, etc.) directly next to his flesh *and I cringed!*

How would a cowboy react if he put chaps next to his skin without the protective liners and pants ~ *he would suffer!*

The analogies show what happens when we choose to ignore doing things the LORD's way. The result of not having a protective inner garment causes a lot of pain, distraction, discomfort, and suffering. We need to "take off" our dirty undergarments (earthly nature) that have been soiled by worldly influences [Col. 3:5] before we put on God's righteous armor. They are incompatible! Wrong thoughts and attitudes have the same effect on our spiritual body. It would be counterproductive, to say the least, if we did not invite the Holy Spirit to search our hearts, to learn if we have sinned in His sight *before* we put on the armor of God [Eph. 6:11]. Our heart is to be conformed to His heart.

Like warriors today, it is important to put on our safety paraphernalia to keep from unnecessary suffering, ours or others. Christ's "inner armor" ~ clean hands and pure heart ~

was Jesus' safety factor that He walked in to keep His thoughts and attitudes in readiness. Christ walked in obedience to God's purposes and plans. His earthly life, death in His flesh and death *to* His flesh, ultimately triumphed over sin and death. Likewise, our inner armor must agree with the ***mind of Christ*** [1 Cor. 2:16] to be protected and equipped for victory over our flesh.

DO WE DAILY SUBMIT OUR MINDS TO GOD FOR CONSECRATION so we can successfully resist the devil? Do we set our minds apart so that our attitudes can be molded to reflect the LORD's attitudes? Or "put in" our hearts His anointed thoughts of forgiveness, grace, mercy and unconditional love to conquer and dissolve obstructive thoughts of presumption, resentment, immorality, impurity, passion, evil desire, greed (covetousness amounting to idolatry), and on and on, that brings God's wrath? [Col. 3:5] Or refuse fleshly, negative, accusing thoughts? Do we substitute righteous, Christ-like hearts, to God?

WE HAVE BEEN RAISED WITH CHRIST [Col. 3:1]. We are to "put in" our hearts ***the attitude of Christ, the mind of Christ***, by setting our hearts and minds (our attitudes) on things above [Col. 3:1, 2]; so that our thoughts will be ***hidden with Christ in God*** [Col.3:3]. We are to put on our new self, renewed in knowledge in the image of its Creator [Col.3:10]. Above all, we are to clothe ourselves with the ***love of Christ*** [Col.3:14], which binds compassion, kindness, gentleness, patience, forbearance, and forgiveness together, and enables our inner self (armor) and outer self (armor) to walk **in *unity with Christ*** (perfection in Christ) [Col. 3:14, 15].

We are told to let ***the peace of Christ*** (His integrity and well-being) [Col. 3:15] rule in our hearts with thanksgiving [Col. 3:15]. The ***mind of Christ***, the **Word of Christ** [Col. 3:16], is God's provision that is to dwell in us richly as we teach and admonish one another with all wisdom. The ***mind of Christ and the love of Christ combined*** is like a woven mesh, a protective inner armor, that will set our inner self free. When we look at the LORD, He radiates from within [Ps. 34:5]. The ***peace of Christ*** is His wholeness, His oneness, which includes judging (discerning), deciding, controlling and ruling in the hearts of believers.[4] (Emphasis Added.)

THERE ARE SO MANY QUESTIONS THAT WE CAN ASK OURSELVES. Do we allow Christ to judge, decide, control, and rule our hearts? Do we allow Christ to richly dwell within our hearts with all wisdom and teaching? [Col. 3:16] Do we think upon the Word of Christ? Do we tell Christ of our love for Him? [John 21:17] Do we sing spiritual songs to Him about His Holy Names, His character, His accomplishments, His blessings? Do we speak or sing about our thankfulness and gratitude to Him? Do we praise Him from within our inner self (armor)? Do we uplift each other with psalms that exalt bless His Holy Name? Do we encourage one another through His Word with hymns of joy unto His Majesty? [Col. 3:16-17]

WE ARE CALLED TO WALK IN THE JOY OF CHRIST, have an attitude of gratitude, and put on the full armor of God so that we can be *defensive* and *offensive* Soldiers of Christ. We often hear about the defensive aspect of God's armor. Armor is for war; it is designed to be used offensively *and* defensively! Soldiers are to go to war to be *victorious!* Christ Jesus, our leader and defender, taught that we are to take a stand in obedience to His principles, using His armor and victorious blood, while He guards, protects and wards off all the flaming missiles of the enemy. His righteous thoughts throughout eternity have and will continue to be offensive to the enemy!

We can have victory in Jesus over our thoughts and attitudes ~ they are freely provided through the living blood of Christ. His blood voluntarily continues to undertake our defense and cleanse us from sin. It is important to understand what the life of Christ's un-perishable blood does for us. The Son of God, the Son of Man, His deathless Blood, still avails itself to transfuse and redeem our thoughts and actions! Christ's Blood is our gift of eternal life [Rom. 6:23]. His triumph cancels all of the enemy's judgments against us.

CHRIST'S BLOOD LIVES TO CLEANSE AND PROTECT OUR MINDS (thoughts and attitudes) and our hearts (what we say). His blood still carries life! His sinless Blood[5] is spiritually transfused to us through the Holy Spirit. We can proclaim that the Blood of the LORD Jesus Christ is incorruptible, indestructible, and lives to cover the portals of our thoughts and attitudes. We are armed by Christ's triumph on Calvary's Cross, His resurrection, and His ascension. We should put our trust in the fact that Christ's innocent atoning Blood has *infused* our blood to convict, cleanse, sanctify, justify, redeem, and arm us within with His righteous thoughts.

DR. DE HAAN WROTE:

Blood is sacred and the life of the blood is the peculiar and particular contribution of divine life to man.[6]

Then there was one man who gave His sinless blood on the Cross of Calvary. It needed no preservative for it was sinless, incorruptible, deathless blood. *There is a blood bank which was opened at the hill of Calvary, and into that bank went the blood of the Son of God Himself, the Lord Jesus Christ.* It suits every type, avails for everyone, is free to all who will submit to its transfusion by the Holy Spirit.[7]

The blood of the Lord Jesus Christ was *incorruptible, indestructible blood* and therefore could not perish . . . it is in existence today [Heb. 13:20; 1 John 1:9] and that blood will remain forever and ever. It is called innocent blood [Matt. 27:14]; sanctifying blood [Heb. 13:12]; justifying blood [Rom. 5:9] and redeeming blood [Col. 1:14].[8]

Blood is life in the physical, but more important, and the thing that we are now interested in, *blood is life in the spiritual as well*. For it is the Blood of Jesus Christ His Son that cleanseth us from all sin.[9] (Emphasis added.)

THE BLOOD OF JESUS AND THE ARMOR OF GOD ARE VITAL to battle our wrong thoughts and attitudes. Paul instructed us to put on the armor of God, His spiritual authority, to protect and strengthen us to stand against the enemy (body, soul and spirit). It is joyful and faith building to hear ourselves trustingly state out loud that each aspect of His armor is active on our behalf [Eph. 6:10-18]. We are taught to put on God's armor and are exhorted to be powerful *in* the LORD and *in* the strength of His might.

THE JEWISH NEW TESTAMENT **interpreted Ephesians 6:10-18:**

[10]Finally, grow powerful in union with the Lord, in union with his mighty strength![11] Use all the armor and weaponry that God provides, so that you will be able to stand against the deceptive tactics of the Adversary. [12]For we are not struggling against human beings, but against the rulers, authorities and cosmic powers governing this darkness, against the spiritual forces of evil in the heavenly realm. [13]So take up every piece of war equipment God provides; so that when the evil day comes, you will be able to resist; and when the battle is won, you will still be standing.
[14] Therefore, stand! Have the belt of truth buckled around your waist, put on righteousness for a breastplate, [15]and wear on your feet the readiness that comes from the Good News of shalom. [16]Always carry the shield of trust, with which you will be able to extinguish all the flaming arrows of the Evil One. [17]And take the helmet of deliverance, along with the sword given by the Spirit, that is, the Word of God; [18] as you pray at all times, with all kinds of prayers and requests, in the Spirit, vigilantly and persistently, for all God's people.

AFTER WE PUT ON GOD'S ARMOR, we should rebuke wrong thoughts and attitudes in the Name of Jesus and tell them we are armed by God, His power and authority and tell them they must leave! We endeavor to put on the mind of Christ, have righteous thoughts, and commit our unrighteous thoughts to God, then declare, "Not I, but Christ" [Gal. 2:20].

His Word teaches us to yield our carnal nature to His authority so that our habits might conform to His will [Col. 3:10; 2 Pet. 1:4]. We are instructed to examine everything carefully, abstain from evil, and hold fast to that which is good [1Thess. 5:21-24]. It is a continual battle in our thoughts and attitudes.

SCRIPTURE POINTS OUT THAT TO FORGIVE OTHER BELIEVERS in the presence of Christ is a disadvantage to the enemy who schemes "to divide and conquer believers in Christ" [2 Cor. 2:10, 11]. We need to ask ourselves if we have any roots of bitterness, resentment, or possible feelings of being threatened by person(s) or circumstance(s).

WE ARE TO SEEK GOD'S COUNSEL AND WAIT FOR HIM to impress our heart before we speak, then we are to walk in His guidance. His fruits of the Spirit are love, joy, peace, patience, kindness, goodness, faithfulness, gentleness and self-control. Against such things there is no law! [Gal. 5:22]

Since it is best to remember to take inventory and to confess our sins before putting on Christ's armor, I normally do it in the morning, or whenever quickened by the Holy Spirit. I verbally put on the armor of God before getting out of bed or as soon afterward as possible. It *is* faith-building.

PAUL TAUGHT US THAT FAITH COMES BY HEARING AND HEARING BY THE WORD OF CHRIST [Rom. 10:17]. I never put on the armor of God by rote. My heart needs to allow the Holy Spirit to freshly, devotionally, impress me with God's provisions. I take up the sword of the Spirit then continue putting on God's armor at my most vulnerable area ~ the top of my head! I thank Jesus that He is faithful and just to forgive my sins and to cleanse me from *all* unrighteousness [1 John 1:9]. Praise the LORD, that must mean that He even forgives the sins I do not see. Following is a sample of putting on the armor of God [Eph. 6:10-18], in a way that helps me to remember things, by doing them in sequence.

I TAKE UP THE SWORD OF THE SPIRIT, THE WORD OF GOD, to ward off all of the flaming arrows of the enemy in the Name of Jesus, saying that I am strong in the LORD and in His Mighty Power. I resist demon powers, principalities, powers of this present world darkness, and evil spirits of the heavenly spheres [Eph. 6:10-12

FATHER GOD, I PLEAD THE PRECIOUS UNBLEMISHED BLOOD OF THE LAMB over me, my family and my efforts today. Thank You for telling me to be strong in You and Your mighty power. Bless You for telling me to put on Your full armor, that my struggles are not against flesh and blood but influencing spirits around me and others.

I PUT ON THE HELMET OF SALVATION, the sinless Blood of Jesus, to cover my mind, my memory, my nerve cells, my subconscious, my flesh and any other area that I have not thought of . . . Thank You, Father God, that Jesus' blood sanctified me, reconciled me, justified me, redeemed me, and made me innocent in Your sight. Father God, You are so good.

I PUT ON THE BREASTPLATE OF YOUR RIGHTEOUSNESS and thank You that You look at me through the righteousness of Jesus.

I GIRD MY LOINS WITH YOUR TRUTH ~ Oh, Holy Spirit of Christ, Spirit of Truth, invite you and desperately need You to lead me today in paths of righteousness for Your Name's sake. Help me to listen to Your still quiet inner voice.

I SHOD MY FEET WITH YOUR PEACE ~ Your harmony, wholeness, well being and integrity ~ which is the preparation for sharing Your Gospel.

LORD, I TAKE UP THE SHIELD OF FAITH TO WARD OFF THE ENEMY'S FLAMING ARROWS ~ faith in Your love, Your protection, Your promises, Your victory, Your faithfulness, Your plans, Your provisions, Your triumphant victory. Thank You from the bottom of my heart that You watch over me.

*IN THE **VICTORIOUS** NAME OF **JESUS CHRIST**, MY LORD AND **SAVIOR**, I resist* unholy spirits, unrighteous spirits, and all spirits that may be trying to influence me. Thank You LORD, that I can trust You to lead, protect, and inspire me today.

FATHER, THANK YOU, YOUR GLORY IS MY REAR GUARD. [Isa. 58:8]. Hallelujah and Amen! What a mighty God we serve!

Clean hands and a pure heart, armed by God and inspired by the Holy Spirit, will inflame a passionate devotion to the LORD Jesus Christ.

REVEREND CHAMBERS WROTE IN MY UTMOST FOR HIS HIGHEST:
The Service of Passionate Devotion, June 19, A person touched by the Spirit of God suddenly says, "Now I see who Jesus is!" ~ that is the source of devotion. People do not want to be devoted to Jesus, but only to the cause He started. Jesus Christ is deeply offensive to the educated minds of today, to those who only want Him to be their Friend, and who are unwilling to accept Him in any other way.

DAVID DEVOTIONALLY SERVED SAUL AS UNTO THE LORD. He was rewarded by the LORD when he sang worshipfully and intimately unto the LORD to soothe King Saul's heart. Like David, we too are to do all devotionally unto the LORD, not unto leadership, for our personal agendas, or to seek recognition. It is imperative to guard against our flesh in our thoughts and attitudes. We need to persevere when we have no vision, feel that we have nothing to offer, no encouragement, no obvious improvement of our circumstances, that we've been put on a shelf, and so forth.

DAVID WALKED OUT HIS DEVOTION WHEN HE SOUGHT GOD to be able to persevere in his battle against discouragement and things that seemed to go awry. David knew that God establishes and removes leaders. David was *an anointed one,* but he would not touch Saul. "Touch not My anointed" was deeply imbedded in his heart [1 Chron. 16:22]. He did not try to manipulate or help God establish his promised kingship, or do things "his way." Obviously, the enemy attacked David's thoughts but he battled back! David's mind and his character, trained to reflect righteousness, was stayed upon God.

THE LORD JESUS CHRIST, OUR EXAMPLE, never operated in the negative thought arena. His root was centered in the Word. *His Word is our source for prayer. His Word* will remove negative, accusing, and bitter attitudes to produce the fruit of righteousness. *His Word is* to be sown in mercy by those who pursue peace [Rom. 14:19]. We remember and pray His Word through His gift of grace then trust that it will be outworked by His power [Eph. 3:7].

Scripture teaches us: "Submit therefore to God, resist the devil and he will flee. Draw near to God and He will draw near to you. Cleanse your hands you sinners, and purify your hearts, you double-minded. Humble yourselves in the presence of the LORD and He will exalt you" [James 4:7-10].

WALK BY THE SPIRIT and you will not carry out the desires of the flesh which is the area that the enemy invades. But the fruit of the Spirit [Gal. 5:16, 22, 23] is our plumb line to question our thoughts before our actions take hold. "You will guard him and keep him in perfect and constant peace whose mind [both its inclination and its character] is stayed upon You, because he commits himself to You, leans on You and hopes confidently in You. Trust in the LORD ~ commit yourself to Him, lean on Him, hope confidently in Him ~ forever; for the LORD GOD is an everlasting rock ~ the Rock of Ages" [Isa. 26:3, 4 AMP].

Scripture shows that the twelve disciples had to learn to keep their thoughts and attitudes in the right place ~ it did not happen overnight! There was a lack of unity between the twelve disciples. Many were preoccupied with thoughts of position, recognition, a need for appreciation and fleshly lusts! We should seek Scripture to understand how the LORD God would have us respond to Him, circumstances, and people, so that our walk and prayers will be in obedience to His guidance! When we search Scripture for intellectual pursuits, personal gain, or approval, we are not pleasing God.

> ***A TIMELY QUOTE FROM OSWALD CHAMBERS:***
> The Way to Knowledge, July 27. The golden rule to follow spiritual understanding is not one of intellectual pursuit, but one of obedience . . . if he desires knowledge and insight into the teachings of Jesus Christ, he can only obtain it through obedience . . . No one ever receives a word from God without instantly being put to the test regarding it.

We must continuously be on guard and test the origin of our thoughts. *The enemy initiates his attacks in our thoughts, which come from three sources, the devil, our flesh, and the Holy Spirit.*

A.W. TOZER WROTE IN MAN THE DWELLING PLACE OF GOD:

He has given us the Scriptures, the Holy Spirit and natural powers of observation, and He expects us to avail ourselves of their help constantly. "Prove all things; hold fast that which is good," said Paul [1 Thess. 5:21].

"Beloved, believe not every spirit," wrote John, "but try the spirits whether they are of God: because many false prophets have gone out into the world" [1 John 4:1]. From this it is plain not only that there shall be false spirits abroad, endangering our Christian lives, but that they may be identified and known for what they are . . . The human mind is capable of plenty of mischief without help from the devil.[10]

Any doctrine, any experience that serves to magnify Him is likely to be inspired by Him. Conversely, anything that veils His glory or makes Him appear less wonderful is sure to be of the flesh or the devil.[11]

IF SATAN'S PLOTS AND SCHEMES, along with our fleshly, worldly thoughts of mischief, are allowed to remain in our mind, we will accept them and often reflect them. We need to resist (refuse) all questionable, sudden, diverting, procrastinating, accusing thoughts in the Name of Christ Jesus and *forbid them to return.* The Holy Spirit speaks to our inner self, our spirit. The Adversary speaks to our mind.

THE SCREWTAPE LETTERS, by C.S. Lewis, is a small entertaining and enlightening book that gives a lot of practical examples of the enemy's assignments that can influence our relationship with God and destroy God's plans and purposes in our thoughts and lives.

WE ARE TO TEST THE SPIRITS in our imagination and questionable thoughts, wrong thoughts, and take authority over them, and then we submit them to God for forgiveness and cleansing. Tell the Accuser that our thoughts were purchased by the Blood of Christ [Rom. 5:9] that forgives us, and makes our thoughts innocent, sanctified, justified, and redeemed.[12]

An example of how to test the spirits is when we receive an offensive or accusing thought, even a thought that we question or wonder if it really is from God, we are to resist the thought and tell it that it must leave in the Name of Jesus. Occasionally, vain imaginings from our flesh return ~ *simply resist again!* Rebuke, prohibit and command the thought(s) to leave through the power of Jesus' Name! You'll be amazed how it simply fades away. *If the thought returns a third time,* and it still does not seem that it is from God, *(you always want to be sure if it is from God),* test it again and tell it that it cannot come back unless it is from Jesus Christ Himself! It is amazing how God's thoughts will persist and at the same time if the thought is not from God it will vanish.

REFUSING THE ACCUSER'S INFLUENCE LIBERATES US to be the LORD's overcomers. Remember that His provisions will not, cannot, help us if we do not use them! (Rarely is agreement with another trusted believer necessary to breakthrough against an ongoing tormenting thought, but a trusted mature intercessor can edify, help us, and enable us to pray from Christ's perspective and in His character [2 Cor. 10:3-6].

WE NEED TO CRUCIFY OUR FLESH, OUR PASSIONS AND OUR DESIRES in order to crucify our unrighteous attitudes. "Now those who belong to Christ Jesus have crucified the flesh with its passions and desires. Let us not become boastful, challenging one another, envying one another [Gal. 5:24-26], but pray and petition at all times in the Spirit for all the saints" [Eph. 6:18]. Jesus, the Merciful Shepherd, exhibited death to self and revealed the Cross. Paul and the disciples pointed to the Cross! Do our lives point to the Cross? Or, do our fingers point away from the Cross and toward others by judging them with presumptive accusing thoughts or words?

There are times when we feel we have every right to be angry over a deed or circumstance (which might have been meant for good). We have done things or spoken words that seemingly came from nowhere and caused another to go ballistic, perhaps opened a kettle of worms. We may try to minister to a person when it is untimely because we care so much, or to a person who is not receptive or might resent the intrusion. We pray and ask the LORD to put forgiveness toward us in their heart, and ask Him if it, our action(s), warrants an apology. Unless He leads, let it lie dormant.

WHEN I WAS IN THE SIXTH GRADE, Mother was exhausted and had a lot of errands to run, groceries to buy, etc. She commented as she left that she had to come home and mop the floor. I felt so sorry for her and wanted to make her happy so I thought it would be a good thing to mop the floor while she was gone. I used too much water and propped the kitchen door open with Jimmy's bat to sweep the excess water out and let the breeze inside to dry the floor. When Mother got home she could not open the front door ~ the Florida summer heat caused it to warp. She was furious and cursed me out good and proper! I cried that I was so sorry. My heart was shattered as I watched her angrily unload the groceries in the pantry. To make matters worse, a garter snake crawled out from under the refrigerator and she screamed and ran! (It had crawled in on Jimmy's bat.) I got a good spanking. However, years later she retold the episode regaling in laughter.

ANOTHER TIME, MANY YEARS LATER, AN INTERIM CLEANING LADY used Brasso to clean our treated polished brass bathroom fixtures and other finished brass items throughout our home. I returned home several months later to find pink, green, and brown colors on my treated polished brass. I was beside myself ~ in a mixture of shock, anger and unbelief anyone would do such a thing. She was due the next day. I began to cry (probably wailed) and prayed about it because it was tearing me up.

A BATTLE BEGAN WITH THE ACCUSER OVER MY THOUGHTS. An inner voice reminded me that Jesus watched well meaning people crucify Him. His response was, "Father, forgive them for they know not what they do." I asked God to help me forgive her as He would have forgiven me. Determined to forgive, I continued to pray forgiveness into the circumstance, then thanked God that He is greater than the problem and concentrated on all that He is. It brought His wonderful peace that was followed by diplomatic ways (thoughts) to discuss the situation with her.

The cleaning lady must have dreaded facing me. I discerned that she did *not* know what she was doing. She was a sweet, kind hearted lady who would not have ruined all of those things on purpose. *Discernment reflects compassion; criticism reflects judgment!* There was no sense in looking backward. What was done, was done!

THE DIFFERENCE IN THE TWO EPISODES is that Mother did not know the LORD's provisions and instructions, so she took the circumstances out on a child that had received a wrong influence (thought) from a wrong source. On the other hand, while learning a lot of lessons the hard way, I began to study the Word, and tried to practice His provisions to forgive in all circumstances, and to overcome my impatient, critical, and judgmental spirit. It further helped when I read the following devotion by Oswald Chambers, which identified a lot of thoughts and attitudes that I battled and still need to watch.

Reverend Chambers wrote June 17, *BEWARE OF CRITICIZING OTHERS:*

Judge not, that you be not judged [Matt. 7:1] Jesus' instructions with regard to judging others is very simply put; He says, "Don't." The average Christian is the most piercingly critical individual known. Criticism is one of the ordinary activities of people, but in the spiritual realm nothing is accomplished by it.

The effect of criticism is the dividing up of the strengths of the one being criticized. The Holy Spirit is the only One in the proper position to criticize, and He alone is able to show what is wrong without hurting and wounding. It is impossible to enter into fellowship with God when you are in a critical mood.

Criticism serves to make you harsh, vindictive, and cruel, and leaves you with the soothing and flattering idea that you are somehow superior to others. Jesus says that as His disciple you should cultivate a temperament that is never critical. This will not happen quickly but must be developed over a span of time. You must constantly beware of anything that causes you to think of yourself as a superior person. There is no escaping the penetrating search of my life by Jesus. If I see the little speck in your eye, it means that I have a plank of timber in my own [see Matt. 7:3-5]. Every wrong thing that I see in you, God finds in me. Every time I judge, I condemn myself [see Rom. 2:17-24].

Stop having a measuring stick for other people. There is always at least one more fact, which we know nothing about, in every person's situation. The first thing God does is to give us a thorough spiritual cleaning. After that, there is no possibility of pride remaining in us. I have never met a person I could despair of, or lose all hope for, after discerning what lies in me apart from the grace of God.

Prayerfully reading James is invaluable in our ongoing battle to allow the Holy Spirit to convict and bring repentance regarding a possible "log in our eye."

THIS MIGHT BE A GOOD TIME TO TAKE A FEW MOMENTS TO PERSONALLY search our own hearts to see if we are impatient, critical, judgmental, or resent anyone. LORD, show us if we have a log in our eyes. Reveal pride, presumption, disillusionment, resentment, a critical spirit, misunderstanding, bitterness, jealousy, feelings of being threatened, or any negative force that may be influencing us.

Have we misread or misjudged another person's motives? Oh, LORD, open my thoughts to Your truth. Please expose, forgive, and erase my unrighteousness with the Blood of the Lamb that they can be sanctified. Give me Your righteous attitude and renew the conviction that but for Your grace and mercy, there go I!

WE BRING FORTH JOY TO JESUS' HEART when we remember our indebtedness to Christ, confess our sin, repent, ask, and receive forgiveness in belief [1 John 1:9]. Repentance allows our thoughts to be "crucified with Christ" so that we may in truth declare, "I no longer live, but Christ lives in me. The life I live in the body, I live by faith in the Son of God, Who loved me and gave Himself for me" [Gal. 2:20].

Another area of concern is false doctrine. We need to be continually mindful of being too eager to seek out new and wonderful "truths."

REVEREND TOZER WROTE:

> These are times that try men's souls. The Spirit has spoken expressly that in the latter times some should depart from the faith, giving heed to seducing spirits and doctrines of demons; speaking lies in hypocrisy; having their conscience seared with a hot iron. Those days are upon us and we cannot escape them; we must triumph in the midst of them, for such is the will of God concerning us.
>
> Strange as it may seem, the danger today is greater for the fervent Christian than for the lukewarm and self-satisfied. The seeker after God's best things is eager to hear anyone who offers a way by which he can obtain them. He longs for some new experience, some elevated view of truth, some operation of the Spirit that will raise him above the dead level of religious mediocrity he sees all around him. For this reason he is ready to give a sympathetic ear to the new and wonderful in religion, particularly if it is presented by someone with an attractive personality and reputation for superior godliness. Now our Lord Jesus, that great Shepherd of the sheep, has not left His flock to the mercy of wolves.[13]

We are to ask Jesus to sanctify our minds and enable us to recognize seducing spirits. We need to be alert when we hear false doctrine as Paul, John, and others were. When our thoughts are "hidden with Christ in God" they are anointed, consecrated, and set apart. When our hearts are not in Christ, we can trust the Holy Spirit to warn us by condemning or convicting us [1 John 3:21; Rom. 8:1].

WEBSTER'S DEFINES CONDEMN AND CONVICT:[14]

> Condemn: censure, blame, prescribe punishment;
> Convict: prove or find guilty.

THE HOLY SPIRIT CONVICTS/CONDEMNS us soundly, gently, consistently. Negative, nagging, judgmental, tormenting thoughts are not from God. It is written, "Test the Spirits, to see whether they are from God . . ." [1 John 4:1] We must!

Christ our Example dealt with the enemy from His position of Absolute Authority! As imitators of Christ, we are called to know and speak His Word with assurance and authority from our heart in full understanding of Christ's Triumphant and Absolute Authority. Remember how the Jewish exorcists attempted to adjure Jesus' name to cast out evil spirits? The spirits said, "I recognize Jesus, I know Paul, but who are you?" [Acts 19:15] The spirits know when Scripture is prompted by the Holy Spirit, believed, and spoken in faith from the heart. Demons fear and tremble before believing proclamations and prayers that are influenced by, and made in the authority of, the LORD Jesus Christ! Spirits must yield to the Living Word!

DEAN SHERMAN AND BILL PAYNE WROTE:

> The basis for our spiritual authority is a *legal* one. It is a legal reality that does not waiver because of our unbelief, and is as real as any transaction.[15]
> With our authority comes the responsibility to use it for God's purposes. If we don't rebuke the devil, he will not be rebuked. If we don't drive him back, he will not leave. Satan knows of our authority, but hopes we will stay ignorant. We must be as convinced of our authority as the devil is [Eph. 1:18-23].[16]

WHEN WE BECOME CONVINCED THAT THE RISEN CHRIST'S AUTHORITY is not only legally ours, but is also our responsibility, we will want to live our lives *unto Him.* We will endeavor to watch our thoughts and attitudes and daily arm ourselves with the fruit of the Spirit and God's armor. It is an essential, practical, faith-building and joyful experience when we hear ourselves verbally affirm God's provisions. The enemy knows that he must obey and bow (yield) to the stated scriptural truths that are *spoken in belief* from our hearts ~ not our heads!

We are to be powerful in the LORD and in the strength of His might [Eph. 6:10]; to put on the full armor of God and to *stand firm against* the schemes of the devil [Eph. 6:11] who is the accuser of the brethren [Rev. 12:10]. I believe when we "put in" Christ's armor, we are putting the fruit of Christ's

Holy Spirit into ourselves. When we "put on" God's armor, we are putting on God's mighty strength, authority, and character to cover us and lead us into victory over His eternal enemy, and ours.

Our struggle is not against people (e.g., government officials, spiritual leadership, etc.) but against the spirits that operate through them, influencing them. Our struggle is against spiritual rulers, (Satan's angelic dictators); powers (demons of pride, lust, greed, etc.); evil forces of this present dark world (anti-Christ, religious spirits); spiritual forces of wickedness in heavenly places (unclean spirits, unrighteous thoughts, worldly spirits, etc.) [Eph. 6:12 AMP].

Our Lord God does not want us to think, speak, or pray negative thoughts about others. Our *concern* must be with the spirits operating *through* the people! We must constantly guard against critical accusing thoughts. They are not from the Spirit of Christ. To reiterate, unholy, unrighteous thoughts come from our flesh and the accuser of the brethren. They inspire misunderstanding, suspicion, assumption, presumption, torment, etc., about people or circumstances. In that context, think about some of the enemy's influential thoughts, "I'm too tired; they expect too much from me; no one cares enough to help; they don't mean what they say; their agenda motivates them; they really want such and such; I'm being manipulated again; they don't know what honor and accountability mean; they're just promoting themselves; they keep using me, there they go again!" . . . and so forth.

In the lesson, *Taking Authority*, we will discuss how we are to administrate God's righteousness and authority by using the Keys of God's Kingdom, which is His gift to His church.

The flight attendants' advice to us on how to minimize hazards during possible disasters is excellent advice for spiritual success:

Listen! Avoid Obstacles! Follow Directions!

Father God, forgive our impaired vision. Create clean hearts, right thoughts and right attitudes in us! Fill us with Your fullness. Give us strength, courage, and joy. Fill us with Your anointed thoughts that we may proclaim and appropriate the fullness of Your armor. Enable us to take a stand and stand firmly "hidden with Christ in God" [Col. 3:3] to face negative or presumptive thoughts that invade us so often. We thank You and praise Your Holy Name for giving us Christ's inner armor and outer armor to help us overcome! Help us to stand in the strength of Your might and daily "put in" and "put on" Your awesome, enabling armor.

FATHER, GIVE US TEACHABLE, CONTRITE HEARTS that honor and encourage one another [Phil. 2:5-16]. Enable us to walk obediently in remembrance that "He that is in us is greater than he that is in the world" [1 John 4:4]. Give us the wisdom, knowledge, understanding, and blessings [Prov. 3:19-23] needed to win our battles and war against Your adversary.

LORD, anoint our thoughts, arm us with Your love and strategies that will restore righteousness in and throughout Your Church.

LORD, enable us to hold out the word of life as exhorted by Paul to us:

"Your attitude should be the same as that of Christ Jesus, who, being in the very nature God, did not consider equality with God something to be grasped, but made Himself nothing, taking the very nature of a servant, being made in human likeness. And being found in appearance as a man, He humbled Himself and became obedient to death ~ even death on a cross!

"Therefore God exalted Him to the highest place and gave Him the name that is above every name, that at the name of Jesus every knee should bow, in heaven and on earth and under the earth, and every tongue confess that Jesus Christ is LORD, to the glory of God the Father.

"Therefore, my dear friends, as you have always obeyed ~ not only in my presence, but now much more in my absence ~ continue to work out your salvation with fear and trembling, for it is God who works in you to will and to act according to His good purpose. Do everything without complaining or arguing, so that you may become blameless and pure, children of God without fault in a crooked and depraved generation, in which you shine like stars in the universe as you hold out the word of life ~ in order that I may boast on the day of Christ that I did not run or labor for nothing"
[Phil. 2:5-16]

CHRIST IS ALL and IN ALL!
[Col. 3:11]

HOW MAJESTIC IS HIS NAME IN ALL OF THE EARTH!
[Ps. 8:1, 9]

LIFE APPLICATION

1. A. What is our protective inner armor? B. What does it protect us from? C. How do we get inner armor? (P. 2)

2. What are we to do before putting on the outer armor of God? (P. 3)

3. Peter said for us to be self-controlled and alert. What gives the devil legal grounds to attack us? (P. 3)

4. We can triumph over fleshly, distracting thoughts of anger, self-righteousness, bitterness, slander, fault finding, lies, and filthy language by doing what? (P. 3)

5. A. What is this new inner self (inner armor) that Colossians 3:12-13 instructs us to put in? B. What do our thoughts and attitudes constantly choose between? C. Is there a gray area? D. What do we need to replace for our sinful nature that allows Christ to continue to lead us from the enemy's captivity to His captivity? (PP. 3, 4)

6. A. Why is unforgiveness an area of concern for all Christians? (P. 4)

7. A. What does the Jewish New Testament tell you should be your heart's decision maker? B. What does Christ, the Messiah, mean in Hebrew? C. Why does His Spirit indwell us? (P. 4)

8. What attitude of Christ shared in Colossians 3 are we to "put in" our new self? (P. 5)

9. A. What does the **love of Christ** bind together? B. What is the provision of the **Word of Christ** that is to dwell in us? C. What is interwoven to set us free? D. What is Christ's Wholeness and what does it include? (P. 5)

10. A. What is freely provided for victory to cleanse us from our thoughts and attitudes and undertake our defense? B. What should we proclaim? (P. 6)

11. A. What did De Haan tell us about the Blood of the LORD Jesus Christ? B. Is it spiritual? (PP. 6, 7)

12. A. What is vital in battling our thoughts and attitudes? B. What did Paul instruct us to do? (P. 7)

13. A. Is it a disadvantage to the enemy when we forgive other believers in the presence of Christ? (P. 7)

14. A. How do we put on the armor of God? B. Who do we resist in Jesus' Name? C. Who is our rear guard? (PP. 8, 9)

15. A. The enemy initiates his attacks in our _____. B. Thoughts come from what three sources? (P. 10)

16. Why did the author say THE SCREWTAPE LETTERS by C.S. Lewis was an enlightening yet entertaining book? (P. 11)

17. A. Why and how do we test the spirits? B. What do we do when we receive an offensive or accusing thought? C. What if the thought (s) return a second and third time? (P. 11)

18. What do we do about words or deeds that wrongly affect us or another person? (P. 12)

19. A. What guidance did the author receive from the LORD when her brass fixtures were ruined? B. What was the result? (P. 13)

20. Name at least five areas that Reverend Chambers identified in BEWARE OF CRITICIZING OTHERS that we need to watch? (P. 13)

21. How does repentance affect our thoughts and attitudes? (P. 14)

22. A. What is the difference in criticizing and condemning according to Webster? B. How does the Holy Spirit convict, condemn us? (P. 15)

23. If our struggle is not against people (e.g. government officials, spiritual leadership, etc.), who is it against? (P. 16)

24. Our LORD does not want us to think, speak, or pray negative thoughts about others because our _____ must be with the spirits operating _____ the people. (P. 16)

25. At the end of the Lesson, which part in Philippians 2:5-16 impacts you the most? (P. 17)

RIGHT THOUGHTS AND ATTITUDES SCRIPTURE SEQUENCES

Page 1
Phil. 2:5 JNT   [Let your attitude toward one another be governed by your being in union with the Messiah Yeshua]

Page 2
Phil. 2:5 NIV   [Your attitude should be the same as that of Christ Jesus]
Col. 3:10 JNT   [Put on the new self ... to be continually renewed in fuller and fuller knowledge, closer and closer to the image of my creator]
Col. 3:11   [Christ is All and in all]

Page 3
Phil. 2:1-11   [Summarizes that our attitude should be the same as Christ Jesus]
Col. 3:2   [Set your mind on things above; not earthly things]
John 3:17   [For God did not send His son into the world to condemn the world, but to save the world through Him]
1 Pet. 5:8   [Be self-controlled, alert; your enemy the devil prowls around like a roaring lion looking for someone to devour]
Col. 3:8   [Put away flesh: anger, slander, abusive speech, faultfinding, lies, etc.]
Col. 3:10,11 NIV   [Put on new self-renewed to a true knowledge according to our Creator's Image]
Rom. 12:2   [Do not conform any longer to the pattern of this world, but be transformed by the renewing of your mind. Then you will be able to test and approve what God's will is ~ His good, pleasing and perfect will.]
Col. 3:11   [Have a renewed mind without distinctions ~ let it be that Christ is all and in all]

Page 4
Gal. 5:22, 23   [The fruit of the Holy Spirit which is love, joy, peace, patience, kindness, goodness, faithfulness, gentleness and self-control]
Col. 3:12, 13   [God's chosen are to put on compassion, kindness, humility, gentleness, and patience and bear with one another, forgiving one another]
Luke 23:34   [Jesus said, "Father, forgive them, for they do not know what they are doing."]
Col. 3:11   [Have a renewed mind without distinctions ~ let it be Christ is all and in all]
Col. 3:15   [Let peace of Christ rule in our hearts to empower us to walk in peace and thankfulness]
Col. 3:5   [Put to death earthly nature: sexual immorality, impurity, lust, evil desires & greed, which is idolatry]
Eph. 6:11   [Put on the full armor of God so that you can take your stand against the devil's schemes.]

Page 5
1 Cor. 2:16   ["Who has known the mind of the LORD that he may instruct him?" But we have the mind Of Christ]
Col. 3:5   [Put away immorality, impurity, passion, evil desire, faultfinding, and greed which amount to idolatry]
Col. 3:1   [If I have been raised up (elevated) with Christ I would seek the things above where Christ is seated at God's right hand]
Col. 3:1, 2   [Since you have been raised to new life with Christ, set your sights on the realities of heaven, where Christ sits in the place of honor at God's right hand. Think about things of heaven. NLT]
Col. 3:3   [We are to be hidden with Christ in God]
Col. 3:10-11   [Mind of Christ renews us into the image of our Creator]
Col. 3:14   [And over all these virtues put on love, which binds them all together in perfect unity]
Col. 3:15   [The peace of Christ needs to rule hearts to empower us to walk in thankfulness]
Col. 3:16   [The Word of Christ dwells richly within, with all wisdom and teaching]
Ps. 34:5   [They looked to Him and were radiant ~ their faces shall never be ashamed]

II ~ RIGHT THOUGHTS AND ATTITUDES

Page 5 (continued)
John 21:17   ["LORD, You know that I love You." Jesus responded, "Feed My sheep."]
Col. 3:16   [The Word of Christ dwells richly within, with all wisdom and teaching]

Page 6
Col. 3:16   [The Word of Christ dwells richly within, with all wisdom and teaching]
Col. 3:17   [And whatever you do, whether in word or deed, do it all in the name of the LORD Jesus, giving thanks to God the Father through Him.]
Rom. 6:23   [The free gift of God is eternal life in Christ Jesus our LORD]
Heb.13:20   [Through the blood of the eternal covenant brought our LORD Jesus Christ back from the dead]
John 1:9   [He is faithful and just and will forgive us our sins and purify us from all unrighteousness]
Matt. 27:14   [Jesus made no reply, not even to a single charge ~ to the great amazement of the governor]
Heb. 13:12   [And so Jesus also suffered outside the city gate to make the people holy through His own blood]
Rom. 5:9   [Since justified by His blood, how much more shall we be saved from God's wrath through him]
Rom. 5:9   [Since justified by His blood, how much more shall we be saved from God's wrath through him]
Col. 1:14   [In whom we have redemption, the forgiveness of sins]

Page 7
Eph. 6:10-18   [Be strong in the LORD . . . we battle against the enemy . . . put on the armor of God]
Gal. 2:20   [I have been crucified with Christ and I no longer live, but Christ lives in me. The life I live in the body, I live by faith in the Son of God, who loved me and gave himself for me]
Col. 3:10   [...and you have been given fullness in Christ, Who is the head over every power and authority.]
2 Pet. 1:4   [Through these He has given us His very great and precious promises, so that through them you may participate in the divine nature and escape the corruption in the world caused by evil desires.]
1 Thess. 5:21-24 [Examine carefully, abstain from evil, hold fast to good]
2 Cor. 2:10, 11   [If you forgive anyone, I also forgive him. And what I have forgiven ~ if there was anything to forgive ~ I have forgiven in the sight of Christ for your sake, in order that Satan might not outwit us. For we are not unaware of his schemes]

Page 8
Gal. 5:22, 23   [The fruit of the Holy Spirit which is love, joy, peace, patience, kindness, faithfulness, gentleness and self-control]
Rom. 10:17   [Faith comes by hearing and hearing by the word of Christ]
1 John 1:9   [If we confess our sins, He is faithful and just and will forgive us our sins and purify us from all unrighteousness]
Eph. 6:10-18   [Be strong in the LORD . . . Put on the full armor of God . . .Our struggle is against rulers, authorities, the powers of this dark world, spiritual forces of evil in heavenly realms . . .]

Page 9
Eph. 6:10-12   [Be strong in the LORD and in His mighty power . . . put on all of God's armor, stand strong]
Isa. 58:8   [The glory of the LORD shall be your rear guard].
1 Chron. 16:22   [Touch not God's anointed!]

Page 10
Rom. 14:19   [Let us therefore make every effort to do what leads to peace and to mutual edification]
Eph. 3:7   [The gift of God's grace given according to the working of His power]
James 4:7-10   [Submit yourselves, then, to God. Resist the devil, and he will flee from you. Come near to God and He will come near to you. Wash your hands, you sinners, and purify your hearts, you double-minded, . . . humble yourselves before the LORD and He will lift you up.]
Gal. 5:16   [Walk by the Spirit and you will not carry out the desires of the flesh]
Gal. 5:22   [The Holy Spirit's fruit: love, joy, peace, patience, goodness, faithfulness, gentleness, self-control]
Gal. 5:23   [Against these (fruit of the Spirit] there is no law]
James 4:7   [Submit to God, resist the devil and he will flee]
James 4:8   [Draw near to God and He will draw near to you, Cleanse your hands, purify your hearts]
James 4:10   [Humble yourselves in the presence of the LORD and He will exalt you]
Isa. 26:3, 4 AMP [Commit, lean upon and trust in the LORD forever]

II ~ RIGHT THOUGHTS AND ATTITUDES

Page 11
1 Thess. 5:21 [Test everything ~ Hold on to the good]
1 John 4:1 [Test the spirits to see whether they are from God; many false prophets have gone out into the world]
Rom. 5:9 [But God demonstrates His own love for us in this: While we were sinners, Christ died for us!]

Page 12
2 Cor. 10:3-6 [Proclaim His Names and Word ~ take thoughts captive to obedience of CHRIST. He has enabled us to be ministers of His new covenant. This is a covenant not of written laws, but of the Spirit. The old gives death ~ the new gives life]
Gal. 5:24-26 [Those who belong to Christ Jesus have crucified the sinful nature with its passions and desires]
Eph. 6:18 [Pray in the Spirit on all occasions with all kinds of prayers and requests ... be alert and always keep on praying for all the saints]

Page 13
Matt. 7:1 [Judge not lest ye be judged]
Matt. 7:3-5 [Take the plank out of your own eye, then see clearly to remove the speck from your brother's eye]
Rom. 2:17-24 [When I judge others I condemn myself]

Page 14
1 John 1:9 [Repent, confess, ask forgiveness, receive it in belief]
Gal. 2:20 [I have been crucified with Christ and I no longer live, but Christ lives in me. The life I live in the body, I live by faith in the Son of God, who loved me and gave Himself for me]

Page 15
1 John 3:21 [Clear consciences give confidence toward God]
Rom. 8:1 [No condemnation to those IN CHRIST JESUS who walk after the SPIRIT]
1 John 4:1 [Test the spirits to see whether they are from God; many false prophets have gone out into the world]
Act. 19:15 [Spirits must yield to JESUS delegated authority decreed from our hearts]
Eph. 1:18-23 [Christ is far above all rule & authority & power & dominion & every name that is named ~ all is in subjection under His feet ~ He is head over the church His body ~ which is the fullness of Christ Who is all in all]
Eph. 6:10 [Be powerful in the LORD and in the strength of HIS MIGHT]
Eph. 6:11 [Stand firm against the schemes of the devil]
Rev. 12:10 [The accuser of the brethren accuses them before God day and night ~ he will be hurled down]

Page 16
Eph. 6:12 [Our struggle is against enemy forces, not our brethren]
Col. 3:3 [For you died, and your life is now hidden with Christ in God]

Page 17
Phil. 2:5-16 [Christ's attitude: as a servant humbled unto death]
1 John 4:4 [He Who is in you is greater than he who is in the world]
Prov. 3:19-23 [Seek wisdom, knowledge, understanding, and the blessings of God]
Col. 3:11 [Christ is ALL and in all]
Ps. 8:1, 9 [HOW MAJESTIC IS HIS NAME IN ALL OF THE EARTH!]
Ps. 8:9 [O LORD, Our Lord, how majestic is Your Name in all the earth!]

RIGHT THOUGHTS AND ATTITUDES ENDNOTES

1. David H. Stern, *The Jewish New Testament Commentary*, (on a translation of the New Testament that expresses its Jewishness), (Jerusalem, Israel: Jewish New Testament Publications).

    P. 595 Chapter 2 ~ (vv. 1-11): The supreme example of *looking out for* the *interests* of others (v.4) was given by Yeshua's descent from *equality with God* to die for us (vv.6-8). *In union with the Messiah* (vv.1, 5), his *attitude* (v.5) of *humility* (v.3) can be ours. God rewards such obedience (vv.8-11).

2. Ibid. P.271

3. W. E. Vine, *The Expanded Vine's Expository Dictionary of New Testament Words*, (Minneapolis, MN: Bethany House Publishers), p. 182.

4. David H. Stern, *Jewish New Testament Commentary*, A companion volume to the Jewish New Testament, (Clarksville, MD: Jewish New Testament Publication), "For the glory of God, the salvation of Israel and the edification of the Messianic Community."

    P. 613 Shalom here means something more like "wholeness" than "peace" (see Matt. 10:12). The Messiah's wholeness or "oneness," His interest, is to do the judging, deciding, controlling, and ruling in the heart of believers.

5. M. R. De Haan, M.D., *Redemption By Blood*, (Grand Rapids, MI: The Radio Bible Class).

    P. 6 The sinless supernatural, divine blood of the Lord Jesus Christ conceived by the Holy Spirit and received from Him, is God's only remedy for your sinful blood . . . without the shedding of blood there is no redemption.

6. Ibid. P.9

7. Ibid. P.15

8. Ibid. P.21

9. Ibid. P.25

10. A. W. Tozer, *Man The Dwelling Place Of God*, (Camp Hill, PA: Christian Publications, 1966).

    P. 120 He has given us the Scriptures, the Holy Spirit and natural powers of observation, and He expects us to avail ourselves of their help constantly. "Prove all things; hold fast that which is good," said Paul [1Thess. 5:21].
    "Beloved, believe not every spirit," wrote John, "but try the spirits whether they are of God: because many false prophets have gone out into the world" [1 John 4:1]. From this it is plain not only that there shall be false spirits abroad, endangering our Christian lives, but that they may be identified and known for what they are. And of course once we become aware of their identity and learn their tricks their power to harm us is gone. And while dealing with these matters we should keep in mind that not all religious vagaries are the work of Satan. The human mind is capable of plenty of mischief without help from the devil.

11. Ibid. P.122 Any doctrine, any experience that serves to magnify Him is likely to be inspired by Him. Conversely, anything that veils His glory or makes Him appear less wonderful is sure to be of the flesh or the devil. The heart of man is like a musical instrument and may be played upon by the Holy Spirit, by an evil spirit or the spirit of man himself.

12. Tozer, Ibid. P.120
13. Tozer, Ibid. P.119
14. *The New Webster's Pocket Dictionary,* (New York, NY: Lexicon Publications, Inc., 1990).
15. Dean Sherman with Bill Payne, *Spiritual Warfare For Every Christian*, (Seattle, WA: Frontline Communication), p. 110.
16. Ibid. P.123

PUTTING IN THE INNER ARMOR OF GOD

My Christian goal should be to continually practice having my mind and my thoughts, renewed by putting on the new self so that I can continually be "renewed in fuller and fuller knowledge, closer and closer to the image of my Creator" [Col. 3:10 JNT].

Father God, help me to choose Christ like thoughts to put in my heart for my protective *inner armor* to help guard against fleshly suggestions, wrong attitudes, presumptions, and affections. Help me to continually check my thoughts before I speak.

Train me LORD, to listen keenly to Your Word, study Your ways, and seek Christ's thoughts to replace my own. Instruct my thoughts and attitudes to be in union with Christ's thoughts, attitudes, strength through humility, and love, so that I can better look out for the interest of others.

Help me to guard my heart against the things here on earth (threatening, presumptive, unforgiving negative thoughts) that evolve into disobedience and ultimately produce wrong attitudes that grieve the Holy Spirit. I deeply repent and confess my need and desire to have Christ's attitude inside my heart.

Thank you that I can triumph over wrong thoughts and attitudes by repenting and appropriating the mind of Christ and asking to be renewed in the knowledge of my Creator. Holy Spirit empower me to follow the LORD with my mind renewed to that which is good, acceptable, and the perfect will of God.

I "put in" my heart the *attitude of Christ* by setting my heart, mind, and attitude on things above so that my thoughts will be *hidden with Christ in God* [Col. 3:3]. I "put on" my new self, renewed in knowledge, in the image of my Creator [Col. 3:10]. I clothe myself with the *love of Christ* [Col. 3:14], which binds compassion, kindness, gentleness, patience, forbearance and forgiveness together and enables my inner self [armor] and outer self [armor] to walk in *unity with Christ* [perfection in Christ] [Col. 3:14, 15].

I "put in" *the peace of Christ* [His integrity and well-being and His wholeness, His oneness, which includes judging, discerning, deciding, controlling and ruling] [Col. 3:15] to rule in my heart with thanksgiving.

I "put in" the *mind of Christ,* the *Word of Christ* [Col. 3:16], God's provision to dwell in me so that I may teach and admonish others with all wisdom. (emphasis added)

I "put in" my heart, *the fruit of the Holy Spirit* which is love, joy, peace, patience, kindness, faithfulness, gentleness and self-control [Gal. 5:22, 23], plus His compassion, humility, grace and forgiveness.

I "put in" my *heart Christ's anointed attitude,* His Word, to fill my thoughts to be prepared to prevail *through Christ* in my daily battles.

HALLELUJAH AND AMEN!

WHAT A MIGHTY GOD WE SERVE!

PUTTING ON THE ARMOR OF GOD

Clean hands and a pure heart, armed by God and inspired by the Holy Spirit, will inflame a passionate devotion to the LORD Jesus Christ.

FATHER GOD,

I take up the Sword of the Spirit, the Word of God, JESUS my sword, to ward off all the flaming arrows of the enemy. In the Name of Jesus, I remind you, enemy, that I am strong in the LORD and in His mighty power, I resist demon powers, principalities, powers of the present world darkness, and the evil spirits of the heavenly spheres [Eph. 6:10-12] in the Name of Jesus.

I plead the precious unblemished Blood of the Lamb ~ over me, my family, and my efforts today. Thank You that You told me to be strong in You and Your mighty power. Thank You for telling me to put on Your full armor and that my struggles are not against flesh and blood, but the influencing spirits around me and in others.

I put on the Helmet of Salvation ~ the sinless Blood of Jesus, to cover my mind, my memory, my nerve cells, my subconscious, my flesh and any other area that I have not thought of. Thank You, Father God, that Jesus' blood reconciled me, sanctified me, justified me, redeemed me, and made me innocent in Your sight. Oh, Father God, You are so good.

I put on the Breastplate of Your Righteousness ~ thank You that I am righteous through Jesus ~ please lead me in paths of righteousness for Your Name's sake.

I gird my loins with Your Truth ~ Oh, Holy Spirit of Christ, Spirit of Truth ~ I invite You to lead me today in Your Way, Your Truth and Your Life. Help me to listen to Your still quite inner voice in me and Your leading through the Word.

I shod my feet with Your Peace ~ Your harmony, integrity. wholeness and well being to prepare me to share the Gospel.

LORD, I take up the Shield of Faith to ward off all the flaming arrows of the enemy ~ faith in Your love, Your protection, Your promises, Your faithfulness, Your plans, Your provisions and Your Triumphant Victory. Thank You from the bottom of my heart for watching over me and my loved ones.

In the VICTORIOUS NAME of JESUS CHRIST, my LORD and SAVIOR, I resist **unholy spirits, unrighteous spirits, and all negative spirits that may try to influence me.** Thank You LORD, that I can trust the Holy Spirit to lead, protect, and inspire me today.

Father, thank You that Your Word says Your glory is my rearguard [Isa. 58:8].

TO GOD BE THE GLORY!
HALLELUJAH AND AMEN!
WHAT A MIGHTY GOD WE SERVE!

Lesson III

SPIRITUAL WARFARE

*"But the Counselor, the Ruach HaKkodesh,
Whom the Father will send in My name,
will teach you everything; that is,
He will remind you of everything I have said to you."*

*John 14:26
Jewish New Testament*

A Fight To The Finish

And that about wraps it up.
God is strong, and he wants you strong.
So take everything the Master has set out for you,
well-made weapons of the best materials.
And put them to use so you will be able to stand up
to everything the devil throws your way.

This is no afternoon athletic contest that we'll walk away from
and forget about in a couple of hours.

This is for keeps,
a life-or-death fight to the finish
against the devil and all his angels.
Be prepared ~ You're up against far more
than you can handle on your own.

Take all the help you can get,
every weapon God has issued,
so that when it's all over but the shouting
you'll still be on your feet.
Truth, righteousness, peace, faith, and salvation
are more than words.

Learn how to apply them.
God's Word is an indispensable weapon.
In the same way,
prayer is essential in this ongoing warfare.

Pray hard and long.
Pray for your brothers and sisters.
Keep your eyes open.
Keep each other's spirits up
so that no one falls behind or drops out.

Ephesians 6:3-4

THE MESSAGE
Eugene H. Peterson

SPIRITUAL WARFARE

"The Holy Spirit will teach you at that time what you should say."
Luke 12:12

TODAY FEW CAN DENY THAT THE SPIRITUAL FORCES UNLEASHED against us, our families, and the Church as a whole have caused acute pain, grief and disillusionment. Our minds and bodies have slowly become insensitive and vulnerable to the enemy's onslaught that has left us feeling hopeless, threatened, useless, helpless, powerless . . . literally at the end of our rope. Perhaps we have been confused or angry about people or circumstances and as a consequence find ourselves struggling with bitterness, anxiety, isolation, doubt ~ even self-pity.

WE MAY SENSE IN A GENERAL WAY THAT SOMETHING IS WRONG, but do not know what to do or how to begin. This lesson is to show how we are to fight the good fight when we are tired of losing and are desperate to see things change. The good news is that the Bible teaches us and entreats us to trust in and put to use God's principles. God has given us everything we need; it is not too late for victory if we fight the good fight of faith, take hold of the eternal life to which we are called, and make a good confession in the presence of many witnesses [1 Tim. 6:12 NIV].

We are to obtain fulfillment, peace and triumph through Christ [Heb. 4:16; Ps. 119:123, 137-144]. We are to test the spirits and to prevail in spiritual warfare through God's righteousness, wisdom, knowledge, understanding, and guidance over the enemy's manifested unrighteous consequences. *It is vital!*

AGREEMENT IS A POWERFUL FORCE and is available for both righteous and unrighteous forces to manifest good or evil. Spiritual warfare is successful when we trust the Holy Spirit's inspiration to guide our prayers with God's Double-Edged Sword, His Holy Name and His Holy Word. According to Scripture [Ezek. 22:30, 31], God wants us to pray for Him to intervene.

If we trust a Triumphant Sovereign All-Powerful God, are our prayers necessary? Dutch Sheets wrote that "A Sovereign God made a sovereign choice to limit Himself in many ways and situations to the actions, decisions and requests of human beings. His plan is to work on Earth with and through us, His family, not independently of us. Prayer and intercession should be all about friendship, relationship, and partnering with our wonderful Father . . . If my primary motivation for prayer becomes interceding for others, this, too, will ultimately fail as a motivator . . . Intercession is not to use God for what He can do for us . . . We must have a relationship with Him so we can partnership with Him in interceding from His perspective for others."[1]

GOD CALLS US TO MOVE SACRIFICIALLY, effectively, in unity, as one with Christ, and as one with His Body. We are called to sacrificially intercede for all saints ~ globally, corporately, personally. We are to triumph over evil in the strength and power of the Word and the Spirit, God's Double-Edged Sword, that infinitely agrees in all things [Eph. 6:17; Heb. 4:12].The LORD Jesus Christ is our confidence, shield, protector, and enabler. The precious Blood of the Lamb qualifies us and readies us to govern the affairs of man through intercessory initiatives. His provisions position us to boldly approach God's throne of Grace with petitions [Acts 2:36; Deut. 33:29; Matt. 18:19; 21:22] then frees us to pray as He leads. Christ's principles teach us how to pray. Our certainty is that when God leads us to pray according to His heart, He intends to answer our prayers. (Sometimes we are blessed that He allows us to see the answer to our prayers.)

CHRIST HAS CALLED US TO SPIRITUAL WARFARE. Our response to His call upon our lives is realized when we instinctively choose the LORD's principles, promises, and purposes for our daily battles [Heb. 5:12-14; 6:17-20]. We need to honestly and privately deal with our own hearts to prepare for a concerted battle through and in the LORD's power, wisdom, and strength before we counsel with others to better understand the enemy's weak spots.

SPIRITUAL WARFARE SHOULD NOT BE SCARY. We were born into spiritual warfare simply because we were made in God's image. The devil hates God's image and is out to destroy us! If the enemy cannot steal, kill, or destroy God's people [John 10:10], he will try to discourage them, undermine their testimony, cause illnesses, etc., to rob God's glory from their lives! We need to understand the LORD's ways to be victorious in spiritual warfare. We need to overcome the fear of spiritual warfare because it is all around us in today's world. It is not frightening, mysterious, or an exclusive calling to fight the enemy. It is mandatory.

WE ARE INVOLVED IN SPIRITUAL WARFARE as long as we inhale and exhale; we are God's children! The LORD gave us love, power, a sound mind [2 Tim. 1:7] and His authority to trample on serpents and scorpions [Luke 10:18-29]. Warfare without knowing the LORD's ways and guidance is reckless and dangerously irresponsible. It is the same as giving a gun and ammunition to a soldier, without a manual, instruction or training! That is why so many of His children, who may have good intentions, end up shooting themselves in the foot ~ or even worse ~ wounding someone else! They may take off on a "new" teaching without knowing God's conditions for that teaching (*clean hands and a pure heart!*) For instance, they were told to keep declaring a Scripture promise to receive it. They started repeating the Scripture frequently *yet had sin in their heart.* They exposed themselves to the enemy's attack, due to the sin, and did not receive the Scripture promise (instigated by themselves). The following proven principles are biblical and will victoriously strengthen us for the daily battles we face.

PRINCIPLE: RIGHTEOUS AGREEMENT BEGINS IN THE SPIRITUAL REALM.
In Genesis 11, God said, "Let Us" go down ~ the Trinity's agreement originated in heaven then materialized in the physical realm [Gen. 11:7]. Similarly, in Trinity agreement, Jesus came down from heaven to do His Father's will, e.g., Christ came down to earth to complete His Father's work [John 4:34]. Jesus instructed us, "Again, I tell you, if two of you on earth agree [harmonize together, together make a symphony] ~ about anything and everything, including lawful and proper things ~ whatever they shall ask, it will come to pass and be done for them by My Father in heaven" [Matt. 18:19 AMP].

JESUS TAUGHT US TO PETITION OUR FATHER THAT HIS WILL WILL BE DONE on earth as it is in heaven. Christ showed us the proper attitude required for us to have prayers of agreement with our Father God.

Sadly, agreement is not always good nor is it always right! Job's friends, for example, meant well and thought that they were doing the right thing when they conferred, agreed upon, then gave Job multiple reasons for his sufferings. I have wondered if the accusing unrighteous words spoken in agreement by Job's friends contributed to his continual suffering. Job's friends' critical spirits instigated *presumptive* conversations which culminated in conclusions accusing Job of being solely responsible and at fault for all of his maladies.

Could their spoken presumptions and comments have delayed answers to Job's petitions to Almighty God? Could their negative words and attitudes have delayed Job's receiving understanding of the real reason for his losses? Could their presumptions have interfered with God's plan? What do you think? (With friends like that who needs enemies?)

BEFORE SATAN REQUESTED JOB'S POSSESSIONS to be put under his power, God asked Satan, "Where are you coming from?" Satan answered God, "From roaming through the earth, wandering here and there" [Job 1: 7 Complete Jewish Bible]. *Satan still prowls about!* He seeks to devour us [1 Pet. 5:8].

He tirelessly plots and plants unrighteous agreement to bring discord to our conversation and/or initiate division during times of prayer. His goal is to divide and conquer God's people! We need prayers of agreement led by the Holy Spirit to neutralize the enemy's plots against us or our loved ones.

IT IS GOOD TO CONCLUDE OUR SUPPLICATIONS AS JESUS DID, "Nevertheless, Father, not my [our] will, but Thine be done" [Matt. 26:39], or "Thy kingdom come, Thy will be done on earth as it is in heaven" [Matt. 6:10].) We are to agree with the Holy Spirit when we pray. We are to be involved with lawful and proper things. Since agreement brings results for good or for bad, should we be afraid to pray in agreement? No, not if the Spirit of Christ Jesus is *asked* to lead us, *then we trust Him* to do so.

THE LORD PROMISES US THAT THE HOLY SPIRIT WILL TEACH US how to pray and bring to our remembrance all things that He has said to us [John 14:26]. The Holy Spirit does, *I know.* When attacked with a debilitating Central Nervous System Dysfunction (CNSD) in 1998, and left with minimal cognizant memory function, I could not read the Word, pray, or barely converse (a decade later the diagnosis remains undetermined). I was in a mental darkness that is hard to describe. I could not stand on the Word to battle the enemy or remember to ask for prayer. My friends did not know what I was going through and I could not think to call them for help.

For background, I had been to Intercessors for America's 25th Anniversary Conference in Cleveland earlier that day. Late that afternoon I was hitting golf balls on the driving range behind our home and felt weird. I told Gene I was going in to rest and before I got to our gate it felt like a thousand daggers were stabbing me from the waist up. I staggered upstairs to bed.

To make a long story short, the next morning Gene could not wake me and took me to the hospital. My vitals were good, but I was mindless of my surroundings and barely remember being there. I was frozen from the waist up and after three weeks of testing ranging from neurological, to physical, to psychological, etc., plus therapy, I was released to go home with braces on my arms, shoulder and neck.

Our son Dave's wedding was a month away and I was flat on my back, unable to read, pray or think. I am so grateful for my family and friends that drove me to therapy and appointments. The morning of the wedding, my sister Rusty, who arrived from Kansas the previous day, took me to buy a dress (my dress would not go over the braces) and to get my hair done so I could be in the wedding.

It took several years to work out of the frozen state, a little at a time. Thankfully, they took me to Edwin Shaw, a rehabilitation hospital, where they taught another way to grip a golf club so I could be outdoors with my husband. That was wonderful, but I could not remember the stance (how to stand) or various ways to set up to hit the ball (or lessons learned earlier). That required cognizant memory. I could not remember telephone numbers or my Social Security number (essential), much less appointments, etc. The worst part was not being able to read the Bible or any book ~ the words simply ran together. My insecurity was threatened and compounded by no longer remembering the Scriptures that had always been a part of my life and prayers.

Word eventually got out about my debilitating distress. My Prime Time Class (Adult Bible Fellowship at the Chapel, my home church) and some National Day of Prayer Task Force prayed for me. Prayer precedes action. God in His faithfulness did not leave me nor forsake me from His provisions because I was able to remember three things of importance: a song, "Jesus Loves Me This I Know"; a prayer, "Now I lay Me Down to Sleep"; and it was important to plead Jesus' blood over me, but I could not have told you why! That was my defense in spiritual warfare.

Healing began in 2001 when we purchased a winter retreat in La Quinta, California to heighten my health. In 2003, a precious friend, Lynne Dugan, saw me at the Palm Springs Mayor's Prayer Breakfast and we reunited. She came to our home and we began praying together. Lynne had my former Seminar/book, *Christ Calls Us to Prevail In Prayer*. She was concerned about my insecurity and vagueness plus what had happened to me and had her prayer group pray that God would "send the Holy Spirit in Jesus' Name to teach me all things and remind me of everything that He had taught me" [John 14:26]. *The Holy Spirit led them to Scripture to pray for me and their prayers of righteous agreement began my restoration.* God is faithful. Hallelujah!

A decade later, after having Biofeedback, along with years of doctors and physical therapy, I am back to normal and my memory has vastly improved. Reworking this has been a catharsis to me and a marvelous time of remembrance and relearning. Praying or proclaiming God's Word has once more become automatic and an ongoing conversation with our LORD. During that debilitating time people would ask me to pray for them and I didn't want to as I felt inadequate. Yet, the Holy Spirit intervened with a prayer that met the need. Have you felt inadequate to pray, yet learned later that your prayer was right on?

Christ Jesus is faithful to take our prayers to our Father in Heaven. Charles

Spurgeon wrote a devotion about Christ Jesus taking the wrong prayers out of our petitions and inserting His righteous prayers before presenting them to Father God to be a precious incense.[2] Freedom comes when we choose to trust in the power and wisdom of God ~ *in all things!*

PRINCIPLE: *AGREEMENT IN THE SPIRITUAL REALM* **precedes reality in the physical realm.** God used the principle of the *spoken word in agreement* when He created the earth! [Heb. 11:3; Ps. 33:6-9] The power of agreement determines the power of unity. To reiterate, agreement and unity are vital!

Note the Trinity's unity and *their resultant plan of agreement:* They said, "Come, *let Us* go down and *confuse* their language that they may not understand one another's speech" (activating force).

The Righteous Trinity illustrated the importance of agreement in the spiritual realm, and then spoke it into the physical realm. God's proclaimed Word confused and scattered the enemy. We are to proclaim His Word in agreement to energize His Word that prevails over the enemy.

The power of agreement activates ruling forces for good or evil. Unrighteous forces were released by Eve and Adam when they ate the forbidden fruit *in agreement* ~ for wrong reasons. They wanted to *possess* God's knowledge of good and evil ~ they wanted to be as God.

Adam and Eve set the stage for unrighteous agreement through their declarations, desires, and actions that set ungodly forces into motion that produced unrighteous consequences on earth! The Babylonians' agreement, unity of purpose, and their participation in its outworking, gave them a consistent, negative, and unrighteous spiritual potential to eradicate righteousness.

PRINCIPLE: *SEEK AGREEMENT IN HIS NAME.* A few examples of spiritual giants who agreed in the LORD's Name are: Moses, Aaron & Hur, Joshua and Caleb, Daniel and his three friends, and certainly the disciples! Jesus said, "When two or three are gathered [drawn together as My followers] in [into] My Name, there *I AM* in the midst of them" [Matt. 18:20 AMP]. Jesus said, "Truly, I tell you, whatever you *forbid and declare to be improper and unlawful on earth* must be what is *already forbidden* in heaven; whatever you *permit and declare proper* and lawful on earth must be *already permitted* in heaven" [Matt. 18:19 AMP, emphasis added]. Believers are to walk and talk together in agreement with the Holy Spirit.

There are four "C's" of wisdom that are good points of reference for believers to remember when seeking to share or pray in God's righteousness:

- Caring wisdom
- Confirming wisdom
- Constructing wisdom
- Conquering wisdom

PRINCIPLE: *LISTEN INTENTLY TO OTHERS WHEN THEY SHARE OR PRAY.* The Father and the Holy Spirit *listened* to the LORD's report before they scattered and confused the enemy. We need to *listen to* and *hear* righteous requests and prayers that are appropriate to the concern, so that we can agree in corporate prayers that will build living memorials that call upon, acknowledge, exalt and honor the glory and authority of the Trinity [Eph.1:9-23].

PRINCIPLE: *DECLARATIONS AND PROCLAMATIONS* **must line up with God's purposes!** The LORD declared that the Babelites were improper and unlawful *before* The Trinity activated God's spiritual forces to confound the Babelite's language and agenda on earth. Satan *misrepresented* God's Word to *tempt* Jesus. Jesus, indwelt and led by the Holy Spirit during His temptation by Satan in the wilderness, paraphrased Scripture out loud as He declared that Satan's requests were *improper and unlawful.* Jesus refused (forbade, rebuked, prohibited) the tempter's influence and proclaimed God's truth as His standard for proper and legal defense. He countered the enemy's verbal attacks by lining up and declaring His testimony in agreement with the Holy Spirit and God's Word ~ Righteousness is the law of heaven! [Luke 4; Matt. 4]

> *C. Gaebelein wrote in* WHAT THE BIBLE SAYS ABOUT ANGELS:
> The ninety-first Psalm gives a prophetic picture of the second Man. The Devil knew this for he quoted this passage when he had led our Lord on a pinnacle of the temple. But *whenever the devil uses Scripture*, he either *adds to it* or *takes away from it.*
> **the footnote added:* All cults and error systems take away from the Word of God or add to it, the significant marks of the power which stands behind them.[3]

THE TRINITY GAVE US A WONDERFUL EXAMPLE when they declared confusion to the Babelite's unrighteous agenda. They proclaimed confusion to the enemy's camp; their agreement prevailed and scattered the Babelites! Let us, as Christ's warrior's, wield righteous words and thoughts ~ His sword ~ as our declarations to create confusion and strife to the enemy's strategies! [Zech. 9:13]

PRINCIPLE: *TEST THE SPIRITS!* Many years ago that was a hard-learned lesson for this child. I was *visiting* a church that needed to pay an unexpected expense. During their evening service they asked *members* to place a special gift on the altar. I thought about the generous bill my husband gave me for spending money and thought "Wouldn't it be good if 'I' lay that on the altar?" Then I impulsively did so!

That night I struggled and grieved in my sleep because I remembered an earlier impression from the LORD, that I was to give the gift to specific friends that were in a music and communication ministry. Convicting questions followed: What was my motive? Had I wanted to be noticed? Had I tested the thought (spirit) about donating the money?

Lamenting, I remembered that Satan used *"if"* to tempt Jesus. Either my flesh or the enemy planted *"if I"* in my thought and I immediately followed through in direct disobedience to the LORD. Tossing and turning I agonized that I had not tested the spirit before I put the money on the altar ~ consequently I had blown it! It is written, *"Test the spirits!"* [1 John 4:1]

Following conviction, I repented and prayed desperately for God to intervene so that it would not be too late to rectify my disobedience so I could obey His plan. My sole option was to return to the church, despite deep embarrassment, and do all that was humanly possible to get the money back. It required humiliating backtracking to retrieve the money. In doing so ~ *His peace returned!*

Two days later I visited my friends that the LORD had planned to receive the money. They were in a faith ministry and trusted God to provide their needs. No one knew (except the LORD) how desperately they needed money by that evening to register their children in their Christian school for the next semester. Praise God ~ the gift was the exact amount needed! Christ's way proved true [2 Sam. 22:31]. This chastened child learned the necessity of testing the spirits in all things. Thankfully ~ *His joy returned!*

PRINCIPLE: *WALK IN GOD'S AUTHORITY.* Jesus walked in God's authority; His Words were empowered by the Holy Spirit. Paul and the disciples trusted and followed Jesus' example. We, too, are to strive to follow His example, walk in the knowledge of God, listen to His Holy Spirit, trust His authority, and be strong in His mighty power [Eph. 6:10].

LORD Jesus rebuked the Pharisees, "Woe to you Torah experts! For you have taken away the key of knowledge (kingdom of God)! Not only did you yourselves not go in, you also have stopped those who were trying to enter!" [Luke 11:52 JNT] Jesus was angry that the Pharisees' legalism denied the communication of the knowledge of God to the heart and soul of man. The religious leaders had replaced (denied) the Power of Yahweh's Name, authority, and personal inward experience and replaced it with man's dogma, agenda and works ~ their religious idols. Truly, God's children need to recognize that academia alone cannot inspire a deeper life in Christ or reveal Christ's wisdom or power. All teachings and emphasis must deal with Christ crucified, "be Scriptural and apostolic in spirit and temper," wrote A.W. Tozer. He added, "The 'deeper' life is deeper only because the average Christian life is tragically shallow."[4]

> *Wendy Beckett agreed and commented:*
> There is a divine tension between the Word and the Spirit. If we emphasize the Word too much then we're in danger of being in the condition where "the letter killeth" [2 Cor. 3:6]. If, as has been true in the latter half of the 20th century, the emphasis is focused on the Holy Spirit, without the discipline of the Word, then we find ourselves vulnerable to being "carried about by every wind of doctrine" [Eph. 4:14]. Let us seek the Lord who alone knows the balance.[5]

PRINCIPLE: *FAITH IS TRUSTING IN GOD'S WORD AND GOD'S POWER.* "Faith should not rest upon the wisdom of men, but on the power of God" [1 Cor. 2:5]. God alone must be our source!

BILL BRIGHT WROTE IN THE PAMPHLET HAVE YOU HEARD OF THE FOUR SPIRITUAL LAWS?:

Do Not Depend Upon Feelings
The promise of God's Word, the Bible ~ not our feelings ~ is our authority. The Christian lives by faith [trust] in the trustworthiness of God Himself and His Word. This train diagram (shown in the pamphlet) illustrates the relationship between **fact** [God and His Word], **faith** [our trust in God and His Word], and **feeling** [the result of our faith and obedience]. [John 14:21, emphasis added]
   The train will run with or without the caboose. However, it would be useless to attempt to pull the train by the caboose. In the same way, we, as Christians, do not depend upon feelings or emotions, but we place our faith [trust] in the trustworthiness of God and the promises of His Word.[6]

The spiritual giants of old were men who became acutely conscious of the real Presence of God and maintained that consciousness for the rest of their lives.[7]

The essential point, wrote Reverend Tozer, is that they experienced God. "How otherwise can the saints and prophets be explained? How otherwise can we account for the amazing power for good they have exercised over countless generations. Is it not that they walked in conscious communion with the real Presence and addressed their prayers to God with the artless conviction that they were addressing Someone actually there? . . . That eternal life which was with the Father is now the possession of believing men, and that life is not God's gift only, but His very Self."[8]

OSWALD CHAMBERS WROTE IN MY UTMOST FOR HIS HIGHEST, that God never speaks to us in startling ways, but in ways that are easy for us to misunderstand. He also says that every time circumstances press, say, "Speak LORD," and make time to listen . . . Recall the time the LORD did speak to you. Have you forgotten what He said? Was it Luke 11:13, or was it 1 Thessalonians 5:23?

As we listen, our ear gets acute, and like Jesus, we shall hear God all the time.[9]

Elijah heard the power [inherent ability] of God in a still small voice ~ the witness of the Holy Spirit penetrated his spirit and he heard God's guidance [1 Kings 19:12, 13]. By studying God's Word we learn to hear with the ears of our heart and to discern the Holy Spirit's direction. We learn beautiful truths about God's character and inherent ability. God's truth is uncomplicated! His Word is what our faith must rest upon. *The Holy Spirit never instructs us to do anything contrary to biblical standards!* Man's doctrine and feelings have never been reliable. Man is imperfect because his feelings exist in the "flesh realm" and can be easily swayed.

Principle: *Biblical, scriptural discernment is needed to equip believers.* Some Bible studies and resources have confused a number of students of the Bible due to academic, intellectual words written by authors who were perhaps enslaved to certain ideas or theories. The outcome was that their influence devalued the integrity of the written word in the Bible and the role of the Holy Spirit. It denied believers the ability to have biblical discernment and robbed many of understanding the forgiveness, love, grace and power of God (the letter killeth!).

A.W. TOZER WROTE IN *THE DIVINE CONQUEST*, about the end result of academic influence, that within hearts of a growing number of evangelicals in recent days has arisen a new yearning after an above average spiritual experience. Yet, a greater number still shy away from it and raise objections that evidence misunderstanding or fear or plain unbelief. They point to the neurotic, the psychotic, the pseudo-Christian cultist, the intemperate fanatic, lumping them all together without discrimination as followers of the deeper life.[10] There are teachings that are in error [1 John 4:1-6].

> **REVEREND TOZER GAVE A SEVENFOLD TEST FOR ERROR IN *MAN THE DWELLING PLACE OF GOD*:**
> Briefly stated the test is this: This new doctrine, this new religious habit, this new view of truth, this new spiritual experience ~ how has it affected my attitude toward and my relation to God, Christ, the Holy Scriptures, self, other Christians, the world, and sin. By this sevenfold test we may prove everything religious and know beyond a doubt whether it is of God or not . . . we but have to ask about any doctrine or experience, What is this doing to me? and we know immediately whether it is from above or below.[11]
>
> "Biblical discernment is essential to enjoy free fellowship with other believers, otherwise we end up living in fear and confusion, unable to walk confidently in truth and love."[12]

MARTIN LLOYD JONES WROTE IN *SAVED IN ETERNITY*, regarding the loss of biblical discernment, "The one thing we have to do in a situation like this is to avoid becoming slaves to our own theories and ideas and to our own understanding of the truth. In avoiding that danger, we should go to the Scriptures and look at the Bible's plain and obvious teaching with as dispassionate and open mind as we are capable of. . . we come up against something that we cannot quite fit into our doctrinal pattern, and the danger at that point is to *stand on our own doctrine* and to try to *explain away the Scripture*. If ever we find a point that seems to conflict with our clear grasp of doctrine, it seems to me, for the time being, the essence of wisdom is to leave our doctrine where it is. It is not that we deny it, we just leave it for the moment, we return to Scripture and note what Scripture says everywhere about this particular matter. Then having done that, we again attempt to relate this obvious and clear teaching of Scripture with the doctrine of which we are equally sure . . . But it is our bounden duty to go as far as we can to understand the teaching as far as that is possible."[13]

LIKE PAUL'S HEART ATTITUDE, let us confess that we "do not have superiority of speech or wisdom in proclaiming the mystery [testimony] of God" . . . and confess that we are "determined to know nothing among ourselves, except Jesus Christ crucified, to the Glory of God our Father" [1 Cor. 2:1]. The bottom line is that we are not to lean on our own understanding [Prov. 3:5]. If teachings cannot be scripturally supported, tread lightly ~ if at all! [Isa. 55:8-9]

PRINCIPLE: *JUDGE OTHERS BY THEIR FRUIT ~ WALK IN RIGHTEOUSNESS AND OBEDIENCE TO GOD.* Our LORD discussed judging others and said, "We will know them by their fruit." He stressed obedience [Matt. 7]. The criteria established by Jesus for judging (discerning) others is to look for the person's walk to be one of righteousness and obedience to God.

Accusations have been written about laymen and ministries within His Body in a forthright effort to "protect" believers in Christ. The intention was to maintain the purity of the Christian testimony before the world [Isa. 58:4-6]. Sadly, some failed to check with the accused and took written or spoken things out of context and presumed wrongly, or possibly misunderstood the intended meaning, without bothering to verify their intent. Colloquialisms can alter understanding.

> **BOB AND GRETCHEN PASSANTINO'S WROTE:**
> It is easy to slip from mature defense of the faith into unthinking witch hunting even though we are sincere Christians who love God and believe that we have an obligation to protect the Church from harm.[14]
>
> Why do Christians label as heresy anything with which they are unfamiliar, even when there is no clear-cut and deliberate doctrinal deviation evident?[15]
>
> However, sometimes Christians confuse their own perspective with the mistaken idea that any belief or expression of Christianity they are unfamiliar with is (automatically) heretical.[16]

THE SCRIPTURAL PRINCIPLE IS TO JUDGE MINISTRIES and people by the fruit of the Holy Spirit: love, joy, peace, patience, kindness, goodness, faithfulness, gentleness and self-control; *"against such things there is no law."* Satan does not have the right [legal entry] to attack us when we are hidden with Christ in God [Gal. 5:22, 23], i.e., when our hearts are in agreement with Christ's righteousness. It is essential to test (discern) all things ~ to know the key doctrines of Christian Orthodoxy.[17]

Jesus and Paul taught us to be of One Spirit, as One Body in True Unity, in and through our Triune God [1 Cor. 12:11-31; John 17:20-23]. We need to follow biblical principles about correction and first go to the accused in humility and gentleness. "Brethren, if any person is overtaken in misconduct or sin of any sort, you who are spiritual ~ who are responsive to and controlled by the Spirit ~ should set him right and restore and reinstate him, without any sense of superiority and with all gentleness, keeping an attentive eye on yourself, lest you should be tempted also" [Gal. 6:1 AMP].

PRINCIPLE: *ASK THE SPIRIT OF CHRIST TO FILL YOU AND TO ILLUMINATE HIS WORD TO YOU IN PRACTICAL WAYS.* The Holy Spirit enables us to absorb the Bible's spiritual truths so that our thoughts and words may reflect His righteous influence, i.e., what we speak, "not in words taught by human wisdom [imperfect interpretations], but in those taught by the Spirit, combining spiritual thoughts with spiritual words" [1 Cor. 2:2-16]. Though all Christians are *indwelt* by the Holy Spirit [John 14:16, 17] not all Christians are *filled* [directed and empowered] by the Holy Spirit [Eph. 5:18, emphasis added].

> ***CHARLES C. RYRIE WROTE*** regarding the two facets of the Holy Spirit's filling:
> The first (filling) as a sovereign act of God whereby He possesses (occupies) someone for special activity. The second facet of Spirit-filling may be described as the extensive influence and control of the Spirit in a believer's life. It evidences an abiding state of fullness rather than the specific event. It produces a certain character of life, and seems to be a close synonym to spirituality. This facet of the Spirit's filling is the finest character reference one could have. All can experience it, but not all do [Acts 6:3].[18]

WE RECEIVE HIS SPIRIT SO THAT WE MAY FULLY KNOW THE THINGS FREELY GIVEN TO US BY GOD: and *speak* His thoughts that He has made known to us [Num. 23:12]. He speaks to us *through His Word by His Spirit* so that we may *follow* His leading [Acts 16:6, emphasis added]. Some teach that the fullness of the Holy Spirit is received when a specific gift of the Holy Spirit is manifested [1 Cor. 12:4-31]. *The biblical test of the fullness of the Holy Spirit is whether or not the Word of God comes to life, is understood when read, and glorifies the LORD!*

MARTIN LLOYD JONES WROTE SATAN CAN COUNTERFEIT most of the gifts of the Holy Spirit. The test of the gifts of the Spirit is this: do they *testify* to the fact that Jesus is God in the flesh? Do they *glorify* the Son of God? As that is the supreme work of the Holy Spirit, so every spirit must be tested by that particular test. We can put such an emphasis on the Spirit Himself that we do so at the expense of the Son.[19]

By the way, I cannot find any place in Scripture where we are instructed to judge anyone, or any ministry, by the gifts of the Spirit [1 Cor. 12:4-11]. *Scripture tells us that the LORD's gifts and calling are irrevocable and unalterable* [Rom. 11:29]. Do you know if the person who is operating in a particular gift is anointed and inspired by the Holy Spirit? Do you know if they are saved? Does the fact that someone is exhibiting a gift of healing necessarily mean that they are saved? Do they say that Christ is the Son of God and the Son of Man? Does a so-called servant of God manipulate or take advantage of people? What about the gift of service? Administration? Teaching and so forth? We must keep in mind that gifts can be abused, misused, counterfeited, bragged about, lied about, etc.

FURTHER, GIFTS CAN BECOME MORE IMPORTANT THAN THE GIVER OF GIFTS. Sadly, gifts can become idols! God's wisdom was prepared for those who love Him. Let us ask the LORD to take His place on the throne of our life and fill us with the Holy Spirit as promised in His Word.

> **CAMPUS CRUSADE'S PAMPHLET,** *"HAVE YOU MADE THE WONDERFUL DISCOVERY OF THE SPIRIT-FILLED LIFE?"* gives reliable information:
> *HOW TO PRAY IN FAITH TO BE FILLED WITH THE HOLY SPIRIT*
> We are filled with the Holy Spirit by **faith** alone. However, true prayer is one way of expressing your faith. The following is a suggested prayer: "Dear Father, I need You. I acknowledge that I have been directing my own life and that, as a result, I have sinned against You. I thank You that You have forgiven my sins through Christ's death on the Cross for me. I now invite Christ to again take His place on the throne of my life.
> "Fill me with the Holy Spirit as You **commanded** me to be filled, and as You **promised** in Your Word that You would do if I asked in faith, I pray this in the name of Jesus. As an expression of my faith, I now thank You for directing my life and for filling me with the Holy Spirit."
> Does this prayer express the desire of your heart? If so, bow in prayer and trust God to fill you with the Holy Spirit **right now**.[20]

PRINCIPLE: *PRAY IN THE SPIRIT WITH UNDERSTANDING.* We are told to pray in the spirit with understanding [1 Cor. 14:15]. Paul exhorted us to put on God's armor then with all prayer and petition, pray at all times in the Spirit [Eph. 6:18]. Spirit in both verses is *pneuma,* the Greek word meaning "the Spirit, the Holy One," and it stresses the character of the person of the Holy Spirit.

DR. SPIROS ZODHIATES TRANSLITERATED PNEUMA in the *Hebrew-Greek Key Study Bible*:

Spirit is the element in man which gives him the ability to think of God. It is man's vertical window. Psuche, soul, is man's horizontal window making him conscious of his environment.[21]

***PNEUMA* MEANS BY THE POWER AND AID OF THE SPIRIT** ~ prompting, joining. We are to pray in the power and aid of the Spirit so that we can be prompted to join the LORD and one another in agreement with the Word. To pray in the Spirit, we must:

(1) begin by submitting our thoughts to God;
(2) resist the devil (who must flee);
(3) invite the Holy Spirit to prompt us with God's appropriate Word to pray His righteousness into lives and circumstances.

ANDREW MURRAY WROTE THAT PAUL COUNTED ON BELIEVERS' BEING FILLED WITH THE SPIRIT, so that it would be perfectly natural to them, without the thought of burden or constraint, to pray for all who belong to the body of Jesus Christ . . . "That is what we need today, for every believer to yield himself undividedly to Christ Jesus, every day, and be conscious that he is one with Christ and His body."[22]

ONLY GOD'S SPIRIT KNOWS GOD'S THOUGHTS. ". . . the Spirit searches all things, even the deep things of God" [1 Cor. 2:7-16]. The LORD's guidance is revealed through the Holy Spirit Who helps us in our weakness according to the will of God [Rom. 8:26, 27]. He Who searches the heart knows the mind of the Spirit because He intercedes for the saints according to the will of God [Rom. 8:27]. He teaches us what to say [Luke 12:12].

MAN'S FALLEN SPIRIT *is limited to man's thoughts.* We need the Spirit of Truth living in us and guiding us to give our minds understanding of what the Spirit desires [Rom. 8:9]. John, who understood the LORD Jesus Christ's desire for believers, wrote about being "at one" with Father God, the teachings of Jesus, and the role of the Holy Spirit, Our Helper, the Spirit of Truth, Who will perfect and unify us in His love.

The Holy Spirit unifies and activates God's concerns *through* our prayers when we follow Christ's teachings and imitate Him in our prayers [John 14:16, 17, 26, 31]. Jesus said, "But the Helper, the Holy Spirit, Whom the Father will send in My name, will teach you all things, and bring to your remembrance all that I said to you" [John 14:26].

PRINCIPLE: ***EXAMINE YOUR HEART*** ~ ***UNANSWERED PRAYERS MAY BE THE RESULT OF GRIEVING THE HOLY SPIRIT.*** Wrong actions or attitudes can hamper prayers [Ps.80: 4]. Misjudging and unforgiveness in our hearts or the hearts of others can rob our prayers. Wrong actions or attitudes can also hold back His Presence from our hearts [Col. 3:5-9].

BEFORE WE JUDGE OTHERS (pass judgment on) or try to discern (understand) the motives of others, we need to first examine our own heart. Have we entertained thoughts of immorality, impurity, passion, evil desire, greed (idolatry), anger, wrath, malice, slander, presumption, abusive speech or lies? [Col. 3:5-11] Have we allowed these cursed attitudes to be activated into the spiritual realm through our flesh? Unrighteous attitudes and thoughts are simply ugly manifestations of the very same evil spirits and false gods that controlled the Babelites. They were the spiritual strongholds that ran rampant over the Babylonians [Col. 3:5-11; Gal. 5:19-21].

DANIEL PRAYED AND FASTED FOR TWENTY-ONE DAYS while Gabriel continued to battle against unrighteous forces to bring God's answer to Daniel. Gabriel needed to call in Michael to help battle against the princes of Persia and Greece. The battle that raged between God's angels and the enemy's princes is a clear illustration of the power wielded by unrighteousness. You can find the functions of the enemy's prince's "evil fruit" in the above-mentioned strongholds of wrong attitudes and actions! LORD, alert us, protect us, and deliver us!

PRINCIPLE: ***REFUSE WRONG ATTITUDES THAT ALIGN THEMSELVES IN AGREEMENT WITH THE ENEMY.*** Wrong actions or attitudes manifest the enemy's unrighteous fruit. They strengthen the immoral sinful foundation that the enemy exercises to build today's *tower of self-deification*. The attitude of a believer, clothed in God's armor and filled with the Spirit of Christ [Eph. 6:11-18], is to represent the LORD's interests. Believers' righteous attitudes can countermand unrighteous spiritual forces. The LORD's vehicle of righteous attitudes ushers forth victory when God's righteousness, wisdom and power are proclaimed. (Let us check our heart attitude ~ do we grieve the LORD? [Col. 3:8-9])

RIGHTEOUS AGREEMENT IS SYNONYMOUS with fulfillment and the principle of holy unity. Righteous agreement (holy unity) versus unrighteous agreement (unholy unity) is also vividly demonstrated in Genesis 11:1-9, where we readily see that the *entire world spoke one language* ~ the same language spoken on Noah's Ark! Notice that when the inhabitants settled in the land of Shinar they declared, "Come let us build for ourselves [self] a city and a tower whose top will reach into heaven and let us make for ourselves [self] a name, lest we be scattered abroad over the whole earth" [Gen. 11:4].

NAME[23] ~ ***SHEM IN HEBREW*** ~ means: a definite and conspicuous position; a mark, sign or memorial of individuality; honor, authority, character.[24]

PRINCIPLE: *NAME MEANINGS AND WORD MEANINGS ARE IMPORTANT TO GOD!* The Babelites were erecting a tower to *glorify their name!* The LORD changed Babel's name (meaning gate or tower to glory) to Babylon (confusion). The Trinity waged war in Holy Unity. They declared confusion to Babel's language, scattered people that purposed to build a city to symbolize their self-glory. He renamed the city, which dramatically symbolized the end result of man's unrighteousness. It is a clear illustration that name meanings and actions are significant to God or He would not have changed the name of the city.

The meaning behind Babylon's name is engrossing because it illustrates God's Sword of the Spirit and the Trinity's righteous judgment against the enemy's sword of unrighteous agreement. Unrighteous agreement had been exercised to gain the Babelites' unholy goal "to make for themselves" a definite, cohesive representation and conspicuous memorial ~ a tower ~ that would identify, glorify and establish the name of "man" as the owner of the heavens. Their cohesive cause was founded on a common denominator based on their egos that feared that their forces would be scattered!

THE UNHOLY-UNRIGHTEOUS SPIRIT'S SWORD WAS WIELDED ~ in unified agreement ~ by the people of Babel to build a visible sign, a memorial, which *deified self.* It was to be a solid representation that declared *"man is god ~ I am god"* ~ the ruler of the heavens!

YAHWEH SAID, "BEHOLD, they are one people and they all have the same language. This is what they have *begun* to do, now *nothing which they purpose to do will be impossible!"* The Trinity was concerned about the Babelites being *unified in agreement* and *single-minded.* Their commitment energized them in their unrighteous cause [Gen. 11:6]. The power of their agreement is hard to adequately communicate, but it is important! When we look at the other side of the coin we can easily see that the same principle is true for believers. Believers should proclaim God's righteous causes by lining up their testimony to agree with the Holy Spirit's plans and purposes.

OUR MINDS AND HEARTS MUST BE OPEN, AVAILABLE AND DEPENDENT upon the power and strength of God's righteous agreement birthed by the Spirit of Christ [Jude 1:20]. Believers' righteous attitudes and righteous agreement are foundational to effectual fervent prayers. The Babelites' unholy, unrighteous attitude and agreement that *they* were as god, was the basis of their immorality, impurity, pride, licentiousness, selfishness, resentment, and judgmental spirits that governed their lives [Gal. 5:19-21].

Today it does not take much insight to agree that the enemy has loosed torrential rains of unrighteous attitudes, accusations, and unrighteous agreement upon mankind [Isa. 49:22; 59:19 KJV]. Have complacency, resentment, presumption, discouragement, and so forth, hindered us from receiving God's fullness in our prayers and our lives?

WE ARE CALLED TO BE ACTIVELY INVOLVED WITH THE LORD'S PURPOSES and to be His vessels to uphold His Standard! May the LORD use His people and intercessors to raise His Standard against the enemy who has come in like a flood!

These gleanings, and the teachings in the following lessons, are shared to help us grow individually and corporately as believers and intercessors. We may not be theologians, but we can dig into God's Holy Word for His insights and jewels that are meant to clarify His Word and help us individually and corporately know Him beneficially. There is so much more that we have yet to learn.

WILL YOU JOIN WITH OTHER BELIEVERS, along with intercessors worldwide, to press on in obedience to know Him and respond to Christ's call to prevail in prayer?

LET US PRESS ON, communicate, agree in the Holy Spirit's leading, use His Double-Edged Sword and triumph through God's spiritual warfare principles.

LET US UNITE TO DECLARE that we are "determined to press on toward the goal for the prize of the upward call of God in Christ Jesus" [Phil. 3:14].

Let Us Unite to Pray according to the will of God.

Let Us Unite to Pray in agreement with God's WORD and the HOLY SPIRIT.

Let Us Unite to Pray for conviction and the miracle of repentant hearts.

Let Us Unite to Pray for restoration and revival through Christ!

Let Us Unite to Pray prevailing prayers . . .

    AND DECLARE . . .

"WE ARE HIDDEN WITH CHRIST IN GOD!"
[Col. 3:3]

PRAISE GOD FOR HIS WORD AND HIS SPIRIT!

SUMMARY ~ GOD'S SPIRITUAL WARFARE PRINCIPLES

- Agreement in the spiritual realm precedes reality in the physical realm.

- Agreement begins in the spiritual realm.

- Seek agreement in His Name.

- Listen intently to others when they share or pray.

- Declarations and Proclamations must line up with God's purposes.

- Test the spirits!

- Walk in God's authority.

- Faith is Trusting in God's Word and God's Power.

- Biblical discernment is needed to equip believers.

- Judge others by their fruit ~ walk in righteousness and obedience.

- Ask the Spirit of Christ to fill you and to illuminate His Word to you in practical ways.

- Pray in the Spirit with understanding.

- Examine your heart ~ unanswered prayers may be the result of grieving the Holy Spirit.

- Refuse wrong attitudes that align themselves in agreement with the enemy.

- Name meanings and word meanings are important to God!

AN EXCELLENT QUOTE ABOUT SPIRITUAL WARFARE BY ART MCMAHON:

The ***demands*** of the world ~ these we are to ***forsake***. (1 John 2:15)
The ***desires*** of the flesh ~ these we are to ***flee***. (2 Tim. 2:2)
The ***devices*** of the Devil ~ these we are to ***fight***. (1 Pet. 5:9)

III ~ SPIRITUAL WARFARE   PAGE 19

LIFE APPLICATION

1. Agreement in the spiritual realm precedes reality in the physical realm. A. What is it really saying? B. How is spiritual warfare successful? C. Does God want us to pray for Him to intercede? (P. 1)

2. What does Dutch Sheets say that prayer and intercession should be about? (P. 1)

3. A. Is spiritual warfare scary? B. Are we involved in spiritual warfare? C. What did the LORD give us to battle the enemy? (P. 2)

4. A. Whom are we to agree with when we pray? B. We are to be involved with _____ and _____ things. C. Agreement brings results for good or for bad. Who should we invite to lead our prayers? (P. 4)

5. According to Spurgeon, what happens if we pray about wrong things in our petitions? (P. 6)

6. What are the four "C's" that are a good point of reference for believers to remember when they are seeking to pray in God's righteousness? (PP. 6, 7)

7. Declarations and proclamations must line up with _____'s _____! (P. 7)

8. A. If convicted we did something that we think might be wrong, what must we ask ourselves to test the thought (spirit) behind it? B. If it's already done, what can we do? (P. 8)

9. Academia alone cannot inspire a deeper life in Christ. What must all teachings and emphasis do? (P. 9)

10. What does Bill Bright warn you about in his pamphlet *"Have You Heard of the Four Spiritual Laws?"* (P. 9)

11. A. Oswald Chambers wrote in *My Utmost for His Highest* that God never speaks to us in startling ways, but in ways that are _____ to _____ .
B. He also says that every time circumstances press, say, "Speak LORD" We need to make _____ to _____. As we listen, our ear grows acute, and, like Jesus, we shall hear God all the time. (PP. 9, 10)

12. A. Is biblical, scriptural, discernment needed to equip believers? B. Some Bible studies and resources have confused a number of students of the Bible due to academic, intellectual words written by authors who were perhaps enslaved to certain ideas or theories. What was the outcome? C. What did it deny to believers? (P. 10)

13. What is the sevenfold test for error Reverend Tozer gave? (P. 10)

14. A. Martin Lloyd Jones wrote (regarding loss of biblical discernment) that when we question a doctrine or authors of religious works, we should do what?
B. What is the bottom line? (P.11)

15. What is the criterion for judging others? (P. 11)

16. Though all Christians are *indwelt* by the Holy Spirit [John 14:16, 17], not all Christians are *filled* (directed and empowered) by the Holy Spirit [Eph. 5:18].
A. What did Charles Ryrie say are two facets of the Holy Spirit's filling?
B. How do we test the gifts of the Spirit? (PP. 12, 13)

17. What must we do to pray in the Spirit? (P. 14)

18. A. What can hamper prayers? B. Before judging others, how do we examine our hearts? (PP. 14, 15)

19. A. We need to _____ wrong attitudes. B. What do wrong actions or attitudes manifest and strengthen? C. The attitude of a believer, clothed in God's armor and filled with the Spirit of Christ, should represent what? (P. 15)

20. Which of the warfare principles do you need to work on the most?
ANS: Answers vary.

SPIRITUAL WARFARE SCRIPTURE SEQUENCES

Page 1

Luke 12:12	[The Holy Spirit will teach you what to say]
1 Tim. 6:12 JNT	[Fight the good fight of the faith, take hold of the eternal life to which you were called when you testified to your faith before many witnesses.]
Heb. 4:16	[Approach the throne of grace with confidence, so that we may receive mercy and find grace to help us in our time of need]
Ps. 119:123	[My eyes fail with longing for Thy Salvation, and for Thy righteous Word]
Ps. 119:137-144	[Righteous are You, O LORD, and Your laws are right]
Ps. 119:138	[The statutes You have laid down are righteous; they are fully trustworthy.]
Ps. 119:139	[My zeal wears me out, for my enemies ignore Your words.]
Ps. 119:140	[Your promises have been thoroughly tested, and Your servant loves them.]
Ps. 119:141	[Though I am lowly and despised, I do not forget Your precepts.]
Ps. 119:142	[Your righteousness is everlasting and Your law is true.]
Ps. 119:143	[Trouble and distress have come upon me, but Your commands are my delight.]
Ps. 119:144	[Your statutes are forever right; give me understanding that I may live.]
Ezek. 22:30, 31	["I looked for a man among them who would build up the wall and stand before Me in the gap on behalf of the land so I would not have to destroy it, but I found none. So I will pour out My wrath on them and consume them with My fiery anger, bringing down on their own heads all they have done," declares the Sovereign LORD.]

Page 2

Eph. 6:17	[Take up the helmet of salvation and the sword of the Spirit, which is the word of God]
Heb. 4:12 JNT	[The Word of God is alive! It is at work and is sharper than any double-edged sword ~ it cuts right through to where soul meets spirit and joints meet marrow; it is quick to judge the inner reflections and attitudes of the heart.]
Acts 2:36	[God made Jesus both LORD and Christ]
Deut. 33:29	[He is your shield and helper and your glorious sword]
Matt. 18:19 AMP	[What you forbid and declare to be improper and unlawful on earth must be what is unlawful in heaven.]
Matt. 21:22	[If you believe, you will receive whatever you ask for in prayer]
Heb. 5:14 JNT	[But solid food is for the mature, for those whose faculties have been trained by continuous exercise to distinguish good from evil]
Heb. 16:17-20	[Men swear by someone greater than themselves, and the oath confirms what is said and puts an end to all argument. God wanted to make the unchanging nature of His purpose very clear to the heirs of what was promised.]
John 10:10	[The enemy comes to steal, kill, & destroy ~ Jesus came to give life abundantly]
2 Tim. 1:7	[They want to be teachers of the law, but they do not know what they are talking about or what they so confidently affirm]
Luke 10:18-29	["I saw Satan fall like lightning from heaven, I have given you authority to trample on snakes and scorpions and to overcome all the power of the enemy; nothing will harm you, but rejoice that your names are written in heaven."]

Page 3

John 4:34	[Jesus came to do the will of the Father]
Heb. 11:3	[By faith we understand that the universe was formed at God's command, so that what is seen was not made out of what was visible.]
Gen. 11:7	[The TRIUNE Godhead said, let us go down to confuse then scatter them ~ and They did!]
John 4:34	[Jesus came to do the will of the Father]
Matt. 18:19 AMP	[Our declarations forbid or permit what is lawful and proper]
Job 1:7	[Satan answered the LORD, "From roaming through the earth and going back and forth in it."]
1 Pet. 5:8	[Be self-controlled, alert ~ the devil prowls around like a roaring lion looking for someone to devour.]

Page 4

Matt. 26:39	["Father, if possible, may this cup be taken from Me. Yet not as I will, but as You will"]
Matt. 6:10	["Your kingdom come, Your will be done on earth as it is in heaven."]

Page 4 (continued)
John 14:26 JNT ["But the Counselor, the Ruach HaKodesh, whom the Father will send in my Name, will teach you everything; that is, He will remind you of everything I have said to you."]

Page 5
John 14:26 JNT ["But the Counselor, the Ruach HaKodesh, whom the Father will send in my Name, will teach you everything; that is, He will remind you of everything I have said to you."]

Page 6
Heb. 11:3 [By faith we understand that the universe was formed at God's command, so that what is seen was not made out of what was visible]
Ps. 33:6-9 [By the word of the LORD were the heavens made, their starry host by the breath of His mouth . . .]

Matt. 18:20 ["For where two or three come together in My Name, there am I with them."]
Matt. 18:19 AMP ["Again I tell you, if two of you agree (harmonize together, make a symphony together) about whatever [anything and everything] they may ask, it will come to pass and be done for them by My Father in heaven."]

Page 7
Eph. 1:9-23 [And He made known to us the mystery of His will according to His good pleasure, which He purposed in Christ, to be put in to effect when the times will have reached their fulfillment ~ to bring all things in heaven and on earth together under one roof . . . that we might be for the praise of His glory]
Luke 4; Matt. 4 [Jesus indwelt and led by the Holy Spirit rebukes Satan by quoting (paraphrasing) The Word]
Zech. 9:13 [Agreement is a warrior's sword]

Page 8
1 John 4:1 [Test the spirits]
2 Sam. 22:31 [His perfect way and promises are true ~ The LORD is a shield]
Eph. 6:10 [Be strong in the LORD in His mighty power!]
Luke 11:52 JNT ["Woe to you Torah experts! For you have taken away the key of knowledge! Not only did you yourselves not go in, you also stopped those who were trying to."]

Page 9
2 Cor. 3:6 [The letter killeth]
Eph. 4:14 [Do not be carried about by every wind of doctrine]
1 Cor. 2:5 [. . . so that your faith might not rest on men's wisdom, but on God's power]
John 14:21 [Whoever has My commands and obeys them, he is the one who loves Me. He who loves Me will be loved by My Father, and I, too, will love him and show Myself to him.]
Luke 11:13 ["If you then, though you are evil, know how to give good gifts to your children, how much more will your Father in heaven give the Holy Spirit to those who ask Him!"]
1 Thess. 5:23 [May God himself, the God of peace, sanctify you through and through. May your whole spirit, soul and body be kept blameless at the coming of our LORD Jesus Christ.]

Page 10
1 Kings 19:12-13 [God's voice was heard as His inherent ability (power) in Elijah's thoughts]
1 John 4:1-6 [Teachings in error refuse to recognize that Jesus *Christ* came in the flesh]

Page 11
1 Cor. 2:1 [. . . and confess that we are determined to know nothing among ourselves, except Jesus Christ crucified to the glory of God our Father.]
Prov. 3:5 [Trust in the LORD with all your heart; rely not on your own understanding.]
Matt. 7 [Judging not lest ye be judged ~ fruit contrasted; obedience stressed]
Isa. 55:8-9 [My thoughts are not your thoughts; neither are My ways your ways]
Isa. 58:4-6 [well-meaning vessels can write crucifying articles]

Page 12
Gal. 5:22, 23 [But the fruit of the Spirit is love, joy, peace, patience, kindness, goodness, faithfulness, gentleness, and self-control. Against such things there is no law!]
1 Cor. 12:11-31 [The same Spirit distributes at His will; one Spirit, one body]

Page 12 (continued)
John 17:20-23	[Paul and Jesus taught us to be of one Spirit, one Body, in True Unity in and through our Triune God]
Gal. 6:1 AMP	[Scripture shows how to address unrighteousness through the Spirit: pure hearts & clean hands]
1 Cor. 2:6-16	[Seek Christ's mind, then decree His eternal wisdom]
John 14:16, 17, 26	[Jesus comforts ~ Oneness with the Father ~ The Spirit of Truth indwells believers]
Eph. 5:18	[Not all are filled by the HOLY SPIRIT]
Acts 6:3-6	[The twelve disciples chose seven men full of the Spirit and wisdom]
Num. 23:12	[Must I not speak what the LORD puts in my mouth?]
Acts 16:6	[Paul was kept by the Holy Spirit from preaching the Word in the province of Asia]
1 Cor. 12:4-31	[Different gifts, but same Spirit; different kinds of service, but same LORD; different kinds of working, but the same God works all of them in all men]

Page 13
1 Cor. 12:4-11	[The gifts of the Spirit]
Rom. 11:29	[The gifts and calling of God are irrevocable]
1 Cor. 14:15	[Pray and sing with the mind and the Spirit]
Eph. 6:18	[With all prayer and petition, pray at all times in the Spirit]

Page 14
1 Cor. 2:7-16	[The Spirit searches all things, even the deep things of God]
Rom. 8:26, 27	[The Spirit helps us in our weakness according to the will of God]
Rom. 8:27	[The Holy Spirit searches hearts & intercedes for saints (holy ones) according to will of God]
Luke 12:12	[The Holy Spirit teaches us what to say]
Rom. 8:9	[We need the Spirit of Christ]
John 14:16-31	[Jesus comforts ~ Oneness with Father ~ Spirit of Truth indwells believers]
John 14:15, 16	["If you love Me, you will keep My commands; and I will ask the Father, and He will give you another Comforting Counselor like me, the Spirit of Truth, to be with you forever."]
John 14:17 JNT	[The world cannot receive Him, because it neither sees nor knows Him. You know Him, because He is staying with you and will be united with you]
John 14:31 JNT	["He has no claim on Me; rather, this is happening so that the world may know that I love the Father, and that I do as the Father has commanded Me. Get up! Let's get going!"]
John 14:26 JNT	[But, the Counselor, the Ruach HaKodesh, whom the Father will send in My name, will teach you everything; that is, He will remind you of everything I have said to you.]
Ps. 80:4	[LORD, How long will Your anger smolder against the prayers of Your people?]
Col. 3:5-9	[Illustration of wrong attitudes that holds back prayer]
Col. 3:5-11	[Wrongful heart attitudes that grieve the Holy Spirit]

Page 15
Col. 3:5-11	[Wrongful heart attitudes that grieve the Holy Spirit]
Gal. 5:19-21	[Wrongful attitudes bring forth unrighteous fruit that builds a tower to self]
Eph. 6:11-18	[The armor of God: Truth, Salvation, Righteousness, Peace, Faith and the Word]
Col. 3:8, 9	[Get rid of: anger, rage, malice, slander, and filthy language from your lips; do not lie to each other]
Gen. 11:1-9	[Unholy agreement versus righteous agreement is demonstrated]
Gen. 11:4	[Let us make for ourselves a name lest we be scattered abroad over the whole earth]

Page 16
Gen. 11:6	[Babelites were one people, one language ~ what they have begun, nothing they purpose will be impossible!]
Jude 1:20 JNT	[. . . build yourselves up in your most holy faith, and pray in union with the Ruach HaKodesh]
Gal. 5:19-21	[It is obvious what kind of life develops out of trying to get your own way all the time: repetitive, loveless, cheap sex; a stinking accumulation of mental and emotional garbage; frenzied and joyless grabs for happiness; trinket gods, magic-show religion; paranoid loneliness; cutthroat competition; all-consuming-yet-never-satisfied wants; a brutal temper; an impotence to love or be loved; divided homes and divided lives; small-minded and lopsided pursuits; the vicious habit of depersonalizing everyone into a rival; uncontrolled and uncontrollable addictions; ugly parodies of community.] *THE MESSAGE*

Page 17
Isa. 49:22 [I will lift up My banner to the peoples; they will bring your sons in their arms and carry your daughters on their shoulders]
Isa. 59:19 KJV [So shall they fear the name of the L{ORD} from the west, and His glory from the rising of the sun. When the enemy shall come in like a flood, the Spirit of the L{ORD} shall lift up a standard against him.]
Phil. 3:14 [I keep pursing the goal to win the prize offered by God's upward calling in Messiah Yeshua]
Col. 3:3 JNT [For you have died, and your life is hidden with the Messiah in God.]

Praise God For His Word and His Spirit!

GOD'S SPIRITUAL WARFARE PRINCIPLES ENDNOTES

1. Dutch Sheets, *The Beginner's Guide to Intercessory Prayer*, (Ventura, CA: Regal from Gospel Light Worldwide, 2001, Re-Published 2008), pp. 24, 25, 11, 27.

2. Charles H. Spurgeon, *1000 Devotional Thoughts*, (Baker Book House, reprinted 1976), pp. 317-318. (Formerly published under the title, *Flashes of Thought; being One Thousand Choice Extracts from the Works of Charles Spurgeon.*)

   Prayer Accepted Through the Intercession of Christ

   I think it is Ambrose who uses a very pretty figure concerning believers' prayers. He says we are like little children who run into the garden to gather flowers to please their father, but we are so ignorant and childish that we pluck as many weeds as flowers, and some of them very noxious, and we would carry this strange mixture in our hands, thinking that such base weeds would be acceptable to him. The mother meets the child at the door, and she says to it, "Little one, thou knowest not what thou hast gathered."

   She unbinds this mixture and takes from it all of the weeds, and leaves only the sweet flowers, and then she takes other flowers sweeter than those which the child has plucked, and inserts them instead of the weeds, and then puts back the perfect posy into the child's hand, and it (the child) runs therewith to its father. Jesus Christ in more than motherly fashion thus deals with our supplications. If we could see one of our prayers after Christ Jesus has amended it, we should scarce know it again. He has such skill that even our good flowers grow fairer in His hand; we clumsily tied them into a bundle, but He arranges them into a fair bouquet, where each beauty enhances the charm of its neighbor.

   If I could see my prayer after the Lord has prayed, I should miss so much, and I should find so much there that was none of mine, that I am sure its fullest acceptance with God would not cause me a moment's pride, but rather make me blush with grateful humility before Him whose boundless sweetness lent to me and my poor prayer a sweetness not our own. So then, though the prayers of God's people are as precious incense, they would never be a sweet smell unto God, were it not that they are accepted in the Beloved.

3. A. C. Gaebelein, *What the Bible Says About Angels*, (Grand Rapids, MI: Baker Book House, First printed in 1924 by "Our Hope" Publication Office), p. 58.

4. A.W. Tozer, *Keys to the Deeper Life*, Series in Christian Life, *Sunday Magazine, Inc.*, (Grand Rapids, MI: Zondervan Publishing House of the Zondervan Corporation, 1957), p. 28.

   . . . the fact that such confusion exists obliges those who advocate the Spirit-filled life to define their terms and to explain their position. Just what, then, do we mean? And what are we advocating? For myself, I am reverently concerned that I teach nothing but Christ crucified. For me to accept a teaching or even an emphasis, I must be persuaded that it is Scriptural and altogether apostolic in spirit and temper. And it must be in full harmony with the best in the historic church and in the tradition marked by the finest devotional works, the sweetest and most radiant hymnody and the loftiest experiences revealed in Christian biography.

   . . . To speak of the "deeper life" is not to speak of anything deeper than simple New Testament religion. Rather it is to insist that believers explore the depths of the Christian evangel for those riches it surely contains but which we are as surely missing. The "deeper life" is deeper only because the average Christian life is tragically shallow. They who advocate the deeper life today might compare unfavorably with almost any of the Christians who surrounded Paul or Peter in early times. While they may not as yet have made much progress, their faces are toward the light and they are beckoning us on. It is hard to see how we can justify our refusal to heed their call. What the deeper life advocates are telling us is that we should press on to enjoy in personal inward experience the exalted privileges that are ours in Christ Jesus; that we should insist upon tasting the sweetness of internal worship in spirit as well as in truth; that to reach this ideal we should if necessary push beyond our contented brethren and bring upon ourselves whatever opposition may follow as a result.

5. Wendy Beckett, (1993) Intercessors For America, P.O. Box 4477, Leesburg, VA 22075.

6. Bill Bright, *Have Your Heard of the Four Spiritual Laws?* Campus Crusade for Christ International, For materials: *New Life Resources*, Peachtree City, Georgia, P.12.

7. A.W. Tozer, *The Divine Conquest*, (Harrisburg, PA: Christian Publications, Inc.). p 26. Copyright 1950 by the Fleming Revell Company, Old Tappan, New Jersey.

    The first encounter may have been one of terror, as when a "horror of great darkness" fell upon Abram, or as when Moses at the bush hid his face because he was afraid to look upon God. Usually this fear soon lost its content of terror and changed after a while to delightsome awe, to level off finally into a reverent sense of complete nearness to God. The essential point is, they experienced God. How otherwise can the saints and prophets be explained? How otherwise can we account for the amazing power for good they have exercised over countless generations. Is it not that they walked in conscious communion with the real Presence and addressed their prayers to God with the artless conviction that they were addressing Someone actually there?

    Without doubt we have suffered the loss of many spiritual treasures because we have let slip the simple truth that the miracle of perpetuation of life is in God. God did not create life and toss it from Him like some petulant artist disappointed with his work. All life is in Him and out of Him, flowing from Him and returning to Him again, a moving indivisible sea of which He is the Fountainhead. That eternal life which was with the Father is now the possession of believing men, and that life is not God's gift only, but His very Self.

8. Ibid. P.27

    God never speaks to us in startling ways, but in ways that are easy to *misunderstand;* we say, "I wonder if that is God's voice?" Isaiah said that the Lord spake to him "with a strong hand," that is, by the pressure of circumstances. Nothing touches our lives but it is God Himself speaking. Do we discern by His hand or only by mere occurrence? . . . Every time circumstances press, say, "Speak Lord"; make time to listen . . . Recall the time the Lord did speak to you. Have you forgotten what He said? Was it Luke 11:13, or was it 1 Thessalonians 5:23? As we listen, our ear gets acute, and, like Jesus, we shall hear God all the time.

9. Oswald Chamber, *My Utmost For His Highest*, Westwood, NJ: Barbour and Company, Inc.) p. 20. "The Dilemma Of Obedience," January 30th, (1 Sam. 3:15).

    Within the hearts of a growing number of evangelicals in recent days has arisen a new yearning after an above-average spiritual experience. Yet the greater number still shy away from it and raise objections that evidence misunderstanding or fear or plain unbelief. They point to the neurotic, the psychotic, the pseudo-Christian cultist and the intemperate fanatic, and lump them all together without discrimination as followers of the deeper life.

10. A.W. Tozer, Ibid. P. 27

11. A. W. Tozer, *Man The Dwelling Place Of God*, (Camp Hill, PA: Christian Publications, 1966), P. 121.

12. Ibid. P. 122

13. Martyn Lloyd Jones, *Saved In Eternity*, (Westchester, IL: Crossway Books [division of Good News Publishers], 1988).

14. Bob & Gretchen Passantino, *Witch Hunt*, (Nashville, TN: Thomas Nelson, 1990), P. 25, 32.

    Biblical discernment is absolutely necessary for Christians living in a world of many ideas, beliefs, and practices. Without a clear understanding of *biblical truth (2 Titus 2:15)* and *accurate discernment* between good and evil (Prov. 2:1-11), Christians are unable to enjoy free fellowship with other believers and confidence in the face of opposition. Without biblical discernment, Christians end up living in fear and confusion, unable to walk confidently in truth and love.

> P.25 . . . the *one thing we have to do in a situation like this is to avoid becoming slaves to our own theories and ideas and to our own understanding of the truth.* In avoiding that danger we should *go to the Scriptures,* and look at the *Bible's plain and obvious teaching with as dispassionate and open a mind* as we are capable of. We should do that, I say, not only with regard to this problem of prayer, but with regard to any other problem that may arise in our spiritual experience.
>
> There are certain doctrines taught in Scripture quite clearly, but then we come up against something that we cannot quite fit into our doctrinal pattern, and the danger at that point is to *stand on our own doctrine* and to try to *explain away the Scripture.* If ever we find a point that seems to conflict with our clear grasp of doctrine, it seems to me that, for the time being, the essence of wisdom is to leave our doctrine where it is. It is not that we deny it, we just leave it for the moment, we come back to Scripture and we note what Scripture has to say everywhere about this particular matter. Then having done that, we again attempt to relate this obvious and clear teaching of Scripture with the doctrine of which we are equally sure . . . But it is our bounden duty to go as far as we can and to understand the teaching as far as that is possible.

15. Ibid. P.33

16. Ibid. P.35

17. Ibid. P.39

18. Charles C. Ryrie, *Basic Theology*, (Wheaton, IL: Victor Books, 1986), p. 376.

    > The first (filling) as a sovereign act of God whereby He possesses (occupies) someone for special activity. The second facet of Spirit-filling may be described as the extensive influence and control of the Spirit in a believer's life. It evidences an abiding state of fullness rather than the specific event. It produces a certain character of life, and seems to be a close synonym to spirituality. This facet of the Spirit's filling is the finest character reference one could have. All can experience it, but not all do [Acts 6:3(-6)].

19. Lloyd-Jones, Ibid. P.87

    > There are other spirits, and these other spirits are very powerful, and can give wonderful gifts. Satan can counterfeit most of the gifts of the Holy Spirit. For example, there are spirits who can heal. There are strong phenomena in this world in which we live, and the test of the gifts of the Spirit is this: do they *testify* to the fact that Jesus is God in the flesh? Do they *glorify* the Son of God? As that is the supreme work of the Holy Spirit, so *every* spirit must be tested by that particular test. There is a danger that again we put such emphasis upon the Spirit Himself that we do so at *the expense of the Son.*
    >
    > There are some people who are always talking about the phenomena in the Christian life. They like talking about the gifts of the Spirit and boasting that they possess one or other of them: Have you got the gift of healing? . . . Well, thank God, the Holy Spirit does give these gifts, but let us never forget that His main function is to glorify the Son, so that if our life is not always pointing to the LORD Jesus Christ and glorifying Him, we better be careful.

20. William R. Bright, *Have You Made The Wonderful Discovery Of The Spirit-Filled Life?* 1966, Ibid. P.12

21. Spiros Zodhiates, Th.D., *The Hebrew-Greek Key Study Bible*, (Grand Rapids, MI: Baker Book House). P.1722, Strong's Numerical Code #4151

22. Andrew Murray, (1828-1917) *God's Best Secrets*, (Grand Rapids, MI: Clarion Classics published by Zondervan Publishing House, [Reprinted by special arrangement with Biola Book Room, Los Angeles, CA.]).

   May 27 – Paul counted on believers' being filled with the Spirit, so that it would be perfectly natural to them, without the thought of burden or constraint, to pray for all who belong to the body of Jesus Christ . . . Is not this what we need in our daily life, that every believer who has yielded himself undividedly to Christ Jesus, shall day by day, every day, and all the day, live the consciousness that he is one with Christ and His body? May God's people be willing for this sacrifice of prayer and intercession at all times and for all saints!

23. James Strong, LL.D.,S. T. D. , (1822-1894) *The New Strong's Exhaustive Concordance of the Bible*, (Thomas Nelson Publishers, Hebrew and Chaldee Dictionary, 1990). <u>P.117</u>, Name, (shem in Hebrew] #8034

24. Francis Brown D.D., D. Litt., S. R. Driver, D.D. Litt.D., Charles A. Briggs, D.D.. D.Litt, *A Hebrew and English Lexicon of the Old Testament, With An Appendix Containing the Biblical Aramaic*, (1906) 1951, pp. 1027-1028.

MOSES – THE HIGH PRICE OF A HOT TEMPER

Four Scenes from the Life of an Angry Man:

- The Murder of the Egyptian Taskmaster (Ex.2: 10-12; Acts 7:22-24).
- The Furious Response to Pharaoh's Stubbornness (Ex.11: 8).
- The Destruction of the Tablets (Ex.32: 15-20).
- The Striking of the Rock (Num.20: 1-13).

What Is Anger?

Anger is "an emotional state that varies in intensity from mild irritation to intense fury and rage. It is a strong passion or emotion of displeasure or antagonism, excited by a real or supposed injury or insult to one's self or others."

Gods' Feelings About Our Anger

Proverbs 29:11 "A fool gives full vent to his anger: but a wise man keeps himself under control."

Ecclesiastes 7:9 "Do not be quickly provoked in your spirit, for anger resides in the lap of fools."

Eph. 4:26-27 "If you are angry, don't sin by nursing your grudge. Don't let the sun go down with you still angry-- get over it quickly; for when you are angry, you give a mighty foothold to the devil." (TLB)

Eph. 4:31 Get rid of all bitterness, rage and anger, brawling and slander, along with every form of malice.

Colossians 3:8 "But now you must rid yourselves of all such things as these: anger, rage, malice, slander, and filthy language from your lips."

The True Source Of Anger

"Out of men's hearts, come evil thoughts of lust, theft, murder, adultery, wanting what belongs to others, wickedness, deceit, lewdness, envy, slander, pride, and <u>all other folly</u>. **All these vile things come from within**; they are what pollute you and make you unfit for God." Mark 7:20-23TLB

Our anger comes from within and is caused by our realization that we are not getting what we want when we want it. The truth is our anger is often a mirror reflecting our true inner self.

We always want to blame our anger on someone else. (E.g. "he made me angry", "she made me mad", "they ticked me off"). No, the truth is he/she, they didn't make you angry. They acted and <u>you reacted,</u> <u>you chose your reaction,</u> <u>you chose to be angry</u>. Think about it, when we are happy we claim sole responsibility for our feelings and emotions (I'm just a happy, positive person).

WHEN WE ARE ANGRY we blame others for our feelings and emotions. (Victim mentality)

WHEN WE ARE ANGRY we must be honest and identify the internal sources of anger:

- *Our Impatience* – I want my way right now.
- *Our Expectations* – You're not doing what I want. Disappointed desires.
  (James 4: 1-2a ~ *What causes fights and quarrels among you?* Don't they come from your desires that battle within you? You want something but don't get it. You kill and covet, but you cannot have what you want. You quarrel and fight.)
- *Our Intolerance* – You're not my kind, you're inferior / undeserving.
- *Our Pride* – I demand, I deserve, that's my space, get out of my way.
- *Our Arrogance* – Superiority – Do you know who I am?

Strategies To Keep Anger At Bay

WHEN WE ARE ANGRY:

- **We should realize the cost.** Think about the consequences. Anger is one letter away from Danger! Your anger can destroy people. Your anger can destroy your testimony or even your life. Concentrate on the undesirable consequences of becoming aggressive.
- **We should resolve to manage it.** Anger is Typical, Sin is Optional, Aggression is a Choice - Calm down, back away, give yourself time and space and do it now. Anger is a choice.
- **We should reflect before reacting.** Stop - get control – THINK before you speak or react. Don't let pride drive you to anger and aggression. It is not our place to judge and punish all wrongs and injustices.
- **We should put ourselves in the other person's shoes.** Keep in mind that we are all humans, subject to making unintentional mistakes. Give them a break. Try to understand the viewpoint of the other person. Don't assume the worst intentions. Remember you make mistakes.
- **We should release our anger appropriately.** Exercise, walk around the block, quote scripture to self, pray, get away from the place of tension.
- **We should remember external sources of anger:** 1. People are selfish, thoughtless and sometimes cruel. 2. Life is unfair. 3. Life is hard.
- **We should evaluate the provocation** with a commitment to learning from it and turning it into a positive growth experience. I.e. learning how to avoid or better deal with a similar provocation. Attempt to reduce or eliminate your exposure to these negative stimuli.
- **Stop hostile fantasies**. Cease dwelling on issues, situations or people, which have aggravated you. Let it go, get over it, it's not worth it, move on.
- **We should rehearse the ABC's of anger** - what caused you to be angry **(Anger trigger)**, what you did about it **(Behavior)**, what happened because of what you did **(Consequence)** and what did you learn that will help you cope better in the future **(Discern)**?

PASTOR LYNN WARNER ~ PRIME TIME LESSON ~ TEXT: EXODUS 2: 10-12
THE CHAPEL, AKRON, OHIO

TESTING THE SPIRITS

The LORD has given us the Scriptures, the Holy Spirit, and natural powers of observation. He expects us to avail ourselves of their help constantly. "Prove all things; hold fast that which is good," said Paul [1 Thess.5:21]. "Beloved, believe not every spirit," wrote John, "But try the spirits whether they are of God: because many false prophets have gone out into the world" [1 John 4:1].

When we have wrong thoughts or unforgiveness, we need to ask ourselves if we have roots of bitterness, resentment, or possible feelings of being threatened by person(s) or circumstance(s).

We are to seek God's counsel, and wait for Him to impress our heart, before we speak, and then walk in His guidance. The fruit of the Spirit [Gal.5:16, 22-23] is a plumb line to question our thoughts before our actions take hold.

If Satan's plots and schemes, along with our fleshly, worldly thoughts of mischief, are allowed to remain in our mind, we will accept them and often reflect them. We need to resist (refuse) all questionable, sudden, diverting, procrastinating, accusing thoughts in the Name of Christ Jesus *and forbid them to return.*

We are to *test* the spirits in our imagination, questionable thoughts and wrong thoughts. We are to take authority over them and submit them to God for forgiveness and cleansing.

Tell the accuser that our thoughts were purchased by the Blood of Christ [Rom.5:9] who forgives us and makes our thoughts innocent, sanctified, justified, and redeemed.

FOLLOWING ARE SOME EXAMPLES OF HOW TO TEST THE SPIRITS:

When we receive an offensive or accusing thought, even a thought that we question or wonder if it really is from God, **we are to resist the thought and tell it that it must leave in the Name of Jesus.**

Occasionally, vain imaginings from our flesh return ~ *simply resist again!* Rebuke, prohibit, and command the thought (s) to leave through the power of Jesus' Name! You'll be amazed how it simply fades away.

If the thought returns a third time, and it still does not seem that it is from God, (you want to be sure that it *is* from God), *test it again and tell it that it cannot come back unless it is from Jesus Christ Himself!* It is amazing how God's thoughts will persist and at the same time if the thought is not from God it will vanish.

Refusing the accuser's influence liberates us to be the LORD'S overcomers. Remember His provisions will not, and cannot, help us if we do not use them!

Rarely is agreement with another trusted believer necessary to breakthrough against an ongoing tormenting thought, but a trusted mature intercessor can edify, help us, and enable us to pray from Christ's perspective and in His character [2Cor.10:3-6].

KNOWING GOD IN YOUR HEART

SERIES II

THE TRUTH

Lessons IV-VI

TAKING AUTHORITY
GOD'S CONQUERING LASERS
AGAPAŌ LOVE CONQUERS

Lesson IV

TAKING AUTHORITY

*Jesus said, "I will give you the keys to the kingdom of heaven,
And whatever you bind on earth will be bound in heaven,
And whatever you loose will be loosed in heaven."
Matt. 16:19*

*"The thief comes only to steal and kill and destroy;
I have come that they may have life, and have it to the full."
John 10:10 NIV*

MESSIAH'S AUTHORITY

"Salvation and power are established!
Kingdom of our God, authority of His Messiah!

The Accuser of our brothers and sisters thrown out,
who accused them day and night before God,
They defeated him through the blood of the Lamb
and the bold word of their witness.

They weren't in love with themselves;
they were willing to die for Christ.
So rejoice, Oh Heavens, and all who live there,
but doom to earth and sea,
For the Devil's come down on you with both feet;
he's had a great fall;
he's wild and raging with anger;
he hasn't much time and he knows it."
Revelation 12:10, 11

The Message
Eugene Peterson

"And they overcame him because of the blood of the Lamb
and because of the word of their testimony,
and they did not love their lives even to death."
Revelation 12:11 NASB

TAKING AUTHORITY

*"Little children, you are of God [you belong to Him]
and have [already] defeated and overcome them
[the agents of the antichrist] because He Who lives in
you is greater than he who lives in the world."*
1 John 4:4 AMP

*S*CRIPTURE TELLS US that we are to overcome the evils of this world. We need to take authority over our words and thoughts to be more productive in our Christian walk. God provided for His Church to walk in His authority. The enemy watches and waits for the right time to influence his purpose for our lives. God wants His children to take authority over the enemy, His enemy. This lesson shares Scriptures, along with insightful information gleaned during research, for God's direction on how to overcome our trials and tribulations, and how to recognize and discern when we are under attack and how to take authority over the agents of the anti-christ.

Sadly, taking authority, which is spiritual warfare, is a subject that many believers stay away from because they have seen people misuse or abuse the source of our battles. Many times I tried to conquer situations and failed. The failures that led me to study the Word to get help and direction, revealed the Holy Spirit's *unlimited ability* to guide and empower believers to choose overcoming thoughts, attitudes, and actions so that we can fulfill Christ's purposes in our lives [Ps. 68:11].

MANY YEARS AGO I turned on the television and heard a preacher talking about overcoming. Suddenly he jumped up and down, gestured in many directions then flamboyantly pointed and yelled, "In the Name of Jesus, I bind you demon spirits of lust from everyone in this auditorium . . ." the program ended abruptly! I waited and wondered what happened . . . what did bind have to do with overcoming? What did it mean to "bind"? Looking in a concordance, it listed "bind" in three verses of Jesus' discourse in Matthew [16:19; 18:18, 19].

READING IN CONTEXT STARTING WITH MATTHEW, Jesus asked the disciples who did the people say that the Son of Man was? [Matt. 16:13-18 JNT] Then Jesus candidly asked them who did *they* say that the Son of Man was? Peter answered, from a Jewish perspective, "You are The Messiah, the Son of the Living God" [Matt. 16:16 JNT]. Peter proclaimed that "for in Him, bodily, in this human figure, Yeshua the Messiah, the Son of God, lives the fullness of all that God is . . . divine as well as human . . . fully identified with God."[1]

JESUS CONTINUED BY VERIFYING PETER'S REVELATION and said that Peter was blessed because that had been revealed to Peter by God in Heaven. Christ told Peter that he was Kefa (Rock) and that "on this rock [little r] I will build My community [church] and the gates of Sh'ol [Hades] will not overcome it" [Matt. 16:18 JNT]. His church is able to overcome attacks from the gates of Hades.

Note: in Matthew 16, the LORD addressed the foundational necessity of repentant hearts, simplicity in belief, humility, and concern for the salvation of others. He established them as *preparatory* to "binding and loosing" and gathering together to "agree in His Name." He explained "binding and loosing" from the heavenly perspective when He said, "Whatever you bind [forbid and declare to be improper and unlawful on earth] must be what is already forbidden in heaven, and whatever you permit and declare proper and lawful on earth, must be whatever is already permitted in heaven" [Matt. 16:19 AMP].

CHRIST'S FOLLOWERS ARE CALLED to establish and administrate His authority through His Name as led by the Holy Spirit ~ Who leads us in God's perfect will.

> ***THE NEW INTERNATIONAL STANDARD BIBLE ENCYCLOPEDIA DEFINED BIND:***
> Necessarily, certain power for administration must be conferred on the company of men to carry out the purpose of Christ. That this power was not conferred on Peter alone is evident from Matt. 18:18, where it is given to all the apostles. The use of the word in the NT is to declare a thing to be binding or obligatory [John 20:23].[2]

NEGLECTING, MISHANDLING AND ABUSING GOD'S ENTRUSTMENT creates confusion and strife in His children. It also prevents administrating Christ's purposes. Some churches have liberally administrated "binding and loosing" in a frivolous way. They "bind" and "loose" in Jesus' Name so many times that it seems more like a performance than a declaration of God's delegated authority over the enemy. The flippant use of declarations have confused people and literally turned them off because the preacher's (or others) conduct and attitude did not reflect a Holy God.

CHRIST'S CHURCH, THOSE BORN OF GOD [John 1:12], must be cautious against dictatorially abusing or misusing Christ's invested, entrusted power. We must not take Christ's authority extended to believers in a shallow manner. It grieves the LORD, and many believers, to hear declarations that are out of line with the purposes, conditions, and principles of Christ.

The often used word "bind" has brought concern and division to some groups. Yet, for some reason, the words "refuse, rebuke, forbid, denounce, or prohibit" does not appear to do so. Can it be the way that our words communicate God's authority? The Bible version we use? Perhaps our comfort zone?

THE POINT IS THAT WE NEED TO BE SENSITIVE to the Holy Spirit's residence and leading in one another. Our hearts must be prepared for us to discern, individually or corporately, who is leading ~ our flesh, the enemy, or the Holy Spirit?

God is too big to put in a box! What sounds right for one may sound wrong to another. On the other side of the coin, what sounds wrong for one may sound right to another. Let God arise and lead His people corporately and individually, His way, to scatter our enemy ~ and His! [Ps. 68:1]

JESUS SAID, "I WILL GIVE YOU THE KEYS TO THE KINGDOM OF HEAVEN, and whatever you bind on earth will be bound in heaven, and whatever you loose on earth will be loosed in heaven" [Matt. 16:19].

The LORD purposed to build His Church upon the foundational rock of belief that the power and wisdom of God, the Messiah, Who is divinely One with God, had extended and entrusted His wisdom, power, and authority to His church to administrate God's plans and purposes. What does that mean to us today?

THE REVELATION THAT JESUS CHRIST IS THE LIVING GOD'S AUTHORITY is the key that opens heaven's door. Christ's power and wisdom came to operate in and through believers. The Spirit of Christ, God's Master Key, is His gift to His church to overcome the accuser in their daily lives [1 Cor. 12:7].

The LORD told Peter that on this rock (belief and faith that Jesus is the Son of the Living God) that He would give him the keys of the Kingdom of heaven. Peter's Jewish background in all likelihood recognized Jesus' point of reference when He used the word key. It had been used regarding the key to the House of David, when Isaiah spoke about the Valley of Vision. Isaiah referred to Eliakim when he said, "I will clothe him with your robe and fasten your sash around him and hand your authority over to him. He will be a father to those who live in Jerusalem and to the house of Judah. I will place on his shoulder the key to the house of David; what he opens no one can shut, and what he shuts no one can open" [Isa. 22:20-23]. The key to the house of David gave Eliakim absolute authority!

THROUGH HIS LOVE AND GRACE, God reached down and gave Heaven's Master Key to believers through Christ Jesus, Who was descended from the house of David, so that His followers could walk in His authority. Jesus came to save, equip, establish, and give authority to His church. Allegiance to the authority of the Messiah is the foundational rock upon which Jesus builds His church against which the gates of hell cannot prevail ~ *His church is to overcome!* [Matt. 16:18]

Reading about Christ's delegated authority, His promise of answered prayers, and commitment to His personal participation with believers, excited and inspired a deeper desire to learn more about "binding" and "loosing." It was both *challenging* and *convicting* to examine "bind and loose" in Jesus' context. The disciples asked the LORD, "Who is the greatest in the kingdom of heaven?" [Matt. 18:1] Jesus called a child to Him, then answered, "I tell you that unless you repent [change, turn about] and become like little children [trusting, lowly, loving, forgiving], you can never enter the Kingdom of Heaven [at all]!" [Matt. 18:3 AMP] "So the greatest in the kingdom of heaven is whoever makes himself as humble as this child" [Matt. 18:2-4 JNT].

IN OTHER WORDS, GOD'S VIEW OF A FOLLOWER'S GREATNESS (rank in His Kingdom) is conditioned upon their humbleness, change in attitude toward God, and personal relationship with Him. A change is required ~ a change from the sin of self-seeking ambition to be the greatest, to an inward turn to have an intimate response to God.[3] One cannot have proud, legalistic thoughts about God, or self-seeking, self-righteous thoughts about themselves, or their religion (which are stumbling blocks), if they want to have an intimate relationship with the LORD.[3]

CHRIST JESUS TAUGHT THE DISCIPLES that God's awesome authority had literally been appointed to His righteous children to put into practice ~ to administrate on earth as it is in heaven [Acts 6:3]. Jesus proceeded, "Again, I tell you that if two of you on earth *agree* about anything you ask for, it will be done for you by My Father in heaven" [Matt. 16:19; John 15:15-16, emphasis added]. The Jewish disciples certainly understood Jesus from the biblical Jewish perspective, that when two or three witnesses established a fact in a Jewish court, or when an agreement or a decision was made, it was honored as having been issued directly from Father God in Heaven.[4]

JESUS CONTINUED, "FOR WHERE TWO OR THREE COME TOGETHER IN MY NAME, there am I with them" [Matt. 18:20]. He gave a wonderful, but conditional, commitment that His presence will be with His children when their thoughts abide with Him and are in agreement with His thoughts [John 1:12; 15:7].

IN THE JEWISH NEW TESTAMENT, translated by David H. Stern from the original Greek into English for Messianic Jews, we find wonderful insight from the Jewish perspective. The introduction includes the following about "binding and loosing":

BINDING AND LOOSING: Who Has the Authority to determine to Halakah?
At Mattityahu [Matthew] 18:18 the Greek words usually rendered "bind" and "loose" are translated "prohibit" and "permit." This reflects the first-century Jewish application of these concepts to their leaders, who were understood as having authority from God to decide what practices should be followed by the community, i.e., to determine halakhah (a term which dates from a later period). In verses 18-20 the Messiah transfers this power from the rabbis to His own talmidim [disciples]. This authority was not assumed instantaneously [Matt. 23:2], nor was it assumed later when it should have been. But the fact that Messianic Jews and Gentiles have hitherto made little use of Yeshua's far-reaching grant of authority does not cancel it.[5]

These three-fold passages of Scripture are built upon a foundation of faith. We truly need to have the gift of faith in that dimension, to have understanding of God's spiritual gifts and to be able to join others in King Messiah's presence. Paul wrote to the Corinthians not to be ignorant of the spiritual gifts [1 Cor. 12:1] and to earnestly covet the best gifts [1 Cor. 12:31]. Paul concluded that faith, hope, and love are the greatest of the spiritual gifts [1 Cor. 13:13].

HELEN ROSEVEARE WROTE GOD'S GIFT OF FAITH enabled her to believe [1 Cor. 12:9] and that He used Miss Candy's explanation to open the eyes of her young heart:

> "Faith is God's gift in your heart that has made you able to believe," she (Miss Candy) explained, then read to me from another of Paul's letters: "For by grace are ye saved through faith; and that not of yourselves, it is the gift of God: not of works, lest any man should boast" ~ unmerited mercy and love reaching out to save me from my sins, planting in my heart His faith that I might be able to believe it![6]

A GNAT BEGAN TO IRRITATE ME while reading the above in *Living Faith*. The distraction was frustrating to say the least! A gentle impression came to "prohibit" the gnat from annoying me, so I "resisted" it and told it to leave the room, and "loosed" the peace of Christ to replace it ~ and it left me alone! Amazing! I had not purposed to "prohibit" the gnat, but in faith obeyed the unexpected still small voice in my heart. Praise God, that my thoughts were already centered "in Christ" when the gnat bothered me. My heart leaped with joy! The LORD allowed a simple gnat to show me the truth of "prohibit" and "permit" or "bind" and "loose." His illustration, in a practical way, confirmed that His invested authority in His children can even govern distractions.

WE NEED TO RECOGNIZE ONE OF THE ENEMY'S STRATEGIES: distraction that is meant to destroy God's purposes and plans for our lives! We need to refuse the distracting thoughts, and by faith put on the mind of Christ [1 Cor. 2:16], to be transformed by the renewing of our mind [Rom. 12:2].

The enemy tried to distract Jesus with temptations. He refused [rebuked, bound, forbade, prohibited, denounced] Satan during His wilderness temptation [Luke 4].

His heart was indwelt by the Holy Spirit before, during, and after the time that He combated the enemy. Jesus recognized the earthly power of the devil, but refused to give him accessibility or the legal rights to oppose Him. Jesus did not have a pity party in the wilderness ~ His eyes were focused on the battle ahead as He prepared for it. We need to be prepared, empowered, and wait for the Holy Spirit to lead us before combating the enemy. We need to follow Christ Jesus' example of clean hands and a pure heart.

WE CONTINUOUSLY NEED TO DEAL WITH STUMBLING BLOCKS and it is self-evident that *stumbling blocks begin in our mind.* Jesus recognized and denounced Satan for using Peter by influencing Peter's thoughts which were spoken to Jesus. The LORD turned and addressed Satan's influence in Peter, "Get behind me, Satan! You are a stumbling block to Me; you do not have in mind the things of God, but the things of men" [Matt. 16:23]. Even Jesus was tested by another person's stumbling block! We must follow Jesus' example by asking for and depending upon the Holy Spirit for discernment, guidance, and enablement to help us overcome stumbling blocks that the Adversary uses against us, our loved ones, and the body of Christ in general. Remember, Mark said for us to be on our guard as even the elect can be deceived [Mark 13:22, 23]. An important fact to remember!

Our thoughts must be aligned with Christ's before we "prohibit or permit" or "bind or loose" or do anything "in Jesus' Name." Impure hearts, criticism, judgment, backbiting, jealousy, and bitterness are some of the wrong attitudes that position believers for a painful fall. Some have suffered defeat by acting flamboyantly, cocky, or arrogant. Some have been careless or flippant when dealing with God's eternal enemy. Some have been overcome by the enemy because they let their guard down during times of illness, grief, disillusionment, fatigue, demands from others, etc. The enemy knows who, where, and when to attack God's children. And he certainly knows how!

WE HAVE BEEN CALLED TO SET OUR MINDS ON HEAVENLY THINGS [Col. 3:2]. Christ is *ALL* and *in all* [Col. 3:11]. If He is *in* all, we can afford to allow (non-doctrinal) differences in one another without being threatened. Other believers may hold different interpretations than ours, such as how or when to serve communion, etc. Shouldn't we *honor* the diversity within His body? Shouldn't we center upon our core belief ~ the *oneness* in Christ ~ that He lived, was crucified, resurrected, is standing at the right hand of God and is coming again? Shouldn't we allow others to make mistakes and not hold it against them? Or nag them about it? The LORD Jesus calls us to forgive, work, and pray corporately *in Christ* [Col. 3:23]. He calls us to be one! [Col. 3:15] If there is honor among *thieves,* cannot His children do better?

HAVE YOU EVER BEEN SO HIGHLY INSTRUCTED that words buzzed around in your thoughts like bees in a bonnet? Have foundational truths failed to change your life? I well remember the time that I found myself in a state of disillusionment and battling a broken heart. I had reached a saturation point on teachings about overcoming. Frankly, I could have recited many overcoming scriptural truths backward and forward, yet I was not an overcomer, nor could I see the fruit of the Spirit in my life. Admittedly, deplorably, I had become a self-righteous know-it-all!

ONE MORNING, AFTER BEING CONVICTED that my heart was not in the right place, I wept brokenly before the LORD. I confessed that I had blown it again and implored Him to help me recognize the mean, negative, self-righteous thoughts that came from the enemy, and to help me to refuse them. I prayed for the LORD to forgive me, and sobbed, "Why can't I be an overcomer?" The LORD gently turned my thoughts toward Calvary. I *knew* that my sins were forgiven and nailed to the CROSS, but the knowledge had not permeated my heart in a practical way.

Sorrowfully, I cried out to the LORD to show me my heart. In His infinite mercy He allowed my mind's eye to see an infinitesimal microscopic glimpse of my Heart. I cannot help but weep as I share this because I could see myself drowning in sin's turbulent waters. A slimy piling was within reach but I could not *bear* to touch it ~ it was *covered* with the most horrible, despicable, worthless parasites this gardener has ever known ~ *SLUGS!*

IT WAS HORRIFYING TO REALIZE THAT THE SLUGS on the piling depicted my carnal heart and that I would drown because I could not bear to touch it. I could not save myself! Helpless, hopeless and sinking, the eternal truth of Jesus' saving love, mercy, and grace reached down and put hope in my heart as He lifted me out of sin's slimy dominion. In awe of His mercy, that I did not and could not deserve, I tearfully sang *"LOVE LIFTED ME":*

> I was sinking deep in sin, far from the peaceful shore,
> Very deeply stained within, sinking to rise no more;
> But the Master of the sea heard my despairing cry,
> From the waters lifted me, now safe am I!
> Love lifted me, Love lifted me,
> When nothing else could help . . . *Love lifted me!*

A WONDERFUL DEVOTIONAL TIME OF PRAISE AND THANKSGIVING FOLLOWED. Jesus' love had saved a wretch like me from drowning in my sins. He lifted me out of that odious evil ~ He did what I could not do ~ His love reached out and touched my slug-like heart, convicted, forgave, and set me free!

PRAISE HIS HOLY PRECIOUS NAME, my beloved LORD died for this sinking sinner. Christ's awesome miracle at Calvary continues to lift us out of our sins and set us on solid ground. Hallelujah!

Afterward, deeply blessed by the new understanding of the saving grace of the Lamb of God, I burst into singing "Calvary Covers It All," because Christ's innocent blood paid, rescued, and redeemed this sinful child from the helplessness and hopelessness of always having to live with sluggish defiling thoughts, bad attitudes, sinful circumstances, etc. [Matt. 26:28].

MESSIAH SAID, "IT IS FINISHED!" Jesus' love, fused with the awesome power of His atoning Blood, will continue to alert me when slug-like thoughts threaten my heart [Heb. 9:22]. His marvelous blood, His Heaven sent love, is available when I blow it again. His blood will continue to cleanse me, lift me, and wash my repentant heart white as snow. Understanding what He did for me, I gratefully sang:

Jesus paid it all, all to Him I owe,
Sin had left a crimson stain,
He washed it white as snow.

HIS LIVING BLOOD CONTINUES to call me, call each of us, to believe in Him, to trust His Word, to appropriate His blood, and to walk in His righteousness. My mind had accepted the fact that Jesus saved my life. The insight about my slug-heart taught me that the grace of Jesus' powerful blood had not only saved me, but His love had washed me white as snow. It *is* all to Him I owe.

> ***DR. M. R. DE HAAN, RADIO BIBLE CLASS FOUNDER, WROTE:***
> Beloved, that blood has never lost its power, but is still available. By our first birth we inherited Adam's sinful nature, and unless born again, and washed in the blood of the Lord Jesus Christ, we shall have to perish forever.
> The question, therefore, becomes a personal one. It is, are you willing to submit to Him Who gave Himself upon the Cross of Calvary, by believing on Him, trusting His Word, and receiving Him as your only hope of salvation. It is a personal matter. There is no such thing as mass salvation or mass transfusions, but it must be a personal, individual thing, settled by you as a sinner in the sight of God and in need of salvation, and so . . . will you not appropriate that precious blood now, because tomorrow may be too late?
> . . . And then it is not only available to wash away our sins, but after we have been saved, when we fail and become defiled and when we fall, that precious blood is still available for our cleansing, for we read: "If we confess our sins, He is faithful and just to forgive us our sins, and to cleanse us from *all* unrighteousness" (1 John 1:9). Will you trust Him now?[7]

IT BECAME QUITE CLEAR THAT IT WAS GOD'S CONDITION that I had to recognize my sins and repent, submit them to God, and then appropriate the Blood of Jesus Christ to overcome my enslavement to dysfunction, rejection, guilt, unforgiveness, self- righteousness, or whatever area I had sinned in.

DR. DE HAAN WROTE:

> Adam sinned. The penalty was death. Blood originally pure and sinless became sinful and corruptible and Adam died. He died immediately spiritually; progressively morally; ultimately physically. The blood of the Lord Jesus Christ (the second Adam) was incorruptible, indestructible blood and therefore could not perish. Because it was incorruptible, it must, therefore, still be in existence somewhere today. Seventy years after Jesus shed His blood, it was still in existence, for John tells us it is the blood of Jesus Christ, His Son, that cleanseth us from all sin [1 John 1:7]. And that blood will remain forever.[8]

> Blood is life in the physical, but more important, and the thing we are now interested in, blood is life in the spiritual as well. For it is the blood of Jesus Christ His Son that cleanseth us from all sin. Each organic tissue in a human body has different functions yet all are fed, sustained and cleansed by the one tissue common to all the living tissues, the blood . . . the blood is the common denominator of all the tissues of the human body . . . it alone is mobile and fluid and flows constantly. . . . What the physical blood is in our veins to bodies, and to every cell of which it is composed, the blood of the Lord Jesus Christ is to the Body of our Lord, the church, and to every member of that body [Eph. 5:30].[9]

THE MARTYRS OF CHRIST'S CHURCH OVERCAME THE ACCUSER of the brothers and sisters through the cleansing blood of the Lamb, their testimony, and they loved not their life unto death. They shared Yahweh's indwelling unconditional love as a community of believers. Oh! His fathomless love! I sang His praises with gratitude and joy ~ Jesus saved me by His indestructible, incorruptible, incomparable blood!

THE REALIZATION THAT THE DEBT FOR MY SINS WAS PAID IN FULL, FOREVER, introduced a liberating, but responsible truth, a sobering truth that I needed to face. I had been purchased for a purpose at a great price! [Heb. 9:14; Titus 2:14] Free! Responsible! *Entrusted!* I owed my Master my heart, my soul, and my spirit. In trembling awe, I asked the LORD to teach me how to be the overcomer that Calvary had freed me to be, and prayed for His Holy Spirit to be my enablement.

I was once more led to Revelation 12:11. This time, something new stood out when I read, "that they overcame Him . . . *because of the 'word' of their testimony!*" My eyes zoomed in on "word" in the word of their testimony, and it began an extensive search on the meaning of word, logos.

INVESTIGATING VARIOUS INTERPRETATIONS OF LOGOS, it seemed The Expanded Vine's Expository Dictionary of New Testament Words was most appropriate:

(1) The revealed word of God (direct revelation given by Christ);

(2) The Gospel (as the message from the LORD) delivered with His authority and made effective by His power;

(3) Discourse, speech, instruction;

(4) Doctrine;

(5) Personal Word of God ~ title of the Son of God; His personal manifestation that represents the whole Deity.[10]

WANTING TO UNDERSTAND "WORD" in a comprehensible and relevant way, plus keep it in context, I began my research at the previous verse, Revelation 12:10 and looked up each word in both verses to the end of Revelation 12:11. Obedience turned the knob that opened the door to a better and practical understanding of logos.

WE NEED TO BE VIGILANT IN THE AREA OF OUR THOUGHTS AND WORDS, obedient to be renewed in the spirit of our mind, put off our old self which is being corrupted by its deceitful desires, and be made new in the attitude of our mind [Eph. 4:22, 23]. Obedience is a deeply challenging, ongoing, but essential condition to overcome areas where we fall flat on our face! *It is an ongoing process.*

IT WAS AMAZING TO STUDY THE GREEK LEXICONS and learn that "word" (logos), translated from Revelation 12:11, is twofold: one part relates to speech; the other relates to thoughts. They are *interrelated!*[11] Logos meant more than I had perceived ~ *it included thoughts!* Were my thoughts as important as my words? You probably know the computer adage regarding bad programming: "GI ~ GO!" for "Garbage In ~ Garbage Out!" Since our brains are like computers, let's use a secular adage for a spiritual one to remind us to program God's Word into our hearts so the Holy Spirit can program it out! *"God's Word In ~ God's Word Out!" or GWI ~ GWO.!"*

IT TAKES CHRIST'S THOUGHTS WITHIN AND WITHOUT TO OVERCOME! "His Word is a lamp to our feet and a light to our path" [Ps. 119:105] and "Thy Word have I hid in my heart that I might not sin against Thee," [Ps. 119:11] are verses which confirm that we need to learn His Word so that our thoughts can reflect His thoughts. What is in our heart comes out in our thoughts, words, and/or attitudes [Matt. 15:18].

Brains can be like computers: God's Word In ~ God's Word Out! GWI ~ GWO! Get rid of wrong thoughts that become the enemy's domain: Garbage In ~ Garbage Out! GI ~ GO! We need to *learn to think God's Word;* it is the source of righteous thoughts, words, deeds and prayers. It is essential to devote time to absorb Scripture so that the Holy Spirit can prompt our thoughts with God's principles and enable us to pray His Word into the heavenlies for people or circumstances.

Excitement mounted as the word study moved to "testimony." The following insights amazed me and enlarged my understanding of how to overcome. Testimony depicts involvement! We will always learn more by studying the Bible. Praise God, His Spirit is alive within us, ready and waiting to teach us!

Testimony (Greek ~ marturia) in THE NEW STRONG'S EXHAUSTIVE CONCORDANCE in a generic sense means:

(1) Witness [Isa. 59:12]; witness as a token, signs [Mark 14:55, 56, 59; Luke 22:71];
(2) Instruction, (solemn) precepts, (solemn) charge, etc. (i.e., that which anyone witnesses or states concerning a person or thing) [Job 15:6; Isa. 59:12];
(3) Declare, expose, exclaim, etc. [Acts 2:40, 10:42; Heb. 2:6];
(4) Affirm, insist on, assure, speak urgently, [Gal. 5:3; Eph. 4:17];
(5) Witness against [Heb. 10:28] and so forth.[12]

Let us compare our conversations and daily thought choices, in a legal yet practical meaning of "testimony" under the following definitions found in *Thayer's Greek-English Lexicon of the New Testament*. The definitions will lend further light to overcoming.[13]

(1) Testimony used as what one says, to what one testifies."[14]

Words and thoughts are utilized either by Christ or Satan. The word of our testimony is an *ongoing battle!* Unstable tongues are full of "death-dealing poison!" [James 3:8 JNT] The enemy will continue to bombard us with harassing accusing thoughts if we permit him (let him). Dwight Moody is credited for saying, "You can't keep the birds from flying over your head, but you can keep them from building a nest in your hair." We need to diligently guard against thoughts and words that build a nest in our mind and hearts and grieve the Holy Spirit. We are held accountable for the way our words are used [Matt. 12:36, 37]. We are to resist negative thoughts! We are to determine to make the devil's attacks *unsuccessful!* We are to resist the devil and he must flee! [James 4:7]

The enemy's goal is to influence us to follow his deviousness just as he influenced Eve and Adam. David allowed himself to be wrongly influenced to take a census of Israel[15] [1 Chron. 21:1]. The devil tried and failed to influence Christ. Calvary gave us both freedom from and responsibility to resist diverting, accusing, unrighteous, unclean, malicious, or presumptive thoughts.

Hearing a wrong thought is not sin ~ dwelling upon or accepting a wrong thought is! We need to refuse wrong thoughts, ask the LORD Jesus to wash our thoughts clean with the power of His Blood, and tell the thoughts that they cannot return because of the Blood of the Lamb.

(2) "Testimony used in a legal sense as a testimony before a judge" [15] [Luk. 22:71; Mar 14:55].

WE ARE HELD ACCOUNTABLE FOR THE WAY THAT OUR WORDS ARE USED [Matt. 12:36, 37]. When we stand before The Judge on Judgment Day, we shall render account for every careless word spoken [Matt. 12:36, 37]. What a sobering thought! We are warned to be continually on the alert ~ to watch out for the devil who plants wrong thoughts and wrong attitudes into our minds. He *often* suggests what someone else *is* thinking, doing or their motives. Satan's influence can easily cause us to misunderstand another person's words, actions and/or intentions to sway us to do and say things that grieve the Holy Spirit. Our testimony can be used for us, against us, or against others. *We must test our testimony!*

(3) "Testimony used as a witness: According to Jewish law there must be at least two witnesses to bind a person legally, to actually qualify making one a prisoner" [Deut. 19:15].[16]

What we testify (think, witness to, agree to, speak) has *dire consequences!* The disciples' Jewish background prepared them to understand the fullness of Christ's teachings about testimony in relation to both the Jewish legal system and the spiritual realm. They understood that their testimony was central to their witness and walk. It is important to carefully choose our thoughts and our words [Matt. 12:36, 37].

Past occultists, redeemed by Christ, have said that Satan cannot hear our thoughts or know our heart. However, his emissaries *can* interpret and report our *body language along with our spoken or written words.* The devil is stopped when we submit our thoughts to God, resist the devil's influence, and tell him that he must flee [James 4:7]. He loses his lawful rights to cause us mischief. Satan can put thoughts in our mind, but it is our action or inaction that will reveal if we have accepted or resisted them. We must always remember that *Only God can know our thoughts!*

(4) "Testimony used to objectively accuse: The chief priests and the whole council kept trying to obtain testimony against Jesus, to put Him to death, and they were unsuccessful" [Mark 14:53-59].[17]

The chief priests were merely vessels used by Satan. They did not have authority to take legal action against Christ without God's permission [Job 1:8-12]. Nor were they able to obtain a "testimony" that objectively accused Jesus. To illustrate objective accusations, in a personal way, I will share how the enemy used my accusing thoughts, and the accusing words of another, to inflict rejection, low self-esteem, self-hatred, self-pity, and so forth ~ they are instruments of destruction!

While growing up, my attitude toward my parents and our circumstances was probably a testimony against my parents. Their actions toward me were most likely instruments inspired by the enemy to keep me from God's purposes at that time. During my teenage years my heart froze "protectively" toward my parents in order to insulate me against the suffocating pain of their continual criticism and rejection.

LATER ON IN LIFE, AFTER I WAS BORN AGAIN, I changed and wanted to honor my parents and reached toward them with new found love. But all attempts to share with them were misunderstood and rebuffed. Nothing I did was right or acceptable. They either lectured or criticized what I shared, so I simply stopped communicating beyond holiday greetings and birthdays.

I wanted to honor my parents, yet I had to keep my distance as I could not afford to continue taking their devastating rejection and reproaches out on my own family. Providentially, in the LORD's goodness and grace, He allowed me to marry into a family who unconditionally loved, encouraged, and edified me.

A GODLY TEACHING AT A CHRISTIAN CONFERENCE exposed the harm that unforgiveness was doing to me and prepared my heart to repent (again) and release forgiveness to my parents. I gave it to Jesus. The LORD revealed to me that they had merely been vessels used by the enemy to undermine God's purpose for my life. My resentment and bitterness dissolved! It was a miracle! After I forgave my parents for misunderstanding and rejecting me, I felt affection growing for them again and began to remember many positive things that I had been blind to before. I chose to leave the painful memories to press on with Christ. It was wonderful to experience freedom from rejection of past failures (mine, others) simply through giving the pain to Jesus.

WHEN I FORGAVE MY PARENTS AT THE CONFERENCE, I received an inner joy, peace, and new strength. I had not realized how much unforgiveness had drained my energy. When I went home, my pastor, family, and friends asked what had happened to me and they said that I literally glowed with joy! *Choosing* to forgive changed my testimony, my heart, and my countenance.

Soon afterward I led Mother to Christ and she asked for forgiveness for all of the years that she had not accepted me for myself. She thought that I was putting on airs because we had different lifestyles. She also asked me to forgive her for the extraordinary amount of discipline given to me. Mother said that because I was the oldest she had concentrated her efforts for perfection on me. She believed if she could get me to do everything right that my sister and brother would fall in line ~ *like dominoes.*

ABOUT SIX MONTHS AFTER FORGIVING MY PARENTS, along with the circumstances of my youth, I attended another Christian conference for leaders. A lady joined our joyful group at lunch and started talking bitterly about her husband who was a well known church leader. She accused him of not loving, understanding, or accepting her ~ "he just performs the duties of a Pastor to impress others . . . he doesn't practice what he preaches!" I naively grumbled inwardly that she couldn't possibly know what problems, forgiveness, or rejections were really all about! My self-reflections increased to the point that all I could think about was how badly I had been mistreated and I wanted to tell her that she didn't even know what abuse and problems were ~ *mine had been much worse!*

THE THOUGHT THAT I SHOULD EXCUSE MYSELF FROM THE TABLE, and I should have, became stronger and stronger. But my prideful desire to help her (?) was stronger! I chose to reject the wisdom from above. My pride became full blown over what *I* had forgiven. I decided to help her! (The others had left the table.) Immediately, I launched into my traumatic and somewhat dysfunctional life, in hopes that my stories would stop her shallow complaints and help her appreciate all that she had. I desperately wanted to impress her that I had forgiven much worse.

HEAVINESS DESCENDED UPON ME and dissipated my earlier freedom and joy as we continued to talk. Dormant memories and forgiven episodes (I thought) came back and depressed me all over again because I had willed to bring back the past. I doubt if I could have helped her ~ do wrong motives help anyone? When I talked specifically against my parents, I objectively accused them again, and aligned my testimony with the enemy's accusations and re-opened my heart to anguish. My testimony became the devil's witness against two precious people that I had forgiven. Unforgiveness had invaded my heart again through my testimony.

I HAD FORGIVEN, BUT I DIDN'T KNOW THAT FORGIVENESS SHOULD BE ONGOING and that I needed to be on guard and continually resist negative utterances and painful memories. Nor did I understand that my freedom was vulnerable. Jesus taught us that if we do not have mercy from our hearts and forgive their sins, that Father God will not forgive our sins and will turn us back over to the demands of our canceled debt [Matt. 6:15, 18:33-36]. My sins of judgment, rejection, presumption, and criticism had probably been the open door for illness and heartbreak in the past. *Was it any wonder?*

That night I lay in bed beaten, exhausted, dismayed, and wrestling with tormented thoughts of hostility, self-justification, and grief. My descent into the past had opened Pandora's Box. It absolutely *was not* "well with my soul."

Why hadn't I tested my first impression to leave the table? Hadn't I been alerted by the Holy Spirit? What was my motive? Surely, I was not the one that the LORD intended to "help" the bitter and injured lady. My unrecognized pride, assertiveness, and immaturity could not have helped a flea.

REMEMBERING MY "SLUG INFESTED" heart, I wept, "LORD, forgive me. Change me. Help me to better understand how this happened so that it won't happen again!" Right away the thought came that instead of "thinking upon the enemy's things" I needed to wash my heart with the Word and "think upon God's things." My thoughts turned toward Jesus' trial, when He stood mute against the accusations of the religious leaders before they handed Him over to Pilate and demanded that He be crucified.

PILATE ORDERED JESUS FLOGGED, and then handed Him over to the soldiers for crucifixion. Because of Calvary, the blessing that was now mine penetrated deeply. I clearly saw . . .

> *The soldiers put a crown of piercing thorns on Jesus Christ's head (His mind)* ~ for me!
>
> *His blood ran down His brow* ~ for me!
>
> *The Unblemished Lamb of God was flogged* ~ for me!
>
> *Christ Jesus stood in unutterable pain* ~ for me!
>
> *His skin hung in shreds* ~ for me!
>
> *Messiah stank, was bruised, beaten, chose to be powerless, and vulnerable* ~ for me!
>
> *LORD Jesus was mocked and went to the Cross* ~ for me!
>
> *The Savior said, "Father, forgive them for they know not what they do."* ~ for me!
>
> *He forgives* ~ for me!
>
> *He died* ~ for me!
>
> *He rose* ~ for me!
>
> *He lives* ~ for me!
>
> *His Eternal Word, His thoughts, were recorded* ~ for me!

COULDN'T HIS WORD HELP ME COUNTER the painful unprofitable memories that lead to self-pity? Couldn't turning to Jesus, and His Word, be better than taking hold of someone nearby or calling a friend to pray it through? Couldn't His Word supersede hours of being counseled above and beyond the time an advisor could take to help me? Couldn't His blood help me forgive? Only the Blood of Jesus can save us from being maneuvered into a position to be used as the enemy's vessel. Only the Blood of the Lamb can erase our past sins. *That was it!* I could choose to forbid and replace the exceedingly painful memories with Jesus' Victory on the Cross for my example and protection. I could choose to prohibit wrong accusations. I could choose to think with the mind of Christ!

Then it hit me! If I choose to take the enemy's thoughts and memories back into my heart, *(which the Lord never inspires),* I would be objectively agreeing with the enemy and my thoughts/testimony would be used by unrighteous, unholy spirits. I would be in agreement with the same spirits that motivated the Pharisees and Sadducees (deceived vessels) when they accused Jesus. Wrong thoughts prompted the soldiers to spit on Jesus. They were merely vessels inspired by Satan. Accusations and talking about my dysfunctional past undermined the victory that had been gained through the triumph of the Cross. I was convicted that taking the gunk back into my heart was tantamount to "spitting on the Cross!" What a horrifying and sobering thought.

Instead of allowing Jesus' righteous influence to overcome my wrong thoughts, I had allowed the enemy's unrighteous influence to crucify virtuous thoughts. My thoughts that wrongly began in the spiritual realm and manifested in the physical realm became objective accusations. The enemy had robbed me of the freedom that Christ purchased for me. Jesus is in me. I need to be on guard against harboring presumptive thoughts and accusations toward others, or myself, to honor Jesus.

Jesus is in us! We can and must choose to refuse and refute the enemy's accusing thoughts by saying or praying, "Father, forgive them, for they know not what they do," or "Father, forgive them, they knew not what they did!"

We are called and chosen to walk in the freedom and joy of His Light! When we know the reality of God's forgiveness and the power of His Blood, why would we choose to think upon ugly things of the past? Why would we choose to be a victim of the enemy's well-executed plans that inflict depression? Why would we choose to allow him to suffocate us with grief? Rob us of God's power? Render us helpless and hopeless? Why???

(5)   **"Testimony used to subjectively accuse: Satan the chief legalist**

prosecutes us in this realm" [Mark 14:55].[18]

Satan not only prosecutes us, but he continually prowls about the earth in readiness to steal, kill, and destroy *God's purpose* for our lives [John 10:10]. Remember Joshua the high priest stood before the Angel of the LORD and Satan was standing at his right hand to oppose him [Zech. 3:1, 2].

One night I was pondering a passage of Scripture and fell asleep only to be awakened in the wee hours with a practical analogy for that passage. I got out of bed to record it while it was fresh on my mind. The telephone rang as I groped in the dark down the steps to my office. I dashed to answer the telephone before it awakened my husband. A relative was calling during that untimely hour to ask a pointed question. While I adjusted my thoughts and before I could say anything, she misinterpreted my silence and angrily yelled something incoherent. I tried to reason with her but her mind was closed. She had presumed wrongly, then "subjectively" accused me of something(?) then hung up! Her wrong presumption of what my answer would be caused her to be angry with me.

SAD, AND PUZZLED, I replaced the receiver and asked the LORD, "Why did You allow the call to come at that time?" The confrontation had merely been a test. The Holy Spirit reminded me that I had allowed sudden distractions and subjective accusations to throw me off the target many times, and had ultimately lost out on God's best by allowing the enemy's influence to interfere.

THE ENEMY DISTRACTS OR DIVERTS US TO ROB US of God's blessings, purposes, or to drain us of our energies. When allowed, distractions and wrong thoughts can easily deter us from the LORD's course, change our priorities, or become so big in our minds that the thoughts interfere with our call and commitment to the LORD. How often have we blown it or could blow it again? It is an ongoing battle. We need to test the spirits at all times.

When the untimely incident was shared with a friend, she suggested that a sudden diversion could also come at the very time our LORD might purpose to answer an earlier petition. Our response is a key factor in seeing God's hand move at that time, or our response can delay His answer. To reiterate, our thoughts, actions, and testimonies cooperate with God or the enemy. Our testimony usually determines whether or not our petitions receive breakthroughs.

Thankfully, the LORD enabled me to choose rightly that night. I forgave my relative as she obviously knew not why she accused me. I prayed for her to forgive me for what she had presumed, then turned it over to the LORD and trusted Him to vindicate me. (The *LORD* eventually did!)

Resting in Christ, I returned to the analogy that I had set out to record, which, incidentally, added light to this lesson.

SATAN USES AT LEAST FIVE TYPES OF TESTIMONY to prosecute mankind. Compare "testimony" to "witness" as contributed by Paul Levertoff in: *THE INTERNATIONAL STANDARD ENCYCLOPEDIA:*

[a] ***"False witnessing was prohibited*** **[Exod. 20:16], it was done to the false witness [supporting testimony] what he had purposed to be done to the accused"** [Deut. 19:16-21].[19]

Jesus told us that by our words we shall be justified and by our words we shall be condemned [Matt. 12:36, 37]. *Words bear consequences.*

[b] ***"The Mosaic Law insisted*** **on the absolute necessity of witnesses [agreement/mutual accusation] to testify in all cases that came before a judge. It was necessary to have at least** ***two*** **witnesses to make a case stand against a person"** [Deut. 17:6; Num. 35:30; Matt. 18:16; John 8:17; 2 Cor. 13:1; 1 Tim. 5:19].[20]

We are to submit our thoughts to God, resist unrighteous thoughts and *refuse* to dwell upon others' wrong actions. Negative and presumptive thoughts are merely the enemy's devices to line up *our* testimony to be used as his witness. We must keep in mind that *HE Who is in us is greater* than he that is in the world! [1 John 4:4] *Amen!*

[c] ***"Important legal agreements required attestation of witnesses"*** [Ruth 4:11-16; Zech. 3:1, 2]. Satan, the chief legalist, accuses us before God [Zech. 3:1; Rev. 12:10]. Jesus, our advocate, *stands* ever in intercession and readiness to rebuke Satan [Heb. 7:25; Rev. 12:10].

It was customary at that time, among Romans and Jews, to stand when they made accusations or bore testimony [Acts 7:56; Luke 23:10]. Various scholars suggest that when Stephen was dying and he looked up and saw the Son of Man *standing* at the right hand of God, that Jesus may have stood up to bear testimony against Stephen's persecutors.

[d] ***"No oath was required of witnesses.*** **If a person knew truth and withheld it, he would have to bear his iniquity/guilt. This was a solemn adjuration [command] of the judge to all those with knowledge of the case to come forward as a witness"** [Lev. 5:1].[21]

DO WE ALLOW CONVERSATIONS, GOSSIP, MISINFORMED CONVERSATIONS, OR PRAYERS to continue when we know that they are in error and that we could bring restoration to someone in His Body? Many times silence will allow wrong assumptions about another's words or actions to flourish. When we are in a position to set matters straight that will clear someone, our silence about it can easily become a wrong witness and a mighty tool for the enemy. Do we strive to be instruments of the LORD's righteousness or do we allow the enemy to reign in our hearts and lives when we do not witness to the truth?

[e] *"The Pharisees decreed that false witnesses were liable to be executed the moment the death sentence had been passed on the falsely accused.* **In spite of the prohibitions, false witnessing was a very common crime among the people"** [Deut. 19:16-21; Ps. 27:12; Matt. 26:60; Acts 6:13].[22] Embellishment, tale bearing, and gossip are the same as accusations. Careless words can be misunderstood and serve as false testimony. Things are not always the way that they are perceived! When concerned about another person's conduct, do not talk about it or fret over it, but *pray that Father God gives them the spirit of conviction, and that God will grant them repentance that will lead them to the knowledge of His Truth* [John 16:8; 2 Tim. 2:25].

WITH REGARD TO BACKSLIDING BELIEVERS, church leadership has scriptural instructions, along with the responsibility, to confront false teachings and the misconduct of their members, found in I Timothy.

DAVID, THE SHEPHERD KING, KEPT SHORT ACCOUNTS WITH GOD. Let us be like David when we "blow it" and quickly, readily, confess our sin, repent and gratefully receive God's mercy and forgiveness. Praise God, Christ's blood purifies our unrighteousness [Titus 2:9-15; 1 John 1:9] and enables us to walk in the riches of His glory and power. His headship is *over* every name, dominion, rule, and authority [Eph. 1:18-23].

When I discussed the legal implications of "testimony" and "witness" with my husband, an attorney, and our son Dave who was studying law, my excitement mounted and intensified. Understanding my *responsibility* in application of the "testimony of His Word" began to grow. Subsequent Scriptures convinced me that Revelation 12:11 was the truth that I needed to walk in, moment by moment, second by second, if I wanted to be a light of Christ Jesus to unbelievers and believers. I prayed for help to exercise my thoughts and words more carefully.

Let us envision our minds in a court of law. The prosecutor (enemy) stands to accuse us, or another person or circumstance, with a negative thought. If one of us chooses to receive, agree with, or repeat the negative thought, we are in effect aligning our thoughts, or words, with the enemy to be used as his witness against them, or us. *It works both ways!* The enemy uses the reinforcement of our thoughts, words or actions *against the accused!* Unknowingly, a pure and simple agreement can be made with the accuser of the brethren which can give the unrighteous spirit legal rights to inflict punishment against a person, circumstance, or even us ~ *God's kingdom suffers!*

IF WE CHOOSE NOT TO LEND SUPPORT (receive, agree with, or repeat) to the accuser's implanted thoughts (tempting, manipulating, scheming, tormenting, presumptive accusations, etc.), the intended punishment for the accused can boomerang back to the accuser. In turn, the accusing spirit suffers the consequences instead of an innocent victim ~ *Satan's kingdom suffers!*

OUR THOUGHTS ORIGINATE FROM THREE SOURCES: the Holy Spirit, the enemy, and our flesh! The enemy attacks us in our *minds* just as he attacked Eve and Adam. Invading thoughts are designed to kill, cripple, and destroy our testimony, our relationship with God and with others. Wrong thoughts can ultimately derail God's plan and call upon our lives ~ or others. A major tactic of the enemy is to inflict deceptive thought patterns! The battle of unrighteous thoughts and decisions versus righteous thoughts and decisions starts in our minds and is a statement for or against biblical teaching [Titus 2:9-15]. Choosing righteous thoughts will maintain daily victory to forgive affronts and forgive ourselves ~ even our circumstances. Absorbing wrong thoughts multiplies temptations that can cripple us, or others. Innocent people can become *victims* of the enemy. We must recognize and overcome the accuser's *tactics*.

THE ACCUSER IS NOT ALL-KNOWING, ALL-POWERFUL, OR SOVEREIGN. Only the LORD God is Sovereign. We need to understand that Satan is the *second* most powerful force in the spiritual realm and is not to be dealt with flippantly or arrogantly. Jesus didn't take Satan's authority lightly ~ the disciples didn't ~ Paul didn't! Nor should we! Satan is *eternally* underneath the absolute authority of the LORD Jesus Christ. Jesus *legally canceled* our powerless position so that we can resist *enslavement* to wrong thoughts, negative utterances, self-glorification, ambition, wrong attitudes, selfish actions, and so forth. The enemy endeavors to lead the whole world astray [Rev. 12:9]. The enemy has no legal authority over our choices, or actions, *unless we allow him* to influence us and change our priorities. Unfortunately, many times the wrong choice is not recognized until it is carried out. The gate is narrow that leads to life [Matt. 7:12-14].

My desire to recognize and choose godly thoughts had begun and must continue for the rest of my life. The new discernment enabled me to look beyond suspicious, hindering, and tormenting thoughts so that I could sincerely pray as our LORD did:

"Father, forgive them (insert the person's name, object, or subject of the invading thought) for they do not know what they are doing" [Luke 23:34]. Help us LORD, to be conscious of our own sins and unworthiness balanced with the gratitude that Christ has cleansed us once and for always.

> ***A.W. TOZER WROTE IN KEYS TO THE DEEPER LIFE:***
> It has been the unanimous testimony of the greatest Christian souls that the nearer they drew to God the more acute became their consciousness of sin and their sense of personal unworthiness. The purest souls never knew how pure they were and the greatest saints never guessed that they were great. The very thought that they were good or great would have been rejected by them as a temptation of the devil. They were so engrossed with gazing upon the face of God that they spent scarce a moment looking at themselves. They were suspended in that sweet paradox of spiritual awareness where they knew that they were clean through the blood of the Lamb, and yet felt that they deserved only death and hell as their just reward.[23]

UNWORTHY TEMPTING THOUGHTS ARE TO BE TAKEN CAPTIVE TO CHRIST ~ in turn we are to replace them with thoughts of our Messiah [2 Cor. 10:3-6] and worship Him. It is wonderful how thoughts of Jesus will dissolve pride or negative thoughts. Let us worship and thank the One Who is Worthy to be praised!

A friend asked me what happens when our words or actions open a kettle of worms, repeats gossip, or a confidence. Is there a pat answer? No, sometimes His grace allows it to fade away, but normally we have to face the music! However, we never have to face accountability alone. He will be with us and lift us into His high tower of peace and grace.

VICTORY COMES WHEN WE RESIST NEGATIVE UTTERANCES and "soul prayers" (praying from our own understanding or desires). When we recognize the source of a thought, we should take authority over it and declare, "Not I, but Christ!" We simply need to reiterate to the enemy, or our flesh, that we submit our thoughts to God, resist the devil, and that he must flee! [James 4:7]

A cartoon showed a lady that had opened her front door and found Satan standing in front of her. She looked back over her shoulder, and yelled, "Jesus, this one is for You!" I copied it and put it in several places! It has been a good reminder of what I need to do.

When we declare that we have submitted our thoughts, meaning invading thoughts, to be crucified with Christ, we can tell the enemy that the life we now live in the body, we live by faith in the Son of God, who loved us and gave Himself for us [Gal. 2:20]. We are to turn down counter impressions that could be used against us, or others, and invite Christ's righteous thoughts of whatever is true, honorable, right, pure, lovely, of good repute, of excellence, or praiseworthy to take over our thoughts [Phil. 4:8].

THERE HAVE BEEN TIMES WHEN IT HONESTLY SEEMED IMPOSSIBLE to think of one good thought to replace the negative attack invading my mind. Frankly, there were times that I wanted to accept the self-righteous or accusing thoughts that tormented me and have a good old "pity party." Sometimes temptation triumphed. Freedom came when I heard and obeyed the Holy Spirit's inspiration and allowed Christ to be my enablement. Praise God for His faithfulness and forgiveness!

A.W. TOZER WROTE IN KEYS TO THE DEEPER LIFE:

> If we are alert enough to hear God's voice, we must not content ourselves with merely "believing" it. How can any man believe a command? Commands are to be obeyed, and until we have obeyed them we have done exactly nothing at all about them. And to have heard them and not obeyed them is infinitely worse than never to have heard them at all, especially in the light of Christ's soon return and the judgment to come.[24]

WE, CHRIST'S CHILDREN, HOLD IN OUR HANDS JESUS' TESTIMONY and command to overcome the accuser's snares, along with the privilege and responsibility to be His instruments of glory. We hold in our hands His free gift of choice. *Will we, His church, use His priceless gifts that we hold in our hands?*

The early church believed that the Lamb triumphed! They believed that Jesus, Who was within them, could not fail! They believed and obeyed at all cost! Today we need to have the same consuming vision of the Lamb of God burning in our hearts, as it burned in the hearts of the believers of the early church. We need allegiance to the Lamb of God.

CHRIST'S OVERCOMING THOUGHTS STAND VICTORIOUSLY between us and the enemy. He put His overcoming authority *in our* hands ~ *it's a choice!*

CHRIST'S CHURCH HOLDS HIS HEART IN OUR HANDS ~ His Word in our hands ~ His purposes in our hands. His church holds His love in our hands ~ His ability to forgive in our hands ~ His prevailing power in our hands . . . and His authority to overcome the enemy in our hands.

PAUL TOLD US:

> *"And the peace of God, which surpasses all comprehension,*
> *shall guard your hearts and your minds in Christ Jesus.*
> *Things that we have learned and received and heard and seen in me,*
> *practice these things and the God of peace shall be with you."*
> *Philippians 4:8-9*

LIFE APPLICATION

1. A. Who did Peter say that Jesus is? B. How did the Jewish New Testament interpret Peter's answer? C. What does it mean to you personally? (P. 1)

2. How did Jesus verify Peter's revelation? (P. 2)

3. The LORD addressed the foundational necessity of repentant hearts, simplicity in belief, humility, and concern for the salvation of others in Matthew 16. The LORD established them as _____ to "binding and loosing" and gathering together to "agree in His Name." (P. 2)

4. How did the *International Standard Bible Encyclopedia* define bind? (P. 2)

5. What keys to the kingdom of heaven did Jesus say He was giving the church (believers)? (P. 3)

6. A. What is the Master Key that God gave to His Church to overcome the accuser? B. What is the Foundational Rock Jesus builds His church on? (P. 3)

7. A. Who did Jesus say was the greatest in the kingdom of heaven? B. What is God's view of a follower's greatness (rank in His Kingdom)? C. What change is required? (P. 4)

8. Jesus taught the disciples that God's awesome authority had literally been appointed to His righteous children to put into practice ~ to _____ on earth as it is in Heaven. (P. 4)

9. A. What did Jesus promise believers who gather in His Name? (P. 4)

10. What is the conditional commitment for Jesus' presence when two or more pray? (P. 4)

11. A. How are "bind" and "loose" translated? B. Who was given the authority to do them as written by David Stern in the JNT. C. Has it been cancelled? (P. 5)

12. A. What was the practical way that the author first learned to prohibit and permit through the example of a gnat? B. What did she bind/resist and what did she loose? (P. 5)

13. A. We must be _____, _____, and wait for the Holy Spirit to lead us before _____ the enemy. B. We also need to follow Christ's example of _____ hands and a _____ heart. (P. 6)

14. A. Where do stumbling blocks begin? B. Jesus recognized and _____ Satan for influencing Peter's thoughts which were spoken to Jesus. C. How did Jesus address Satan's influence in Peter? D. Why did Mark say to be on guard? (P. 6)

15. We can afford to allow differences (that do not affect doctrine) in others. What is the one center core belief we should center upon? (P. 6)

16. What is God's condition before we appropriate the Blood of Jesus Christ to overcome dysfunction, rejection, guilt, unforgiveness, self-righteousness, and so forth? (P. 8)

17. Revelation 12:11 says the Martyr's of Christ Church overcame the accuser because of three things. What are they? (P. 9)

18. What is the Holy Spirit able to do when we devote time to absorb Scripture? (P. 10)

19. In the *New Strong's Exhaustive Concordance of the Bible,* what are the generic definitions of testimony? (P. 11)

20. A. Which of the *five legal definitions of testimony* broadened your understanding of caution and responsibility in your testimony, personal or legal? [See bolded numbers 1-5 (PP. 11-16)] B. Which one impacted you the most?

21. A. The Lord revealed to the author that her parents had merely been _____ used by _____ to undermine God's _____ for her life. B. Choosing to forgive changed her _____ _____, and _____. (P. 13)

22. A. Why did the author stay with the bitter lady and review old memories of her parents that had been forgiven? B. What did her testimony become when she stayed with the bitter lady and whose witness did she become? C. What invaded her heart again? (P. 14)

23. A. Distractions from the enemy can do what to us? B. Our thoughts, actions, and testimonies cooperate with _____ or the _____. (P. 17)

24. Name five types of testimony [a-e] that Satan uses to prosecute mankind? (PP. 18, 19)

25. Where are three sources that our thoughts come from? (P. 20)

26. Unworthy, tempting thoughts are to be taken captive to _____ and replaced with what? (P. 21)

TAKING AUTHORITY SCRIPTURE SEQUENCES

Page 1
1 John 4:4	[God's children belong to Him, have already defeated and overcome the enemy and greater is He that lives in us than He that lives in the world].
Ps. 68:11	["The LORD announced the word; great was the company of those who proclaimed it."]
Matt. 16:19	["I will give you the keys of the kingdom of heaven; whatever you bind on earth will be bound in heaven, and whatever you loose on earth will be loosed in heaven."]
Matt. 18:18	[Whatever you bind on earth will be bound in heaven, and whatever you loose on earth will be in loosed in heaven (JNT renders prohibit for bind; permit for loose)]
Matt. 18:19	[If two of you on earth agree about anything you ask for, it will be done for you by My Father in heaven]
Matt. 16:13-18	["God bless you, Simon, son of Jonah! You didn't get that answer out of books or from teachers. My Father in heaven, God himself, let you in on this secret of who I really am. And now I'm going to tell you who you are, *really* are. You are Peter, a rock. This is the rock on which I will put together my church, a church so expansive with energy that not even the gates of hell will be able to keep it out." (The Message vv. 13-18.)]
Matt. 16:16	[Peter answered, "You are Christ (Messiah), the Son of the Living God."]

Page 2
Matt. 16:18 JNT	[. . . and the gates of Hades shall not prevail against it (Messiah's church)]
Matt. 16:19 AMP	[I will give you the keys of the kingdom of heaven; whatever you bind on earth will be bound in heaven, and whatever you loose on earth will be loosed in heaven]
John 20:23	[If you forgive anyone his sins, they are forgiven; if you do not forgive them, they are not forgiven]
John 1:12	[Yet to all who received Him, to those who believed in His name, He gave the right to become children of God]

Page 3
Ps. 68:1	[Let God Arise, let His enemies be scattered!]
Matt. 16:19	["I will give you the keys to the kingdom of heaven, and whatever you bind on earth will be bound in heaven, and whatever you loose on earth will be loosed in heaven."]
1 Cor. 12:7	[Now to each one the manifestation of the Spirit is given for the common good.]
Isa. 22:20-23	[I will clothe him with your robe . . . I will place on his shoulder the key to the house of David . . . what he opens no one can shut, and what he shuts no one can open.]

Page 4
Matt. 16:18	[The gates of hell shall not prevail against Christ's church]
Matt. 18:1a	["Who is the greatest in the kingdom of Heaven?"]
Matt. 18:2	[He called a little child and had him stand among them]
Matt. 18:3	[And He said: "I tell you the truth, unless you change and become like little children, you will never enter the kingdom of heaven."]
Matt. 18:4	[Therefore, whoever humbles himself like this child is the greatest in the kingdom of heaven]
Acts 6:3	[Brothers, choose seven men from among you who are known to be full of the Spirit and wisdom. We will turn this responsibility over to them and will give our full attention to prayer and ministry of the word.]
Matt. 16:19	[I will give you the keys of the kingdom of heaven; whatever you bind on earth will be bound in heaven, and whatever you loose on earth will be loosed in heaven]
John 15:15-16	[. . . You did not choose me, but I chose you to go and bear fruit ~ fruit that will last. Then the Father will give you whatever you ask in My name]
Matt. 18:20	["Again, I tell you that if two of you on earth agree about anything you ask for, it will be done for you by My Father in heaven. For where two or three come together in My Name, there I am with them."]
John 1:12	[He gave believers the power to be His children]
John 15:7	[Abide in Me and My Words abide in you ~ ask and it shall be done unto you]

Page 5

Matt. 18:18	[If two on earth agree asking in Jesus' Name it will be done by My Father in heaven]
Matt. 23:2	[The teachers of the law and the Pharisees sit in the chair of Moses]
1 Cor. 12:11-31	[The same Spirit distributes at His will; one Spirit, one body]
1 Cor. 13:13	[And now these three remain: faith, hope and love. But the greatest of these is love]
1 Cor. 12:9	[regarding gifts . . . to another faith by the same Spirit, to another gifts of healing by that one Spirit]
1 Cor. 2:16	[For who has known the mind of the LORD that he may instruct him? But we have the mind of Christ.]
Rom. 12:2	[Do not conform any longer to the pattern of this world, but be transformed by the renewing of your mind.]
Luke 4	[Jesus' temptations in the wilderness]

Page 6

Matt. 16:23	[Jesus said to Peter "Get behind me Satan! You are a stumbling block to me; you do not have in mind the things of God, but the things of men."]
Mark 13:22, 23	[For false christs and false prophets will appear and perform signs and miracles to deceive the elect ~ if that were possible. So be on your guard; I have told you everything ahead of time.]
Col. 3:2	[Set your minds on things above, not on earthly things]
Col.3:11	[Here there is no Greek or Jew, circumcised or uncircumcised, barbarian, Scythian, slave or free, but Christ is all, and is in all.]
Col. 3:23	[Work at it with all your heart, as working for the LORD, not for men]
Col. 3:15	[Let the peace of Christ rule in your hearts, since as members of one body you were called to peace.]

Page 8

Matt. 26:28	[This is My Blood of the Covenant, which is poured out for many for the forgiveness of sins]
Heb. 9:22	[. . . the law requires that nearly everything be cleansed with blood, and without the shedding of blood there is no forgiveness.]
1 John 1:9	[If we confess our sins, He is faithful and just and will forgive us our sins and purify us from all unrighteousness]

Page 9

1 John 1:7	[But if we walk in the light, as He is in the light, we have fellowship with one another, and the blood of Jesus, His Son, purifies us from all sin.]
Eph. 5:30	[. . . for we are members of His body]
Eph. 5:30-32	[The mystery is great ~ Christ's love is revealed for His church . . . we are members of His body]
Heb. 9:14	[How much more, then, will the blood of Christ, who through the eternal Spirit offered himself unblemished to God, cleanse our consciences from acts that lead to death, so that we may serve the Living God!]
Titus 2:14	[. . . Who gave Himself for us to redeem us from all wickedness and to purify for Himself a people that are His very own, eager to do what is good.]
Titus 3:5	[He saved us, not because of righteous things we had done, but because of His mercy. He saved us through the washing of rebirth and renewal by the Holy Spirit]

Page 10

Rev. 12:10	["Now have come the salvation and the power and the kingdom of our God, and the authority of His Christ. For the accuser of our brothers, who accuses them before our God day and night, has been hurled down."]
Rev. 12:11	[To overcome: His Blood ~ His Word spoken or thought, and love not life unto death (to self)]
Eph. 4:22, 23	[. . . put off the old self, which is corrupted by its deceitful desires, to be made new in the attitude of your minds, and put on the new self, created to be like God in true righteousness and holiness.]
Ps. 119:105	[His Word is a lamp to our feet and a light to our path]
Ps. 119:11	[Thy word have I hid in my heart that I might not sin against Thee]
Matt. 15:18	[What is in our hearts comes out in our attitudes]

Page 11

Ps. 59:12	[For our offenses are many in Your sight, and our sins testify against us. Our offenses are ever with us, and we acknowledge our iniquities . . .]
Mark 14:55, 56, 59	[The chief priest and Council kept trying to obtain testimony against Jesus to kill Him]
Luke 22:71	[They needed no further testimony as they had heard it from His own mouth]
Job 15:6	[Your own mouth condemns you, not Mine; your own lips testify against you]
Isa. 59:12	[For our offenses are many in Your sight, and our sins testify against us. Our offenses are ever with us, and we acknowledge our iniquities]
Acts 2:40	[With many other words Paul warned them; and he pleaded with them, "Save yourselves from this corrupt generation."]
Acts 10:42	[He commanded us to preach to the people and to testify that He is the one whom God appointed as judge of the living and the dead.]
Heb. 2:6	[But there is a place where someone has testified: "What is man that You are mindful of him, the Son of Man that You take care of him?"]
Gal. 5:3	["I declare to every man who lets himself be circumcised that he is obligated to obey the whole law."]
Eph. 4:17	["So I tell you this, and insist on it in the LORD, that you must no longer live as the Gentiles do, in the futility of their thinking."]
Heb. 10:28	[Anyone who rejected the law of Moses died without mercy on the testimony of two or three witnesses]
James 3:8 JNT	[But the tongue no one can tame ~ it is an unstable and evil thing, full of death-dealing poison]
Matt. 12:36, 37	[We render account for our careless words ~ our words justify or condemn us]
James 4:7	[Submit to God, resist the devil and he will flee from you]
1 Chron. 21:1	[Satan rose up against Israel and incited David to take a census of Israel]
Testimony:	[Bearing witness, certifying]
Luke 22:71	[They needed no further testimony as they had heard it from His own mouth]
Mark 14:55, 56, 59	[The chief priest and Council kept trying to obtain testimony against Jesus to kill Him]

Page 12

Matt. 12:36, 37	[We are accountable toward ourselves & others through careless, useless words]
Deut. 19:15	[Two witnesses were needed to imprison]
Matt. 12:36, 37	[By our words we are justified and by our words we are condemned]
James 4:7	[Resist the devil and he will flee from you]
Mark 14:53-59	[Testimony that accuses]
Job.1:8-12	[The LORD put all of Job's possessions into Satan's hand, except Job himself]

Page 14

Matt. 6:15	[But if you do not forgive men their sins, your Father will not forgive your sins]
Matt. 18:33	[Shouldn't you have had mercy on your fellow servant just as I had on you?]
Matt. 18:34	[His master angrily turned him over to jailers to be tortured, until he paid back all he owed]
Matt. 18:35	[This is how My heavenly Father will treat each of you unless you forgive your brother from your heart]

Page 17

Mark 14:55	[The Chief priests and the whole Council tried to find testimony to put Jesus to death]
John 10:10	[The thief comes to rob, steal, and destroy; Jesus came that we might have life abundantly]
Zech. 3:1, 2 NKJV	[Then he showed me Joshua the high priest standing before the Angel of the LORD, and Satan standing at his right hand to oppose him.]

Page 18

Exod. 20:16	[False witnessing is prohibited]
Deut. 19:16-21	[Satan prosecutes to destroy God's purposes]
Matt. 12:36, 37	[We are accountable toward ourselves & others through careless, useless words]
Deut. 17:6	[Two witnesses are required to make a case stand]
Num. 35:30	[No one is to be put to death on the testimony of one]

PAGE 28   IV ~ TAKING AUTHORITY

Page 18 (continued)
Matt. 18:16	[By the mouth of two or three witness every fact (word) may be confirmed]
Job 8:17, 18	["I am He Who bears witness of Myself and the Father Who sent Me bears witness of Me."]
2 Cor. 13:1	[Every fact (word) is to be confirmed by the testimony (mouth/thoughts) of two or three witnesses]
1 Tim. 5:19	[Do not receive an accusation against an elder, except on the basis of two or three witnesses]
1 John 4:4	[God's children have overcome them; greater is He that is in them than he that is in the world]
Ruth 4:11-16	[Boaz required legal rights before witnesses for Ruth's hand]
Zech. 3:1, 2	[The LORD testifies, "The LORD rebuke you, Satan! Is this not a brand plucked from the fire?"]
Zech. 3:1	[Satan stood at the right hand of the angel of the LORD]
Rev. 12:10	[The accuser accuses day and night; he has been tossed down because of the Salvation, Power, & the kingdom of our God, and the authority of His Christ has come]
Heb. 7:25	[He saves forever those who are drawn near to Him ~ He lives to make intercession for them]
Rev. 12:10	[The accuser accuses day and night; the Salvation, Power, & the kingdom of our God, and the authority of His Christ defend us]
Acts 7:56	[Stephen's persecutors heard him say, "Behold, I see the Son of Man standing at the right hand of God."]
Luke 23:10	[The chief priest & scribes accused Jesus vehemently]
Lev. 5:1	[We are held responsible for withholding testimony]

Page 19
Deut. 19:16-21	[False witnesses will suffer the consequences designated for the accused]
Ps. 27:12	[Do not deliver over to the adversaries desires ~ their false witness has risen against me]
Matt. 26:60	[Many false witnesses came forward ~ but the Council could not settle upon any]
Acts 6:13	[False witnesses testify that He spoke against the holy place and the Law]
Job 16:8	[SPIRIT convicts of sin, righteousness and judgment]
2 Tim. 2:25	[God grants repentance and gives us the knowledge of the truth]
Titus 2:9-15	[Unrighteous thoughts versus righteous thoughts begin in our hearts]
1 John 1:9	[When we confess our sins He is faithful & just to forgive & cleanse us of *all* unrighteousness]
Eph. 1:18-23	[We are to walk in glory and power over every name, dominion, rule & authority in Christ's Name]
Rev. 12:11	[Overcome by His Blood, His Word spoken or thought, and love not our life (self) unto death]

Page 20
Titus 2:9-15	[Unrighteous thoughts versus righteous thoughts begin in our hearts]
Rev. 12:9	[The great dragon was hurled down, that ancient serpent called the devil, or Satan, who leads the whole world astray.]
Matt.7:12-14	[The gate is narrow that leads to life and few are those who find it.]

Page 21
Luke 23:34	["Father, forgive them, for they do not know what they are doing."]
Matt.7:13-14	[The gate is narrow that leads to life]
2 Cor. 10:3	[For we live in the world ~ we do not wage war as the world does.]
2 Cor. 10:5	[Demolish arguments & pretensions set against the knowledge of God]
2 cor. 10:5	[Take every thought captive to the obedience of Christ]
James 4:7, 8	[Submit yourselves to God, resist the devil, and he will flee from you. Draw near to God and He will draw near to you]
Gal. 2:20	[I have been crucified with Christ and I no longer live, but Christ lives in me. The life I now live in the body, I live by faith in the Son of God, who loved me and gave Himself for me.]

Page 22
Phil. 4:8	[Think on these things: whatever is true, noble, right, pure, lovely, admirable ~ anything excellent or praiseworthy]
Phil. 4:8-9	[Think on what is true, honorable, right, pure, lovely, of good repute, of excellence, worthy of praise ~ let your mind dwell on these things]

TAKING AUTHORITY ENDNOTES

1. David H. Stern, *Jewish New Testament Commentary*, (Clarksville, MD: Jewish New Testament Publications), p. 607; paragraphs 1, 4, 5.

2. *The International Standard Bible Encyclopedia*, Volume One A-D, (Grand Rapids, MI: William B. Eerdman's Publishing Company).

3. Ibid. P.56 Mattity Ahu (Matthew) Chapter 18:3 *Unless you change.* Greek strephó ("turn") can mean inward turning, hence "repent" or "change." KJV renders the phrase, "except ye be converted." The "conversion" needed is not from Judaism but from the sin of self-seeking ambition to be the "the greatest" (v.1). The conversion is not to Christianity or to an "-ism," but to God and relating personally with Him through Yeshua the Messiah.

4. Ibid. P.58

5. David H. Stern, *Jewish New Testament*, (Clarksville, MD: Jewish New Testament Publications), p. xxiii (of the Introduction).

6. Helen Roseveare, *Living Faith*, (Minneapolis, MN: Bethany House Publishers), p. 22.

7. M. R. De Haan, M. D., *Redemption By Blood*, The Radio Bible Class, (Grand Rapid, MI), p. 26.

8. Ibid. P.15

9. Ibid. P.21

10. W. E. Vine, (1873-1949) *The Expanded Vine's Expository Dictionary of New Testament Words*, (Minneapolis, MN: Bethany House Publishers, 1984), p. 1241.

11. Vine, P.1241

12. *The New Strong's Exhaustive Concordance of the Bible*; James Strong, L .L. D., STD, (Nashville, TN: Thomas Nelson Publishers, 1984), 2. Marturia ~ Testimony (Strong's 3141): evidence given (judicially or genitive): record, report, testimony, witness.

13. Joseph H. Thayer, (1885) 1977, *Thayer's Greek-English Lexicon of the New Testament*, (Grand Rapids, MI: Baker Book House), p. 391.

14. Ibid.

15. Ibid.

16 bid.

17. Ibid.

18. Ibid.

19. Paul Levertoff (contributor), *The International Standard Bible Encyclopedia*, James Orr, M.A.D.D., (Grand Rapids, MI: William B. Eerdmans Publishing Co., 1984), p. 3099, See: "witness" Vol. IV.

20. Ibid.

21. Ibid.

22. Ibid.

23. Tozer, *Keys to the Deeper Life*, Ibid. <u>P.30</u>

24. A.W. Tozer, *Keys to the Deeper Life*, From the Series in Christian Life, by *Sunday Magazine*, Inc., (Grand Rapids, MI: Zondervan Publishing House, of the Zondervan Corporation, 1957), p. 31.

STRONGHOLDS

(It is helpful to write the Scriptures down and commit to memory.)

Overcoming Idolatry ~ Isaiah 44:6, 8; Deuteronomy 30:20; Nehemiah 9:6; Jeremiah 29:11; 1 Chronicles 29:11; Psalm 40:5; 95:3-5; 145:13, 16-17; Job 36:26-29; Psalm 90:1-2

Overcoming unbelief ~ Isaiah 43:10; Mark 9:24; Ephesians 1:18-19; Hebrew 11:6; Romans 11:20, 23; Psalm 78:18; Hebrews 3:19; Psalm 78:18; Hebrews 3:19; Psalm 78:32-33; Psalm 119:66; Mark 5:35-36

Overcoming Pride ~ 2 Kings 19:22; 2 Chronicles 26:16; 32:26; Psalm 10:4; Psalm 73:6; Prov. 11:2; 13:10; 16:18; 29:23; Isaiah 2:17; 13:11; 60:15; Jeremiah 13:17; 49:16; Daniel 4:37

Overcoming Deception ~ Psalm 119:30; Genesis 3:13; 2 Corinthians 11:3; Psalm 25:4-5; 26:2-3; 31:5; 40:11; 43:3; 45:4; 51:6; 86:11; 119:43; 145:18; Proverbs 23:23; Isaiah 45:19

Overcoming Insecurity of Feeling unloved ~ Isaiah 54:10; Lamentations 3:22-24; Hosea 14:4; John 3:16-17; 4:2; 15:9; 16:27; 1 Corinthians 2:9; 1 John 3:19-20; Romans 5:8

Overcoming Addiction ~ Jeremiah 32:17; Matthew 5:35; 1 John 1:8-9; Psalm 139:14, 23-24; Proverbs 13:10, 20; 19:20; 27:7; 28:14; 28:26; Isaiah 26:9, 13; Romans 6:14, 16, 19, 22; 7:18; 8:1-2,9

Overcoming Food-related Strongholds ~ Proverbs 16:3; James 1:22; Jeremiah 15:16; Psalm 21:5-7; 2 Peter 2:19; 1 Corinthians 6:12; Galatians 5:1, 13; Psalm 62:5-8; Jeremiah 32:17

Overcoming Feelings of Guilt ~ 2 Kings 22:19; Lamentations 1:20; Psalm 40:2-4, 11-12; 41:4; 32:5; Isaiah 55:7; Psalm 51:1-2, 10; 2 Corinthians 7:9-10; 2 Chronicles 6:29-31; Psalm 139:23-24

Overcoming Despair from Loss ~ Lamentations 3:22-25; Habakkuk 3:17-19; Isaiah 46:4,9; 53:4,5; Jeremiah 29:11; Romans 4:20-22; 5:3; 11:33-36; Ecclesiastes 7:13-14; 3:1-4; Prov. 16:9

Overcoming unforgiveness ~ Matthew 6:14; 7:1,2; 1 John 1:8; Romans 2:1-2; Matthew 7:3-5; 18:21, 22; 33-35; Mark 11:25; 5:23, 24; Romans 14:10-13; 1 Corinthians 4:4-5; James 2:12-13

Overcoming Depression ~ Psalm 42:5-6 Lamentations 3:21-23; Luke 24:17,21; 2 Corinthians 7:6; Isaiah 61:1-4; Psalm 143:4; Isaiah 41:10; Psalm 4:1; 18:6; Isaiah 63:9; Psalm 55:2

Overcoming Sexual Strongholds ~ Romans 7:15-21, 22-25; Psalm 139:1-3, 13-14; 1 John 1:9; Jeremiah 32:17; 1 John 3:7-9, 19; 1 Corinthians 6:13-15, 19-20; 5:5; Romans 1:24-25; 2:5-7

Overcoming the Enemy ~ Exodus 3:7-8, 14-15; 15:1-3, 6-7, 9-12; Deuteronomy 28:13-14; 33:26-27, 29; Joshua 7:13; Psalm 16:1-2; 17:7-9, 11-13; 18:1-3, 4-6, 8-10, 14,16

Permission granted by Arthur J. McMahon,
ajmncm71@yahoo.com

DEVICES OF SATAN

Lest Satan should get an advantage

~

We are not to be ignorant of his devices
2 Corinthians 2:11
Satan has wiles or fiery arrows
Ephesians 6:11, 16

1. Satan tempts us to sin ~ Luke 4:1-13
2. Satan lays snares or traps ~ 1 Timothy 3:7
3. Satan can bring oppression ~ Acts 10:38
4. Satan seeks to devour ~ 1 Peter 5:8
5. Satan plants doubts in God's Word ~ Genesis 3:1-5
6. Satan seeks to alter true doctrine ~ 1 Timothy 4:1-2
7. Satan beguiles or deceives ~ 2 Corinthians 11:3
8. Satan appears as an angel of light ~ 2 Corinthians 11:14
9. Satan has his ministers or agents ~ 2 Corinthians 11:15
10. Satan puts evil ideas into open minds ~ John 13:2
11. Satan enters willing hearts ~ John 13:27
12. Satan hinders Christ's servants in carrying out a desired task ~ 1 Thessalonians 2:18
13. Satan resists servants of God in the prosecution of their work ~ Zechariah 3:1; Daniel 10:13
14. Satan shakes Christ's disciples up and sifts them ~ Luke 22:31
15. Satan accuses the brethren before God day and night ~ Revelation 12:10
16. Satan has power over all the unsaved ~ Acts 26:17,18; 1 John 5: 19
17. Satan makes an attempt to deceive the very elect of God ~ Matthew 24:2
18. Satan sows tares (weeds) in God's field ~ Matthew 13:24-30; 36-39
19. Satan blinds the minds of unbelievers from the light of the Gospel ~ 2 Corinthians 4:3,4
20. Satan takes away the Word from hearts ~ Mark 4:4, 14, 15
21. Satan will cast some of Christ's servants into prison ~ Revelation 2:10
22. Satan will give power to the lawless one (Antichrist) to deceive the perishing ~ 2 Thessalonians 2:9, 10

DON'T GIVE PLACE OR A HANDLE TO THE DEVIL
Ephesians 4:27

Permission granted by Arthur J. McMahon,
ajmncm71@yahoo.com

Lesson V

GOD'S CONQUERING LASERS

*"They went away at the light of Thine arrows,
at the radiance of Thy gleaming spear . . .
For the salvation of Thine anointed
Thou didst strike the head of the house of evil."
Habakkuk 3:11-15 KJV*

"Is not my word like a fire," saith the LORD,
*"and like a hammer that breaketh the rock in pieces?"
Jeremiah 23:29 KJV*

*"Thy Word is settled in Heaven."
Psalm 119:89*

BE PREPARED

TAKE UP THE SWORD OF THE SPIRIT

"Be prepared.
You're up against far more than you can handle on your own.

Take all the help you can get,
every weapon God has issued,
so that when it's all over but the shouting
you'll still be on your feet . . .

God's Word is an indispensable weapon.
In the same way prayer is essential in this ongoing warfare.

Pray hard and long."

~

"Take up the Sword of the Spirit,
which is the Word of God,
With all prayer and petition,
pray at all times in the Spirit,
be on the alert with all perseverance,
petition for all the saints."

Ephesians 6

The Message
Eugene H. Peterson

GOD'S CONQUERING LASERS

*The LORD announced the word,
and great was the company of those who proclaimed it.
Psalm 68:11*

G*OD'S LASERS WILL VAPORIZE THE ENEMY'S FLAMING MISSILES. LASER* is used throughout this lesson as an acronym that represents the *Light* of Christ, *Amplified* by the Holy Spirit, *Stimulated* by believers, who are *Empowered* to speak God's *Righteous Word* in declarations and prayers that vaporize the enemy's flaming missiles. God's Word is living, active, sharper than any two-edged sword [Heb. 4:12-13] and will not return void [Isa. 55:11]. That is a fact! I know, because one morning while singing to the LORD and making the bed, I suddenly knew beyond the shadow of a doubt, that my daughter Diane's life was in danger. I dropped to my knees and prayed desperately for her protection and for God to bring her home safely. I interceded until His peaceful assurance came and I *knew, that I knew,* she was safe.

S*OON AFTERWARD, A TREMBLING DIANE APPEARED* at the front door. She was as white as a sheet! A motorcycle had spooked Zack, her horse, and he had galloped toward a ravine with her helplessly clinging to him for dear life! She was scared to death that she would be killed, when suddenly ~ it must have been an angel ~ Zack stopped at the very edge of the deep ravine!

I hugged Diane with tears of immense relief and a grateful heart, and thanked Father God that the Holy Spirit had warned me, guided my prayers, and brought her home safely. Later that day, I realized that when I had prayed for Diane I had inserted her name into the Scriptures that were quickened to me by the Holy Spirit. The prayers flowed naturally although I had never thought about praying the Word of God by "taking up the Sword of the Spirit, praying in the power of the Spirit, and being alert with all perseverance" [Eph. 6:18].

O*UR NEAR DISASTER HAPPENED SOON AFTER* I had participated in Campus Crusade's "I FOUND IT" campaign as one of many volunteers that called people to lead them to Jesus. Anne sat next to me and led many people to Jesus. Every day I used the same format without one conversion! It was frustrating, disheartening, and agonizing to say the least. When I confessed my concern to Anne, she recognized my problem immediately. I'll never forget how her crystal blue eyes penetrated my soul when she asked, "Did you receive the Holy Ghost when you believed?" [Acts 19:2] Her question shocked me. I was saved but did not know about a Holy Ghost, and said, "Frankly, it sounds spooky!" Anne said because she prayed for the Holy Ghost to make her sensitive to their needs, she was enabled by the Holy Ghost to introduce the people she called to Jesus' salvation. She directed me to Luke 11:13, and said that I should "ask the Father for the filling of the Holy Ghost, so He could teach me, bring His Word to my remembrance [John 14:26], and confirm His guidance" [Rom. 9:1].

THE NEXT DAY, Anne gave me Campus Crusade's booklet *"HAVE YOU MADE THE WONDERFUL DISCOVERY OF THE SPIRIT-FILLED LIFE?"*[1]

I took it home and studied its Scripture references which ministered truth to my soul and manna to my spirit. I longed for the Spirit-filled life and for Christ to have more of me after I read the following paragraph in Campus Crusade's booklet:

> Jesus promised the abundant and fruitful life as the result of being filled (directed and empowered) by the Holy Spirit. The Spirit-filled life is the Christ-directed life by which Christ lives His life in and through us in the power of the Holy Spirit [John 15].[2]

I learned that I needed to ask the Holy Spirit to direct and empower me to be more fruitful for Christ and prayed Bill Bright's suggested prayer[3] to ask for the Holy Spirit's fullness to work through me. I professed in faith that I needed the filling of the Holy Spirit, asked forgiveness for "doing my own thing," invited Jesus to take His place on the throne of my heart, and prayed to witness and walk in the power of the Holy Spirit. I remember adding a P.S. that my life would "radiate Christ" like Anne's life did. I also read in A.W. Tozer's *Keys to the Deeper Life*, that "Almost all Christians want to be full of the Spirit. Only a few want to be filled with the Spirit." Tozer's book gave insight and conviction regarding the filling of the Holy Spirit of Christ.[4]

AT FIRST I WAS DISAPPOINTED because I didn't feel different like I thought I would. *But, better than feelings, something wonderful happened ~ Scripture came to life!* I was blessed as His Holy Word began to penetrate my understanding, saturate my heart, and reveal precious, practical, and meaningful truths to me. My understanding was opened in a profound way as God filled me with His Holy Spirit just as His Word promised! God's Word became so exciting, inspiring, and down-to-earth, that I sought more time to absorb it.

It was amazing and comforting to know that God really does want to daily lead us and that He wants to empower our thoughts. I knew that I would never be the same and praised God, with deep gratitude, that I had received the Holy Spirit's prompting of Scripture, His directive, perfect timing, and the empowerment to pray for our daughter's life.

Diane's near tragedy taught me that it was time to grow beyond enjoying His love. I needed to learn to let His indwelling influence guide me into an abiding state of His fullness. So I purposed to set my thoughts on the LORD and to desire the good, true and righteous "fruit of His Spirit" [Gal. 5:22], the "fruit of the Light" [Eph. 5:8-10]. Scripture spoke volumes to my spirit as I sought to mature in His Word and have an uncomplicated, consecrated prayer life.

MY INTROVERTED PRAYERS WERE REDIRECTED. I cried out, "LORD, enlarge my understanding and give me unshakable faith! Fill me with the knowledge of Your will through all spiritual wisdom and understanding; be the inspiration of all that I think, say, and do!" [Eph. 1:17, 18; Col. 1:9] My self-centered prayers changed to self-*less* prayers. I pled for God to teach me Christ's way to pray for people and to be more than a conqueror ~ a light in the world [Matt. 5:16]. We are called to trust Jesus, the True Light, to guide us, to watch over us. *Praise God! He does!*

MANY BOOKS HELPED ME UNDERSTAND MY RESPONSIBILITY TO GOD, what Christ accomplished at the Cross, His Resurrection, and the role of the Holy Spirit. They were profoundly precious books written by His proven servants that taught God's principles. Their shared insights simplified my walk, gave practical illustrations, convicted, freed, and challenged me to change. Their writings put a hunger in my heart to spend more time in prayer to seek God's wisdom as revealed by the Holy Spirit[5] [1 Cor. 2:10]. I literally stole time to spend in my prayer closet (a metal desk in the laundry room) which became my favorite place where I could privately rejoice in His Word and His love.

(Please don't get the idea that I was a hermit in the Word or very spiritual. Most of my time was demanded as a typical suburban mother with church activities, driving children *everywhere* for their activities, refinishing furniture, painting, landscaping and organic gardening [with my own rotor-tiller!], canning and freezing, cleaning house, volunteering and entertaining groups for my husband.)

THE HOLY SPIRIT UNFOLDED SCRIPTURE IN PRACTICAL, definite, realistic ways. Whether I pondered His Word, worshiped Him, did my chores, or was driving the car, I found myself seeking graphic illustrations and practical portrayals of God's scriptural truths.

The Holy Spirit did not fail me. He gave inspired analogies and illustrations of God's principles and providence in action that ultimately helped me become a better Sunday School teacher. His inspired thoughts, and Scripture Press' solid Sunday School lessons, kept their attention and challenged the thoughts of *seven* third and fourth grade boys that were so active the elementary school kept them separated in *seven* different classrooms. God was faithful. I not only survived, but looked forward to preparation and teaching!

WHILE TEACHING A GROUP OF LADIES, I needed an analogy to help me better understand a verse in the lesson that contained the "washing of the water with the word" [Eph. 5:26]. It was a struggle to comprehend what that verse meant to me as a believer, a wife, and a mother.

PRAYING WHILE SITTING AT MY LAUNDRY ROOM DESK, the LORD provided an analogy about "God's Sanctifying Machine." Thoughts came that Christ's blood, as purifier par none, would cleanse the filthy garment of my heart to make it holy and acceptable in "God's Sanctifying Machine" that is filled by His Living Water [Isa. 64:6]. My unrighteous thoughts and actions would be agitated by God's Words of righteousness to convict me and cause my heart to repent and be cleansed by His sanctifying soap, His Blood, that loosened the worldly dirt [John 17:17; 1 John 1:9].

"God's Sanctifying Machine" would spin the sins and unforgiveness out of my heart. I would die to self as His holy redeeming wringer squeezed carnal desires out of my heart [Gal. 2:20]. Then I would be hung out to be blown dry without a wrinkle by His justifying wind of grace, mercy, and faithfulness. The warmth of His absorbing love would renew my heart and prepare me for His use. The analogy helped me understand "washing of the water with the Word" in a practical, housewifely way.

THE HOLY SPIRIT LED ME TO A BIBLE STUDY GROUP that was starting a study based on *WHAT HAPPENS WHEN WOMEN PRAY* by Evelyn Christenson. We saw a radical difference when we prayed Scripture with the principles taught in her book. We learned to be more effective in prayer. It was exciting as the LORD led our group forward, one step at time, while we witnessed awesome answers to our prayers.

The Bible became a personal letter that edified, convicted, directed, and exhorted us to learn more about God's ways. We looked to His Word [precepts] for guidance [Ps. 119:89] and purposed to walk obediently in faith [Rom. 1:5]. We believed in His Name and trusted Him to guide us as we sought to follow Him [John 1:12, 43].

DURING THE EARLY 1970'S I was seeking to learn more about prayer and learned it was not a frequently taught subject in churches or seminaries. I purchased Hebrew and Greek lexicons and other resourceful aids and then began to study word meanings in both. They enlarged Scripture and helped me glean a more direct and practical understanding of God's Word, which truly is more precious than gold. His Word is settled [stands firm] in the heavens [Ps. 119:89].

It was important to "go beyond the reaches of faith based upon knowledge", as mentioned by **MARTIN LLOYD-JONES IN SAVED IN ETERNITY:**

> ". . . that the possession of eternal life, which is from God, leads to such a knowledge of God if we but realized it and cultivated it and developed it . . . is something that goes beyond the reaches of faith based upon knowledge. Genuine faith, established upon the full doctrine of the Bible, leads us to a knowledge of God which is more immediate and direct, what the Puritans called a spiritual knowledge of God, over and above the knowledge of faith."[6]

STUDYING ABOUT GOD AND HIS WAYS STRENGTHENS OUR FAITH, increases the awareness of our need to repent, and enhances our worship. Worshiping the LORD opens our hearts to communicate our love to Him and fellowship with the Most High God. The LORD Jesus Christ becomes our focus, our most frequently thought of and trusted friend. Telling Him of His worth uplifts and enlarges our understanding of His character and principles; it gives us an awareness of His ways and helps us line up with the perspective of His Word. Our hearts are enveloped in awe of His glorious holiness.

My heart, so full of love, could scarcely take in the awesome truth that Christ Jesus is LORD of the universe, yet, He was my trusted, beloved, best Friend. The consciousness of His nearness was beyond expressing!

> **MARTIN LLOYD-JONES WROTE** ABOUT JONATHAN EDWARD'S EXPRESSION of "just finding himself in the presence of the glory of God" . . .
> "There was no vision but just the sense, the consciousness, of the reality and nearness, and the holiness and majesty, of the glory of God." . . . Dwight Moody was walking along Wall Street, in New York City, when God revealed and manifested Himself in an immediate way; he had believed in Him before, he had been used by Him, he was a great Christian man, but here was something new, this consciousness of the immediate presence of God, the Glory of God."[7]

Our English language is inadequate to fully praise the glory of God's Name. Although the Word states it in its fullness, it is awesome when we absorb in our hearts that our LORD is the great *"I AM Who I AM,"* that told Moses to tell the Israelites that *the LORD sent Him to them.* "This is My Name forever; the Name by which I am to be remembered from generation to generation" [Exod. 3:14, 15] . . . and, "I AM the LORD; that is My Name! I will not give My glory [Everlasting Power and Divinity] to another, nor My praise to graven images [idol]" [Isa. 42:8 AMP; John 8:58].

GRAVEN IMAGES! THAT MADE AN IMPACT! We had just returned from a trip abroad where prolific graven images were pointed out by enthusiastic travel guides as being used by people to worship (glorify) pagan gods. I grieved and felt helpless about their ignorance then came home only to find graven images in the homes of social acquaintances and Christians. Some were beautiful art pieces, some were bizarre art objects.

The owner's excited conversations about them were peppered with words like "karma," "points of light," and so forth (you get the picture). It was extremely uncomfortable to be around their idolatry. It was even more uncomfortable to learn during research that some of our own beautiful art objects from our travels were included in the growing list of graven images. I took them out and destroyed them with an axe and hammer or burned them.

ALTHOUGH THE TERM "POINTS OF LIGHT" and other expressions are popular with the New Age, we must not label all who use the terms as New Agers. Many churches, businesses and governments have innocently embraced occult terminology unaware the phrase implies supernatural power points to New Agers, etc. We need to discern how people speak and where they are coming from. *Concern and caution are needed.*

I wept before the LORD over the revival of graven images and false gods and anguished over the hateful insult that the enemy intended for the Holiest ONE of all. My heart broke for the naive believers and nominal Christians who had openly, *eagerly,* advocated the (veiled) ways of the occultic New Age, false religions, the One-World and One Religion Movement forbidden by God.

> *REVEREND BENNY CLARK,* Trinity Baptist Church at Beaver Creek, Colorado said:
> "Everybody I come in contact with who is not a born-again Christian ~ and by that I mean someone who has turned their life around and dedicated it to God ~ has trappings of New Age . . . Anyone who hasn't relinquished their center to God and is keeping that selfish core could be called New Age."

It was grievous to see Satan's New Age deception expounded through adulation toward self, pantheism, false gods, paraphernalia, etc. It was painful to learn that it was being taught in the Christian realm and glamorized by Christian leaders. Many had unknowingly cooperated due to seminars, advertising, talk shows, etc. An explosion of other religions (false gods) and New Age practices and agendas were subliminally and/ or openly taught by the media, schools, the medical professions, etc., to capture both the children's minds and ours. Satan's hour had arrived to subtly establish humanism through pseudo-science, drugs, exercises, false religion and idol worship!

MARK BUBECK SAID IN THE SATANIC REVIVAL:

> I believe we're seeing a carefully orchestrated conspiracy at work, too sinister and subtle to be entirely of human origin. This conspiracy flows out of the realm of evil supernaturalism, and our only hope for any change necessitates divine, supernatural intervention. Only God's power, manifested in the hearts of a caring, concerned citizenry, can stop this onslaught of evil.[8]

WHAT STRATEGY DOES GOD'S WORD TEACH His caring, concerned citizens to use to stop the onslaught of evil? How does Jesus want us to resist the anti-Christ influence and the New Ager's widely documented psychic (PSI) and subliminal warfare conducted by governments, institutions, media advertising, etc., to brainwash and immobilize civilians, nations, and the world? How are we to counteract the effects of the perceptions and efforts of the anti-Christ forces who openly laud, publicize, exhibit and promote false doctrine, ungodly agendas and occult practices?

WHAT IS GOD'S BATTLE PLAN? Weeping in distress over the devastating and seemingly unchallenged dominance of the unleashed evil forces around us, the thought came: "God's laser beams!" With intense interest, turning to the dictionary I found that laser is an acronym.

> **L** ~ signifies *LIGHT*
>   **A** ~ represents *AMPLIFICATION by*
>   **S** ~ stands for *STIMULATED*
>   **E** ~ symbolizes *EMISSION of*
>   **R** ~ represents *RADIOACTIVE BEAMS*

THE DEFINITION OF A LASER included microchips and microwaves as common examples! It obviously called for further investigation! Research absorbed and excited me in spite of the technical words that sometimes blurred together. I found in each word of the acronym words that I pondered, in relation to a spiritual truth, a possible simile that would counteract unrighteousness.

CLEARLY, SPIRITUAL LASERS ILLUSTRATE PRAYING GOD'S WORD TO OVERCOME the forces of darkness! Wow! THE WORD of God triumphs as the *ABSOLUTE LASER that slays in judgment like a light* [Hos. 6:5-6] and vaporizes the enemy's flaming missiles! (My joy could hardly be contained!)

DR. TERRY D. MYERS WROTE IN *EXECUTIVE HEALTH*::

Just What Is a Laser?
> The word laser is an acronym . . . Lasers require an active medium and an outside energy source to stimulate the active medium. Unlike ordinary light from an incandescent bulb, lasers emit light that is monochromatic (meaning one color), directional, and usually of a single wavelength.
> Laser light is generated when certain atoms are stimulated sufficiently so as to emit energy in the form of a brilliant beam of coherent light. By placing highly polished mirrors at either end of the active medium ~ as is commonly done in a laser ~ the emitted photons are guided back through the active medium. This amplification of energy accounts for the remarkable qualities of lasers.[9]

PLEASE KEEP PROCLAMATIONS OF GOD'S WORD AND PREVAILING PRAYERS in mind as we further review lasers. Spiritually celebrating, ***LASER*** represents the *Light* of Christ *Amplified* by God's Holy Spirit Stimulated by believers who are *Empowered* with *Righteous declarations and prayers of agreement*. God's inspired Word is the Light of Christ that guides His Conquering Lasers. Lasers are indeed remarkable weapons in the spiritual realm as well as the physical realm!

GOD'S ETERNAL WORD is living, active, and will not return void [empty] [Isa. 55:11]. We are to polarize, vaporize, the enemy with declarations and prevailing prayers that affirm Christ's authority. A diagram of a functioning laser helped me envision intercessors waiting upon the LORD for the Holy Spirit to communicate the knowledge of God to their hearts. Jesus, the Word, *listens* to the intercessor's entreaties and *sends* His Light/Word down to *reveal* His wisdom to *guide* their prayers that are *energized* by the Spirit of Christ then God *facilitates* the answers. Intercessors *reflect* His righteousness by *proclaiming* God's inspired Word/Light into the spiritual realm. His Spirit-empowered Laser is *energized* and *organized* by the LORD's heavenly forces. In turn, His Laser is *beamed* to *hit the mark* to establish the *Light* of His perfect will in *answer* to our petitions.

THE GREEK TRANSLATION OF LIGHT,[10] *PHOS,* is "light that is unquenchable." The following verses illustrate Jesus as the True PHOS, the Unquenchable LIGHT. Jesus was transfigured when He was praying. His face shone like the sun and His clothing became white and gleaming as PHOS/Light [Luke 9:29]. LIGHT, of such intense brilliance, flashed around Paul and blinded him [Acts 9:3-16]. Moses was hidden in the cleft of the rock for protection from the LORD's face, i.e., His Presence, His Shekinah glory, *His LIGHT!* [Exod. 33:18-23; 1 Tim. 6:13-16] *His LIGHT* breaks forth as morning and our health springs forth speedily. His Glory is our reward! [Isa. 58:8] Amen! Hallelujah!

THE LIGHT OF GOD, THE WORD, created all that we know. His Word will not return without accomplishing its purpose; He hastens His Word to perform it [Isa. 55:11; Jer. 1:12]. His Power is unleashed through prayers that harmonize with His Word that "lay with judgments like light that goes forth" [Hos. 6:5 NAS]. *THINK ABOUT CHRIST'S . . .*

> *Light*
>> *Amplified* through our prayers, expands, enlarges;
>>> *Stimulates,* energizes;
>>>> *Emits*, discharges;
>>>>> *Radioactive* energy, as we
>>>>>> *Speak forth the Word of God.*

***WE ARE TO SHARE IN THE INHERITANCE OF THE SAINTS IN* LIGHT** [Col. 1:12]; *the children of LIGHT* [John 12:35-36; 1 Thess. 5:5]. We are to put on the *full armor of LIGHT* [Rom. 13:12], *believe in God's LIGHT* [John 12: 35-36] and *serve the* LORD *Jesus Christ ~ THE LIGHT!* [John 8:12; 1 John 1:5-7] The LORD qualified us, and Paul exhorted us, to reflect *CHRIST'S LIGHT.*

Light in the New Webster's Dictionary (under physics) is designated as luminous energy, radiant energy, and electromagnetic radiation to which the organs of sight react.[11] Light is further defined as "a wave band of electromagnetic radiation, which by its actions, upon the retina of vision, enables the eyes to perform their function of sight which the brain interprets; light's most important phenomenon is: reflection, refraction, dispersion, interference and polarization."[12]

CHILDREN OF CHRIST'S LIGHT ARE TO REVEAL CHRIST. We are to REFLECT (imitate); REFRACT (break up, deflect); DISPERSE (dissipate, sow); INTERFERE (hinder, obstruct) and POLARIZE (unify, focus, zoom in on the enemy*)* WITH HIS LIGHT that RADIATES Righteousness into darkness. Soldiers of Christ's Light reflect the Word of Righteousness by refracting, dispersing, interfering and polarizing the enemy! Let us, as believers, polarize and neutralize the enemy with proclamations and prevailing prayers that affirm Christ's Authority!

Another advantage of God's Word declared and prayed is we activate His Lasers. Lasers are a probe that goes where light as we see it cannot go. Lasers penetrate the body where light or physical elements cannot penetrate. HIS LIGHT, HIS WORD, goes where we cannot ~ to unseen spiritual realms to affect impregnable strongholds ~ to the enemy's dominions that we cannot see and should not enter.

LASERS ARE THE HIGHEST FORM OF CONCENTRATED ENERGY known by man to date. Yet lasers cannot begin to compare with the Triumphant Energy released through God's Word when He prompts us to pray it into circumstances. His Word brings His Light and light reveals things that were previously hidden by darkness [1 Cor. 4:5].

TEXE MARRS WROTE IN MEGA FORCES, SIGNS AND WONDERS OF THE COMING CHAOS:
> The New High-Tech Arsenal ~ The newest tools of armed conflict are frighteningly reminiscent of those seen in Star Wars and Buck Rogers movies. If this sounds like an overstatement, take a look at some of man's new life-destroying military weapons. Each of these is either available now or will be in a few years: Smart Bombs, called precision guided munitions, take themselves directly to a minute, well-hidden target. Stealth aircraft, armed with nuclear bombs that are invisible to radar . . . Laser beams that cut holes in airplanes and can even cause supersonic aircraft and speeding missiles to disintegrate or vaporize in flight, etc.[13]

LASERS OPERATE AT OPTIMAL FREQUENCIES that produce high energy beams of light, or infrared radiation. They can repair with precision and correct in the physical realm what surgical instruments cannot. As a positive force, lasers dissolve and eradicate problems without side effects. Yet, as a negative force, they disintegrate objects and cause missiles to vaporize.

DR. TED YAMAMORI WROTE:
> The near future holds a final epic that Christians must not watch from the living rooms and churches. We Christians must act ~ become active players by reaching out in both mind and spirit.[14]

CHRIST'S WORD, INCONCEIVABLY POWERFUL, whether spoken or prayed, causes the Light of His Righteousness to penetrate concerns, persons or circumstances ~ without harmful side effects!

THE NEW AGE DISCIPLES' COUNTERFEIT OF WORSHIP, OR PRAYING SCRIPTURE FROM THE BIBLE, is to harmonize with occultic names and words whether in worship or conversations. They gather in dedicated zeal at Harmonic Convergences, or other sites, to "usher in" Lucifer's force from the spiritual to the physical realm. New Ager's believe it will empower them to usher in world peace, one world government, and one world religion that declare that man or woman are as gods, and mandates the worship of Mother Earth ~ Venus, Gaius, Isis, Diana, Kali, etc.

MANY INNOCENT PEOPLE HAVE BECOME INVOLVED IN NEW AGE teachings or various addictions because their church did not teach them the power of God nor the power of a Christ-directed life. They do not need Christians pointing fingers, gossiping, or condemning them. They need Holy Spirit compassionate inspired prayers for God to set them free *from seduction, bondage and delusion.*

WE MUST REMEMBER THAT BUT FOR THE GRACE OF GOD, THERE GO I! The battle will be won through praying His Word as led by the Holy Spirit ~ prayers that are empowered by the Blood of the LAMB's forgiveness, grace and mercy.

Marie Barnes attended sessions of *God's Peerless Names* and *God's Conquering Lasers*. She wrote to me that the LORD had previously shown her "during a NASA laser demonstration an analogy of the awesome power of His Word as lasers." She shared that "believers needed more of His Word revealed to their hearts to experience His power, and that as we become stronger in His Truth, we'll receive His revelation more clearly and brightly. We will be enabled to walk in His Truth with His power flowing out of us."

Lasers are an analogous truth that illustrates how prayers that availeth much begins in the spiritual realm before they are manifested in the physical realm. The LORD said a thousand shall flee at the rebuke of one [Isa. 30:17]. His all-powerful Word enables us to resist the enemy so that we may maintain and prevail until He returns [Heb. 4:12]. Jesus quoted Scripture throughout His ministry ~ even when He was dying for our sins on the Cross. Doesn't that illustrate that His Word spoken out loud is the highest weapon of warfare?

HEARING THE WORD "RADIATION" PAINED MY DEAR FRIEND MARGARET, my prayer partner now with the LORD. It brought back memories of cancer treatments that were hard to endure. Margaret shared that radiation, cited in the role of lasers, have positive functions. She said that she was briefly attached to the Light Brigade, which functioned as Great Britain's search light battery during World War II. It was amazing to see the searchlight "lock in" the enemy aircraft until it was brought down. *There was no gray area!* If they did not "lock in" and "destroy" the enemy, they would *give access and power* to the enemy to "lock in" and "destroy" all that England held dear.

IT IS A PHYSICAL REALITY THAT PARALLELS A SPIRITUAL REALITY that a searchlight battery can illustrate both the power and energy of God's Word. The Light of His creative power is unleashed to "lock in" the enemy's missiles ~ even the source of the missiles to defeat the missiles of the enemy of darkness. The searchlight is effective because its *light is concentrated, **amplified**, and stimulated* to *emit* its focused beam to *radiate* in the dark.

IT IS A SPIRITUAL REALITY THAT LASERS PARALLEL GOD'S WORD. Lasers illustrate the Light of His creative power unleashed to deflect and defeat the enemy of darkness; God's Lasers prompted by His Holy Spirit "lock in" to vaporize and bring down the enemy. His lasers are to be discharged through prayer for the salvation and deliverance of mankind [Hab. 3:11-15].

> Jesus commanded us to be lights in the world, saying that spiritual battles are not only inevitable, but will escalate during the final days. We cannot afford to falter and accept battle plans from anyone but God.[15]

WE ARE APPOINTED TO BE A LIGHT TO THE NATIONS, to open blind eyes and free prisoners [Isa. 42:7]. Yeshua's Light, Deliverance/Salvation[16] reaches to the ends of the earth! [Isa. 49:6] Christ's Light not only sheds Truth upon hearts to reveal His salvation, goodness, righteousness, and justice, but His Light exposes the unholy, unfruitful deeds of darkness [Eph. 5:8-13]. His *clear* transmitters receive and communicate redemptive prayers that "lock in" and bring down the enemy. The fine tuning that lasers require demonstrate that we need to consistently work at being fine-tuned and clear vessels.

WE NEED TO BE AVAILABLE AND READY TO DISPERSE HIS LASERS ~ HIS LIGHT ~ IN TIMES OF DARKNESS! Lasers are devices that contain crystals or other suitable substances such as *copper.* Pagans, occult worshipers, New Agers, pantheists, drug addicts, etc., use *crystals, rocks, copper, pyramids, paraphernalia,* and so forth, as their aids to help them *seek the light.* They pursue ways to *commune with a higher power*, and to *invite* the spiritual entity that the device or medium represents to possess them. The desired evil power is ultimately for self glorification or gratification. Symbols, emblems and devises are used as seductive aids. They may signify that the wearer communes with a specific god or goddess. There is a potpourri of personalities that represent evil spirits and their manifestations that the *seekers commune with and obey.*

THE HIGHLY SOUGHT "CHRIST CONSCIOUSNESS" is merely anti-Christ deception, i.e., the counterfeit of Christ's LIGHT! *There cannot be a counterfeit of Christ unless there is a genuine Christ!* Christ is the bona fide LIGHT and the only Light we are to receive and walk in [Eph. 5:14]. When people meditate, chant, invoke, or decree various generic names, or specific names of false gods or spirit beings, they are literally inviting evil spirits to manifest themselves into and through their bodies. They open themselves to activate *evil fruit* in their areas of influence. Unbeknownst to some, they are literally seeking to become *channels* that receive information (to be relayed) from "a higher level of spiritual reality outside the physical realm."[17]

Copper, crystals, pyramids, drugs, etc., are used in a *physical* sense for NIRVANA or spiritual transmission. They use copper[18] as the main conduit for both crystal and pyramid power to receive wisdom and guidance. Copper enhances meditation with spiritual forces; it is used to communicate with or channel the higher self, as their point of light. They invoke, or call down, the "highest power of the ascended master" whom they know as "the great white light" or other names or terms.

RANDALL BAER WROTE IN INSIDE THE NEW AGE NIGHTMARE:
Seeking after truth, I found only masterful counterfeits disguised as the truth. Yearning for inner fulfillment and peace, I found glittering fragments and pieces that eventually would crumble to dust. So deep did the seduction lead that the bizarre became accepted as the norm, fantastical lies saturated my mind and Satan's demons masqueraded as my guiding angels of light.[19]

One of the most commonly held views in the New Age is that Jesus was just one of many enlightened masters. Jesus, though, in many ways and in many different Bible passages, states clearly that this is definitely not the case. This is the most crucial issue that separates Bible-based Christianity from New Age philosophy.[20]

TAL BROOKE, A NEW AGE RESEARCHER AND FORMER DISCIPLE OF INDIA'S SUPER-GURU SAI BABA, WROTE IN HIS BOOK WHEN THE WORLD WILL BE AS ONE:

Esoteric spiritual paths that I had explored for years, placing me in a distinct minority, have become by now almost the consensus view of America. The plan is unfolding with the force of a charging freight train. 1987 starts out with a bang. As 1986 passes by on New Year's Eve, millions have gathered in convention halls and stadiums and even churches to invoke the New Age. It is International Meditation Day for World Peace. Hundreds of organizations in 60 nations have sponsored this event.

New Age leader John Randolph Price identified the event, "A planetary affirmation of love, forgiveness and understanding involving millions of people in a simultaneous global mind-link. The purpose: reverse the polarity of the negative force in the race mind, achieve a critical mass of spiritual consciousness, usher in a new era of Peace of earth, return mankind to God kind (man is god)."[21]

The summer of 1987 brought in the Harmonic Convergence, with scores of people world-wide invoking the higher powers from the spiritual realms as they flock to the Great Pyramid in Egypt, Stonehenge in England, Machu Picchu in Peru, and Mount Tamalpais in California's Marin County, plus thousands of other 'sacred places.'[22]

MARK BUBECK INCLUDED IN THE SATANIC REVIVAL:

This is the kind of condition we face now in our society. It's a desperate hour. Our culture is being demonized before our very eyes, and nothing can confront it or change this accelerating problem but a God-authored, revolutionary revival. It is important that God's people know why nations fall.

The satanic revival presently underway demands a spiritual response from God's people that is strong enough to meet the challenge. Only the power of the Gospel, unleashed through a concentrated season of prayer and repentance, is mighty enough to dismantle a satanic revival. Believers must know that and act upon it. In Israel and Judah's time, there was no gospel message to confront and defeat the satanic rule the people had brought on themselves.

That's the difference between then and today. We have such a message. The death, burial, resurrection, ascension and glorification of the Lord Jesus Christ has released sufficient grace to meet the challenge. The Holy Spirit has come. He is able and ready to convict any individual or an entire culture (nation) of sin, righteousness and judgment to come. We believers must rise up and use our weapons of warfare. God has equipped us with all we need to win this great battle. Survival demands revival.[23]

Celebrities like actress Shirley MacLaine have given the movement fanfare and popular appeal, but it is much deeper than tinsel and lights. New Ageism promotes a dark, sinister element that elevates man to god status. Death is denied; good and evil are declared illusions. A blind optimism emerges based upon a false, unbridled hope for the world and humanity. This excited hope fuels the movement. In our day of so much despair and darkness, the New Age holds much appeal. The younger, more educated leaders of the world are being drawn by the thousands into this false hope.[24]

The redeeming blood of Christ is revealed [1Pet. 1:18-22] as being sufficient to free us from all that has been handed down from our forefathers. Salvation through the shed blood of our Lord Jesus Christ cancels all legal claim of demonic powers upon a believer's life . . . Believer's must know and aggressively, continually, apply victory in the Lord Jesus Christ. Resisting the devil steadfastly in the faith effects the enemy's defeat and the believer's freedom.[25]

LET US PRAY THAT THE NEW AGE TEACHINGS and other ungodly influences will be revealed to its victims as counterfeit. Pray that the New Agers will see Christ's LIGHT, as Truth, and be set free from drugs, addictions, hallucinations, imaging, meditating upon pyramids, fire, crystal, nature, graven images, and other things God created. *Pray for their deliverance from bondage, astrology, palm reading, brainwashing, drugs, seduction, etc.* They are the major strongholds that control or influence New Agers.

JESUS TOLD US THAT IN THE END DAYS EVEN GOD'S ELECT WILL BE DECEIVED. We must spend every conceivable opportunity getting to know the *TRUE MESSIAH*. We must learn to pray and walk in His Word! God's people need to recognize, combat and resist the anti-Christ deceptions with prevailing prayers from the Word of God. How would God have us, as His soldiers, combat the New Age "points of light"?

PONDERING HOW BELIEVERS ARE TO OVERCOME the *influence of the counterfeit points of light,* I was reminded of the Scripture, "If I have been *risen with Christ* I would *keep seeking things above,* where Christ is sitting at the right hand of God ~ the highest place of power [Col. 3:1]. I would set my mind on things above [eternal fruit] not the things of this earth" [Col. 3:1-4].

THE WORDS "RAISED UP," "SEEK THINGS ABOVE," and "set my mind on things above," reminded me of an allegory about *"ANNA, THE BURNED OUT WARRIOR."* The setting was on the battlefront in a hospital ward, full of battered women from the armed forces who were suffering "burn out," apathy, disillusionment, rejection, broken hearts, and so forth. They were depressed, bitter, and wrapped up in their current and past dysfunctions [Prov. 18:14]. Anna was ten to fifteen years older than the other patients who were "first-timers." Anna, the *poor little drill sergeant,* was a veteran of the *Pity Party Ward* and felt that all she did was give, give, give, and do, do, do, without one bit of thanks or recognition. She was burned out from good works (battle fatigue)! Seething with anger and resentment, her thoughts were dominated by harassing and tormenting accusations.

ONE NIGHT, SHE WAS JARRED AWAKE BY A CHARACTER that looked like Daniel Boone, a frontier scout with a coonskin hat, moccasins, and a big old musket. He appeared strong and assured with eyes that emitted a shining *inner* radiance. His joyful expectation was totally out of place in the Pity Party Ward on a battlefront. He asked Anna for directions to the elevator. She grudgingly gave him directions while resenting his calm assurance. She sneered to herself, "How could he seem so sure of himself with such an obsolete weapon?" Anna had better weapons than that, yet look where she had ended up ~ *in the Pity Party Ward!* Huffing, she turned back over to get her much needed rest.

ANNA WAS JOLTED AWAKE. This time it was a radiant conquistador who was also seeking the elevator and carrying the same obsolete weapon. The disturbing thought came, "He is pressing on toward the goal for the *upward call* of God in Christ Jesus" [Phil. 3:14]. She ignored the thought. Infuriated, she angrily told him how to get to the elevator! "What in the deuce is going on? What's so important about that elevator? Why don't they leave me alone? Why can't they understand that I'm here to recuperate from battle fatigue?" Anna thought angrily. Sleep finally returned.

Again, she was jarred awake. This time she fumed, "If it's another one of those radiant, determined, confident musket-carrying, characters . . . . .!" It was a Pakistani, or Indian, dressed in the British Empire uniform, carrying the same obsolete weapon! The Imperial soldier seemed peacefully assured, sensitive, caring and excited about Anna being his ally. "Ally for what?" she wondered. "His citizenship is in heaven," flickered in her thoughts [Phil. 3:20]. However, her heart reflected that "many walk as enemies of the Cross of Christ; enemies whose end are destruction, whose God is their driving desires [self-realization, self-comfort] whose glory is in their shame, who set their minds on *earthly things*" [Phil. 3:18-19, emphasis added].

HER HARD HEART DEFINITELY DID NOT REFLECT HEAVENLY THINGS! She did not want to be involved and angrily directed the radiant warrior to the elevator. Resisting conviction, Anna finally fell asleep again only to be awakened by a short oriental warrior that looked ridiculous to her. He was holding on to a huge worn out musket too large for him to handle. Yet, he, too, was radiant, gracious, and intent in his purpose. She knew what he wanted, but he could not comprehend her directions.

CONVICTING THOUGHTS OF SCRIPTURE bounced about in Anna's mind. "Could the scout and the warriors represent believers who are allies ~ peoples, nations and men of every language that are being raised up to serve The LAMB?" [Dan. 7] The enemy deflected her thoughts with "What's their urgency? What are they seeking? Is a strategic battle coming? Am I good enough to train soldiers, *but not good enough for battle?* Don't they think I can fight the good fight? Haven't I religiously followed instructions to the last jot and tittle? Where is the elevator taking them? Am I being passed over?" That was just a few of the tormenting thoughts Anna struggled with.

THE CHINESE SOLDIER CUPPED HIS HANDS as if in prayer and pointed up because he couldn't understand Anna. She knew that he wanted the same elevator. She angrily got up from her cot and jerked him toward the elevator, punched the button and shoved him on the elevator. Confused and dismayed, she turned around and headed back down the hall to the haven of self-destruction ~ the Pity Party Ward! Suddenly, she felt ashamed and chastened and could no longer resist the LORD's spirit of conviction. She got a mental picture of her own despicable attitude and began to weep with tears of repentance. She desperately wanted to change.

BOOM! LIKE A BOLT OF LIGHTNING, Anna's heart was transformed! She saw herself reflected in the window pane . . . she too was radiant like the soldiers. She was becoming conformed into the image of His Glory, armored in the same Light the soldiers reflected! By the exertion of His power, Christ Jesus subjected her rebellious heart to Himself and *transformed it* [Phil. 3:20-21; 2 Cor. 3: 18]. Petty things that had dominated her thoughts and controlled her actions were gone! They simply dissolved! Anna finally understood that the scout and warriors sought the elevator of God's *upward call* [Phil. 3: 12-14]. They literally mirrored God's LIGHT in their desire to be "raised up to seek things above" with their "minds set on things above" to get His mightiest weapon! The soldiers were undaunting in their quest to exchange their outmoded muskets (weapons) of ineffectual prayers for God's most effective artillery to prepare for the major warfare ahead! They sought God's perfect weapons, His "smart bombs," His *Lasers.* They needed them for their prayers to be effective so they could hit the mark and vaporize the enemy's missiles [Heb. 4:12; Eph. 6:17]. Their purpose was undaunting!

ANNA WAS RENEWED IN CHRIST. She no longer thought of herself. With compelling urgency she returned and told the Pity Party Ward casualties about her joyful new purpose to get God's Lasers, the Sword of His Spirit, His Word, to use in the major battles ahead. She warned them to put all concerns behind as a traumatic event was about to happen. Life would never be the same.

The parable of Anna and the soldiers convicted me of my laziness and carnality. I repented and in His infinite mercy and grace He forgave and cleansed me [Ps. 143]. I purposed to exchange the old thought patterns for the *upward call of God* to *"set my mind on things above."* I wanted to be equipped like the scout and warriors so I could use God's perfect weapon for warfare, His LIGHT, HIS WORD, *HIS LASERS!*

WE FACE UNKNOWN HEINOUS FORCES IN THE DAYS AHEAD. We are called to RISE UP to be part of an allied army that fights the enemy as one, an army of pray-ers that pray in line with His will, reflect His Nature, and maintain righteousness so that we can radiate *HIS LIGHT.*

JESUS IS THE LIGHT OF THE WORLD [John 8:12]. The radiance of God's Glory sustains all things by His Powerful Word [Heb. 1:3]. Intercessors who fervently and effectively follow His direction and battle with His LIGHT ~ *His WORD* ~ *will prevail!*

THE SOVEREIGN COMMANDER-IN-CHIEF is calling His Soldiers to a renewed commitment in the major warfare ahead. It is time to learn His assignment and how He wants it performed. "And the LORD utters His voice before His army; surely His camp is very great, strong is he who carries out His word" [Joel 2:11].

> **PAUL LITTLE WROTE: KNOW WHY YOU BELIEVE, A RADICAL POWER IS NEEDED:**
> Today's society is experiencing a profound power failure ~ a moral power failure. Parents know what is right for themselves and their children, but for lack of backbone they find it easier to go along with the crowd. Children readily pick up this attitude . . . The result is rapid deterioration of the moral fabric of society . . . What is needed is radical power. Christianity is not the putting of a suit on a man, but the putting of a new man into the suit [John 10:10]. He offers us His power.[26]

SPENDING TIME IN OUR PRAYER CLOSETS, as well as in corporate gatherings, is essential. Our thoughts need to rise up to seek Christ so we can reflect His laser prayers and proclamations.

We need Christ's inspired prayers that HIT THE MARK!
Prayers that go right through steel chains and prison doors!
Prayers that penetrate darkness!
Prayers that give the LIGHT of His instruction [Prov. 6: 23].

LET US SEND LASER'S THAT RADIATE CHRIST'S WORD in our petitions to Father God to give us prayers that loose His forgiveness into our sphere of influence [Acts 7:55, 59]. Some say, "We are in the end times ~ all of these things have been prophesied so we can't change anything or be involved!"

The LORD sent Jonah to Nineveh with an end time prophecy. They repented and were saved! Noah listened and became God's seed! Why would God warn Moses if He did not want to change *His* mind? [Exod. 32:9, 11, 14 Living Bible] That happened before Christ! There are too many lost souls to stop interceding!

SURVIVAL DEMANDS REVIVAL AND REVIVAL ACCOMPANIES TRIBULATION. Let us listen and be prepared for His Harvest! Colossians 3 continues to blare as a loud siren in my thoughts! We must put divisions and diversions aside to press forward.

We are to be about our Father's business. We are to reflect His righteousness. We need to proclaim His living, active, effective Word, that is sharper than any two-edged sword [Heb. 4:12] for the major battles ahead.

CONCERTED PRAYERS AND PROCLAMATIONS RECEIVED FROM THE WORD OF GOD ARE HIS LIGHT that probes through darkness and brings forth His Absolute Power [Heb. 1:3] over man's plans and mere words.

WE ARE TO REJOICE! We will be mirrors that reflect His Righteousness to defeat evil. The LORD in turn transforms His inspired Word into overcoming weapons ~ *GOD's Conquering Lasers.*

HIS WORDS PRAYED AND PROCLAIMED ARE THE . . .

> *Light of His illumination*
>> *Augmented by*
>>> *Spurred believers who are*
>>>> *Exalting Him as His*
>>>>> *Radiant dispatchers in harmony*
>>>>>> *Set to intercede and*
>>>>>>> *Tread out God's will!*

LET GOD'S ALLIES,
>**LAUNCH HIS LASERS**
>>**AIM HIS ARTILLERY**
>>>**ACTIVATE HIS AUTHORITY**
>>>>**ADMINISTRATE HIS STRATEGY**
>>>>>**ACCLAIM HIS ABSOLUTENESS**
>>>>>>**ARISE AND SHINE!**
>>>>>>>**FOR HIS LIGHT HAS COME!**

***CHRIST'S IMAGE REFLECTED!* [Gen. 1: 26-27]**

GOD'S LASERS ~ HIS WORD ~ PROCLAIMED FOR VICTORY!

THE LORD'S QUICKENED WORD PREVAILS IN THE SPIRITUAL REALM!

"I have slain them by the words of My mouth;
And the judgments on you are like the LIGHT that goes forth.
For I delight in the knowledge of God rather than burnt offerings."
Hosea 6:5, 6

V ~ GOD'S CONQUERING LASERS   PAGE 19

LIFE APPLICATION

1. What does the acronym LASER represent in this lesson? (P. 1)

2. A. What did Anne say that enabled her to lead people to salvation? B. Which Scripture backs this up and what does it tell us? (P. 2)

3. What happened to the ladies in the Bible Study based on *What Happens When Women Pray* by Evelyn Christenson? (P. 4)

4. A. What does studying about God and His ways do for us? B. What does worshiping the LORD do? C. What does telling the LORD about His worth do? (P. 5)

5. A. What must we do to be careful that we don't label all those who use "points of light" or other expressions as New Agers? B. How did Reverend Benny Clark describe a New Ager and what must we do to discern? (P. 6)

6. How do we polarize and neutralize the enemy? (P. 8)

7. A. Why have innocent believers and people become involved in New Age teachings and various delusions, bondages, and seductions? B. What can set them free? (P. 10)

8. What is God's highest weapon in spiritual warfare? (P. 11)

9. A. Explain how lasers parallel God's Word. B. Why do we discharge His lasers? (P. 11)

10. A. What devices do New Agers, etc., use to seek the light? B. Who are they inviting to posses them when they commune with a higher power? C. What do they desire? (P. 12)

11. A. How does Brubeck say that a satanic revival can be dismantled? B. Why? (P. 13)

12. How do we pray for New Age teachings and the other ungodly influences to be revealed? (PP. 13-14)

13. A. Why was Anna in the Pity Party Ward? (P. 14) B. What transformed Anna's heart and attitude about the four warriors? C. What did the four warriors want to exchange and why? (PP. 14,16)

14. A. _____ accompanies Tribulation. B. How does Colossians 3 affect this statement? (P.17)

GOD'S CONQUERING LASERS SCRIPTURE SEQUENCE

Page 1
Ps. 68:11	[. . . the LORD announced the word, and great was the company of those who proclaimed it.]
Heb. 4:12-13	[For the Word of God is living and active, sharper than any double-edged sword, it penetrates even to the dividing of soul and spirit, joints and marrow; it judges the thoughts and attitudes of the heart. Nothing in all creation is hidden from God's sight. Everything is uncovered and laid bare before the eyes of Him to Whom we must give account]
Isa. 55:11	[" . . . so is My Word that goes out from My mouth: it will not return to Me empty."]
Eph. 6:18	[Take up the sword of the Spirit and pray in the power of the Spirit, be alert with all perseverance]
Acts 19:2	[Did you receive the Holy Spirit when you believed? No, we have not heard there is a Holy Spirit.]

Page 2
Luke 11:13	[. . . how much more will your Father in heaven give the Holy Spirit to those who ask Him?]
John 14:26	[But the Counselor, the Holy spirit, whom the Father will send in My name, will teach you all things and will remind you of everything I have said to you.]
Rom. 9:1	[I speak the truth in Christ ~ I am not lying, my conscience confirms it in the Holy Spirit.]
John 15	[Jesus promised the abundant and fruitful life as the result of being filled (directed and empowered) by the Holy Spirit. The Spirit-filled life is the Christ-directed life by which Christ lives His life in and through us in the power of the Holy Spirit.]

Page 3
Gal. 5:22	[But the fruit of the Spirit is love, joy, peace, patience, kindness, goodness, faithfulness, gentleness and self-control ~ against such things there is no law]
Eph. 5:8-10	[Live as children of light (for the fruit of the light consists in all goodness, righteousness and truth) and find out what pleases the LORD]
Eph. 1:17, 18	[May the Father of Glory give us the spirit of wisdom & of revelation so we may know Him better]
Col. 1:9	[. . . be filled with the knowledge of His will in all spiritual wisdom and understanding]
Matt. 5:16	["Let your light shine before men, that they may see your good deeds and praise your Father in heaven."]
1 Cor. 2:9, 10	[No eye has seen, no ear has heard, no mind has conceived what God has prepared for those who love Him . . . but God has revealed it to us by His Spirit. The Spirit searches all things, even the deep things of God.]

Page 4
Eph. 5:26	[So that He might sanctify her, having cleansed her by the washing of the water with the Word. AMP]
Isa. 64:6	[Our sins are like filthy garments]
John 17:17	[Sanctify them by the TRUTH; Your Word is truth]
1 John 1:9	[He is faithful and just to forgive our confessed sins and cleanse us from *all* unrighteousness]
Gal. 2:20	[I have been crucified with Christ and I no longer live, but Christ lives in me. The life I now live in the body, I live by faith in the Son of God, who loved me and gave Himself for me.]
Ps. 119:89	[Thy Word is settled in heaven.]
Rom. 1:5	[Through Him, for His Name's sake, we received grace and apostleship to call people from among all the Gentiles to the obedience that comes from faith.]
John 1:12	[He gave us the right to be His children]
John 1:43	[Finding Philip, He said to him, "Follow me."]
Ps. 119:89	[Thy Word is settled in heaven.]

PAGE 22   V ~ GOD'S CONQUERING LASERS

Page 5
Exod. 3:14, 15   ["I AM WHO I AM . . . This is My Name forever, the Name by which I am to be remembered from generation to generation."]
Isa. 42:8   [I am the LORD that is My Name! I will not give My glory to another or praise to idols]
John 8:58   ["Truly, truly, I say to you, before Abraham was born, I am."]

Page 7
Hos. 6:5-6   [Therefore have I cut you in pieces with My prophets, I killed you with the words of My mouth, My judgments flashed like lightening upon you.]

Page 8
Isa. 55:11   [My word from My mouth will not return to Me empty, but will accomplish what I desire and achieve the purpose for which I sent it]
Acts 9:3-16   [Suddenly a light from heaven flashed around Paul . . . he got up & could see nothing for three days until he received the Holy Spirit]
Exod. 33:18-23   [Moses was hidden in the cleft of rock to be protected from God's glorious   Light]
1 Tim. 6:13-16   [God, the blessed and only Ruler, the King of kings and LORD of lords, Who alone is immortal and Who lives in unapproachable light . . .]
Isa. 58:8   [And the glory of the LORD will be your rear guard.]
Isa. 55:11   [My word from My mouth will not return to Me empty, but will accomplish what I desire and achieve the purpose for which I sent it.]
Jer. 1:12   [He hastens His WORD to perform it]
Hos. 6:5 NAS   [His Words slay with judgments like the light that goes forth.]

Page 9
Col. 1:12   [. . . giving thanks to the Father, Who has qualified you to share in the inheritance of the saints in the kingdom of light]
John 12:35-36   [Trust in the Light while you have it, so that you may become sons of Light]
1 Thess. 5:5   [You are all sons of the light and sons of the day. We do not belong to the night or to the darkness.]
Rom. 13:12   [Let us put aside the deeds of darkness and put on the armor of light]
John 12:36   [While you have the light, put your trust in the light, so that you may become people of light]
John 8:12   [Yeshua spoke to them again: "I am the light of the world; whoever follows Me will never walk in darkness but will have the light which gives life." JNT~ He IS LIGHT!]
1 John 1:5-7   [God is Light and in Him there is no darkness]
1 Cor. 4:5   [. . . wait till the LORD comes. He will bring light to what is hidden in darkness and will expose the motives of men's hearts.]

Page 11
Isa. 30:17   [One Thousand shall flee at the threat of one man; you shall flee at the threat of five until you are left as a flag on the mountain]
Heb. 4:12   [For the Word of God is living and active. Sharper than any double-edged sword, it penetrates even to dividing of soul and spirit, joints and marrow; it judges the thoughts and attitudes of the heart.] (i.e., The WORD penetrates everything ~ everything is uncovered and laid bare before His eyes)]
Hab. 3:11-15 KJV   [They went away at the light of Thine arrows, at the radiance of Thy gleaming spear . . . for the salvation of Thine anointed Thou didst strike the head of the house of evil.]
Isa. 42:7   [We are called to righteousness, appointed as a covenant; a light to the nations; to release prisoners from darkness]
Isa. 49:6   [The LORD is a light to the Gentiles]
Eph. 5:8-13   [The fruit of Christ's light consists in goodness, righteousness, truth ~ All things become visible when exposed by the light, everything that becomes visible is light]

Page 12
Eph. 5:14   [But everything exposed by the light becomes visible. That is why it is said: "Wake up, O sleeper, rise from the dead, and Christ will shine on you]

Page 13
1 Pet. 1:18-22   [Christ's redeeming blood is revealed]

Page 14
Col. 3:1   [If I have been raised up (elevated) with Christ, I would seek the things above where Christ is seated at God's right hand]
Col. 3:1-4   [I would set my mind on the things above, not on the things of this earth]
Prov. 18:14   [. . . but a crushed spirit who can bear?]

Page 15
Phil. 3:14   [Pressing on toward the goal for the upward call of God in Christ Jesus]
Phil. 3:20   [Our citizenship is in heaven]
Phil. 3:18-19   [Many live as enemies of the Cross of Christ. Their destiny is destruction, their god is their stomach, and their glory is in their shame. Their mind is on earthly things]
Dan. 7:14   [. . . all peoples, nations, and men of every language worshiped him. His dominion is an everlasting dominion that will not pass away, and His kingdom is one that will never be destroyed]

Page 16
2 Cor. 3:18 NASB   [But we all, with unveiled face beholding as in a mirror the glory of the Lord, are being transformed into the same image from glory to glory, just as from the Lord, the Spirit.]
Phil 3: 21 NASB   [. . . Who will transform the body of our humble state into conformity with the body of His glory, by the exertion of the power that He has even to subject all things to Himself.]
2 Cor. 3:18 NIV   [And we all, who with unveiled faces contemplate the Lord's glory, are being transformed into His image with increasing glory, which comes from the Lord, Who is Spirit]
Phil. 3:12-14   [Press on to the upward call of GOD in CHRIST JESUS]
Heb. 4:12   [The word of God is living and active and sharper than any two-edged sword . . .]
Eph. 6:17   [Take up the SWORD of God ~ *His WORD!*)
Ps. 143   [David's Psalm]
John 8:12   [JESUS is the LIGHT of the world]
Heb. 1:3   [The Son is the radiance of God's glory and the exact representation of His being (nature), and upholds all things by His powerful word]

Page 17
Joel 2:11   [Strong is he who carries out His word]
John 10:10   [Christianity is not the putting of a suit on a man, but putting of a new man into the suit.]
Prov. 6:23   [His teachings (commands) are light]
Acts 7:55, 59   [Stephen, filled with the Holy Spirit, gazed at God's Glory and saw Jesus standing at His right hand ~ he fell on his knees and cried out, "LORD, do not hold this against them."]
Exod. 32:9, 11, 14   [God warned Moses; Moses interceded and God changed His mind.] TLB
Heb. 4:12   [God's Word is living, active, sharper than a two-edged sword & can judge the intentions of the heart]

Page 18
Heb. 1:1-3   [He reflects the glory of God . . .upholding the universe with His word of power]
Gen. 1:26-27   [Man is made in God's image]
Hos. 6:5   [I have slain them by the words of My mouth]
Hos. 6:6   [For I desire and delight in dutiful steadfast love and goodness, not sacrifice, and the knowledge of and acquaintance with God more than burnt offerings.]

GOD'S CONQUERING LASERS ENDNOTES

1. William R. Bright, President, Campus Crusade for Christ International, For materials: *New Life Resources*, Peachtree City, Georgia, 1-800-827-2788, Fax: (770) 631-9916.

2. Bright, P.8

3. Bright, Ibid. P.3

    HOW TO PRAY IN FAITH TO BE FILLED WITH THE HOLY SPIRIT. We are filled with the Holy Spirit by *faith* alone. However, true prayer is one way of expressing your faith.

    The following is a suggested prayer: Dear Father, I need You. I acknowledge that I have been directing my own life and that, as a result, I have sinned against You. I thank You that You have forgiven my sins through Christ's death on the Cross for me. I now invite Christ to again take His place on the throne of my life.

    "Fill me with the Holy Spirit as You *commanded* me to be filled, and as You *promised* in Your Word that You would do if I asked in faith, I pray this in the name of Jesus. As an expression of my faith, I now thank You for directing my life and for filling me with the Holy Spirit."

    Does this prayer express the desire of your heart? If so, bow in prayer and trust God to fill you with the Holy Spirit *right now*.

4. A.W. Tozer, *Keys to the Deeper Life*, (Grand Rapids, MI: Clarion Classics, Zondervan Publishing House), PP.49-50 *Brimming Over with the Spirit* ~ Almost all Christians want to be full of the Spirit. Only a few want to be filled with the Spirit. But how can a Christian know the fullness of the Spirit unless he has known the experience of being filled? It would, however, be useless to tell anyone how to be filled with the Spirit unless he first believes that he can be. No one can hope for something he is not convinced is the will of God for him and within the bounds of scriptural provision. Before the question "How can I be filled?" has any validity, the seeker after God must be sure that the experience of being filled is actually possible. The man who is not sure can have no ground of expectation. Where there is no expectation there can be no faith, and where there is no faith, the inquiry is meaningless.

    The doctrine of the Spirit as it relates to the believer has over the last half century been shrouded in a mist such as lies upon a mountain in stormy weather. A world of confusion has surrounded this truth. The children of God had been taught contrary doctrines from the same texts, warned, threatened and intimidated until they instinctively recoil from every mention of the Bible teaching concerning the Holy Spirit.

    PP.50-51 The Church can have light only as it is full of the Spirit, and it can be full only as the members that compose it are filled individually. Furthermore, no one can be filled until he is convinced that being filled is a part of the total plan of God in redemption; that nothing is added or extra, nothing strange or queer, but a proper and spiritual operation of God, based upon and growing out of the work of Christ in atonement . . . He must believe that God wills that he be anointed with a horn of fresh oil beyond and in addition to all the ten thousand blessings he may already have received from the good hand of God . . . Unless he is persuaded from the Scriptures, he should not press the matter nor allow himself to fall victim to the emotional manipulators intent upon forcing the issue. God is wonderfully patient and understanding and will wait for the slow heart to catch up with the truth.

    P.52 To the interested inquirer I ask these questions: Are you sure that you want to be possessed by a Spirit Who, while He is pure and gentle and wise and loving, will yet insist upon being Lord of your life? Are you sure you want your personality to be taken over by One Who will require obedience to the written Word? Who will not tolerate any of the self-sins in your life: self-love, self-indulgence? Who will not permit you to strut or boast or show off? Who will take the direction of your life away from you and will reserve the sovereign right to test you and discipline you? Who will strip away from you many loved objects which secretly harm your soul?

P.53 . . . if your soul cries out for God, for the living God, and your dry and empty heart despairs of living a normal Christian life without a further anointing, then I ask you: Is your desire all-absorbing? Is it the biggest thing in your life? Does it crowd out every common religious activity and fill you with an acute longing that can only be described as the pain of desire? If your heart cries "Yes" to these questions you may be on your way to a spiritual breakthrough that will transform your whole life.

PP.55-56 The infilling itself is not a complicated thing. While I shy away from "how to" formulas in spiritual things, I believe the answer to the question "How can I be filled" may be answered in four words, all of them active verbs. They are these: (1) surrender (Rom. 12:1, 2), (2) ask, (Luke 11:13), (3) obey (Acts 5:32), (4) believe (Gal. 3:2).

P.56 True faith invariably brings a witness. But what is that witness? It is nothing physical, vocal nor psychical. The Spirit never commits Himself to the flesh. The only witness He gives is a subjective one, known to the individual alone. The Spirit announces Himself to the deep, inner spirit of the man. The flesh profiteth nothing, but the believing heart knows. Holy, Holy, Holy.

P.57 In my sober judgment the relation of the Spirit to the believer is the most vital question the church faces today. The problems raised by Christian existentialism or neo-orthodoxy are nothing by comparison with this most critical one. Ecumenicity, eschatological theories ~ none of these things deserve consideration until every believer can give an affirmative answer to the question, "Have ye received the Holy ghost since ye believed?"

5. Brother Lawrence's *The Practice Of The Presence Of God* simplified my walk. Further blessings came from applying scriptural truths learned from reading Hannah Whitehall Smith's *The Christian's Secret of a Happy Life*, Catherine Marshall's *The Helper*, Evelyn Christenson's *What Happens When Women Pray*, plus *Lord, Change Me* ~ which should change anyone! A. W. Tozer's *Keys To The Deeper Life* brought conviction, insight and freedom. Andrew Murray's *With Christ In The School Of Prayer* challenged and inspired me to spend more time in my prayer closet seeking God's Wisdom as revealed by His Holy Spirit (1Cor. 2:10).

6. Martin Lloyd-Jones, *Saved In Eternity*, (Westchester, IL: Crossway Books (division of Good News Publishers), p. 612.

7. Lloyd-Jones, P.162

8. Mark I. Bubeck, *The Satanic Revival*, (San Bernardino, CA: Here's Life Publisher's, Inc., 1991), p. 21.

9. Terry D. Myers, D.D.S., *Lasers in Dentistry: The future is Here Now*, Executive Health's Good Health Report, September 1992 Volume 28 Number 12, p. 1.

10. Spiros Zodihates, Th.D., Compiler and Editor, *The Hebrew-Greek Study Bible,* (Grand Rapids, MI: Baker Book House, 1984), p. 1738; phos (coded to Strong's #5457); is never kindled and therefore, never quenched.

11. Noah Webster, W.T. Harris, Ph.D., L'ISLET, Editor in Chief, *Webster's New International Dictionary of the English Language*, (Springfield, MA: Published by G.& C Merriam Co., 1933), p. 1248.

12. Webster, Ibid.

13. Texe Marrs, *MEGA FORCES, Signs and Wonders of the Coming Chaos*, (Austin, TX: Living Truth Publishers, 1988), p. 93.

14. Ibid. PP.19,20 Dr. Ted Yamamori, Chairman, Spiritual Mapping Track, A.D. 2000 Movement, Adjunct Professor of Sociology, Arizona State University.

15. George Otis, III, *The Last Of The Giants*, (Tarrytown, NY: Chosen Books, R.H. Revell Company, 1991) P.20 (Please note: This book is must reading to understand how to witness, pray effectively for the salvation of Muslims and how to recognize Islamic spirits.)

16. *The New Strong's Exhaustive Concordance* (James Strong 1822-1894), (Nashville, TN: Thomas Nelson Publishers, 1990).

    P.53 #3444 Yᵉshuw`ah something saved, i.e. deliverance; aid, victory, prosperity, salvation, etc. feminine passive particle from the primary. From the *root word:* #3467 Yasha' (yaw-shah'); a primary root; to be open, wide or free, i.e.(by implication) to be safe; causative to free or succor: avenging, defend, deliver (-er), help, preserve, rescue, be safe, bring (having) salvation, save(iour), get victory.

    P.47 (From #3068 and #3467: Jehovah-saved; Jehoshua [Joshua], #3068 Yᵉhovah, [yeh-ho-vaw']). P.48 (For #3091; Yᵉhowshuwa or Yᵉhowshu`a [both pronounced yeh-ho-shoo'-ah]; he will save.

17. Randall N. Baer, *Inside The New Age Nightmare*, (Lafayette, LA: Huntington House, Inc., 1989).

    P.103 Note: For further gleanings please refer to: PP. 96-121; 122-141

18. David B. Guralnik, Editor in Chief, *Webster's New World Dictionary of The American Language,* (The World Publishing Company, New York and Cleveland, Second College Edition, 1970).

    P.313 Copper: a reddish-brown, malleable, ductile, metallic element that is an excellent conductor of electricity and heat.

19. Baer, P.1

20. Ibid. P.185

21. Tal Brooke, *When The World Will Be As One*, (Eugene, OR: Harvest House Publishers, Inc., 1989), p. 67.

22. Ibid. P.68

23. Bubeck, PP.51,52

24. Ibid. P.29

25. Ibid. P.48

26. Paul E. Little, *What and Why Book, Know What You Believe*, (Minneapolis, MN: World Wide Publications), Little, p. 244.

PRAYING THE WORD FOR AREAS OF INFLUENCE
PRAYERS PROCLAIMING GOD'S POWER

"Pray without ceasing." [1 Thess. 5:17]
"The effectual fervent prayers of a righteous man availeth much." [James 5:16]
"Seek from the Book of the LORD..." [Isa. 34:16]

The Power that created the universe is available to guide and answer prayers. We are to cease striving, "be still and know that I am God" [Ps. 46:10; Phil. 3:7-11]. We are to humbly submit to Him so that we may know His guidance [James 3:13, 17]. Heaven's wisdom and power [1 Cor. 1:18-31] is available to His children [John 1:12, 13], as His representatives on earth [Mark 13:33, 34 KJV], to build and plant His Word [Jer. 31:27-34] through prayer [James 5:7-10; Jer. 1:9, 10].

There *is* power in agreement. When two or more gather *in His Name*, we are promised that *"I AM"* is in our midst [Matt. 18:20]. When we gather *in the LORD's Name*, we gather as *ambassadors of His character* and *authority*. We gather as the LORD's earthly representatives, to *seek His council,* so that we may *proclaim* His intentions in cooperation with the Holy Spirit. When we gather in the LORD's Name, we *invite* His Holy Spirit to guide us into prayers that are based on the perspective of His Word that He promises to answer [Jer. 51:12, 15, 19-22]. Praying "in the Name of the LORD" is proclaiming *agreement with* the LORD *and with one another.*

His Sovereign authority, character and attributes are solicited. Direction for prayer that *conforms* to His nature, wisdom, knowledge and understanding is received [Prov. 3:19-26; Jer. 1:6-9]. We gather together in belief that our *obedience* to His guidance will *bring forth His answer* [Jer. 1:12]. In thankful anticipation and faith *we believe* [John 7:38] that the LORD *will respond* to our obedience of *active participation* in the advancement of His Kingdom [James 5:16b].

The following prayer samples illustrate the value of praying God's Word for effectual prayers that reflect Christ, by praying within God's principles, conditions, and character. Invite the Holy Spirit to enlarge and deepen your prayers appropriately so that many may be blessed. You are encouraged to look up the Scriptures and use your Bible's Scripture references. Insert actual names in the (parentheses of examples) for righteous effectual fervent prayers (James 5:16b).

Father God, Triumphant Spirit of Christ, revive us according to Your Word [Ps. 119:25] which is a fire and hammer that breaks a rock in pieces [Jer. 23:29]. Energize our prayers through Your Word that is active and sharper than any two-edged sword [Heb. 4:12]. Motivate our prayers with Christ's wisdom and knowledge [Col. 2:2, 3]. Encourage and knit our hearts in love so that we may triumph in Christ's fullness over *every* power and authority [Eph. 2:4; Col. 2:9-15].

Father, we ask You to fill us with the Spirit of Christ [Phil. 1:19]. We praise and thank You for giving us the Holy Spirit. We invite Your Spirit to teach us how to pray [Luke 12:12] so that we may go boldly to Your throne [Heb. 4:16] to receive prayers from Your perspective, proclaim Your revealed Word into circumstances, then in faith with anticipation, wait for the success of Your Word prayed in the matter for which You bring it forth [James 1:5-12, 17, 18].

LORD, Your Word tells us that Your ways are not our ways [Isa. 55:8] and that Your Word will not return without accomplishing Your intentions [Isa. 55:11]. We ask for mutual assurance and confirmation [Dan. 9:12] so that we can understand how You would have us proclaim and pray Your Holy Living Word.

Father, put Your Word into our mouths as Your appointed ambassadors, intercessors, and emissaries over nations and kingdoms, so that we may be Your builders and planters [Jer. 1:10]. Show us how You would have us make entreaties and prayers, petitions and thanksgivings on behalf of all men, kings, and leaders in authority, so that we may lead tranquil and quiet lives in all godliness and dignity [1 Tim. 2:1, 2].

PRAYERS FOR OUR JUDICIAL SYSTEM

Father, may (judge/bailiff, etc.) allow you to be the Judge and Lawgiver. Your Word says that You are Lawgiver and King and that You will save us [Isa. 33:22]. May (he/she) understand You, know that You exercise loving-kindness and justice and may You delight in them [Jer. 9:23]. We pray that (Justice/Judge/bailiff/etc.) will be righteous and obedient to the morality of Your Commandments [Matt. 28:20; Exod. 20:1-17], endeavor to restore families [Ps. 127:3-5; Eph. 5:22-23] and conduct themselves in holiness and godly sincerity.

Father, we pray that (Attorney General/Prosecutor/Recorder, etc.) will walk in Your house with a blameless heart [Ps. 101:2], guard our City/State/Nation [Ps. 127:1] with commitment to You [1 Sam. 7:3b], judge the poor in righteousness [Isa. 11:4]. LORD, grant (Safety official/police/guard/dispatcher/etc.) Your counsel and strength through the Spirit of knowledge and fear of the LORD [Isa. 11:2]; protect them, preserve their life and bless them [Ps. 41:2].

PRAYERS FOR OUR GOVERNMENT

Suggestions for General Prayers:

Father, Your Word says righteousness exalts a nation, but sin is a reproach to any people [Prov. 14:34]. Please forgive us, and our leaders, for knowingly or unknowingly sinning against You. Give them and us humble hearts and changed hearts that can be actively involved in healing our land [2 Cor. 7:14].

Father, enable us to select able men of truth who hate dishonest gain. Appoint them as officials over thousands, hundreds, fifties, and tens [Exod. 18:21] and enable them to approve the things that are excellent in order to be sincere and blameless until the day of Christ [Phil. 1:10].

Suggestions for Specific Prayers:

Father, may (President/Governor/Mayor, etc.) honor You [Prov. 3:6], learn righteousness [Isa. 26:9b], and be courageous and responsible to confront the threats to the moral fabric of our nation [Isa. 35:4; Rom. 13:11-14]. Father, enable (Director of Energy/Health/Education, etc.) to trust in You with all of their heart and rely not upon their own understanding [Prov. 3:5].

LORD, protect and keep (President/Governor/Congressman/Councilman, etc.) and their families from evil [John 17:15]. Give them the fear of the LORD so that they may attend You in truth [1 Sam. 12:24], know You as LORD [Phil. 2:10, 11], and be people of prayer [Luke 22:46].

Father God, may our (elected/appointed official) listen to what You have to say, have a compassionate heart for the poor, and be charitable [Prov. 29:14] so that we may have peace [Ps. 85:8]. LORD, we put the heart of (name of elected/appointed official) into Your hands [Prov. 21:1,] and pray that they will hold fast to the Word of Life [Phil. 2:16]. May (they) encourage the work of Your people in Your house [Ezra 6:22].

PRAYERS FOR CHRIST'S CHURCH

LORD, we pray that (a spiritual leader) will be full of Your Spirit and Wisdom [Acts 6:3]. Sanctify them in Your Word of Truth [John 17:17]. Give (the spiritual leader) Your words when they open their mouth so that they will fearlessly make known the mystery of the Gospel for which they are ambassadors in chains [Eph. 6:20; Rom. 1:5].

LORD, may (pastor/elder/deacon/deaconess/teacher/organist/etc.) lead us with a servant's humility in paths of righteousness for Your Name's sake [Prov. 2:20], so that You may exalt them [Matt. 23:11, 12]. May (same leader) make Your Name known through the revelation of Your Christ-like character to the people of this (city/county/state/nation).

Father, may (religious leader/s) be one in You, as an example of unity, without regard to ethnic differences or previous divisions, that they may join together to pray and seek Your face for our (nation, municipality/county/ state, etc.).

Father, may the world see that (religious leader/s) represent the LORD, Whom You sent [John 1:21], and may they glorify You [2 Chron. 5:11-14]. Protect and enable Your stewards (spiritual leaders) to be above reproach [James 4:7-12], hospitable, lovers of what is good, sensible, just, devout and truthful. Help them to exercise self-control [Titus 1:7, 8].

LORD, we pray that (elders/deacons/choir directors/etc.) will hold Your Word fast in accordance with Your teachings, so that they may be able to both exhort sound doctrine and refute those in contradiction to the Way, the Truth and Life [Titus 1:6; John 14:6]. Provide for (custodian/organist/secretary/etc.) so that they shall not want [Ps. 23:1]. Vindicate those who have been wrongly judged [Ps. 26:1] so that all may reach forward to gain what lies ahead [Phil. 3:13].

LORD, we lift up (missionary/ministry/etc.) and pray that everywhere their feet shall tread that You will give it to them [Josh. 1:3], that they will be strong and courageous, and know that You are with them wherever they go [Josh. 1:9].

LORD, may Your people love the habitation of Your house and see Your Glory dwell therein [Ps. 26:8]. Give us the desire to meditate in Your house, plant Your Word in good soil to bring forth a great harvest, and learn to behold your beauty while we sing praises to Your Name [Ps. 27:4-6].

Father, may Your house of worship once more be called Your house of prayer, [Matt. 21:13]
so all will know . . . *CHRIST IS ALL* and *IN ALL!* [Col. 3:11]

Prepared for the International Bible Reading Association
P.O. Box 1501 ~ Murfreesboro, TN 37133-1501

Lesson VI

AGAPAŌ LOVE TRIUMPHS

*"This is how we know what love is:
Jesus Christ laid down His life for us.
And we ought to lay down our lives for one another."*

1 John 3:16

THE MESSAGE

The Way Of Love

"Love never gives up.

Love cares more for others than for self.

Love doesn't want what it doesn't have.

*Love doesn't strut,
Doesn't have a swelled head,
Doesn't force itself on others,*

*Isn't always 'me first,'
Doesn't fly off the handle,
Doesn't keep score of the sins of others,
Doesn't revel when others grovel,*

*Takes pleasure in the flowering of truth,
Puts up with anything,
Trusts God always,
Always looks for the best,
Never looks back,
But keeps going to the end."*

Excerpted from 1 Corinthians 13

*THE MESSAGE
Eugene H. Peterson*

AGAPAŌ LOVE TRIUMPHS

*"They weren't in love with themselves;
They were willing to die for Christ."*
Revelation 12:11   THE MESSAGE

JESUS IS THE HIGHEST EXAMPLE OF GOD'S LOVE! The blood of the Lamb is God's gift of love to us paid in full on the cross to conquer sin's claim on mankind.

Christ's legal ownership was established on the Cross. His life sacrifice for us glorified and demonstrated God's infinite love. *No more ~ no less!* Martyrs over the centuries loved not their lives unto death. We need to emulate their example. We need to walk in that same fullness of power that God has given us. We also need to exercise His victory through sharing His agapaō love. We will now investigate how to demonstrate God's agapaō, *unconditionally.*

Love does not accuse! Love rejects unrighteous thoughts! The words of our testimony should proclaim Christ's victorious legal ground within, without and through us. Our words can give the enemy legal ground in our lives or the lives of others. The Bible teaches that the Accuser of the brethren, who accused the brethren day and night, was overthrown, thrown out, by God's heavenly forces. It also says that the Enemy is wild and raging with anger. He knows he doesn't have much time [Rev. 12:10, 11].

WE MUST BE ON GUARD, WATCHFUL, CAUTIOUS. The enemy's ongoing warfare requires ongoing vigilance over our minds and hearts. We need to practice agapaō love at all costs to walk in God's glory and power!

ANDREW MURRAY WROTE IN *THE BLOOD OF THE CROSS*, that we must fix our attention on the LOVE of the CROSS to learn the full glory and power of the blood of the cross:

> What we need is a right view of Jesus Himself, and of His all-conquering, eternal love. The blood is the earthly token of the heavenly glory of that love; the blood points to that love. What we need is to behold Jesus Himself in the light of the cross. All the love manifested by the cross is the *measure* of the love He bears to us today. The love which was not terrified by any power of opposition of sin will now conquer everything in us that would be a hindrance. The love which triumphed on the accursed tree is strong enough to obtain and maintain a complete victory over us. To know Jesus in His love, to live in that love, and to have the heart filled with that love is the greatest blessing that the cross can bring to us. It is the way to the enjoyment of all the blessings of the cross. *Glorious Cross!*
>
> Each drop of that blood points to the surrender and death of self-will, of the *'I'* life, as the way to God and life in Him. Each drop of that blood assures you of the power obtained by Jesus on the cross to maintain that inner nature, that crucified life, in you. Each drop of that blood brings Jesus and His eternal love to you, to work out all the blessing of the cross in you, and to keep you in that love.[1]

THE BLOOD OF THE LAMB SHED ON THE CROSS was spiritually transfused into our veins to set the stage for believers to defeat the enemy's exploits.

> "They defeated him through the blood of the Lamb
> and the bold word of their witness.
> They weren't in love with themselves;
> they were willing to die for Christ."
> [Rev. 12:11] The Message[2]

AFTER EXPERIENCING FIRSTHAND THE FRUIT OF HIS OVERCOMING TRUTH about taking authority, I taught that the righteous words of our testimony would bring victory when it is based on the strength of His Word. Afterward, the godly worship leader *privately* pointed out that I was not teaching the full truth. "What about 'they did not *love* their lives unto death?'" she asked. She explained that my teaching had not been in context. Her non-confrontational question demonstrated God's way to handle differences of opinion or doctrine.

THE WORSHIP LEADER'S QUESTION RAISED A PAINFUL TRUTH I needed to hear. I had omitted the end of the verse simply because it seemed *obvious*. That fact alone kept the teaching from being in context. Sadly, her exhortation stung ~ pride crept in. Didn't I always teach precept upon precept? Driving home, I rationalized in defense of the completeness of *my* teaching. "What did love unto death have to do with overcoming?" I turned to *The Teacher* and it was confirmed that I had heard truth through His devoted servant. Who was I to pick and choose which words I thought were important? Was it precept upon precept? The Holy Spirit convicted me of my self-righteous defensiveness. It was past time to lay my heart on the altar.

ANDREW MURRAY WROTE IN THE BLOOD OF THE CROSS:

> The body has a head ~ we speak of the head with the brains as the seat of understanding. The head with all its thoughts must be laid on the altar. I must consecrate my understanding entirely to the service of God, placing it entirely to the service of God, placing it entirely under His control and direction to be used by Him: I must "bring into captivity every thought to the obedience of Christ" [2 Cor. 10:5] . . . By my mouth, I reveal what is in me, what I think and see and will. By it I exercise an influence over others. My mouth and tongue and lips must be consecrated so that I will not speak; anything except what is in accordance with God's will and to His glory.[3]

IT WAS IMPORTANT TO REPENT AND ASK for my understanding, thoughts, eyes, ears, and mouth to be consecrated to speak God's teachings, not mine. It was high time that I got quiet before the LORD to investigate *all* of the areas of my heart before I began a word search based on the martyr's love. The Holy Spirit wanted a clean submitted vessel that would resist evil according to God's conditions to work His will in me. [James 4:7-12]

> *"So let God work His will in you. Yell a loud no to the Devil and watch him scamper. Say a quiet yes to God and he'll be there in no time. Quit dabbling in sin. Purify your inner life. Quit playing the field. Hit bottom, and cry your eyes out. The fun and games are over. Get serious, really serious. Get down on your knees before the Master; it's the only way you'll get on your feet. Don't bad mouth each other, friends.*
>
> *It's God's Word, His Message, His Royal Rule, that takes a beating in that kind of talk. You're supposed to be honoring the Message, not writing graffiti all over it. God is in charge of deciding human destiny. Who do you think you are to meddle in the destiny of others? As it is, you are full of your grandiose selves. All such vaunting self-importance is evil. In fact, if you know the right thing to do and don't do it, that, for you, is evil."*[4]

I GOT SERIOUS AND CRIED MY HEART OUT BEFORE THE LORD wondering how pride had entered. When I felt His peace that passes understanding embrace me, I knew that I was forgiven. Soon afterward I saw a sign on a church marquee that made me giggle:

Try swallowing your pride once in a while ~ It's non-fattening!

A CHURCH'S HUMOROUS TRUTH REMINDED ME HOW PRIDE had overindulged my thoughts and actions. Was there anything I could take pride in? What righteous act had I ever done that originated outside of His wisdom and grace? Instead of excitement about The Teacher, I realized that I had fallen into the trap of pride over the teaching. Paul said, "But may it never be that I should boast, except in our LORD Jesus Christ, through Whom the world has been crucified to me, and I to the world" [Gal. 6:14]. "A righteous man receives nothing unless it has been given him from heaven" [John 3:27].

WHEN WE PRACTICE THE CORRECT TESTIMONY, and apply God's Word as "our witness" against negative thoughts, God's victory is maintained God's way! It is an *ongoing battle*, yet rewarding, to watch His thoughts in action when they wash our thoughts with His Word to triumph over the Accuser. We cannot overindulge in His love ~ *it is non-fattening!*

I knew, that I knew, it was time to dig in and pursue the martyrs "love" in Revelation 12:11.

EXAMINING LOVE IN REVELATION 12:11, in various Greek lexicon translations, I learned that *agapaō love* is not the brotherly love that I had taken for granted. I experienced a deep appreciation for the godly leader who obeyed the Holy Spirit and told me my teaching was incomplete.

In the New Testament, agapaō means (1) "the active love of God for His Son and His people, and (2) the active love His people are to have for God, each other, and even enemies."[5] (Agapaō is pronounced: ahh guh *pay* oh!*)*

HOW DO WE APPLY AGAPAŌ LOVE PRACTICALLY? There is a tremendous difference between agapaō and other words for love. Agapaō is a love that *chooses* to supplement another's deficiency, with unconditional love, even though that person may not recognize God's requirement of love. What does it mean in our life or circumstances to love by a choice of our will which stands higher than other love due to its moral influence? My head spun trying to figure out, and separate in a concrete way, the various translations of love versus agapaō, but my heart was not enlightened. It was a struggle to grasp how we are to apply agapaō in a personal and practical way.

"AGAPAŌ" AND "LOVE" ARE INTERCHANGEABLE IN THIS SESSION, and will be used interchangeably as we proceed. They are to be understood as His unconditional love ~ the *love* of Christ that we are to substitute and extend to others.

THE HEBREW-GREEK KEY STUDY BIBLE stated:
> Agapaō love, indicates a direction of the will and finding one's joy in anything. It is used of God's love toward man and vice versa; it is used of love toward our enemies. Doing what the one who loves deems is needed by the one who is loved, a love that is a conscious decision to love our enemies.[6]

JESUS LAID DOWN HIS LIFE TO PROVIDE FOR US WHAT WE NEED but we do not recognize that we need salvation and the Holy Spirit actively involved in our lives. His death on the Cross was the greatest example of agapaō love ever known to mankind. The question is, how do we receive and walk in His agapaō love in a realistic way, day to day? When we die to ourselves by not thinking wrong thoughts or insisting on our way (lay down our lives for our brother) we can demonstrate His agapaō love. When we love with our actions and in truth then others will see His love reflected through us [1 John 3:16].

W.E. VINE COVERED AGAPAŌ MORE EXTENSIVELY IN LAYMEN'S LANGUAGE:
> The deep and constant love and interest of a perfect Being towards entirely unworthy objects, producing and fostering a reverential love in them toward the Giver, and a practical love towards those who are partakers of the same, and a desire to help others to seek the Giver . . . Love is only known from

the actions it prompts. God's love is seen in the gift of His Son. It was an exercise of the Divine will in deliberate choice, made without assignable cause save that which lies in the nature of God Himself.

Christian love, whether exercised toward the brethren, or toward men, generally, is not an impulse from the feelings, it does not always run with the natural inclinations, nor does it spend itself only upon those for whom some affinity is discovered. Love seeks the welfare of all and works no ill to any . . . Love seeks opportunity to do good to all men, and especially toward them that are of the household of the faith.[7]

QUESTIONS BEGAN TO POP: Love my enemies? Choose to love? As this truth was revealed, situations began to challenge my peace with new and old hurts that seemed to crawl out of the woodwork! Choosing to love others is not easy! I chose to love, over and over, but it wasn't working like I thought it should. Then I read that my heart was the meeting place of my desires and endeavors of all that I choose, of love and hatred, and that I must *give up my right* to love or hate after my own desire.

ANDREW MURRAY WROTE IN THE BLOOD OF THE CROSS:

The body has a heart, the center of life, where the blood, in which the soul dwells and flows in and out. In the heart is the meeting place of all the desires and endeavors of men, of all they will choose, of love and hatred. The heart of Jesus was pierced on the cross. Everything that flows in or out of our heart must be laid upon the altar. I must renounce the right to seek or will anything after my own wish, to love or hate after my own desire. In the case of Jesus the cross meant: "My will is of no account: the will of God is everything"; "The will of God, cost what it may, must be done, even if it costs my life." In the smallest as well as in the greatest things God's will must be done. In nothing must my will be done ~ in everything God's will.[8]

UNCONDITIONAL LOVE, the right to choose between love and hate, became an intensified battle in my mind. Sometimes it seemed like my heart was a raw wound that salt had been poured in, especially when certain personalities openly manipulated and mocked me to my face. I poured my heart out to the LORD. The dismay and disillusionment of frequently "blowing it" suffocated me. Why did I feel like I had to defend myself? Why didn't anyone understand the whole picture? Why couldn't I grasp the truth of agapaō in a practical way? Why couldn't I yield to God's will in my heart? Why was it so easy to give in to smoldering feelings? Why couldn't I be still and allow the LORD to exonerate me? Or just put it in His hands and let it go? Why?

DURING PRAYER I WAS PROMPTED TO TURN ON THE TELEVISION (which I seldom watched). I knew that the thought was not from God, because it was contrary to what I thought the LORD would lead me to do. I refused the thought in Jesus' Name and it promptly came back two times. I turned on the television and my heart jumped up to my throat when I heard a pastor say that he wanted to leave the "Gifts of the Spirit" Seminar that he had been teaching and talk about the greatest gift of all, although it had not been listed in the program, *agapaō love!* He had my full attention! The pastor spoke about his difficulty in making the truth of agapaō love applicable to his everyday life in a manner that had staying power. I knew, that I knew, that the Holy Spirit had led me to turn on the television so I took notes and listened keenly to what the pastor had to say!

FOLLOWING THE PASTOR'S RESEARCH ON AGAPAŌ LOVE, he too, had been unable to put it into practical application. He shared that his "moment of truth" came as a consequence of an elder's angry outburst toward him at a committee meeting before the elder stormed away. The next day the pastor had a chance encounter with the angry elder. It was obvious that the elder wanted to cross to the other side of the street to keep from acknowledging the pastor, but it was unavoidable! The pastor, having studied agapaō, recognized that he was being tested. He knew that he was required to respond to the elder with "agapaō", so he obediently, simply, rendered a hearty "hello." The exasperated elder inaudibly returned the pastor's greeting and rushed pass him.

The decision the pastor faced at that point was critical! How was he to apply agapaō love toward the elder's snub as the LORD required? He *had* forgiven and extended a 100 percent friendly salutation yet the elder rebuffed it with a mumbled 6 percent salutation. That left a whopping gap! How was the pastor to react? It was edifying when the pastor shared that he *chose* to substitute the love of God in the 94 percent gap left by the elder, then *released* the elder from *any apologies or requirements*. The elder would not have to respond 100 percent, 73 percent, or even 1 percent. The pastor put God's perfect love into the gap! *He forgave him.* Finally, I understood what agapaō required. I got so excited! The pastor substituted *a love that stood higher* which neutralized the angry snub. That's how it worked! His explanation confirmed and enlarged my research. Overcoming is possible through agapaō. The LORD's agapaō love freed the pastor *and the elder.* The elder was released by the pastor from apologies or restitution. The good news is that the pastor was free from dwelling upon it.

THE PASTOR BEGAN PRACTICING GOD'S PRINCIPLE of his "newly found agapaō" on his family and church. A week later they asked him to tell them what had changed him. That was the moment that God's love began to cover it all!

Agapaō love is higher than any other type of love in the Bible. Agapaō was used 137 times as a verb and 116 times as a noun. Agapaō is our divine substitute on the Cross and is our substitute in attacks from others! Agapaō transcends our ability to love, dies to self, and cancels all demands that "self" makes for recognition or apology.

TESTS SEEM TO FOLLOW NEW UNDERSTANDINGS, DON'T THEY? That night my husband came home after having a *very* bad day. I greeted him with 100 percent love, and it would be fair to say that he responded with, maybe, 4 percent (?). More than a whopping gap stood between us! A little light bulb turned on! I remember thinking, "LORD, I'm going to put Your 96 percent agapaō there to replace the hurt that I feel. I free Gene. He does not have to make amends about this ~ ever! Gene's debt is canceled! Christ's love is going to replace Gene's rejection!" Amazing Grace! Waves of peace fell over me. I remember looking up at the ceiling and whispering, "LORD, that was a test! Your love enabled me to pass it!" Joy exploded! I honestly cannot remember to this day if Gene ate dinner that night. I *do* remember that negative thoughts did not stand a chance.

THE LONG-SOUGHT UNDERSTANDING OF HOW TO APPLY AGAPAŌ LOVE in a practical way had arrived! *Freedom in Christ* came into my circumstances because I asked, then allowed, the Spirit of Christ to enable me to choose His Love that "covers it all" [1 Pet. 4:8]. The freedom of requiring nothing in return, by applying the truth of Christ's love within, was real! How I wish I could say agapaō love has been perfected in my life, but we (the LORD and I) are still working on it. However, I have improved with God's grace, and can testify that joy abounds when agapaō reigns in my heart.

I deeply regretted that I had taken it for granted that agapaō love would be understood generally as love, and neglected learning about the essence of agapaō, which is the love that "loves not themselves *even* unto death!" [Rev. 12:11]

AGAPAŌ OPERATES HAND IN GLOVE WITH THE WORDS OF OUR TESTIMONY, Christ's thoughts that we speak or think, based upon His crucified yet living love. The manger at Bethlehem and the Cross of Christ illustrate agapaō's fullest substitution for an offender's shortcomings with Christ's unconditional love that values and esteems others regardless of their offense. Our forgiving heart, in communion with the *power of His agapaō,* testifies that His agapaō within has freed us to be slaves of Christ [Eph. 6:6].

CHRIST'S GIFT OF ETERNAL UNCONDITIONAL LOVE, in spite of our deficiencies, lives on within us, when we, in turn, extend His unconditional love to others then require nothing in return for their offenses or omissions. His love frees both parties and allows the Holy Spirit to minister truth where it is needed!

Should anyone point to another's sin against us? Pointing out another's sin toward us or an injustice, should be done only if, and when, it can be ministered through the agapaō love of Christ, not before!

Please note: As painful as it can be, and as much as we want to be exonerated, sometimes it is best to leave an injustice toward us alone as God may have another way He wants to handle the situation. When we remember that everything is not about us, but about God's overall plans and purposes, we can freely give it to the LORD and trust Him to do what is best in the long run. For all we know, there may be areas of spiritual growth that someone else needs to develop and we could be interfering.

REGARDING AN INJUSTICE, *if we are prompted by the LORD to intervene,* we are to pray for God to put forgiveness in all of the hearts involved, and to prepare the heart of the person He may lead you to speak to. Prayerfully go to the person in the agapaō love of Christ and present the error or misunderstanding [Matt. 18:15]. It is good to have prayer covering by a trusted intercessor before we talk to the offender. The person giving prayer covering *does not need to know all about it*; just that you are facing a difficult discussion and you need God's grace, mercy, forgiveness, protection and love to dominate the situation. We also need to ask the LORD to forgive those who willingly took the accusation and ran with it, or who might have innocently spread it further by asking for prayer about it in a prayer group. Many times repeating an offense (first or second hand) can easily produce unrighteous gossip. We can ask for prayer for a situation or circumstance but do not need to give names or details ~ God knows the details ~ we do not need to tell Him, nor do others!

No apologies, acknowledgments or requirements are needed from offenders when we become Christ's instruments of unconditional love and choose to forgive offenses toward us. Praise God that His servant was obedient to correct me. It was constructive criticism. To God be the glory!

CHRIST CALLS US TO BE OVERCOMERS! Praise God that Jesus esteemed us enough to make us innocent and righteous in God's sight. Christ's victory on the Cross, through obedience to Father God's agapaō love, canceled all of our legal debts of sin and death's claim.

CHRIST CALLS US TO HUMBLY OBEY HIS GUIDANCE, be righteous stewards over the Keys of God's Kingdom, love not our lives unto death, and maintain the purposes of Christ. It is exciting and wonderful at the same time, to know that believers can overcome because the salvation, and the power, and the kingdom of God, and the authority of His Christ is in our hearts.

MESSIAH'S AGAPAŌ LOVE OVERCOMES!

*And I heard a loud voice in heaven, saying,
"Now the salvation and the power
and the kingdom of our God
and the authority of His Christ have come,
for the accuser of our brethren
has been thrown down,
who accuses them before our God
day and night.*

*And they overcame him
because of the blood of the Lamb
and because of the word of their testimony,
they did not love their lives even to death.*

*For this reason,
rejoice,
O heavens and you who dwell in them.*

*Woe to the earth and the sea, because the devil
has come down to you,
having great wrath,
knowing that he has only a short time."
Revelation 12:11, 12*

~~~~~~~~~~~~~

NOTE: MAJOR LOVE WORDS IN GREEK

The major Greek words "love" and "loved" references in Strong's Exhaustive Concordance of the Bible (in King James). Strong's numbers are in (parentheses):

- **Agapaō** - (25) love in a social or moral sense, judgment, deliberate will as a matter of principle & duty - **OF THE HEAD** (Joh. 3:16; Rev. 1:5 - "Unto Him that loved us, and washed us from our sins in His own blood, …"
- **Philëō** - (5368) to be a friend, affection, kiss, outward love - **OF THE HEART**
- **Agapĕ** - (26) affection or benevolence, charity, dear, love
- **Thĕlō** - (2309) desire, determined

PAGE 10   VI ~ AGAPAŌ LOVE TRIUMPHS

LIFE APPLICATION

1. A. Our _____ can give the enemy ground in our lives. B. Andrew Murray said that we must fix our attention on the _____ of the _____ to learn the full glory and power of the blood of the Cross. C. What does each drop of the blood on the cross point to? (P. 1)

2. A. What did the author need to do when she felt self-righteous anger and resentment about a teaching she had done? B. What did she do before she began a word search based on the martyr's love? (P. 2)

3. How is God's victory maintained God's way? (P. 3)

4. A. What was the greatest example of *agapaō love* ever known to man? B. How do we demonstrate His agapaō love in a practical way? (P. 4)

5. W.E. Vine wrote that there are different definitions of Agapaō love. A. Which do you prefer and why? B. What does he say Christian love is? (PP. 4, 5)

6. A. According to Andrew Murray, when your heart is at the meeting place of your desires, and endeavors of all that you choose, of love and hatred, do you have to give up your right to love or hate? B. In the case of Jesus, what does the cross mean? (P. 5)

7. A. What did the pastor choose to do when the elder gave him a mumbled six percent salutation? B. What happened as a result? (P. 6)

8. A. What is the highest type of love in the Bible? B. How many times was it used? C. What does it substitute for? D. What does it transcend? (PP. 6, 7)

9. How did freedom in Christ, the freedom of requiring nothing in return, come in the author's test to substitute the agapaō love of God in the gap left by the love not shown to her? (P. 7)

10. A. What is the essence of agapaō love? B. How does His unconditional love live within us? (P. 7)

11. A. Should anyone point to another's sin against us? B. How do we proceed against an injustice? C. How do we pray? D. Is it wise to ask for prayer covering? E. What information do we give when we ask for prayer? F. Do we ask forgiveness for anyone else? G. How do we ask for prayer groups to pray about it? (PP. 7, 8)

12. A. Who calls us to be overcomers? B. Christ calls us to humbly obey His guidance, to be righteous stewards over the _____ of God's _____, to _____ not our lives unto death, and maintain the _____ of Christ. (P. 8)

AGAPAŌ LOVE TRIUMPHS SCRIPTURE SEQUENCES

Page 1
Rev. 12:11   [… and they did not love their lives unto death]
Rev. 12:10b, 11   [For the accuser of our brothers accuses them day and night, and has been hurled own ~ the martyr's overcame him by the blood of the Lamb, the word of their testimony and they did not love their lives unto death]

Page 2
2 Cor. 10:5   [We demolish argument and every pretension that sets itself up against the knowledge of God, and we take captive every thought to make it obedient to Christ.]
Rev. 12:11   [They defeated him through the blood of the Lamb and the bold word of their witness. They weren't in love with themselves; they were willing to die for Christ.] The Message

Page 3
2 Cor. 10:5   [We demolish argument and every pretension that sets itself up against the knowledge of God, and we take captive every thought to make it obedient to Christ.]
James 4:7-12 [Submit, draw near, clean hands, pure heart, humble yourself]
Gal. 6:14   [May I never boast except in the cross of our LORD Jesus Christ, through which the world has been crucified to me, and I to the world.]
John 3:27   [John the Baptist said, "A man can only receive what is given him from heaven."]

Page 4
1 John 3:16   [This is how we know what love is: Jesus laid down his life for us. And we ought to lay down our lives for other.]

Page 6
Note: [Agapaō was used 137 times as a verb and 116 times as a noun]

Page 7
1 Pet. 4:8   [Above all, love each other deeply, because love covers over a multitude of sins.]
Eph. 6:6   [… like slaves of Christ, doing the will of God from your heart.]

Page 8
Matt. 18:15   ["If your brother sins against you, go and show him his fault, just between the two of you. If he listens to you, you have won your brother over."]
Rev. 12:10-12 [Christ's power has come. The accuser is overcome by the Blood of the Lamb, the words of our testimony and we are to love not our lives unto death]

AGAPAŌ LOVE TRIUMPHS ENDNOTES

1. Andrew Murray, *The Blood of the Cross*, Copyright © 1981 by Whitaker House, U.S.A.

    PP. 32-36

    We have spoken of the inner nature of which the cross is the expression and of the powerful influence that inner nature exercises in and through us if we allow the blood of the cross to have its full power over us. The fear, however, often arises in the mind of the Christian that it is too much of a burden always to preserve and manifest that inner quality . . . This is because the exercise of that power depends to some extent on our surrender and faith. *I see it!* What we need is a right view of Jesus Himself, and of His all-conquering, eternal love. The blood is the earthly token of the heavenly glory of that love; the blood points to that love.

    What we need is to behold Jesus Himself in the light of the cross. All the love manifested by the cross is the *measure* of the love He bears to us today. The love which was not terrified by any power of opposition of sin will now conquer everything in us that would be a hindrance. The love which triumphed on the accursed tree is strong enough to obtain and maintain a complete victory over us. To know Jesus in His love, to live in that love, and to have the heart filled with that love is the greatest blessing that the cross can bring to us. It is the way to the enjoyment of all the blessings of the cross. *Glorious Cross!*

    Beloved Christian, whose hope is in the blood of the cross, give yourself up to experience its full blessing. Each drop of that blood points to the surrender and death of self-will, of the *'I'* life, as the way to God and life in Him. Each drop of that blood assures you of the power obtained by Jesus on the cross to maintain that inner nature, that crucified life, in you. Each drop of that blood brings Jesus and His eternal love to you, to work out all the blessing of the cross in you, and to keep you in that love.

2. Eugene H. Peterson, *The Message*, (Colorado Springs, CO: The New Testament in Contemporary Language, NAVPRESS Publishing Group), p. 529.

3. Murray, The altar sanctified by the blood; The offering sanctified by the altar.

    P. 46

    The body has a head ~ we speak of the head with the brains as the seat of understanding. The head with all its thoughts must be laid on the altar. I must consecrate my understanding entirely to the service of God, placing it entirely to the service of God, placing it entirely under His control and direction to be used by Him: I must "bring into captivity every thought to the obedience of Christ" [2 Cor. 10:5].

    The head has its members also, the eyes and mouth and ears. By the eye, I come into touch with the visible world and its desires; the eyes must be turned away from vanity and be wholly His, to see, or not to see, according to His will. By the ear, I enter into fellowship with my fellow-men. The ear must be consecrated to the Lord and is not to listen to language or conversation that pleases my flesh, but it is to be attentive to the voices which the Lord sends to me. By my mouth, I reveal what is in me, what I think and see and will. By it I exercise an influence over others. My mouth and tongue and lips must be consecrated so that I will not speak anything except what is in accordance with God's will and to His glory.

4. *The Message,* Peterson, Ibid. P.483, 484

5. James Strong, LL.D.,S.T.D. (1822-1894) *The New Strong's Exhaustive Concordance Of The Bible*, (Thomas Nelson Publishers, Hebrew and Chaldee Dictionary, Greek Dictionary, 1990), p. 7, Strong's #25, Agapaō.

6. Zodhiates, *The Hebrew-Greek Key Study Bible*, Lexical Aids To The New Testament, p. 1656.

7. W.E. Vine, *The Expository Dictionary of New Testament Words* (Minneapolis, MN: Bethany House Publishers, 1984 [a Special Edition Keyed to *Strong's Exhaustive Concordance for the Bible*]), P. 693.

8. Murray, Ibid. P.48

IMITATING CHRIST IN OUR PRAYERS

As Imitators of Christ ... we know, speak, and pray His Word with assurance anchored in our hearts. The LORD declared to Jeremiah (29:30) that His "Word is like a fire" and "a hammer that breaks the rock in pieces."

Christ's Word is ... "a lamp to our feet; a light for our path" (Psa.119:105); "the entrance of His words gives light; it gives understanding to the simple" (Psa. 119:130).

The LORD said that ... He is the Way, the Truth, and the Life (John 14:6). Our prayers are to reflect His Way, His Truth, and His Life.

The Psalms teaches us to ... "serve the LORD with fear, and rejoice with trembling" (2:11) and to "be still and know that He is God" (46:10); and "he who has clean hands and a pure heart" ... will "receive blessings from the LORD" (24:4, 5).

We are told to ... "Submit therefore to God, resist the devil and he will flee from you ... Draw near to God and He will draw near to you ... Cleanse your hands you sinners, purify your hearts you double-minded ... Humble yourselves in the presence of the LORD and He will exalt you" (James 4:7-10).

We are to confess ... "your sins to each other and pray for each other so that you may be healed." The prayer of a righteous man is powerful and effective. "The effectual fervent prayers of a righteous man availeth much" (James 2:15).

We are reminded to ... "Lift up holy hands in prayer, without anger or disputing" (1 Ti. 2:8).

We are assured that ... The LORD will guard him and keep him in perfect and constant peace whose mind [both its inclination and character] is stayed upon Him, because he commits himself to the LORD, leans on the LORD, and hopes confidently in the LORD (Isa. 26:3).

We are taught that ... "The Word of God is living and active and sharper than any two-edged sword ... able to judge the thoughts and intentions of the heart' (Heb. 4:12).

We are to begin with the Word of God ... in order to have effectual prayers from Christ's heart. The LORD is our Shepherd, we shall not want ... He will guide us in paths of righteousness for His Name's sake (Psa. 23:1-3).

The LORD declared that ... "My thoughts are not like your thoughts, neither are My ways your ways" (Isa. 55:10); His Word goes out from His mouth and will not return to Him empty, but will accomplish what He desires (v. 11).

Christ resisted the Devil ... Jesus declared to the Devil, "It is written ..." and concluded his declarations with a paraphrase of God's Eternal Word (Matt. 4:4-10).

We are directed to ... "Be steadfast in mind, trust in the LORD... commit yourself to Him, lean on Him, hope confidently in Him forever; the LORD GOD is an everlasting rock ... the *ROCK OF AGES*" (Isa. 26:3, 4).

We are instructed to ... "Finally, be strong in the LORD and in His mighty power." (Eph. 6:10).

We are required to ... "Take up the shield of faith, with which to extinguish all the flaming arrows of the evil one. Take the helmet of salvation and the sword of the Spirit, which is the Word of God" (Eph. 6:10).

We are informed that ... "Our struggle is not against flesh and blood, but against the rulers, against the authorities, against the powers of this dark world and against the spiritual forces of evil in the heavenly realms" (Eph. 6:12).

We are commanded to ... "Put on the full armor of God, so that when the day of evil comes, you may be able to stand your ground ... Stand firm then, with the belt of truth buckled around your waist, with the breastplate of righteousness in place, and with your feet fitted with the readiness that comes from the gospel of peace" (Eph. 6:13-15).

We are exhorted to ... "Pray in the Spirit on all occasions with all kinds of prayers and requests. With this in mind be alert and always keep on praying for all the saints" (Eph. 10:18).

We are to learn that ... "This is good, and pleases God our Savior, who wants all men to be saved and to come to a knowledge of the truth" (1 Ti. 2:3).

We are prompted to ... pray for spiritual leaders "That whenever they open their mouths, words may be given so that they will fearlessly make known the mystery of the gospel, for which they are ambassadors in chains" (Eph. 6:20).

The LORD prayed for His disciples ... "Now they know that everything You have given Me comes from You. For I gave them the words You gave Me and they accepted them ... sanctify them in Thy truth; Your word is truth" (John 17:7, 8, 17).

The LORD asked our Righteous Father ... to give us another Counselor to be with us forever, the Spirit of Truth, to teach us all things and remind us of all that the LORD hath said (John 14:16, 17, 25).

As imitators of Christ ... we go boldly to the throne of grace with confidence to receive mercy and help in our time of need (Heb. 4:16) ... we know, speak and pray His Word with assurance through His Triumph on the Cross, asking our Father to teach us to pray His Living Word for others, and circumstances, that we may prevail over the enemy.

As imitators of Christ ... we pray positive prayers for others, as the LORD prayed:

Father, forgive (name of person), for they know not what they do.
Father, sanctify (name of person) by Thy truth; Your word is truth.
Father, give Your abundant grace and gift of righteousness to (name of person).
Father, may (name of person) trust in the LORD with all their heart and lean not upon their own understanding.

Personalize prayer for others. Imitate the Christ-like prayer in Paul's letter to the Philippians:

Dear LORD, *thank You for* _____. You Who have begun a good work in _____ will continue developing it. _____ is very dear to me (the Word prayed can convict us when our heart is not in the right place. Can we tell the LORD something that is not true, yet should be?). I share Your grace with _____ (we need to be reminded that we *share* it). *Father,* I long with the deep love and affection of Christ for _____'s spiritual companionship (change *my* heart if it's in the wrong place). I pray that _____ may have still more love, a love full of knowledge and every wise insight, and that _____ will recognize the highest and best, and live a sincere and blameless life until Christ comes.

Father, may _____'s life be full of goodness produced by the power of the Holy Spirit, so that _____ will be a credit and a joy to Your praise and glory. May _____'s bondage/s (or mine) be changed so that we will glorify You. May _____'s circumstances turn around so that _____ may become a personal witness of Christ, daily take fresh heart in Christ, and *have courage in the Word of God ...* (excerpts from Philippians One).

We are reminded ... "Faith by itself, if it is not accompanied by action, is dead" (James 2:17).

We are responsible ... "First of all, that requests, prayers, intercession and thanksgiving be made for everyone, for kings and all those in authority". . . that "we may live peaceful and quiet lives in all godliness and holiness" (1 Ti. 2:10).

Our LORD prayed for us:
"Holy Father, keep them in Your care ~ all those You have given Me, so that they will be
united just as We are, with none missing ~ make them pure and holy through teaching them Your
words of truth ~ protect them by the power of Your Name ~ the Name You gave Me ~ that they may
have the full measure of My joy within them"
(John 17:11b, 17-19 Living Bible)

"For you died and your life is now hidden with Christ in God." (Col. 3:3)

To confirm the value of praying the Word
Prepared for the International Bible Reading Association
P.O. Box 1501 ~ Murfreesboro, TN 37133-1501

KNOWING GOD IN YOUR HEART

SERIES III

THE LIFE

LESSONS VII - IX

PREMIER PRAISE

GOD'S PEERLESS NAMES

CHRIST THE PANORAMA OF HEAVEN

Lesson VII

PREMIER PRAISE

*"Blessed are those who have learned to acclaim You,
who walk in the light of Your presence,
They rejoice in Your Name all day long;
they exult in Your righteousness."*

Psalm 89:15, 16

PASSWORDS OF PRAISE

*"Blessed are the people who know the passwords of praise,
Who shout on parade in the bright presence of Yahweh."
Excerpted from Psalm 89*

*"Be good to me, God ~ and now! I've run to you for dear life.
I'm hiding out under your wings until the hurricane blows over.
I call out to High God, the God who holds me together.
He sends orders from heaven and saves me,
He humiliates those who kick me around.*

*God delivers generous love, he makes good on His word.
I find myself in a pride of lions who are wild for a taste of human flesh;
Their teeth are lances and arrows, their tongues are sharp daggers.
They booby-trapped my path; I thought I was dead and done for.
They dug a mantrap to catch me, and fell headlong themselves.*

*I'm ready, God, so ready, ready from head to toe,
Ready to sing, ready to raise a tune:
"Wake up, soul! Wake up, harp! Wake up lute!
Wake up you sleepyhead sun!"*

*I'm thanking you, Yahweh, out loud in the streets,
singing your praises in town and country.
The deeper your love, the higher it goes;
every cloud is a flag to your faithfulness.*

Psalm 57

THE MESSAGE
Eugene H. Peterson

PREMIER PRAISE

*"Blessed are those who have learned to acclaim You,
Who walk in the light of Your presence."
Psalm 89:15*

GOD WHERE ARE YOU? I'M CRACKING UP, I'M BEATEN ~ I've prayed and prayed and nothing's happened ~ "O God! I can't take it anymore!" I sobbed uncontrollably. My pity party was at a full throttle. I couldn't pretend to be grateful about anything! It was the fifth day that our home was without heat in our hardest winter of the twentieth century. I got very little sleep because I needed to keep vigil over the new waterlines to our unfinished addition so they would not freeze.

Devastated, feeling all alone because my husband was out of town, I had to "farm out" our children so they could be warm, bathe, do homework, eat, sleep and live somewhat normally.

Further, my heart was resentful because the owners of the barn, where we boarded Diane's horse, were in Florida enjoying the beaches while I was left behind barn-sitting! The water lines to their barn had frozen below the three-foot line, so several times a day I had to heat gallons upon gallons of water and haul them to the barn. I was at the end of my rope.

I WAS DISCOURAGED, EXHAUSTED, LONELY, HELPLESS, and desperately homesick for both my family and normalcy to return. Hauling the water, "mucking" the horrible smelling stalls and living and sleeping in ski clothes without a bath for four days were minor in comparison to the condition that my heart was in. The "straw that broke this camel's back" was the "mucky" circumstances beyond my control!

The furnace repairman had totally disassembled and reassembled the furnace for four days in a row. He was working downstairs with it torn apart again. Each evening before he left, he told me that he could not understand why it didn't work because he couldn't find anything wrong.

Numbly, I walked to the French doors and stared at the frozen pond. I was reminded that God's Word says not to be anxious about anything, but in everything by prayer and supplication, *with thanksgiving*, to let my requests be made known to Him [Phil. 4:6, 7]. I *knew* that I should count all things joy, but all I could count were *problems upon problems!*

"GOD," I SOBBED, "I'M GOING TO STAND HERE AND THANK YOU UNTIL YOU HELP ME MEAN IT! LORD, CHANGE ME!"

Several years earlier I had read Evelyn Christenson's book *Lord, Change Me!* The truths learned from it once more confronted and challenged my self-righteousness and self-pity.

"*O God!* Have mercy on me," I groaned. *"Sing Hallelujah to the LORD"* began to run through my thoughts and I *knew that I knew* that God wanted me to sing it. I tried, but I could not even articulate "Sing Hallelujah . . ." because I simply choked on the words. I don't know how long I stood there and tried to sing, but gradually, surely, my sobbed words turned from guttural sounds into a song. As I sang on and on, the suffocating heaviness began to lift . . . up to my ankles . . . up to my knees . . . and on upward. My heart grew lighter and lighter as I continued singing. God's Word had proved itself again ~ *the sacrifice of praise* had literally lifted my blind despair up toward God [Heb. 13:15] as I obediently sang, *"Sing Hallelujah to the LORD!"*

The furnace repairman entered the living room and jolted me back to reality when he said, "I don't know what I did that was any different, but this time the furnace started like it should have all along!" When had it started? My hands were warm! I was warm! Joy exploded in my heart ~ *the LORD had intervened!* I know, that I know, that the furnace was repaired as a direct answer to obedience to the command to be *thankful in anxiety* and to *rejoice in Him always* [Phil. 4:4-7].

Reverend Jack R. Taylor wrote in The Hallelujah Factor:

> Hallelujah looks in all directions. It looks backward to salvation commenced and forward to salvation crowned. It looks upward to God enthroned and downward to the devil enchained. It looks inward to fear diminished and faith established. It looks outward to righteousness and readiness. I have one word at this juncture. You might easily guess what it is. You're right. Hallelujah![1]

Singing "Sing Hallelujah to the Lord" actually worked the torturing trials and tribulations right out of *my mind.* God's presence came into my heart in a profound way as my thoughts turned from hopelessness and despair into thoughts of rejoicing and thanksgiving about *Who He Is* and *His awesome eternal worth.* Singing to the LORD, about the LORD was providential. Singing Hallelujah fixed my heart upon *THE ONE* Who is worthy to be praised! [Ps. 57:7-11 KJV] Sing Hallelujah to the LORD!

Reverend Taylor continued:

> Hallelujah seems to be the only response that is reasonable in the light of God's greatness. . . . Hallelujah is inescapably eternal. When we say it, sing it, or shout it we are lining up with eternity . . . Hallelujah brings us to breathe the air of heaven, accords the greatness due God's name, and affords us a view of God as He is and things as they are.[2]

Hallelujah[3] means Praise ye Jah. Jah (Yah) means *Yahweh* in abbreviated form and suggests the presence of God in everyday life and His present activity and oversight on behalf of His own.

> **HERBERT LOCKYER WROTE IN *ALL THE NAMES AND TITLES IN THE BIBLE*:**
> JAH is a shortened form of Jehovah, which though compelled to mention such a name, the transcribers dared not write it in full . . . this name signifies, He *is,* and can be made to correspond to I AM, just as Jehovah corresponds to the fuller expression I AM THAT I AM. The name *Jah* first occurs in the original, in the triumphal Song of Moses, Exodus 15:2. Among the references, the one of Isaiah is suggestive, "Jehovah is Jah, the rock of ages" [Isa. 26:4 KJV], implying that Jehovah is what is meant by Jah, the everliving, eternal one, and so, an everlasting refuge and defense. . . It is affirmed that as Jah is the present tense of the verb "to be," it suggests Jehovah as the PRESENT LIVING GOD ~ the *Presence* of God in daily life, or His *present* activity and oversight on behalf of His own.[4]

IT WAS A BLESSING TO LEARN THAT JAH MEANT THAT YAHWEH IS EVER-LIVING and ever-present in my daily life and I could call upon His Name. One evening that truth was experienced. I was really scared as I rode in an automobile recklessly driven by a relative. I prayed in silent desperation and was led to sing to God in my thoughts His name JAH, to the tune of *"Alleluia" ... "JAH-JAH, JAH-JAH-JAH-JAH-JAH-JAH..."*

I KNOW, THAT I KNOW, THAT JAH HEARD ME CALL UPON HIS NAME! [Ps. 68:4 KJV] Praise God, His presence and power were activated on my behalf. I witnessed my relative's attitude (and driving) take an amazing 180-degree turn! If God can change the hearts of kings, who is mere man before Him? [Gen. 20:1-10] JAH, LORD, proved that I could rest my trust in Him and that He is my refuge and defense. "Thy right hand, O LORD, is majestic in power. Thy right hand, O LORD, shatters the enemy" [Exod. 15:6].

> ***JACK TAYLOR WROTE ABOUT THE WORD HALLELUJAH:***
> Because of the providence of God, I believe, the original word was such in majesty and completeness that instead of being translated, it was transliterated. This means that it is pronounced essentially the same as it was in the original... We have in this marvelous word a combination of two Hebrew words. The first, hallal, means "to boast, to brag on, to laud, to make show, even to the point of looking foolish." The second, "jah," is simply the shortened name for God. Thus Hallelujah became the spontaneous outcry of one excited about God, the exclamation of one upon whose consciousness part of the majesty of God has dawned.[5]

I WONDERED WHY I HAD PREVIOUSLY FOUND IT OFFENSIVE when people exclaimed "Hallelujah!?" Why had it sounded *so "Holier than thou!!!???"* Realizing my self-righteousness, I repented over my attitude and wondered why had I thought that it was acceptable to *sing* "Hallelujah" but not *speak it?* In my ignorance, I did not know that Hallelujah *was* and *is* spoken universally. Hallelujah, Alleluia as some articulate it, is transliterated and pronounced recognizably the same worldwide.

The Greek text renders it Allelouia.

REVEREND TAYLOR WROTE:

> We will discover the word most often used for praise in the Old Testament was *hallal* . . . but now I want to treat a remarkable word derived from hallal, the most commonly used word for praise in our Bible. (It is used some ninety-nine times!)
>
> The word of which I speak is *HALLELUJAH*. The Hebrew word *hallal* forms the first part of this splendid word which I have labeled the premier word for praise. I am told this word has transcended the language barrier among the major languages of the world.[6]

HALLELUJAH TRANSCENDED LANGUAGE BARRIERS. During the Global Consultation On World Evangelization (GCOWE) in Seoul, South Korea, May 16-26, 1995, I was awed when I first heard Hallelujah and Amen transliterated! What an incredible and humbling experience it was to be one of twenty-one delegates for the Women's Mobilization of North America's AD 2000 and Beyond Tract (United States and Canada). We were blessed to be a small part of 186 countries with more than 4,000 delegates worldwide.

We met, learned from one another, repented, prayed and praised the LORD together in our mother tongues. We shared that it must be the way Heaven will be peopled ~ many cultures, races, tongues and creeds ~ *a rainbow of God's glory!* Our praise and worship seemed like a foretaste of Heaven as we heard *Amen* and *Hallelujah* transliterated by people from all over the world. They were so excited about the LORD! It was awesome! It was vital! It was real! They *believed* in God's promises. They *believed* that His Holy Book (that's what our Russian friends called it) speaks truth today as it did when the LORD and His disciples walked on this earth.

WE WERE THRILLED TO HEAR THEM TESTIFY ABOUT THE MIRACLES, revival and restoration happening in their countries and yearned and prayed for God to bring revival to America. They believed God's Word unconditionally and literally. *One man shared that he had stood on the Bible because it said to stand on His Word.* They expected and received miracles upon miracles!

AS DELEGATES, WE WERE INVITED TO BE HONORED GUESTS at Seoul's Olympic Stadium. (We witnessed *80,000 students dedicate themselves to world evangelism.*) They assembled all GCOWE delegates in the center of the field to honor and pray for us. Following South Korea's President Young-Sam Kim's welcome to us, a "wave" erupted with a tremendously thrilling burst of energy that swept around the stadium. We watched and puzzled over what was taking place. It was awesome to behold. Later, when we were seated, the wave happened again and when it passed us, the Koreans around us jumped up spontaneously, arched their arms from the left upward then down to the right in such inexpressible joy, excitedly exclaiming *"Amen ~ Hallelujah!"* In one breathless moment they lifted (hallaled) God's premier word of praise to their heavenly Father. They demonstrated their love as they honored their Savior and LORD!

A.W. TOZER RELATED, IN WHATEVER HAPPENED TO WORSHIP?, an impression that he had when he met a believer from India "who *was neither a label* nor a denomination but was *simply a brother in Christ* who had been born into the Hindu religion." He became a disciple of Jesus Christ by reading and seriously studying the New Testament record of the death and resurrection of our LORD. Reverend Tozer pondered if the day would come when primitive areas will send gospel missionaries to Canada and the United States. He said "unless we arouse ourselves spiritually, unless we are brought back to genuine love and adoration and worship, our candlestick could be removed." He wrote in 1962 that he questioned if we may need missionaries coming to us to show us what genuine and vital Christianity is![7]

GCOWE illustrated that to be different is not wrong. Nor is it sin. We have a lot to learn from our sisters and brothers in the LORD! Later we concurred that we deeply missed being with our global sisters and brothers. Many returned to their communities and churches in deep sorrow when they realized how ineffective and stagnant lives and ministries were in comparison to the vital energetic testimony, worship, and adoration of fellow believers from around the world. The GCOWE international delegates' continual enthusiasm and joy about the LORD was contagious, colorful, convicting and an incredible blessing! Was it a foretaste of Heaven? [Rev. 19:1-6]

When I look back upon that frigid winter of despair, discouragement and helplessness, my thoughts turn to God in deep gratitude and awe for what He did and once more I celebrate that "Hallelujah!" is the premier word of praise [Rev. 19:1-9].

HALLELUJAH IS A HEAVENLY PRAISE THAT HONORS GOD [Ps. 89:5]. Hallelujah, spoken or sung, acclaims the LORD's Sovereign Authority. Hallelujah brings awareness of His love, character and holiness to bring holiness to our hearts to replace *un*righteous thoughts. Hallelujah turns our hearts toward the wedding of the Lamb and His bride [Rev. 19:6-8]. Hallelujah consummates the LORD Jesus Christ as the *Supreme ONE* of the universe ~ *KING of kings* and *LORD of lords* [Rev. 19:16].

HALLELUJAH HALLALS THE SAVIOR we are commanded to boast in! [Ps. 117;

Rom. 13:11]. Let us join the angelic choirs [Rev. 19:1-6] and others around the world and fearlessly, foolishly, joyfully, eagerly boast in Jesus, the Alpha and Omega, *the Triumphant "Amen ~ Hallelujah!"* [Rev. 21:6; 22:13]

I BELIEVE THAT HALLELUJAH INVITES THE LORD'S PRESENCE AND POWER ~ literally all that He is ~ to come and take control of our circumstances. Little did I know that when I sang Hallelujah that freezing morning that it was a *verbal banner* unfurled that proclaimed to the heavenlies that *The Great I AM* was actively involved in my behalf. *"Sing Hallelujah to the LORD"* was the premier song of praise in my circumstances. Obedience in singing praise to His Name, YAH, took me into the highest realm of *offensive* spiritual warfare waged in allegiance to, and faith in, the power of Yahweh's Presence! *Sing Hallelujah to the LORD!*

JAH IS YAHWEH ~ LORD[8] ~ YAHWEH IS THE SIGNIFICANT, sacred, personal Signature Name of the LORD. A few synonyms for signature are logo, stamp, seal, notary, trademark, endorsement, inscription, underwriter. Stop for a moment and celebrate what *Yahweh's matchless, incomparable Signature Name* means for you, and to you. We can further rest our trust in Him when we come to know and understand the inner meaning and message of God's *peerless names* which we will discuss in the next lesson.

> *Dr. Herbert Lockyer wrote*:
>
> All down the ages there has been a disposition to recognize conditions of peculiar blessing as set forth in divine names, seeing that they manifest the glorious virtues of Deity, and also the ever-expanding purposes of the divine Persons themselves. . . There is a great deal in a name, especially if it is the Name above every other name. To the Hebrews of old, the *name* of God meant the revelation of His nature, hence the various Old Testament names are very important as showing the different conceptions of the Deity held by them in the successive stages of revelation. God jealously guarded His successive names, particularly His signature one, *I, Jehovah.*
>
> Among the primitive people, and the ancient Jews were no exception, the name of a deity was regarded as his manifestation, and therefore was treated with the greatest respect and *veneration* ... That God *Himself* sets great store upon His names is evident from the revelation given to Moses [Exod. 6:3]. That He also attached importance to His several names is found in the prohibition not to take any one of them in vain [Exod. 20:7]. Further, it is only as we come to know and understand the inner meaning and message of His peerless names that we can repose our trust in Him [Ps. 9:10].
>
> As we come to classify all His glorious names, may our faith and confidence in Him be strengthened, and may our lives reflect the virtues many of them represent . . . Of this we are confident, that all the grand names of Deity, conspicuous and sublime, will stand, not only in the spacious firmament of time, but also of Eternity. Such names will never be *unsung, unwept, unrecorded, lost and gone.*[9]

JEHOSHAPHAT PRAYED in his hour of desperation because he understood that he faced insurmountable forces [2 Chron. 20]. Then, in obedience to the LORD, he then commanded his people to believe in and to be established in Yahweh. He delegated singers to praise *(hallal)* the beauty of God's holiness. His platoon of singers *led the army into battle hallaling* "Praise the LORD *(Hallal-u-JAH),* for His mercy endureth forever!" [2 Chron. 20:21 KJV] Their verbal banners boisterously proclaimed that God's presence was with them. They *proclaimed* and *acclaimed* His Absolute Sovereignty. They established their thoughts *in* the LORD, announced their fidelity *to* the LORD, and identified themselves *with* the Highest Authority of all creation ~ *Absolute YAH!*

    THE LORD SET AMBUSHES AND SMOTE THE ENEMY when they began to sing and praise His Name. The LORD's manifested presence and active involvement came as a direct answer to their obedience, prayers, confessions, acknowledged defenselessness and praises to Yahweh. Yahweh was faithful to His Covenant that when His people were in distress, returned to the LORD their God, and listened to His voice, He would not fail them, destroy them, nor forget His covenant with their fathers [Deut. 4:29-31]. Paul and Silas were praying and singing hymns of praise to God in prison when suddenly an earthquake opened the doors and unfastened their chains [Acts 16:24-26]. *A coincidence?*

    Standing broken in front of the French doors that frigid day, the Holy Spirit led me to audibly acclaim Hallelujah as a verbal banner. His help came after I called upon the Name of the LORD! [Ps. 124:8] I sang a hymn of premier praise to Yahweh and He set me free! *A coincidence?*

    SOON AFTERWARD, THE HOLY SPIRIT BEGAN TO TEACH me through the Word to exalt the LORD's Name by praising His manifold, multifaceted character. Praise God, the Word gave light and understanding to this simple child [Deut. 4:29-31]. Our Sovereign King Jesus, the Yahweh of creation, transcends all barriers to unfold understanding and precious truths ~ even to the simple who seek Him [Ps. 119:130]. The LORD proved that He is not partial nor a respecter of persons and that He does not show favoritism [Rom. 2:11].[10]

    The Holy Spirit led me to Exodus 3:14 where God answered Moses, "My Name is Yahweh. *This is My Name forever and this is My Memorial Name to all generations"* [Exod. 3:13-15]. That really puzzled me! If God, Himself, said that Yahweh was His *Memorial* Name, why didn't I hear anyone say it? Why didn't we acclaim, exalt, memorialize or even allude to *Yahweh when God's Word said it is Jesus' Memorial Name?*

    WHEN HAD WE LOST RECOGNITION OF HIS MEMORIAL NAME? His Signature Name? The question triggered a biblical search to find out when and why we stopped calling the LORD Yahweh.

AMAZINGLY, I COULD NOT FIND ONE PLACE IN SCRIPTURE where the LORD even intimated that His Memorial Name was to be declared null and void or terminated. Encyclopedias, lexicons and various books explained how it evolved. Tradition and biblical history teach that the Scribes and Pharisees (man, not god) declared that Yahweh was "too holy" to be written or pronounced. They must have been influenced by the enemy when they substituted *YHWH* and instructed readers when reading YHWH to pronounce "Adonai" in lieu of Yahweh. The LORD's *self-proclaimed* Memorial Name. His Signature Name lost recognition.

DAVID STERN WROTE IN THE JEWISH NEW TESTAMENT COMMENTARY:
Long before Yeshua's day, however, the word "Adonai" had, out of respect, been substituted in speaking and in reading aloud for God's personal name, the four Hebrew letter yud-heh-vav-heh, variously written in English as "YHVH" "Yahweh," and "Jehovah." The Talmud made it a requirement not to pronounce the Tetragrammaton (the word means the "four-letter name" of God), and this remains the rule in most modern Jewish settings. (The Greek word here is "kurios," which can mean (1) "sir," (2) "lord" in the human sense, as in "lord of the manor," (3) "LORD" in the divine sense, or (4) God's personal name YHVH.)[11]

PRAISE GOD! THE LORD JESUS CHRIST CAME TO EXPLAIN GOD'S GRACE and truth to us [John 1:16-18]. Jesus scolded the religious leaders for complicating Scripture because they had neutralized, nullified and annulled the simplicity of God's Word [Luke 11:39-44]. As a consequence God's people have not been taught *to call upon,* or *hallal,* His name *YAHWEH.* God's people have been robbed of blessing, appropriating, worshiping, and calling upon His Chosen Personal Name . . .

. . . *to know as His Memorial and Signature Name;*
. . . *to keep us mindful of His absolute authority, worth and esteem;*
. . . *to remember our identity with Him;*
. . . *to remind us of His covenant;*
. . . *to confirm His defense of His people in times of trouble;*
. . . *to testify to His ever expanding purposes;*
. . . *to love and reverence in our hearts;*
. . . *to proclaim that Jesus Christ is LORD!*

A SHORT TIME LATER IN JUNE OF 1987, I chanced upon an article in the *READERS DIGEST* about YAHWEH which was entitled *THE MYSTERY OF THE BURIED AMULET.*[12] The article reported a discovery made by Gabriel Barkay in 1973 that prompted digs that began in 1975. (By 1979, nine burial caves were uncovered from the First Temple period [Solomon's Temple].)

JUDITH HADLEY OF TOLEDO, OHIO *(A GRADUATE ASSISTANT)* discovered *"a silver cylinder that looked like a cigarette butt."* It turned out to be the discovery of the first of two silver bits uncovered that were rolled tightly in cylinders and were amulets that were worn by ancient Israelites. Although Barkay was convinced that they contained writing, it took several years before a technique could be developed that allowed them to protectively unroll the amulets. According to the *READERS DIGEST* when they were able to look inside they discovered faint etchings of ancient Hebrew letters. The article reported:

> In the basement laboratory of the Israel Museum in Jerusalem, Gabriel Barkay stared through a microscope at four Hebrew letters ~ Y H W H ~ etched on a tiny silver scroll. "Yahweh," he said softly. The name of God, "Jehovah" as others pronounce it, had ~ for the first time ~ been found on an ancient object in the holy city of three great religions.

THE AMULET'S CONTENTS REMAINED A MYSTERY UNTIL 1986 when Ada Yardeni, Jewish graphic artist and expert on ancient scripts, found the key ~ it was Aaron's Priestly Benediction with God's Memorial Name, YHWH, inscribed three times [Num. 6:24-27]. Although it had not been spoken out loud for centuries, Barkay softly said "Yahweh."

FOLLOWING BELOW IS AARON'S PRIESTLY BLESSING, copied directly from the *READERS DIGEST* with Yahweh inserted for YHWH. Hopefully, it will give an inkling of the exhilaration that was surely felt by Barkay, Judith, Ada and all involved, when the contents of the discovery were concluded:

> *"Yahweh bless you and keep you;*
> *Yahweh make His face to shine upon you*
> *and be gracious unto you;*
> *Yahweh lift up his countenance upon you,*
> *and grant you peace."*

YAHWEH CONCLUDED AARON'S PRIESTLY BENEDICTION, "So they shall invoke My name on the sons of Israel, and I then will bless them." [Num. 6:27] Names are very important to God![13]

GOD'S PROCLAIMED NAMES and descriptions of Himself tell us how His character, authority, and power were manifested in behalf of His people in the past. When we proclaim, pray, or *call upon His Name* in believing faith, we establish His banner of Divine Glory and His Presence as the Authority that we have entrusted to settle our concerns. When we call upon His Living Memorial Name, Yahweh, *we invite* His Righteousness and ever expanding purposes *to intervene*.

"SING HALLELUJAH TO THE LORD" entreats God's Sovereign participation.

WHEN WE SUBMIT OUR THOUGHTS AND WORDS TO GOD AND RESIST negative thoughts from the enemy's realm, by replacing them with God's higher thoughts, we invite and permit the Spirit of Christ to protect, instruct, and guide our lives [James 4:7-8]. Had I remained in that pit of self-pity after four traumatic days of blaming everyone and everything, including the furnace repairman, for my misfortune and misery, my attitude and behavior would have *continued* to invite, invoke and support the enemy's influence and harassment. Providentially, my angry thoughts were miraculously transformed into praises of God's Majesty. *Hallelujah!*

Studying the LORD's Names introduces a deeper awareness of God's love, character, attributes and nature. It magnifies the Word in a totally fresh way that intensifies our awareness of what is true and what is false. His Names implant an intimate biblical understanding of the LORD and our Triune God's ways into our hearts in such a way that we can only adore and worship Him.

OUR WORSHIP REFLECTS HIS AWESOMENESS BACK TO HIM the way a mirror reflects an image back to its viewer. We soon find ourselves exalting His awesomeness and telling Him of His goodness. Our love and admiration culminates in humility, repentance and heartfelt gratitude for all that He has done and Who He is. We become more secure in the LORD when we spend time sitting at His Holy feet, studying His nature, responding in obedience to His guidance and exalting Him in our worship [Ps. 18:3]. An additional protection is that the enemy cannot bear to be in the presence of God's worshipers when they embrace and enjoy His presence. Worshiping the LORD brings restoration.

This is a serious time. We must *discern our thoughts and actions,* along with conversations or actions of other people [Phil. 1:10], recognize the *enemy's tactics* and *counterfeits* of God's ways and principles. Ignorance, apathy, hoping it will not happen, or "sticking our head in the sand," will not protect us, or our families, or give us victory over our flesh or the enemy. We cannot fight an enemy if we are ignorant of his ways. We need to recognize the enemy's plots "lock in God's smart bombs," deflect, polarize and vaporize the enemy's missiles and destroy his objectives.

IT HAS BEEN SAID THAT WHAT WE WORSHIP IS WHAT WE BECOME, what we *think* is what we are and what we *believe* reveals itself in our lives! That is why we need to believe in and learn about God ~ His character, His ways and how He would have us think, worship and reflect His fullness in our lives. A good way to do that it is to study His Names.

THIS LESSON NOT ONLY FOCUSES ON PRAISING GOD, which is paramount, but it also needs to recognize that there are praises meant for the enemy that can be made by innocent or purposeful people. Universally, thinkers from antiquity have believed that the pronunciation of the name of any god will cause him to appear and his force (power) to operate (manifest). The name spoken is the *audible form* ~ banner, memorial, mark, sign ~ of a pagan god whose evil fruits are called upon to manifest with power. Satanically inspired chants are literally counterfeit verbal banners that call upon false gods and their underlings to actively manifest their personalities, characteristics and attributes. In other words, pagans believe that their acclamations, their chants and proclamations call out to a spiritual force ~ the god of the whole universe, visible and invisible ~ to unleash a physical force of unrighteousness.[14]

ACCORDINGLY, BELIEVERS NEED TO BE CONCERNED ABOUT THE WORD AUM. It is highly used by the enemy's followers, deceived devotees, and oblivious unmindful persons as they align themselves with anti-Christ forces. The word Aum, or OM, used in exercises, video games, articles, advertisements, commercials, commerce, and so forth, is a Hindu word, a name (unholy word) that is intentionally proclaimed and acclaimed by the devil's disciples.

Aum, is Satan's *supreme premier name.* Cultists, even uninformed people, use Aum to meditate or relax the mind into a trance state as they chant, acclaim, invoke, exalt and proclaim the universal verbal banner of Satan. Aum, OM, glorifies Satan as "I am" and calls his presence and demonic spirits into activity.[15] See endnote.[16] Research established aum is also the verbal banner chanted to Kali, Shiva, and their cultural or mythological counterparts to call down and/or invoke manifestations of Lucifer as "I am."[17]

SIMILARLY, THEY BELIEVE THAT LUCIFER IS SAID TO BE NEITHER EVIL NOR GOOD. They also believe that he simply *is* and *formerly* was a destroyer, but Lucifer now becomes a god ~ perhaps the god chosen to shepherd mankind into the brightness of a New Age. He is Shiva and Kali of the New Age.[18]

Aum, the enemy's counterfeit title for Yahweh, *The Great "I AM"* [Exod. 3:14, 15], is undeniably the imitation *name* for god that the majority chant to invoke the devil's evil forces. Hindu yoga, shamanistic mantras, chants, prayers and fasting are made to empty the mind and in turn it simply opens the mind to multitudes of unrighteous gods, goddesses, spirit guides, etc., worldwide.

BOB LARSON WROTE IN LARSON'S NEW BOOK OF CULTS (REVISED 1989):

A major text on yoga states, "The aim of all yoga is the realization of the Absolute Brahman." The God of yoga is an impersonal deity who pervades the universe as an *energy force*. Hindu belief teaches that God (Brahman) is unknowable, inexplicable, and at the same time present in all living things. Sometimes Brahman is referred to as the Universal Being, the Supreme Absolute, or Pure Consciousness. Whatever the name, his manifestation to men is known through the Hindu god Shiva. And it is Shiva, the Hindu divinity who is the manifestation of destruction, who plays an integral part in the practice of yoga.[19]

THE BABYLONIANS OF ANTIQUITY CHANTED the *same names and words* that are commonly heard today on television, in advertisements, programs, cartoons, video games, mind techniques, programs, some school curriculums, fraternal symbols, etc. The *mantra's* are a product right out of Satan's dominion.

For instance, when New Agers and occultists meditate and chant to Kali, the goddess of destruction, and wife of Shiva whom they believe to be the god of the universe, they verbally declare, proclaim, decree and invoke destruction and unrighteousness into the physical realm. The power of agreement *prevails* whether for righteous or unrighteous forces! God used *His principle of agreement* to create this universe and to confuse the Babylonians! [Gen. 11:7] Didn't the LORD say, "And this is what they began to do, and now nothing which they purpose to do will be impossible for them [withheld from them]?" [Gen. 11:6] Agreement is destructive or constructive!

THE "LITTLE GODS" PAGANS VERBALLY CHANT, PRAY, AND FAST TO are *counterfeit* names, *generic* names, mantras to rally unrighteous spirits that operate under Satan's authority! Pagans are diligent and dedicated in calling forth, invoking and praying for the false gods or evil spirits to manifest into the physical realm.

Dungeons and Dragons, some video games that can reprogram the brain to maim and kill, even some exercises that orally speak out and evoke the little god's names (Om or Aum, etc.), are a few examples of the deadly games that use Babylonian and mythological names, etc., to unfurl verbal banners of unholiness and unrighteousness. Participants are assigned activities, which in reality are curses, omens, and spells that they are to act out or speak forth. *They are real!* They are *dangerous* counterfeits of the LORD's Eternal Absolute Truth. The LORD commanded us to *leave* them *alone!* [Exod. 22:18; Lev. 19:31].

A GOOD EXAMPLE IS THE RELIGIOUS EXTREMISTS AND RADICALS that pray and verbally proclaim verses of the Koran to Allah five times a day to release destructive forces against believers and others that do not agree with their theology. Other religions also chant their beliefs. Do we pray enough? Do we proclaim God's authority enough to reverse the enemy's designs and defeat his evil purposes?

WE MUST COUNTERMAND THE ENEMY'S DEMONIC COUNTERFEIT mantra's, prayers, invocations, Harmonic Convergences, curses, omens and spells, etc., *by declaring, decreeing, proclaiming, and acclaiming the verbal banners of truth that JESUS CHRIST IS LORD!* We need to declare our belief that the ONE TRUE GOD, *Yahweh Yeshua H'Maschiah,* is the Sovereign Eternal and Absolute *"I AM"*. We need to launch verbal banners about Yahweh's eternal Triumph at the Cross. We need to proclaim that the LORD Jesus' power and authority triumphs over every stronghold that influences the lives of our loved ones, churches, governments and the world.

THE NAMES OF GOD ARE HIS GENUINE NAMES! We need to proclaim His Names and Scripture verses *often* to countermand Satan's counterfeit names and curses. We should include both calling upon Jesus' Name and His original genuine Hallowed Names to countermand the evil forces. Our children and grandchildren need to be protected and *snatched back from the snares of Satan.* Are we looking away while our children are overcome by the New Age evils that are taught in many schools under the guise of science, counseling and health? We, without exception, will stand before our LORD and be accountable.

WE MUST BE OFFENSIVE, proclaim His Names, and pray fervent, righteous Holy Spirit inspired prayers to undermine the enemy's strategies to capture our families.

WE NEED TO BE AWARE OF THE TIMES WE LIVE IN. If some within a prayer group/s would read accurate reports, books, periodicals or newsletters (and *at the proper time* share documented truths), then seek God to lead them in His prayers, churches could wake up and claim many lost souls. Many have sacrificed at great personal cost to alert and activate Christians to stand up to be counted and involved. Highly documented books, literature, broadcasts, etc., help Christians recognize the heinous forces unleashed on our families, marriages, churches, tragically our children. There are excellent Christian Magazines and periodicals that print timely articles.

INCIDENTALLY, A FEW ORGANIZATIONS that have regular broadcasts or send out newsletters to inform and give timely prayer topics are: Intercessors For America, Focus on the Family, Concerned Women for America, Eagle Forum, The Christian World Report, The WallBuilder Report, Capitol Hill Prayer Partners, Family Talk, American Family Association, etc. Be wise, sensitive and informed. We need not agree with one another's theology to utilize their timely information when the source is accountable. Like Paul, we are to pray with our spirit and our mind [1 Cor. 14:15].

THIS LESSON POINTED OUT WHY IT IS ESSENTIAL TO REVERSE THE ENEMY'S INROADS. GOD'S CHILDREN ARE EMPOWERED AND COMMANDED TO COMBAT UNRIGHTEOUSNESS and to establish His authority on earth as it is in Heaven. Satan's deceived, or unaware followers, are enunciating mantras or proclaiming ungodly names or unholy verses that call evil spirits from the heavenly spheres to establish curses and Satan's influence into our sphere! [Matt. 10:16] We must be diligent to spend as much time as the enemy's minions spend *by calling upon ~ hallaling, invoking, proclaiming, establishing ~ the righteous influence personified in the Name of the LORD!*

I am eternally grateful that the presence of the LORD's love manifested itself in my heart before the furnace was repaired! I am fully convinced that the furnace did not work until my full attention turned to the LORD and His Name was hallaled. Praise be to our LORD Jesus Christ, the Holy Spirit turned my tears of despair and repentance into a song of joy that called upon His Name, rejoiced, celebrated and blessed His exalted Name that endures forever [Ps. 135:13].

GOD'S INSTRUMENT OF PRAYER AND PRAISE RESTORED MY HEART AND HOME. It required sincere confession, brokenness, surrendered grief, repentance and an obedient heart determined to give thanks to the LORD by *singing "Sing Hallelujah to the LORD"* in spite of overwhelming circumstances, until the song that He put in my heart turned despair into a song of praise.

> *It was . . .*
> *a song that rose from the pits of my heart.*
> *a song that cried out to Him to end the unbearable burdens [Prov. 18:10].*
> *a song that invited His presence to be revealed.*
> *a song that looked inward to my fear and established faith in its place.*
> *a song that beamed the Light of His hope and love upon my head.*
> *a song that enabled me to walk out of the tunnel of darkness and despair [Job 29:3].*
> *a song that called out to His love.*
> *a song that embraced the heights of His mercy and grace.*
> *a song that restored my soul.*
> *a song that boisterously sang praises to Yahweh.*
> *a song that decreed "Let God arise and His enemies be scattered!" [Ps. 68:1]*
> *a song that called upon the Name of the LORD . . .*

"SING HALLELUJAH TO THE LORD!"

VII ~ PREMIER PRAISE   PAGE 15

LIFE APPLICATION

1. What does God's word tell us to do when discouraged, anxious and in turmoil? (P. 1)

2. A. Define Hallelujah and JAH. B. What happened when the author was scared while riding in an automobile and inwardly sang "JAH" in her thoughts? (PP. 2, 3)

3. A. What does transliterate mean? B. What two Hebrew words are transliterated universally? (P. 3)

4. What is the premier word of praise to the LORD? (P. 4)

5. What does the name Yahweh mean? (P. 6)

6. A. What did Jehoshaphat and his people do before battle? [2 Chron. 20] B. How did God respond? Personal ~ Should we follow their examples in our battles? (PP. 6, 7)

7. A. What did the Holy Spirit lead the author to audibly acclaim when she stood broken that frigid morning before French doors? B. What happened? (P. 7)

8. Why did His Memorial Name lose recognition? (P. 8)

9. A. How is YHWH spoken by Jewish People? B. Explain why Jewish people use Adonai. (P. 8)

10. A. How was Aaron's Priestly Benediction concluded? B. What do God's Proclaimed Names describe? (P. 9)

11. A. Why do we submit our thoughts and words to God? B. We invite and permit the _____ of _____ to protect, instruct, and guide our thoughts and our lives. (P. 10)

12. Why must we discern our thoughts and actions along with the conversations or actions of other people? (P. 10)

13. A. Whose name does Aum or OM represent? B. What will chanting acclaiming, invoking, exalting and proclaiming Aum, the universal banner of Satan, cause? (P. 11)

14. A. Curses, omens, and spells are _____ . They are _____ of the LORD's Truth. B. The LORD commands us to _____ them _____ . (P. 12)

15. A. How should believers' countermand counterfeit pagan chants, etc.? B. Name some ways. C. What must our offensives be? (P. 13)

16. What are God's instruments of prayer and praise that restores our hearts? (P. 14)

17. What are some ways to lift our hearts from despair to praise? (P. 14)

PREMIER PRAISE SCRIPTURE SEQUENCES

Page 1
Ps. 89:15 ["Blessed are those who have learned to acclaim You, Who walk in the light of Your presence."]
Phil. 4:6, 7 [Do not be anxious about anything, but in everything, by prayer and petition, with thanksgiving, present your requests to God. And the peace of God, which transcends all understanding, will guard your hearts and your minds in Christ Jesus.]

Page 2
Heb. 13:15 [Through Jesus, therefore, let us continually offer to God a sacrifice of praise ~ the fruit of our lips that confess His Name.]
Phil. 4:6,7 [Be not anxious about anything, with thanksgiving make your requests to God]
Ps. 57:7 [My heart is steadfast, O God . . . I will sing and make music]

Page 3
Exod. 15:2 [Song of Moses]
Isa. 26:4 NASB [Trust in the LORD forever, for the LORD, the YAH, is the Rock eternal]
Ps. 68:4 [Sing to God, sing praise to His name, extol Him who rides on the clouds ~ His Name is the LORD ~ and rejoice before Him.]
Gen. 20:10 [Abraham's treachery]
Exod. 15:6 [Thy right hand, O LORD, is majestic in power. Thy right hand, O LORD, shatters the enemy.]

Page 5
Rev. 10:1-6 [After this I looked and there before me was a great multitude that no one could count, from every nation, tribe, people and language, standing before the throne and in front of the Lamb.]
Rev. 19:1-9 [Multitudes in heaven shout: Hallelujah! . . . for our LORD God Almighty reigns . . . these are the true words of God.]
Ps. 89:5 [The heavens praise your wonders, O LORD, Your faithfulness too, in the assembly of the holy ones.]
Rev. 19:6-8 [Let us rejoice and be glad . . . for the wedding of the Lamb has come, and His bride has made herself ready.]
Rev. 19:16 [The King of kings and LORD of lords]
Ps. 117 [Praise the LORD all you nations; extol Him all you peoples. For great is His love toward us, and the faithfulness of the LORD endures forever.]

Page 6
Rom. 15:11 [Praise the LORD all you Gentiles, and sing praises to Him, all you peoples.]
Rev.19:1-3 [Hallelujah! Salvation and glory and power belong to our God, for true and just are His judgments . . . and again they shouted: "Hallelujah! The smoke goes up from her forever."]
Rev. 21:6 ["I AM the Alpha and the Omega, the Beginning and the End.]
Rev. 22:13 [I Am the Alpha and the Omega, the First and the Last, the Beginning and the End.]
Exod. 6:3 ["I am the LORD, I appeared to Abraham, to Isaac and to Jacob, as God Almighty (El Shaddai), but by My name the LORD, I did not make Myself known to them."]
Exod. 20:7 ["You shall not misuse the name of the LORD your God, for the LORD will not hold anyone guiltless who misuses His name."]
Ps. 9:10 [Those who know Your name will trust in You, for You, LORD, have never forsaken those who seek You.]
2 Chron. 20 [God's battle plan is believer's high praise ~ The LORD set ambushments against the enemy and they were smitten ~ because of their praise and obedience]

Page 7
2 Chron. 20:21 KJV [Singers praised (hallaled loudly) the beauty of His holiness as they led forth the army]
Deut. 4:29-31 [Seek the LORD ~ search with all your heart to find Him; return to the LORD; listen to His voice. He is compassionate; He will not fail you, destroy you, nor forget the covenant sworn to your fathers]

Page 7 (continued)

Reference	Content
Acts 16:24-26	[Songs of praise brought forth rescue energized through an earthquake]
Ps. 124:8	[Our help is in the Name of the LORD, the Maker of heaven and earth.]
Deut. 4:29-31	[Seek the LORD ~ search with all your heart to find Him; return to the LORD; listen to His voice ~ He is compassionate; He will not fail you, destroy you, nor forget the covenant He swore to your fathers]
Ps. 119:130	[The unfolding of Thy words gives light ~ it gives understanding to the simple]
Rom. 2:11	[For God does not show favoritism.]
Exod. 3:14	[MY NAME is YAHWEH ~ "I AM"]
Exod. 3:15	[This is MY NAME FOREVER ~ His memorial name to all generations]

Page 8

Reference	Content
John 1:16-18	[Jesus explains God to us]
Luke 11:39-44	[Jesus scolds the religious leaders]

Page 9

Reference	Content
Num. 6:24-26	[The LORD bless you and keep you; the LORD make His face to shine upon you and be gracious to you; the LORD turn His face toward you and give you peace.]
Num. 6:27	[So they will put My Name on the Israelites, and I will bless them.]

Page 10

Reference	Content
James 4:7.8	[Submit yourselves, then, to God. Resist the devil, he will flee from you. Come near to God and He will come near to you. Wash your hands, you sinners, and purify your hearts, you double-minded.]
Ps. 18:3	[Call upon the Who is worthy to be praised, & we shall be saved from our enemies!]

Page 11

Reference	Content
Exod. 3:14, 15	[God said to Moses, "'I AM Who I AM.' This is what you are to say . . . 'I AM has sent me to you.'"]

Page 12

Reference	Content
Gen. 11:7	["Come, let us go down and confuse their language so they will not understand each other."]
Gen. 11:6	[The LORD said, "If as one people speaking the same language they have begun to do this, then nothing they plan to do will be impossible for them."]
Exod. 22:18	[You shall not allow a sorceress to live]
Lev. 19:31	[Do not turn to mediums or spiritists; so do not seek them out and be defiled by them]

Page 13

Reference	Content
1 Cor. 14:15	[Pray with the mind also]

Page 14

Reference	Content
Matt. 10:16	[. . . Therefore, be as shrewd as snakes and as innocent as doves.]
Ps. 135:13	[Your Name O LORD, endures forever, Your renown, O LORD, throughout all generations.]
Prov. 18:10	[The Name of the LORD is a strong tower; the righteous run to it and are safe.]
Job 29:2, 3	[. . . when God watched over me, when His lamp shone on my head and by his light I walked through darkness.]
Ps. 68:1	[Let God Arise, let His enemies be scattered!]

PREMIER PRAISE ENDNOTES

1. Jack R. Taylor, *The Hallelujah Factor*, (Nashville, TN: 1983, Broadman Press, 1983), p. 80.

2. Ibid PP.74,75

3. W. E. Vine, M.A., *An Expository Dictionary of New Testament Words*, (Iowa Falls, IA: Riverside Book and Bible House), p. 520, Hallelujah signifies 'Praise ye Jah.' Alleluia, without the initial H, is a misspelling.

4. Herbert Lockyer, *All the Divine Names and Titles In The Bible*, (Grand Rapids, MI: Lamplighter Books, Zondervan Publishing House, 1975), p. 17.

5. Taylor, P.71

6. Ibid. P.80

7. Tozer, *Whatever Happened To Worship?*, (Camp Hill, PA: Christian Publications), pp. 81-82.

8. *Master Study Bible* ~ See *TO KNOW GOD*, Endnote #5, Principles of Translation.

9. Lockyer, P.1, 2

10. Martin Lloyd-Jones, *Saved In Eternity*, (Westchester, IL: Crossway Books).

    P.89: In this matter of recognition of the Lord Jesus Christ we are all exactly on a level, we are all in the same position. The greatest brain is never big enough to understand and grasp it, but the Holy Spirit can enable the most ignorant and the most unintelligent to understand.

11. David H. Stern, *Jewish New Testament Commentary*, (Clarksville, MD: Jewish New Testament Publications), p. 4.

12. Claire Safran, *The Reader's Digest*, pp. 95-99.

13. Ibid. P.45 The many names of God in Scripture provide additional revelation of His character. These are not mere titles assigned by people but, for the most part, His own descriptions of Himself. As such they reveal aspects of His character.

    Joseph Campbell, *The Masks of God: Primitive Mythology*, (New York, NY: Viking Penguin, Inc., 1959).

14. P.85: In the Hebrew Kabbala, for example, the sounds and forms of the letters of the Hebrew alphabet are regarded as the very elements of reality, so that by correctly pronouncing the names of things, of angels, or even of God, the competent Kabbalist can make use of their force. The pronunciation of the name of God (YHVH), indeed, has always been guarded with great care. In ancient times the sages communicated the pronunciation of the name to their disciples only once in seven years. A scribe inditing biblical scrolls was required to place his mind in a devotional attitude when writing the name of God, and if he made an error in the name, in certain cases the mistake was irremediable and the whole column on which the error occurred had to be withdrawn from use; for the name itself could not be erased.

Comparably, in mystical disciplines of the Indian Tantric tradition, where not Hebrew but Sanskrit is regarded as the primal language of the universe, the pronunciation of the name of any god will cause him to appear and his force to operate, since the name is the audible form of the god himself. The supreme Word, of which the whole universe visible and invisible is the manifestation, is in the Indian tradition the syllable *AUM*.

15. Ibid. P.277 *Book Endnote 25*

16. Texe Marrs, *Dark Secrets Of The New Age*, Satan's Plan For a One World Religion, (Westchester, IL: Crossway Books, [division of Good News Publishers], 1987).

   P. 114 Unholy Words ~ During meditation the New Age believer often uses a mantra, a mystical holy word of power, to invoke the demon spirit guide to come. A mantra also serves to relax the mind into a trance state. Elizabeth Clare Prophet's Church Universal and Triumphant teaches "that the repeated chanting of a mantra "magnetizes" the "Presence" whom the meditator desires to communicate with. The magic word recommended is *aum* in Sanskrit (Hindu) or *I am* in English." Prophet also says that this is the word originally used to command the universe into existence.

   In the article "OM: The Sacred Syllable and Its Role in World Peace," in the New Age publication *Life Times*, Winter 1986-87, (P.35), the author states, "He who meditates on OM attains to Brahman (God). Hindus and Tibetan Buddhists have consciously used the *power of OM* for centuries, especially chanting OM while sitting in the configuration of a circle . . . OM is sometimes also pronounced AUM."

   P.114 (Book endnote #23, P.277: Mark and Elizabeth Prophet, The Science of the Spoken Word [Colorado Springs, CO: Summit University Press, 1974], pp. i, ii, 12, 13).

17. Ibid. P.85

18. Ibid. P.87

19. Bob Larson, *Larson's New Book of CULTS*, (Wheaton, IL: Tyndale House Publishers, 1989). p. 474.

PURSUE GOD'S NAMES

L̇ᴏʀᴅ (O.T.), (all small caps) YAHWEH, YEHOVAH,
(Strong's #3068) KURIOS, CHRIST JESUS in O.T.

Lord (O.T.), (ord, small case) ADONAI, GOD ALMIGHTY,
(Strong's #136) DIVINE TITLE

GOD (O.T.), (all upper case) YAHWEH, YEHOVAH,
(Strong's #3068) CHRIST JESUS in O.T.

God (O.T.), (od, small case) ELOHIM, HOLY TRIUNE GOD,
(Strong's #430) MAJESTIC DEITY

GOD MOST HIGH (Strong's #5945) EL YON, SUPREME

SABAOTH (Strong's #6635) GOD OF HOSTS

EL SHADDAI (Strong's #7706) ALMIGHTY GOD

IMMANUEL, EMMANUEL, from EL GOD WITH US (EL)
(Strong's #410)

Lᴏʀᴅ NISSI (Strong's #5251) BANNER, STANDARD, SIGN,

AB, ABBA (Strong's #1 FATHER, OUR SOURCE,
  DADDY

MESSIAH (Strong's #4899) THE CHRIST, ANOINTED, Lᴏʀᴅ,
  CHOSEN ONE, CREATIVE POWER
  PASSOVER LAMB, CONSECRATED

YESHUA, YESHUWAH (Strong's #3444) JESUS, YAHWEH IS SALVATION,
  DELIVERANCE, LION OF JUDAH,
  VICTORY, HELP, Lᴏʀᴅ
  MESSIAH, WORD OF GOD, THE AMEN

LAMB OF GOD (Strong's #3532) JESUS' MESSIANIC TITLE
  SON OF MAN, KING OF KINGS,
  SUFFERING SERVANT

Let every tongue confess that:

YESHUA H' MACHIACH IS YAHWEH, TO THE GLORY OF ELOHIM, THE AB (Phil. 2:9-11)
Amen!

This is a limited rendition. Strong's Exhaustive Concordance can be used to study the Lᴏʀᴅ's many NAMES. It identifies His Names by number and includes both Hebrew and Greek Dictionaries. Other lexicons are numerically coded to Strong's and can be used as well. It will bless you to record your impressions in a notebook.

Lesson VIII

GOD'S PEERLESS NAMES

*"Praise the LORD.
Sing to the LORD a new song,
His praise in the assembly of His faithful people."*

Psalm 149:1

GOD'S PEERLESS NAMES

Oh my soul, bless God.
From head to toe, I'll bless His holy name!
Oh my soul, bless God, don't forget a single blessing!
He forgives your sins ~ every one.
He heals your diseases ~ every one.
He redeems you from hell ~ saves your life!
He crowns you with love and mercy ~ a paradise crown.

He wraps you in goodness ~ beauty eternal.
He renews your youth ~ always young in His presence.
God's love, though, is ever and always,
eternally present to all who fear Him,
Making everything right for them and their children
as they follow His Covenant ways
and remember to do what He said.

God has set His throne in heaven;
He rules over us all. He's the King!
So bless God, you angels, ready and able to fly at His bidding,
quick to hear and do what He says.

Bless God, all you armies of angels,
alert to respond to whatever He wills.
Bless God, all creatures, wherever you are,
everything and everyone made by God.
And you, oh my soul, bless God!

Excerpts from Psalm 103
THE MESSAGE
Eugene H. Peterson

Bless the LORD, O my soul;
And all that is within me, bless His Holy Name.

Psalm 103:1

GOD'S PEERLESS NAMES

*"O, LORD, they rejoice in Your name all day long,
they exult in Your Righteousness,
for You are their glory and strength,
and by Your favor You exalt our horn."*
Psalm 89: 16, 17 NIV

IT WAS A BEAUTIFUL AUGUST DAY IN 1988 when I got in the car to leave the produce stand. Suddenly, the world around me grew fuzzy and I fainted. When I came to, I saw two men talking and gesturing toward me, so I motioned for help. They laughed at me. I was frightened, foggy and drained of energy. Not knowing what to do or where to turn, I realized that it took less strength to drive the car home than to open the door for help, so I put the emergency hazard lights on and began driving at a snail's pace along the berm. This happened before I had a cell phone.

The fainting spell started again and I stopped the car in time. When consciousness returned, a woman was standing in front of the car, next to her mail box, mumbling and vigorously shaking her finger at me. She abruptly turned away and crossed the street. Did she think I was drunk?

Alone and petrified, I cried out would *anyone* help me? Once more I started the car and crept slowly along the berm with my hazard lights blinking ~ once more I fainted. The fainting spells happened four more times before I was able to pull into the entry to our condominium and passed out. Judy, my neighbor, found me and got others to help carry me from the car to my bed. They used the garage door opener to get me in the house.

GENE CAME HOME AND THOUGHT THAT I WAS NAPPING and decided to let me rest. Providentially, Mary Anne called to see how I was doing and told Gene how they had found me. Shocked, Gene examined me and when he saw my condition rushed me to the hospital. They admitted me because I was unstable and barely responsive. The next thing I remember is being in a totally dark room. Nurses thought I was in a coma and unable to understand them. I heard one say as they left the room, "Do you think she will make it through the night?"

The other nurse responded, "I don't think so ~ her vital signs are deteriorating."

In the pitch dark I moaned, *"LORD, what happened? Where am I? Help me!"* I no sooner called to Him for help, when He put a song in my heart! I began to sing it inwardly and it built a bridge of hope ~ hope that I would be healed of whatever was wrong. The room grew lighter and lighter ~ *the lights were on all along!* I whispered "thank You" to my Father for the new song He gave me.

The LORD then impressed me that I was to get out of bed and *stand up!* I was to sing the new song out loud! I well remember protesting, *"LORD, how can I? I'm too weak to stand ~ I can't even talk! I'm hooked up to oxygen and all of this other stuff! Do you really want me to get out of bed and stand up and sing out loud to You? O God, You'll have to help me!" He did!*

I STRUGGLED OUT OF BED and stood up holding unto the IV stand and was amazed to feel myself getting some strength as my vision grew clearer. The LORD had surrounded me with *a song of deliverance* [Ps. 32:7 NAS], then helped me sing it to Him:

> *"Your Banner of Love flies over me,*
> *Your Banner of Love has set me free,*
> *Your Banner of Love now covers me,*
> *I'm protected by LORD Nissi."*

THE NURSE CAME IN AND SAW ME STANDING CLINGING TO THE IV STAND and heard me singing about His banner of love! Her eyes were huge and she turned pale, then got excited. I had cried out to the LORD and He gave me a song that hallowed, proclaimed and invited His control, authority, and Presence. My weakness called upon God's strength to protect me and rescue me from the dark pit that I was lying in.

The Holy Spirit led me to *"call upon the name of the LORD"* and I thanked Him and worshiped Him. Our help comes in the Name of the LORD [Ps. 124:8] and to call upon the Name of the LORD is to worship Him [Gen. 21:33].[1]

I was diagnosed with Legionnaires Disease. It later turned out that I was one of three in the nation, according to the Center for Disease Control, who incubated Legionnaires Disease for eight months from December of 1987 through August of 1988. The common denominator was an old theater in New York City where we had watched the closing performance of a musical.

HE WILL NEVER LEAVE US NOR FORSAKE US *[Heb. 13:5-6]*. In my despair, I had called upon His Name and God put *LORD NISSI* in my heart. Ever since He gave me that song, I love to think of *LORD NISSI* as the banner that represents His protection, freeing love, and the comprehensiveness of the Triune Godhead.

Later I pondered if *NISSI* (meaning standard, banner, flag, signal) could symbolize the *fullness of* and the *realness of* the Godhead? Could *NISSI* be the banner

Name that rallies His Heavenly forces, rallies the fullness of His Compound Names,[2] rallies the personage of God to gather, meet and unite for battle? WOW! What a thought!

Praying, worshiping, and victoriously proclaiming appropriate titles of God's revelations of Himself, invites (permits) and establishes the LORD's intervention in our interests and concerns. For example, when we worship, acclaim, sing, read Scripture, proclaim, or invite Yahweh Shammah (the LORD *is* Present! Jehovah *is* there!), we invite, confirm, and acknowledge that the LORD's presence is with us! [Ezek. 48:35; Job 22:28] Yahweh Shammah, LORD Shammah, represents Yeshua Jesus there in action, speech, and concerning all matters.

I will always thank the LORD that in the fall of 1982, I attended a National Lydia Fellowship Conference at Lake Junalaska for lady intercessors. When it was over, an unopened package with lists of the Names of God was given to me to take home for possible use. I'll never forget how *"strange, foreign and unappealing"* they looked! I could not begin to imagine the impact that His Peerless Names would make in my life.

The Names of God had been prepared by Shelagh McAlpine, founder of Lydia Fellowship International (for intercessors), and her prayer partner, Tryna Bahl. Shelagh's demeanor blessed, yet convicted me. She had been born in the United Kingdom and understood what "honor" meant, particularly the honor due royalty (in a manner democracy cannot teach) *and especially the honor due THE HIGHEST ROYALTY!* Her deep reverence and love for the LORD put a hunger in my heart to know God that same *real* way. I yearned to have thoughts and words to honor my LORD so I could better express my love to Him. I prayed that studying His Names would be the Holy Spirit's vehicle to help me understand how to better relate to the LORD, and one another, along with enlarging my vocabulary to honor and praise Him. Studying the names of God radically enlarged my life and walk with the LORD.

The Lord's Peerless Names gave me a broader understanding of Christ's Authority and opened my heart to a deeper relationship with Christ Jesus and His ways. The resulting study, which is ongoing, magnified and enlarged our LORD Yeshua's *awesome role* as Yahweh in the Old Testament. It reinforced the reality of His blessings, covenants, virtues, and promises. His Name itself speaks volumes: *YAHWEH IS SALVATION!* [Ps. 14:7]

To call upon His Name, or one of His Hallowed Names, is to call upon, or proclaim, a particular facet of His character to intervene on our behalf, or on others behalf, and it confesses that we trust the LORD to do so! Whenever we acclaim one of God's Compound Names, whether to worship or resist the enemy, it advises the enemy that we have chosen that facet of the *fullness* of God's Authority to have dominion over that area. The New Testament is built upon and confirms the Old Testament in the same way that the Compound Names of Yahweh are not additional Names of God, but reveal additional facets of the Character of God. They are designations of titles that often grew out of commemorative events. When we submit ourselves to God and resist the devil, he must flee ~ *Satan has no choice* ~ he must yield to God's Sovereign Power! [James 4:7]

During the pursuit of God's Names, I noticed that *in the name of the LORD* was woven like a thread throughout the Bible. That seemed odd! I wouldn't refer to anyone as *in the name of* Gene, or *in the name of* Diane, Charlotte, Judy or David, I would simply say their names! Using Strong's Exhaustive Concordance, I looked up and recorded word by word all of the verses that used "in the Name of the LORD." What a blessing that proved to be! By studying His sovereign, sacred and unique holy Names they were reinforced in my heart in a practical way ~ a real way!

Dr. David Stern wrote in the Jewish New Testament Commentary:
> His Name is not a magic word. Greek onoma corresponds to Hebrew shem, which biblically, means not just a name but everything that the Named individual is and represents ~ his work, personality, power, authority and reputation.[3]

Shem means name in Hebrew. Strong's Concordance lists the three major understandings of name (shem) in reference to the LORD:

(1) Honor, Authority, Sovereign Character (revealed through His manifold manifestations), or His Image (as reflected by His people);
(2) Mark or memorial of individuality (His indwelling character and attributes), to set apart, to distinguish (as His);
(3) The Sign of His protection.[4]

The Name of the Lord epitomizes Christ Jesus' eternal role as the actively involved Absolute, Self-Existing, God (Yahweh).[5] The Name of the LORD represents Jesus' intervention, reputation, power, character, etc. The Name of the LORD heralds Yahweh's *Presence* and represents His authority, power, and protection.

John Frame wrote in The Doctrine of the Knowledge of God, A Theology of Lordship:

Presence involves authority, for God is never present apart from His Word [Deut. 30:11ff; John 1:1ff] etc. To summarize, knowing God is knowing Him as Lord, "knowing that I AM the LORD." And knowing Him as LORD is knowing His control, authority, and presence.[6]

LORD, ALL CAPITAL LETTERS IN THE OLD TESTAMENT, IS JESUS.[7] Knowing and proclaiming His Peerless Name's memorializes and hallows the LORD Jesus Christ. To hallow is to make sacred ~ to revere as holy. We hallow a spectrum of His attributes, control, authority, and nature. We proclaim His Peerless Names to call upon the LORD and to tell the LORD that we know that His Presence is with us and that His forces will fight for us. Proclaiming His Hallowed Names sets us apart, distinguishes us and marks us as God's people ~ people that know that Jesus is LORD and acknowledge His control, authority, and presence.

Peter, Stephen, Paul, etc., called upon His Name ~ they trusted Him to intervene and they were committed to serve Him. They knew Jesus was YAHWEH, their Messiah, and that they were *marked* as God's people! We, God's people, are marked, signed and sealed by His protection. We call upon His Name because we belong to Him and are committed to serve Him.

WE ARE MADE IN HIS IMAGE, called to walk in His image, to communicate His image, created to be His friend, to walk in His character, to serve and worship Him as LORD "so that His life may be revealed in our mortal body" [2 Cor. 4:4, 11].

Six months after I received the packet with the lists of God's Names that I had been studying, I attended a Lydia Leadership Conference at Mt. Hermon, California. I had never seen a banner in a Christian setting and I will never forget how I sat, with tears running down my face, as I gazed in awe at a beautiful ivory satin banner standing on the platform. It had a large *"I AM"* in purple with twelve of His compound Names beautifully stitched underneath it in purple cursive. Six pennants (small banners) also stood on each side of the podium ~ one for each of the Hallowed Names on the *I AM* banner.

WE WERE GIVEN THE LYDIA BROCHURE *STEPS TO THE THRONE*.[8] It listed the same twelve Names of God and included their Scripture references. We used it for meditation and learned more about His mercy, love, holiness, omnipotence, faithfulness, justice and grace. Each lady that attended received a purple miniature silk handmade pennant memento to use for meditation [Gen. 14:18-20] and for a bookmark. My memento introduced me to one of *His Peerless Names, EL YON.* I love my memento ~ *JEHOVAH EL YON* ~ which means God Most High, Possessor of Heaven and Earth!

I TREASURED THINKING UPON, THEN REVERENTLY WHISPERING TO THE LORD (Jehovah) what *EL YON* meant to me. Deep within my heart I wanted to know Him more. We experienced pure worship when we became so filled with the awareness and awe of Who He is, His Holiness, and His absolute Majesty, that all else faded away. Awe entered our hearts as we discovered precious truths about our Master. We surrendered our hearts in deep worship to Him as our meditations reflected a new awareness of His holiness, His Majesty ~ He is a *holy* God! I cannot verify this, but I doubt if there was one lady there who did not come face to face with her unworthiness in the presence of her Maker, her Master, who loved her unconditionally. Surely all there wept from the depth of their hearts, "Woe is me, for I am ruined! I have unclean lips and live among people of unclean lips [Isa. 6:5] . . ." When we face *Truth,* our inward sob can only be, *"HOLY, HOLY, HOLY . . ."*

DURING WORSHIP AT THE END OF THE CONFERENCE, some of our leaders spontaneously took the twelve pennants with His Name's on them from the platform and handed them to us to pass back. As we joyfully acclaimed the LORD's Name's, we were blessed passing the pennants back, row by row, then forward again to return to their stands. I'll never forget the waves of devotion toward the LORD and the reality of His love experienced when passing the *EL YON* pennant! I was doubly blessed when I saw that the pennant that I had passed each way was *EL YON,* the Name on my memento! The spontaneous worship of His Names will always be a beautiful indelible memory.

DURING AN EARLIER TIME (1977), I was blessed to feel His awesome Presence at the Garden Tomb in Jerusalem, following the communion served to our church group while we sat on the benches facing the tomb. Afterward, each person went into the tomb. I sat there overwhelmed with awe as I faced, then grasped in deep reverence and gratitude, that Jesus' Triumphant act of love, that I did not, or could not deserve, merit, or take for granted, was for *me.* His wondrous loving Presence became so real that I could hardly breathe. Gramma Grosh startled me when she said, "Sweetie, if you want to go into the Tomb, you better do it now as the group is getting ready to leave." I entered the Garden Tomb, knowing that it represented all that Christ had done for me, for us, and sat down and closed the door. A ray of light came down through the upper hole in the wall to the area where many believe that Christ had been laid. It was breathtaking. When I got up to leave, a sign on the door said *"HE IS NOT HERE ~ HE HAS RISEN!"* That had happened ten years earlier.

AFTER I RETURNED HOME FROM THE CONFERENCE, I concentrated on *El Yon* for my daily devotions using Strong's Concordance and numerically traced El Yon throughout the Bible. El Yon became real, awesome and exciting! The Holy

Spirit taught me to take the verses and "headline" them into subjective and objective thoughts that I used in prayer and praise.

> ***MANY NEW DESCRIPTIONS AND ATTRIBUTES OF HIS LORDSHIP EMERGED:***
> EL MEANS GOD, YON MEANS EMMANUEL   A few blessed insights from studying *EL YON* are: El Yon is Most High God, Most Powerful, Awesome, Possessor of Heaven and Earth, Almighty, Holiest, Glorious, Sovereign, Supreme, Exalted, Strongest, Jealous, Compassionate, Mightiest Hero . . . *GOD WITH US.*

EL YON, MOST HIGH GOD, became my focus. El Yon became more than a word, a name of inspiration, a commentary, or insight written by someone else. El Yon became real, and personal. The magnitude of El Yon's character and provisions burst alive in my heart and enlarged my vocabulary in prayer and to praise the LORD. Renewed faith and courage will enter our hearts when we verbally honor our Master, our LORD, our Savior and King! Faith truly comes by hearing the Message and the Message is heard through the Word of Christ! [Rom. 10:17] I urge you to stop now and reverently, thankfully, prayerfully and verbally tell the LORD what El Yon means to you starting with the short list above. Watch how it strengthens your faith when you hear His attributes spoken out loud.

YAHWEH SABAOTH WAS MY NEXT NAME STUDY. WOW! They talk about David's slingshot killing Goliath, I think when he confidently proclaimed the Name of Yahweh Sabaoth, the LORD of Host's, that he was strengthened with clear vision and empowered by the Holy Spirit with a steady hand. David's confidence, trust, and battle strategy was to *call upon* the fullness of the LORD Sabaoth ~ the LORD of Hosts ~ to manifest victory and his stone hit the mark!

I began to resist the enemy's attacks by proclaiming the authority of Christ's Holy Name. I used Yahweh's Peerless Names that encompassed antonyms or the opposite meaning of the enemy's attack, that is, his character and nature in evidence. Christ Jesus' Old Testament Names reflect the LORD's power, control and character. To *reflect* the LORD's Name is to *deflect* the enemy!

THE NEXT VENTURE WAS TO LIST SYNONYMS OF THE TWELVE NAMES OF GOD listed in *Steps To the Throne* by using concordances, lexicons and a favorite thesaurus.[9] I listed the titles of His Names represented by His nature or character with their corresponding synonyms on slips of paper. My prayer partners joined me and we used them for scriptural meditation, praise, worship, learning and praying His Names. Our understanding and our hearts were definitely enlarged! We saw the LORD demonstrate His providence, care, and love as a direct result of praising and praying *His*

Peerless Names into the burdens that He put in our hearts.

We were blessed to study Adonai knowing that the Jewish people prayed and praised His name, Adonai (pronounced Ad-o-noy) for Yahweh. Adonai is the Proper Name of *GOD* and is exclusive to *YAHWEH* [Gen. 15:2, 5]. Some synonyms for Adonai are:

> ***ADONAI:*** Self-existent One, Eternal, Sovereign, Majesty, Holy One, Controller, Master, Superior, Monarch, Leader, Noble, Potentate, Chief, Headman, Governor, Emperor, Royal, Princely, Kingly, Authority, Primary, Paramount, Magnificent, Shield, Lofty, Regal, First, Source, Wellspring . . .

WE CALL UPON ADONAI, THE HOLY ONE, THE POTENTATE OF THE UNIVERSE, and so forth, to be our Source, our Authority, our Shield, our Royal Leader, our Wellspring. We call upon El Yon, the Strongest, and Yahweh Rapha to overcome spiritual and physical weaknesses. When facing a need, we call upon Yahweh Yireh, the Provider (Jehovah Jireh), and so on. The synonym prayer cards helped us identify facets of His nature, character, qualities, integrity, etc., deepened our understanding and enlarged prayers and worship. You can imagine how amazed I was when I learned that the following descriptions incorporated *NISSI!*

> ***LORD NISSI:*** (nis-si) ~ BANNER! (altar) STANDARD! FLAG! SIGN!*
> [Exod. 7:15] Signal! Warning! Conspicuous! Display! Eternal Victor! GOD'S Victory Symbol! *Fiery Serpent ~ Lifted to Heal!* HIS NAME! Truth that Delivers and Saves! Military Standard of Love! Awesome! Comes Speedily! Executes God's Anger! His Own Assemble To Stand Before Him! To Be Seen By All! Solitary Signal! Lift Against Babylon! His Sign Appears in Heaven!
>
> * Sign/Distinguishing Mark: signpost, guide, beacon, pointer, attribute, quality, objective, standard, label, symbol, manifest, reveal, rank, represent, personify, etc., Yahweh's victory Logo!

HIS NAMES ARE PRACTICAL AND PRECIOUS TO USE for situations, attitudes, and prayer concerns in today's world. When I had Legionnaires Disease, and called upon the LORD, He gave me a song about His Name that proved most appropriate for my malady! Had *I* chosen, I probably would have called upon *YAHWEH RAPHA* ~ the LORD my Healer ~ I would not have known that more was needed! When I called upon LORD Nissi it was a signal to the enemy that declared that I stood assembled before the LORD, body, soul and spirit. The Truth, Who delivers and saves us, came speedily! In essence and reality, in my frailty, I believe that the LORD led me to *stand* to declare *NISSI* because it was a Victory Symbol, a symbol that encompassed the Fiery Serpent being lifted to heal me. It was His banner of protection and truth! I was released in much improved health twelve days later!

Incidentally, we had two prescheduled prayer meetings during my hospitalization. We did not let the situation keep us from our scheduled time with the LORD. What an Awesome Victor we serve! God's hallowed names give us a catalog of praises that span the Old Testament and New Testament. Studying His Names enlarges our capacity to express our love to Him. When we know more about His Character, the Holy Spirit opens our understanding to enable us to make choices to reflect His Image.

MY STUDY OF HIS NAMES LED ME TO LOOK INTO GOD'S REDEMPTIVE NAMES. The study culminated into prayer cards with headline thoughts of Scripture verses. They are useful for praying specific attributes into our concerns. They extend our vocabulary so we can bless His Holy Name, sing a new song to the LORD, and so forth [Ps. 33:3; 40:3; 96:1-13].

A SAMPLE OF SYNONYMS FOR ONE OF GOD'S REDEMPTIVE NAMES:

Jehovah Rapha: (yeh-ho-vaw' raw-faw') HEALER. [Exod. 15:26] Physician, Doctor, Therapist, Mender, Restorer, Repairer, Recuperator, Medical Examiner, Treater, Correction, Renewer, Establisher, Reviver, Regenerator, Refashioner, Refresher, Rehabilitator, Fortifier, Energizer, Strengthener, Revitalizer, Pardoner, Comforter, etc.

CHRIST CAME TO GIVE US THE ABUNDANT LIFE [John 10:10]. Christ's ways are magnified inwardly when we ask the Holy Spirit to illuminate the meaning of Jesus' Names throughout the Bible. We need to understand Christ's authority and have confidence in His authority. His Names enlarge our capacity to be specific when we profess God's character into a situation. His Names demonstrate His never-ending source of victory in our ongoing warfare against our flesh and the enemy.

WE MUST LEARN ABOUT GOD, HIS WAYS, HIS CHARACTER AND HIS CONDITIONS if we want to overcome the Enemy. The Holy Spirit began teaching spiritual warfare through internalizing the character of His Names then externalizing the authority of His Names into prayer concerns, praise, and worship. I dubbed this as *WARSHIP ~ WARfare* through *worSHIP!* ~ a play on words [Ps. 149].

AN INVITATION CAME TO TEACH SPIRITUAL WARFARE in Columbus. Can you imagine how startled I was to wake up that morning, prepared, but troubled I was not to teach Spiritual Warfare? It seemed loud and clear we needed to know God's principles before we were qualified to go into warfare! I was totally unprepared to present an alternate teaching, so I desperately sought God for further direction. The LORD promptly reminded me of my search for His Names and how it had deeply enhanced my security in Him and my understanding of His covenants and invested authority.

THE LORD HAD ALREADY PREPARED ME! I was to begin at the first occurrence of each of His Names and share the wonderful facets of His character and authority in the same Scripture sequence that I had found and highlighted in my Bible. I asked my hostess for index cards, skipped breakfast and began assembling His Names. I literally finished them in her car as we arrived at the meeting!

I shared my impression from the LORD with leadership and secured their approval. After prayer I opened my Bible and had us turn to Genesis 1:1. With great anticipation we began reading the Peerless Names of God as they unfolded in the Bible.

ELOHIM ~ GOD (capital G ~ little OD) IS HIS FIRST PEERLESS NAME MENTIONED. "In the beginning God, (Elohim), created the heavens and earth" [Gen. 1:1]. Elohim, plural God in form and revelation, Supreme God, created the heavens and the earth by His Spirit ~ *RUACH* [Gen. 1:2; Act. 17:24-29].

THE HEBREW LEXICONS TRANSLATE SPIRIT/RUACH HAKODESH AS WIND, or to breathe, a sensible (even violent) exhalation! ~ Divine power of creation, Who, with Yahweh Elohim (Adonai God), made heaven and earth [Gen. 2:4] ". . . and the Spirit of God was moving over the surface of the waters" [Gen. 1:2] Elohim's creative force, Ruach, His wind or violent exaltation, breathed and created Life and Light [John 1:1; Rev. 19:13].

Then Elohim <u>said</u>, "Let there be light," and there was light! [Gen. 1:3] Elohim said! Elohim made! Elohim called! Elohim spoke, Elohim created and Elohim *named* His creation! [Gen. 1:6-8] Elohim said, "Let *Us* [Plural/Triune God] make man in Our image, according to Our likeness; and let *them [man]* rule over the fish, birds, cattle, earth, and every creeping thing" [Gen. 1:26, emphasis added]. That would include serpents and scorpions ~ the unrighteous gods and graven images of antiquity that are worshiped openly today.

WE WERE GIVEN POWER AND AUTHORITY TO TREAD UPON SERPENTS AND SCORPIONS WITHOUT INJURY! [Luke 10:18-20] The Bible teaches us that we were called to walk in Christ's authority, character and attributes! We were told to administrate Yahweh's authority on earth as it is in heaven! We were entrusted as His representatives to administrate His righteousness over rulers and authorities in heavenly places! [Eph. 3:8-11 NAS] Will we prepare our hearts and obey our commission to walk in His delegated authority? Will we?

YAHWEH ELOHIM (LORD God) brought the beasts, etc., to see what Adam would call them.

ADAM CHOSE THEIR NAMES, Adam planted his seed into Eve. Eve birthed Seth, and Seth's seed was Enosh. That was the first record of man *calling upon The NAME of the LORD* [Gen. 4:26].

MY HEART YEARNS FOR YOU TO START YOUR OWN STUDY OF HIS WONDROUS PEERLESS NAMES.

THE FOLLOWING IS COMPILED FROM HIGHLIGHTED MARKINGS IN MY BIBLE used beginning that day to enlarge my understanding of many of His Hebrew Names, translated into English in the Bible, in sequence of their first appearance:

ELOHIM ~ Plural Supreme God [Gen. 1:1];

RUACH ~ Holy Spirit [Gen. 1:2];

YAHWEH ~ Active, Self-Existing, Creator of Heaven and Earth [Gen. 2:4];

EL YON ~ God Most High [Gen. 14:18];

ADONAI, Lord ~ Reverential Title, Divine, Sacred, Owner [Gen. 15:2];

EL ROI ~ The God Who Sees [Gen. 16:13];

EL SHADDAI ~ God Almighty [Gen. 17:1];

EL OLAM ~ Everlasting God [Gen. 21:33];

YAHWEH YIREH (JEHOVAH JIREH) ~ The LORD will Provide [Gen. 2:14];

EL-ELOHE ISRAEL ~ El of Immanuel as the God of Israel [Gen. 3:20];

EL GIBBOR ~ Mighty One of Jacob [Gen. 49:24];

YAHWEH, LORD ~ I AM that I AM [His Memorial Name] [Exod. 3:15];

YESHUA ~ Salvation, Deliverer [Exod. 15:2];

YAHWEH RAPHA ~ The LORD your Healer [Exod. 15:26];

YAHWEH NISSI ~ The LORD is my Banner [Exod. 17:15];

YAHWEH M'KADDESH ~ The LORD Who Sanctifies You [Exod. 31:13];

YAHWEH SHALOAM ~ LORD Covenant of Peace [Num. 25:12];

ABBA, FATHER ~ Bought and Made Us! [Deut. 32:6];

EL HAI ~ Living God [Josh. 3:10];

YAHWEH SABBOTH ~ LORD of Hosts, God of the armies of Israel! [1 Sam. 17:45];

MESSIAH ~ Consecrated, Anointed, Set Apart [Ps. 2:2];

YAHWEH ROI ~ The LORD our Shepherd [Ps. 23:1];

YAHWEH T'SIDKENU ~ The LORD our Righteousness [Jer. 23:6];

YAHWEH SHAMMAH ~ The LORD is Present [Ezek. 48:35].

TO KNOW GOD IS ONE OF THE HIGHEST LEVELS OF SPIRITUAL WARFARE!

ANOTHER TIME OF SHARING HIS NAMES WITH INTERCESSORS, each lady present was given a copy of Lydia's *KNOW YOUR GOD*, which encompassed many of His Names above, along with Scripture sources for individual meditation on one or more of His Names. We sat, two by two, in total silence before God. His Word promises . . .

> *"Silence is praise to you, Zion-dwelling God,*
> *and also obedience. You hear the prayer in it all."*
> *Psalm 65 ~ The Message*

A WHILE LATER, SITTING IN TWOSOMES, we shared our thoughts about our LORD and caught a deeper glimpse of the fullness of our Master Jesus. When we re-gathered to worship, we spoke His names corporately out loud and felt an excitement well up in our hearts. We knew we were glorifying the LORD and He was in our midst. It was exciting to worship and praise His multi-faceted character represented by His Names. *An added plus* was when we sensed the revealed depth of His love it brought us face to face with our own unworthiness accompanied by conviction and repentance. A healing balm fell upon us and ultimately restored broken relationships within the group.

We learned that when we pray *"in the Name of the LORD,"* as the early disciples did, we are acknowledging that *Jesus Christ is Yahweh* of the whole Bible. The best part of all was that we enjoyed inviting and letting the Holy Spirit be our Teacher. He centered us on the Eternal Truth that Jesus Christ is Yahweh and we basked in His precious love. *HE IS LORD!*

THE DEMONS KNOW THAT WHEN WE KNOW AND BELIEVE, that our prayers are proclaimed in the Name of the LORD to establish His authority on earth. They recognize that we are praying by Jesus' authority and they must bow! The earth is the LORD's footstool [Ps. 110:1; Isa. 66:1].

IT IS WONDERFUL TO ACCLAIM MESSIAH'S GREATNESS by speaking, thinking or singing His Names and proclaiming His attributes and Majesty. His Names are a mighty weapon and protection over our spiritual and physical lives. His Sovereign Word is a weapon that is not carnal, but divinely powerful for the destruction of fortresses. We are to "destroy speculations and every lofty thing raised up against the knowledge of God by *taking every thought captive* to the obedience of Christ" [2 Cor. 10:3-5].

During my studies and meditations of the LORD's awesome Names, His attributes and character became a magnet. I paraphrased, then headlined the Scriptures that told of His awesome ways. After sharing them, they were later assembled as *HALLOWED COMMEMORATIVE prayer cards* and subsequently been used as tools to study His Names at conferences, seminars, Bible studies, prayer groups, etc. The accompanying Scripture references and synonyms of His Names were included and used for meditation, worship, praise, and prayer.[9]

The *Hallowed Commemoratives* has been well received as a resource tool that enhances and strengthens believers' relationship with Messiah (Emmanuel) [Isa. 7:14; Matt. 1:23]. The proclamations and prayers shared below came from meditations that were triggered by study and evolved into the prayer cards. They are shared in hopes that you will be encouraged to spend time alone in His Word and record fresh thoughts, medleys of praise, prayers, and guidance that you receive from His throne.

THE FOLLOWING PRAYER MEDLEYS WERE USED throughout Ohio and other states during seminars, sessions or teaching, and are samples of how to weave His Word in thanksgiving, worship, proclamation and prayer:

ABBA FATHER, precious Father God, You are our Eternal Father that bought, made and established us [Deut. 32:6] and kings and thrones. We decree that the people of Ohio and America will bow their knee, and confess with their tongue that Jesus Christ is LORD, to Your Glory [Phil. 2:11]. We pray that You will raise up righteous Cabinet Members and godly Representatives and Senators. For Your Name's sake, appoint anointed spiritual leaders who will recognize and bow to Your Authority.

LORD CHRIST JESUS, precious Self-Existing, Sovereign Anointed Savior, call us to our knees to repent for apathy and prayerlessness. The state of this world rests upon us [Gen. 1:26]. Forgive us for abdicating Your Righteous influence over every realm of our lives. LORD, forgive me, forgive us, for not purposing to take time to be with You that we may be guided by the Spirit and obediently serve You, by serving others.

ADONAI, we praise and thank You. You hear our intercession. We reverently worship and thank You for forgiving our selfish ways. You are *LORD of lords, Mighty and Awesome.* You do not show partiality and cannot be bribed. Thank You for giving guidance when hope seems dim. Rise up, fight for our families and homes ~ Laugh and scoff at the enemy [Ps. 2:4].

LAMB OF GOD, enthroned Yahweh, Messianic Title of our beloved LORD Jesus, protect us from the destroyer [Isa. 53:6]. You are The PASSOVER LAMB and the New Covenant for our families, churches, state and nation. Thank You that Your perfect unblemished innocent Blood purified, sanctified, justified, and set us apart to glorify You. Protect us, Messiah! Rule us and enable us to be the overcomers and bondslaves that You freed us and called us to be! You are worthy to receive power, riches, wisdom, might, honor, blessings, and thanksgiving because You sit at the right hand of Him Who Sits On the Throne!

EL, EMMANUEL or IMMANUEL, God ~Yahweh with us! [Matt. 1:23] Strongest! Most powerful! Highest! Almighty Shield and Defender! Stronghold! Awesome in majesty! The Rock! Savior! Jealous God! Who battles for us with the horns of a wild ox! [Num. 23:22]. Answer us in our distress, share Your divine thoughts and inspirations with us. We beseech You, heal our city, our state, our nation. You accomplish all things, You made us in Your Image. Help us reflect Your Righteousness and Love.

YESHUA, our Salvation and Deliverance [2 Chron. 20:17]; *Living YAHWEH,* Glorious "I AM" ~ save, deliver and give us victory over our troublesome sins. Be our strength and song. Make Ohio a refuge state for Your people. Make America once more a refuge for the nations. Thank You for revealing and explaining our Father to us. May Your Holy Spirit give us prayers to set the captives free! We exalt the *Power of Your Blood shed at Calvary!*

SADLY, DURING TIMES OF PRAYER, I have heard prayer leaders enunciate the precious "Name of Jesus" loudly, repeatedly, obviously, and sometimes pointedly, in order to make a point to convict or proselytize unbelievers. Most people are drawn to Christ through the Holy Spirit using believers' love, actions, testimonies, or written word. Christ taught us to pray to our Father in heaven [Matt. 6:1-15] not horizontally to others to make a point. We are to reflect Christ ~ *would He pray in that manner?*

PAUL COUNSELED US REGARDING OUR WITNESS AND RELATIONSHIP WITH UNBELIEVERS, to "conduct ourselves in a manner worthy of Christ, to stand firm in one spirit, with one mind as we strive together for the faith of the Gospel; in no way be alarmed [or threatened] by our opponents [the spirits influencing the nonbelievers], which is a sign of destruction for them [the unholy, unrighteous spirits], but of salvation for us, and that too, from God" [Phil. 1:27, 28]. His perfect love enables us and casts out fear! [1John 4:18]

WHEN WE ARE ACTIVELY INVOLVED IN SECULAR OR ECUMENICAL ACTIVITIES, and have been *invited* to lead in prayer, we can solemnly honor and establish our LORD Jesus' Presence by ending our prayer *"in the Name of the LORD."* "In the Name of the LORD" establishes and honors Jesus Christ as LORD and Savior of His people, yet it does not alienate or offend Jewish people who have also been invited to participate [Rom. 12:18].[10] To reiterate, it is *when* we are in secular meetings, or are with invited Jewish people, not normal Christian gatherings. Jewish guests are *not offended* when we reverently end our prayers "in the Name of the LORD" or "in Messiah's Name." Jesus knows, and we know, that it reinforces the reality of His blessings, covenants, virtues, and promises which are still in operation today. The demons definitely know that they must yield when we are praying in the triumphant Name of our LORD. They know Jesus is LORD and at His Name they must yield!

IF YOU ARE GIVING THE PRAYER IN A SECULAR ENVIRONMENT, you can include Jewish people in your prayer at the end by saying, "We ask this in the Name of the LORD. All who agree, please say 'Amen!'" I have had Jewish people come to me afterward and thank me for letting them be included in the prayer (usually prayers for our Armed Forces or our Nation).

Prideful, condescending declarations or proselytizing, injures, insults, alienates and angers most Jewish people. Is it good manners? Are we being sensitive? Are our prayers to evangelize? No, our prayer is an audience with The Holy, Majestic, Sovereign God ~ we are *talking with* the Most High God, *not people!*

Always remember that the Scribes and Pharisees of old robbed Jewish people of the Truth and they have not known the blessings of the fullness of Scripture [Luke 11:52]. When we sincerely, reverently, lovingly pray "in the Name of the LORD" and rejoice in the glory of God, it builds a bridge of hope that they can cross over into the New Testament where only the Truth can set man free [John 8:32]. Through Christ's love and Truth the Holy Spirit can draw man out of darkness!

JEWISH PEOPLE HAVE BEEN WON TO CHRIST when they have seen the love, devotion, concern and peace of believers in sickness and health, good times and hard times [Rom. 5:1-5], and by the revelation of His Word into their hearts. Hunger enters the hearts of many Jewish people when they recognize Adonai's Names being hallowed, exalted on high, and honored. Truth dawns in many of their hearts when they hear the LORD confessed adoringly, reverently, and sincerely in worship and in prayer. Messianic Jews have testified that before they were saved, they heard Gentiles make devout proclamations to the "Messiah"[11] and the Holy Spirit used the Gentile's worship as the tool that opened their hearts! They saw that we love the One True God and are not a cult, or pagans as their spiritual leaders had taught them.

JEWS ARE SPIRITUALLY THREATENED when they hear the name "Christ" whereas "Messiah" is the Name of the One they look for and yearn for. In David Stern's Jewish New Testament Commentary, he points out the value of calling Christ the "Messiah" in the presence of Jewish people. He shared that Jews were persecuted and murdered "in the name of Christ." They don't want anything to do with Christ. They are looking for the Messiah ~ *The Promised Anointed One!* Interestingly, Messiah is used in lieu of Christ more than 380 times in the Jewish New Testament which was written specifically for Messianic Jews.[11]

A SCRIPTURAL WAY TO PRAY FOR UNSAVED OR BACKSLIDERS: *ask our Holy Father* (and theirs, we must remember that man was created by Him, for Him, in

His image] to give them to Jesus that they may keep His Word and be kept in His Name [John 17:11]; that they may know Him [John 17:6]; and that Father God will sanctify them in His Truth [John 17:17-19]; that we may be one! [John 17:22, 23]

AS CHRISTIANS, WE SHOULD SPEND AS MUCH TIME studying and imitating our LORD as sports enthusiasts spend studying their idols and cheering for them and what they stand for! We know the Victor! Shouldn't we celebrate and walk in His victory? We are to reflect the Messiah's love and proclaim Yahweh's Character in our thoughts, our lives, our prayers, and in our worship. Christians should idolize the LORD Jesus Christ and be a mirror of The ONE Who made us in HIS IMAGE!

Many idolize sports and cinema stars ~ all types of celebrities! They study their habits, the way they dress, the way they walk, the way they talk, and who they know. They strive to imitate or reflect that star's personality, attributes, and character. We need to remember that the enemy's forces are merely deluded followers who try to become like the star/god they worship. When they talk about, or call out the names of false gods in mantras or songs, they are in actuality (whether they know it or not) asking to be identified with and changed into that personality. Let us *countermand* the hordes of false spirits called forth through unrecognized idolatry, pagan rituals, rebellion, even false religions as mentioned earlier.

A FRIEND GAVE ME PROCLAMATION! BY DEREK PRINCE. Some highlights follow regarding observations that he made during the time that he lived with the Moslem (Muslim) people over a period of many years; facts about the Middle East, and dominant spiritual power of Islam.

> Derek Prince wrote (in the 1990's):
> (Islam's power is) . . . summed up in one word: *Proclamation!* Most of us have heard that faithful Moslems go to their mosques five times a day to proclaim and chant their beliefs about God and their Mohammed. These have been going on daily for more than 1,300 years ~ a total of <u>2,372,500 proclamations!</u> If you multiply that by at least a million mosques, you're into billions. I believe these proclamations are the real basis for the growing spiritual power of Islam.
> I believe that if we as Christians want to see God's will done in the Middle East, we must learn to make intercession for this area, and *specifically to proclaim the victory of Jesus:* the power of His Name, the power of His Blood, what has been accomplished through His death on the Cross, His exaltation in glory as the *SUPREME RULER OF THE UNIVERSE,* and that He is coming back again to establish His earthly kingdom.[12]

DEREK PRINCE STATED THAT HE BELIEVED THAT THE OVERWHELMING AMOUNT OF PRAYER FOR DESERT STORM WAS ITS PROTECTION AND VICTORY. He exhorted us "to continue intercession for this area of conflict by using *proclamation* in prayer, in intercession, and in singing."

WE ARE CALLED TO PREVAIL IN PRAYER ~ TO TAKE A VIOLENT STAND AGAINST THE ADVERSARY! Our proclamations cause violence in the heavenlies when we pray for indoctrinated terrorists to be released from bondage and for their salvation through Christ Jesus our LORD.

We are to pray that they may know the *One True God* and that their *struggle* will be *for truth in behalf of our LORD Jesus Christ!* We need to pray effectively for God to reveal the terrorist's plans, intervene in them, and protect the innocent.

We need to pray forgiving prayers, adoring prayers, prevailing prayers, revival prayers!

DR. ROBERT E. COLEMAN SUMMARIZED IN THE COMING WORLD REVIVAL:
"Revival comes when people prevail in prayer [Isa. 66:8] . . . Jesus has promised, 'I will do whatever you ask in My name' . . . The name of Jesus, of course, is just another way of expressing the person and work of the Master. To pray in His name is to pray in His character, to pray in His Spirit, to pray as Jesus Himself is praying as mediator before the Father.

"Prayer implies our complete identification with the purpose of God. Jesus called out in the inner depth of human emptiness, 'Not my will, but yours be done' [Luke 22:42; Matt. 26:39; Mark 14:36]. His prayer was not passive submission to the Father but a determined plea that God's will prevail over all else. Prayer has its joys, and it always throbs with thanksgiving, but supremely it is seen in Jesus to be active conformity to the will of God."[13]

THE LAST TIME THAT JESUS' NAME IS MENTIONED IS IN REVELATION when Jesus said to John, "I, Jesus, have sent my angel to give you this testimony for the churches. I am the Root, and Offspring of David, and the bright Morning Star" [Rev. 22:16]. Jesus sent His testimony so that we hear, know and understand that He is coming. He calls us to minister to others that they may be saved.

WE ARE CALLED to pray for the salvation of the lost. Let us go before our Father in pure worship and learn how He would have us pray for the lost to be saved from the enemy's grasp.

WE ARE CALLED to use Jesus' Shield of Faith and the Sword of the Spirit and to take a stand against the adversary.

WE ARE CALLED to pray that they may know the One True God and that their struggle will be on YAHWEH's behalf!

WE ARE CALLED to know Him and enter into pure worship of His Majesty.

I recently heard that pure worship is going individually to the LORD *with thanksgiving* to find out what He wants to say, listening in reverent silence as we move deeper into the awareness of all that He is, flowing into ministering to Him as a worshiper, and waiting for Him to reveal Himself to our inner man.

LORD, teach us to proclaim and sing Scripture in worship of You.

LORD, teach us how to countermand darkness and the enemy's forces.

LORD, teach us to proclaim Jesus Christ is LORD to the Glory of God our Father. [Phil. 2, 10, 11]

LORD, teach us to establish Your Banners, Your Peerless Names, Your Passwords of Praise!

LORD, teach us, help us, to remember Your last words to John in Revelation. [Rev. 22:16]

LORD, teach us, lead us, that we may join the myriads of angels that . . .

"Sing HALLELUJAH to the LORD!"
Psalm 149

PLEASE NOTE:

"The Bible refers to our Lord by over 200 names and titles. A few of the familiar ones would include Alpha and Omega (Rev. 22:13); Beloved (Eph. 1:6); Bread of Life (John 6:48); Bright and Morning Star (Rev. 22:16); The Lamb (Rev. 5:6); Lion of the Tribe of Judah (Rev. 5:6), and many others. But of all the names of our Lord, the most common is Jesus, which appears over 800 times in the New Testament.

"By whatever name He is called, the testimony of Scripture is that Jesus Christ is the one person who can provide salvation. All spiritual blessings come through His name, including adoption (John 1:12), salvation (Acts 4:12), forgiveness of sin (Acts 10:43), answered prayer (John 14:13, 14), the Holy Spirit (John 14:26), and it is to Jesus that every knee will bow (Phil. 2:10). Believers are to do everything in His name (Col. 3:17), so that His name will be glorified (2 Thess. 1:12).

Those who name His name must turn away from sin (Tim. 2:19). Peter directs attention away from himself, and John, to Jesus Christ. Peter uses five (5) of the many names of our Lord, all of which have Messianic implications ~ Servant, Jesus, Holy and Righteous One, Prince of Life, and Christ. As he did in his first sermon, Peter presents Jesus as the Messiah, approved by God, yet rejected by the people. By doing so, he again stresses to them that they were in the disastrous condition of being at odds with God."[14]

HIS NAME ON OUR FOREHEADS!

*"His servants . . . shall see His face,
and His name shall be on their foreheads."*
[Rev. 22:3-4]

THE NAMES OF GOD have shown Him to be all that He promised to be, and all that we need Him to be. His names read like a catalog of blessing from the One Who can do exceedingly above all we can ask or think.

Among Hebrews, names were very significant, and were chosen carefully. They often revealed what the parents hoped their child would become.

Apparently God also placed great value on names, for sometimes He changed a person's name in keeping with a development in his life: Abram to Abraham, Jacob to Israel, Cephas to Peter, and Saul to Paul. Perhaps, like me, you have read of those changes and wished for something as dramatic in your own life.

I have good news for you ~ there is a very real sense in which we are going to be known by a different name in heaven.

First, we shall know even as we are known (man of faith, person of love, woman of prayer), by our spiritual characteristics.

Second, when the Spirit records the closing moment of time as we step into eternity, He describes the blessings of our new environment, and then says, "His name shall be on their foreheads."

Imagine! His name, His nature, and character will be the outstanding impression when others look on your face! "We shall be like Him, for we shall see Him as He is." [1 John 3:2] The last time His name is mentioned in Scripture, it is found on your forehead.

What Grace![15]

VIII ~ GOD'S PEERLESS NAMES

LIFE APPLICATION

1. What happens when we call upon "the Name of the LORD"? (P. 2)

2. A. What happens when we proclaim God's revelations of Himself (His Peerless Names)? B. Why should we proclaim His Peerless Names? C. Do we benefit from understanding His Peerless Names? (P. 3)

3. Why should we call upon The Hallowed Names of God? (P. 4)

4. A. Are Yahweh's Compound Names additional Names of God? B. What do they designate? (P. 4)

5. Did Peter, Stephen, and Paul know the comprehensiveness of Who Jesus was? (P. 5)

6. A. What led the author to study EL YON and other Names of God and how did she proceed? B. What tools were used? C. How did she incorporate her study into her prayer life? (PP. 5-7)

7. What was David's battle strategy to defeat Goliath? (P. 7)

8. What was the author's next venture in studying the Names of God? (P. 7)

9. What does Nissi Mean? (P. 8)

10. Why do we study the Hallowed Names of God? (P. 9)

11. A. What did you learn about Elohim? B. Creation? C. What does Ruach mean? (P. 10)

12. Who gives believers' power and authority to tread on serpents and scorpions? (P. 10)

13. What was the first record of man calling upon the Name of the LORD? (P. 11)

14. What makes demons yield to our prayers? (P. 12)

15. Notebooks are good to have on hand during worship. Why? (Answers will vary)

16. What does Emmanuel (Immanuel) mean to us? (P. 14)

17. A. How did Paul counsel us to conduct ourselves around unbelievers? B. If we are called to witness Christ's love, what should we call *Him* in the presence of Jewish people? (P. 14)

18. When Jewish or secular people are present, does it honor and extend the grace of the LORD Jesus Christ to pray "In the Name of the LORD?" (P.15)

19. What is a scriptural way to pray for the unsaved and backslidden? (PP. 15-16)

20. What did Derek Prince say is the sum of Islam's power? (P. 16)

21. We are called to take a violent stand against the Adversary. How do we pray? (P. 17)

22. When is the last time that Jesus' Name is mentioned in Scripture? (P. 17)

23. What is pure worship? (P. 17)

24. When we join the myriad of angels, what will we sing? (P. 18)

25. A. The Bible refers to our LORD by over _____ names and titles. B. By whatever His Name is called, the testimony of _____ is that _____ _____ is to the One Person Who can provide _____. (P. 18)

26. What shall be on our foreheads when we see His face? (P.19)

PAGE 22   VIII ~ GOD'S PEERLESS NAMES

GOD'S PEERLESS NAMES SCRIPTURE SEQUENCE

Page 1
Ps. 89:16, 17   [Acclaim His name ~ walk in the light of His presence]

Page 2
Ps. 32:7 NAS   [You are my hiding place; You will protect me from trouble and surround me with songs of deliverance]
Ps. 124:8   [Our help is in the Name of the LORD, the Maker of heaven and earth]
Gen. 21:33   [Abraham planted a tamarisk tree . . . there he called upon the Name of the LORD, the Eternal God]
Heb. 13:5   [. . . God has said, "Never will I leave you; never will I forsake you."]

Page 3
Ezek. 48:35   [The name of the city from that day shall be called The LORD is there. (Yahweh Shammah ~ is present)]
Ps. 14:7   [Oh, that salvation for Israel would come out of Zion!]

Page 4
James 4:7   [Submit yourselves then to God. Resist the devil and he will flee from you]

Page 5
Deut. 30:11   [What I am commanding you today is not too difficult for you or beyond your reach]
John 1:1   [In the beginning was the Word, and the Word was with God, and the Word was God]
2 Cor. 4:4,11   [Believers are to reflect His Image]
Gen. 14:18-20   [EL YON ~ Possessor of heaven and earth ~ Sovereign ~ Holiest, etc.]

Page 6
Isa. 6:5   [I have unclean lips and live with a people of unclean lips]

Page 7
Rom. 10:17   [Faith comes by hearing the Word of Christ]

Page 8
Gen. 15:2, 5   [ADONAI: Abram said, "O Sovereign LORD, what can you give me since I remain childless and the one who will inherit my estate is Eliezer of Damascus?"]
Exod. 17:15   [Yahweh NISSI: Moses built an altar and called it The LORD is my Banner.]

Page 9
Ps. 33:3   [Sing to Him a new song; play skillfully, and shout for joy]
Ps. 40:3   [He put a new song in my mouth, a hymn of praise to our God. Many will see and fear and put their trust in the LORD]
Ps. 96:1   [Sing to the LORD a new song; sing to the LORD, all the earth]
Exod. 15:26   [YAHWEH RAPHA: If you listen carefully to the voice of the LORD your God, and do what is right in His eyes, if you pay attention to His commands and keep all His decrees, I will not bring on you any of the diseases I brought on the Egyptians, for I am the LORD, who heals you]
John 10:10   [The enemy comes to steal, kill, & destroy ~ Jesus came to give life abundantly.]
Ps. 149   [Worship through warfare = War-Ship]

Page 10
Gen. 1:1   [**ELOHIM** created]
Gen. 1:2   [**RUWACH/HOLY SPIRIT** is HIS INSTRUMENT]
Acts 17:24-29   [**SUPREME GOD** created heavens & earth by His Spirit]
Gen. 2:4   [**YAHWEH ELOHIM** made heaven and earth]
Gen. 2:2   [**THE SPIRIT OF GOD** was moving over the surface of the waters]

Page 10 (continued)

John 1:1	[**His WORD** is God's creative force: in the beginning was the Word, the Word was with God, the Word was God]
Rev. 19:13	[He is clothed with a robe dipped in blood: and His Name is called The Word of God]
Gen. 1:3	[**GOD** said . . . Let there be Light!]
Gen. 1:6-8	[**ELOHIM** said, made, called, spoke, created and named His creation]
Gen. 1:26	[**ELOHIM** made man in Their image to rule over the fish, birds, cattle, earth ~ every creeping thing]
Luke 10:19	[Jesus gave us power/authority to tread upon serpents & scorpions & over all the power of the enemy (unholy forces) ~ nothing is to injure us]
Eph. 3:8-11 NAS	[Believers administer His authority to the rulers and authority in heavenly places]

Page 11

Gen. 4:26	[The first record of **man calling upon the Name of the LORD**]
Gen. 1:1	**ELOHIM**
Gen. 1:2	**RUACH/HOLY SPIRIT**
Gen. 2:4	**YAHWEH/LORD**
Gen. 14:18	**EL YON**
Gen. 15:2	**ADONAI . . . Lord**
Gen. 16:13	**EL ROI**
Gen. 17:1	**EL SHADDAI**
Gen. 21:33	**EL OLAM**
Gen. 22:14	**YAHWEH YIREH**
Gen. 33:20	**EL ELOHE ISRAEL**
Gen. 49:24	**EL GIBBOR**
Exod. 3:15	**YAHWEH** (Memorial name)
Exod. 15:2	**YESHUA**
Exod. 15:26	**YAHWEH RAPHA**
Exod. 17:15	**YAHWEH NISSI**
Exod. 31:13	**YAHWEH M'KADDESH**
Num. 25:12	**YAHWEH SHALOAM**
Deut. 32:6	**ABBA! FATHER!**
Josh. 3:10	**EL HAI**
1 Sam. 17:45	**YAHWEH SABAOTH**
Ps. 2:2	**MESSIAH**
Ps. 23:1	**YAHWEH ROI**
Jer. 23:6	**YAHWEH T'SIDKENU**
Ezek. 48:35	**YAHWEH SHAMMAH**

Page 12

Ps. 65	["Silence is praise to you, Zion-dwelling God, also obedience. You hear the prayer in it all."]
Ps. 110:1	[Sit at My right hand until I make Thine enemies a footstool for Thy feet.]
Isa. 66:1	[Thus saith the LORD, "heaven is My throne, and the earth is My footstool."]
2 Cor. 10:3-5	[Proclaim His Names and the Word ~ take our thoughts captive to the obedience of CHRIST!]

Page 13

Isa. 7:14	[Therefore the LORD Himself will give you a sign: The virgin will be with child and will give birth to a son, and will call him **IMMANUEL**]
Matt. 1:23	[The virgin will be with child and will give birth to a son, and they will call Him Immanuel ~ which means "God with us."]
Deut. 32:6	[**ABBA! FATHER!** ~ bought, made, and established us]
Phil. 2:11	[**Jesus Christ is LORD to the GLORY of God the Father**]
Gen. 1:26	[And let man rule over . . . everything on the earth]
Ps. 2:4	[**ADONAI** laughs and scoffs at the enemy]

PAGE 24   VIII ~ GOD'S PEERLESS NAMES

Page 13 (continued)
Isa. 53:6   [**LAMB OF GOD** protects us from the destroyer]

Page 14
Matt. 1:23   [… and they will call Him Immanuel (Emmanuel) ~ which means, "God with us."]
Num. 23:22   [**EL ~ EMMANUEL** wrestles for us with the horns of a wild ox]
2 Chron. 20:17   [**YESHUA** came on our behalf ~ Salvation of Yahweh on our behalf]
Matt. 6:1-15   [Jesus teaches the disciples how to pray to our Father in heaven]
Phil. 1:27, 28   [Whatever happens, conduct yourselves in a manner worthy of the gospel of Christ . . . stand firm
                      in one spirit, contending as one man for the faith of the gospel . . . without being frightened by
                      those who oppose you. This is a sign to them that they will be destroyed, but you will be saved ~
                      and that by God!]
1 John 4:18   [But there is no fear in love. But perfect love drives out fear, because fear has to do with
                      punishment. The one who fears is not made perfect in love.]
Rom. 12:18   [If possible, so far as it depends on you, be at peace with all men]

Page 15
Luke 11:52   [You have taken away the key of knowledge; and hindered those who were entering]
John 8:32   [And you shall know the truth and the truth shall set you free]
Rom. 5:1-5   [The love of God is poured out through our hearts]
Luke 11:4   [Forgive us our sins, we also forgive everyone who sins against us ~ lead us not into temptation]

Page 16
John 17:11   ["Keep them in Thy Name that Thou hast given Me."]
John 17:6   [Give them (unbelievers) to JESUS that they may know/keep His WORD]
John 17:17-19   [Sanctify them in truth ~ Thy Word is truth]
John 17:22, 23   ["Glorify them that them may glorify Me." ~ be perfected in unity]

Page17
Isa. 66:8 KJV   [. . . for as soon as Zion travailed, she brought forth her children]
Luke 22:42   ["Father, if You are willing, take this cup from Me; yet not My will but Yours be
                       done."]
Matt .26:39   ["Father, if possible, may this cup be taken from Me. Yet not as I will, but as You will."]
Mark 14:36   ["Abba, Father," Jesus said, "everything is possible for You. Take this cup from Me. Yet not what
                      I will, but what You will."]
Rev. 22:16   ["I, Jesus, have sent My angel to give you this testimony for the churches. I am the Root and the
                      Offspring of David, and the bright Morning Star."]

Page 18
Phil. 2:10, 11   [Every knee shall bow and tongue confess that **Jesus Christ is LORD**]
Ps. 149   *[SING HALLELUJAH TO THE LORD!]*

GOD'S PEERLESS NAMES ENDNOTES

1. Charles C. Ryrie, *Basic Theology*, (Wheaton, IL: Victor Books, 1986), p. 45.
   Even when no particular name is used, the occurrence of the phrase "The name of the Lord" reveals something of His character. To call upon the name of the Lord was to worship Him [Gen. 21:33].

2. Ryrie, Ibid.
   P.48 Strictly speaking these compounds (Ryrie is referring to the various Names of Yahweh [Jireh, Shaloam]) are not additional names of God, but designations of titles that often grew out of commemorative events. However, they do reveal additional facets of the character of God.

3. David H. Stern, *The Jewish New Testament Commentary*, Clarksville, MD: Jewish New Testament Publications), p. 229. Acts 3:16

4. Dr. James Strong, *The New American Standard Bible EXHAUSTIVE CONCORDANCE OF THE BIBLE*, Hebrew-Aramaic and Greek Dictionaries, Robert L. Thomas, Th.D., General Editor, (Nashville, TN: Holmann Bible Publishers, 1907, by permission of Oxford University Press, Brown, Driver, and Briggs (Hebrew Lexicon of OT):

   P.117 #8034 *Name, shem:* coded to Strong's Exhaustive Concordance numerical dictionary,

   P.1607, Brown, Driver and Briggs,

   P.1027 (d).

5. Charles C. Ryrie, *Basic Theology*, (Wheaton, IL: Victor Books, 1986).
   P.49 LORD (KURIOS) c. "Christ as Kurios":
   During His earthly life Jesus was addressed as Lord, meaning Rabbi or Sir (Matt. 8:6). Thomas ascribed full Deity to Him when he declared, "My Lord and my God" (John 20:28). Christ's resurrection and exaltation placed Him as Lord of the universe (Acts 2:36; Phil. 2:11). But, to an early Christian accustomed to reading the OT, the word "Lord," when used of Jesus, would suggest His identification with the God of the OT (S.E. Johnson, - Lord [Christ], The Interpreter's Dictionary of the Bible [New York: Abington, 1976], 3:151). This means, in relation to a verse like Romans 10:9, that any Jew who publicly confessed that Jesus of Nazareth was "Lord," would be understood to ascribe the divine nature and attributes to Him (William G. T. Shedd, Romans [New York: Schribner, 1879, P.318]). Thus the essence of the Christian faith was to acknowledge Jesus of Nazareth as the Yahweh of the Old Testament.

6. John M. Frame, *The Doctrine of The Knowledge of God, A Theology of Lordship*, (Phillipsburg, NJ: Presbyterian and Reformed Publishing Company, 1987), p. 18.

7. Ryrie, Ibid. P.49 "Thus the essence of the Christian faith was to acknowledge Jesus of Nazareth as the *Yahweh* of the Old Testament."

8. Lydia Fellowship in the U.S.A. has been renamed. Please contact www.ASKNETWORKUSA.NET for information or Pamphlets: STEPS TO THE THRONE, KNOW YOUR GOD, etc.

9. *THE DOUBLEDAY ROGET'S THESAURUS in Dictionary Form*, Sidney I. Landau, Editor in Chief, Ronald J. Bogus, Managing Editor, (Garden City, NY: Doubleday and Doubleday, Inc., 1977).
"Not based on any other thesaurus . . . Entries were selected from entries in the Doubleday dictionary, first published in 1975."

10. Lee Amber, *CHOSEN, Communicating With Jews Of All Faiths*, (Santa Ana, CA: Vision House Publishers, 1977), p. 135.
"What should be kept in mind when entertaining mixed groups to which Jewish people have been invited? If food is served and a blessing is asked, the blessing should be asked in the name of the Lord, or even Yeshua, but do not ask it in the name of Jesus or Christ."

11. Stern, *Jewish New Testament Commentary*,
<u>P.1</u> The Messiah. ". . . The significance of being known as 'The Anointed One' is that both kings and cohanim (priests) were invested with their authority in a ceremony of anointing with olive oil. Thus, inherent in the concept of 'Messiah' is the idea of being given God's priestly and kingly authority.

<u>P.2</u> The Messiah (continued). ". . . usually in the text of the JNT Greek Christos is rendered by 'Messiah'; 'Christ' does not appear even once. This is because 'Messiah' has meaning in Jewish religion, tradition and culture; whereas the word 'Christ' has an alien ring and a negative connotation because of the persecutions Jews have suffered from those claiming to be his followers. Further, the use of the word 'Messiah' more that 380 times in the text of the JNT is a continual reminder that the New Testament claims Yeshua to be none other than the promised Mashiach for whom the Jewish people have yearned. The English word 'Christ' does not point to Yeshua's fulfillment of Jewish hopes and biblical prophecy."

12. Intercessors For America, P.O. Box 2639, Reston, VA 22090.
Derek Prince *The Power of Proclamation,* excerpted with permission from a taped message on the "Power of Proclamation." <u>NOTE:</u> By proclaiming the Word of God in faith, under His divine authority, we impact God's purposes on the earth.

13. Robert E. Coleman, (Wheaton, IL: Crossway Books, a division of Good News Publishers, 1995), pp. 45,46.

14. Arthur J. McMahon, *Abundant Living*, The Chapel, Akron, OH. ajmncm71@yahoo.com

15. *Haven of Rest*, Box 2031, Hollywood, California 90028, *THE ANCHOR*, p. 32; "How Excellent Is Thy Name": Meditation for Day 31.

PROCLAIM GOD'S PEERLESS NAMES IN THE OLD TESTAMENT!

ELOHIM ~ Plural Supreme God [Gen. 1:1];

RUACH ~ HOLY SPIRIT [Gen. 1:2];

YAHWEH ~ Active, Self-Existing, Creator of Heaven and Earth [Gen. 2:4; Gen. 4:26];

EL YON ~ God Most High [Gen. 14:18];

ADONAI ~ Lord, Reverential Title, Divine, Sacred, Owner [Gen. 15:2];

EL ROI ~ The God Who Sees [Gen. 16:13];

EL SHADDAI ~ God Almighty [Gen. 17:1];

EL OLAM ~ Everlasting God [Gen. 21:33];

YAHWEH YIREH (Jehovah Jireh) ~ The LORD will Provide [Gen. 22:14];

EL ~ God ~ Strongest, Most Powerful, Shield, Awesome in Majesty [Gen. 32:30];

EL-ELOHE-ISRAEL ~ EL of Immanuel as the God of Israel [Gen. 33:20];

EL GIBBOR ~ Mighty One of Jacob [Gen. 49:24];

YAHWEH LORD ~ I AM that I AM (His Memorial Name) [Exod. 3:15];

YESHUA ~ Salvation, Deliverer [Exod. 15:2; Isa. 12];

YAHWEH RAPHA ~ The LORD your Healer [Exod.15:26];

YAHWEH NISSI ~ The LORD is my Banner [Exod. 17:15];

YAHWEH M'KADDESH ~ The LORD Who Sanctifies You [Exod. 31:13];

YAHWEH SHALOAM ~ LORD ~ Covenant of Peace [Num. 25:12];

ABBA, FATHER ~ Bought and Made Us! [Deut. 32:6];

EL HAI ~ Living God [Josh. 3:10];

YAHWEH SABAOTH ~ LORD of Hosts, God of the armies of Israel! [1 Sam. 17:45];

MESSIAH ~ Consecrated, Anointed, Set Apart [Ps. 2:2];

YAHWEH ROI ~ The LORD our Shepherd [Ps. 23:1];

YAHWEH T'SIDKENU ~ The LORD our Righteousness [Jer. 23:6];

YAHWEH SHAMMAH ~ The LORD is Present [Ezek. 48:35];

THE LORD'S SOVEREIGN NAMES IN THE NEW TESTAMENT:

JESUS, YESHUA ~ IESOUS ~ Savior [Matt. 1:1];

CHRIST, CHRISTOS ~ Anointed, Messiah, and Epithet of Jesus [Matt. 1:16];

LORD, KURIOS, (YAHWEH) ~ Supreme in Authority, Controller, LORD, Master, Sir [Matt. 1:20];

GOD, THEOS ~ Divinity, Magistrate, Very God [Matt. 1:23];

FATHER, PATER, ABBA (Aramaic) ~ Parent (Divine in this mention) [Matt. 5:16];

IMMANUEL, ~ *GOD with us* [Matt. 1:23];

MESSIAH ~ H'Maschiah! [John 1:41].

COME YAHWEH YESHUA H'MASCHIAH!

Lesson IX

Christ The Panorama of Heaven

*"To Him Who is able to keep you from stumbling,
and to present you before His glorious presence
without fault and with great joy,
to the only God our Savior be glory,
majesty, power and authority through
Jesus Christ our LORD before all ages,
now and forevermore!
Amen."*

Jude 1:24

The Sound of Hallelujahs

I heard a sound like massed choirs in Heaven singing,

"Hallelujah!
The salvation and glory and power are God's,
His judgments are true,
His judgments are just.
He judged the great Whore
who corrupted the earth with her lust.
He avenged on her the blood of His servants."

Then, more singing:

"Hallelujah!
The smoke from her burning
billows up to high Heaven forever and ever."

The Twenty-four Elders and the Four Animals fell to their
knees and worshiped God on His Throne, praising,

"Amen! Yes! Hallelujah!"

From the Throne came a shout, a command:

"Praise our God, all you His servants,
All you who fear Him, small and great!"

Then I heard the sound of massed choirs,
the sound of a mighty cataract, the sound of strong thunder:

"Hallelujah!
The Master reigns ~ our Sovereign-Strong!
Let us celebrate, let us rejoice, Let us give Him the glory!"

"The Marriage of the Lamb has come;
His wife has made herself ready.
She was given a bridal gown of bright linen,
The linen is the righteousness of the saints."

The Angel said to me, "Write this: 'Blessed are those invited to the Wedding supper of the Lamb.'"
He added, "These are the true words of God!"
REVELATION 19

The
Message

Eugene H. Peterson

CHRIST THE PANORAMA OF HEAVEN

"Thou, O Christ, Who wert tempted in all points like as we are,
yet without sin, make us strong to overcome the desire to be wise,
and to be reputed wise by others as ignorant as ourselves.
We turn from our wisdom as well as from our folly, and flee to Thee,
the wisdom of God and the power of God [1 Cor. 1:24]. Amen"[1]

***C**HRIST, THE VERY ESSENCE OF GOD'S WISDOM AND POWER,* triumphed over flesh and death when He volunteered to shed His innocent, *sinless,* blood on the Cross. Jesus met God's supreme requirement that provided for the Spirit of Christ to indwell, enable, and instruct us.

CHRIST THE MAN, Who was both the Son of Man and the only begotten Son of God, ascended to the right hand of the Father in Heaven as *a man glorified in the flesh.*

CHRIST, CHRISTOS,[2] Whose Holy Spirit came to empower us and mold our character into His likeness, is the Heavenly vision that we are to keep our eyes fixed upon.

> *A.W. TOZER WROTE IN MAN THE DWELLING PLACE OF GOD:*
> One cause of our moral weakness today is an inadequate Christology. We think of Christ as God, but fail to conceive of Him as a man glorified. To recapture the power of the Early Church we must believe what they believed. And they believed they had a God-approved **man** representing them in heaven.[3]

***T**HE EARLY CHURCH AND GODLY SAINTS SPANNING THE GENERATIONS SINCE, WERE SINGLE-MINDED ~ CHRIST-MINDED.* They were always in communion with Christ to seek His living knowledge.

> *REVEREND ANDREW MURRAY WROTE IN THE SPIRIT OF CHRIST:*
> He brings a living knowledge; His light is the light of life. It is not information, an insight into the connection of truths, or appreciation of their beauty and grandeur . . . To know God and Jesus Christ Whom He has sent is life eternal. This knowledge of God, beholding Him and Christ, is the spiritual, never-ending life which the Spirit creates within us. Dead knowledge is not the work of the Holy Spirit ~ knowledge which the Spirit gives is communion. We see the Father and Son as seeing us.
>
> When we behold them by the revelation of the Spirit, it is as beholding us with infinite love, and bestowing upon us the blessings of grace. In other words, adoration, love, petition, listening to God's voice, receiving the love and peace of Christ, communion, is invoked in this knowledge.[4]
>
> The early Christians met frequently and talked about Christ's uniqueness and His Triumph. They shared their knowledge of His Truth and joyfully celebrated the Holy Spirit's indwelling. They discovered the power of His love which they were required to extend to one another. ". . . each was commissioned to carry on the loving life of Jesus."[5]
>
> This knowledge is therefore also an experience of God; when we know, we possess and receive God and His gifts. We know the Father, and He is our Father; we know Christ, we see His mediation; we have come to

the blood of the new Covenant, and we possess Christ, and experience the power and efficacy of His death and resurrection . . . It is the Spirit Himself Who teaches and enlightens. The Truth itself, the preaching of the Gospel, the reading of the Scriptures, has not inherent power to bring knowledge into the soul. These are only the instruments, the Spirit is the agent; they are only the sword, the Spirit is the energy, the hand that wields it. They shall be taught of God. God causes the light of the Gospel to shine into our hearts.[6]

THE NEW TESTAMENT BELIEVERS WERE FOCUSED BODY, SOUL, AND SPIRIT upon the LORD Yeshua Whom they knew as their Messiah. Nothing diverted them from their heavenly vision of the Messiah!

REVEREND MURRAY NOTED:
It was in wisdom, philosophy, and the search after truth, that the Greeks sought their glory . . . Even when in Christ the LIGHT of God in its Divine love shone upon men, they knew it not.[7]

MANY LOST THEIR ORIGINAL QUEST FOR COMMUNION WITH CHRIST because they pursued knowledge devoid of the Spirit of Christ. Believers are to seek the indwelling Living Christ, Who resides within, yet at the same time resides with the Father and the Son. The Spirit is the One in existence Whom believers can rally around to enjoy corporate worship, fellowship and unity. We have the same Spirit of Christ in us, the Holy Spirit, Who indwelt and enabled our beloved LORD Jesus to walk victoriously in communion with God. The Spirit of Truth, The Messiah, indwells believers as God's enabling gift, force, inspiration, and influence.

THE LIVING TRUTH CAN EDIFY, PROTECT, AND ENCOURAGE US through God's indwelling Spirit. We are strengthened by fellowshipping with believers in the Holy Spirit and corporately pursuing the knowledge and expression of Messiah's character ~ the very essence of God. As believers, we need to understand and trust that we have been given the Holy Spirit as Christ's power within us. We are to exercise God's flow from within us [John 7:38]. We are to serve the whole body of Christ through His incredible love that He recycles through us as His living link with believers. Messiah's Spirit within believers becomes increasingly obvious when they conform to His influence in their lives. The believer's life of prayer is to be in continuous harmony and faith; a faith that rejoices that the Spirit has been received yet waits for the "flow" from the Holy Spirit.

WHO IS THE MESSIAH? He was prophesied in the Old Testament, anticipated and scrupulously watched for by the Pharisees. Messiah is none other than God's Creative Spirit Who spoke into existence the heavens, earth, light, and life [Gen. 2:1-26; John 1:1-5].

Why was such an emphasis put upon *The Messiah?* Why were the Wise men seeking The Christ? Why did Herod seek to kill the Christ Child? Why did Matthew begin his Gospel with the lineage of Jesus as *The Messiah?*

What does this Christ, *The Messiah,* mean to a believer?

What does Christ the CHOSEN ONE mean to us personally?

HOW DO WE DISCERN HIS TRUTH FROM OTHER SO CALLED "TRUTH" if even the elect can be deceived? These are just a few of the questions that started the exciting study about the MESSIAH. Scripture teaches us the importance of learning about the *revelation* of CHRIST. We were told to "think upon these things" and were taught that *JESUS, the LAMB OF GOD*, is both LORD and *MESSIAH!*

IN MY PILGRIMAGE TO LEARN ABOUT THE MESSIAH, the Authority of Truth [Matt. 7:29], my spiritual eyes were opened as never before. My prayer is that you will be enlightened by this humble attempt to share the blessing received in the quest to learn more about *THE LIVING MESSIAH*.

While packing to leave for our vacation, I was quickened to do a Bible search on Christ in the Old Testament. The verses were assembled and printed out, but not read. Later, on the airplane, I took out the printed verses about Christ. I sat there in awe reading the verses through and began to whisper a medley of Christ, using His Name, Messiah. My heart burst with joy to see Christ unfold in such a blessed way. I pray that this happens to you.

IN THE FOLLOWING SELECTIONS OF CHRIST throughout the Bible, the inclusion of Scripture references that come after the subject is suspended to reveal the essence of Christ. However, they are listed in Scripture Sequences at the end. It is my hope you will read the medley of Scriptures (even out loud) that reveal Christ from the beginning to the end. I pray you will experience the excitement I did when envisioning the scriptural **PANORAMA OF HEAVEN** unfold about the **MESSIAH.**

MESSIAH . . . is the Enmity between the serpent's seed and the woman's seed! The Passover Lamb! The Standard lifted to save man! The Peace proclaimed as Judah's Scepter and Staff! The Rescuer from oppression and violence! The Chief Cornerstone and Light for those in darkness! The Chosen Exalted Power! The Anointed One! The Strength of Hannah's song! The ONE that David sang about Who laughed at the enemy! The Incorruptible only Begotten Son of the Father! The Fortress of Salvation! The right hand of Yahweh Who intercedes for transgressors! The Holy One! The Oil of Joy! The Victorious unfailing Love pierced *for us!*

MESSIAH, the Unquenchable LIGHT is . . . ***EMMANUEL!***

Angels proclaimed MESSIAH and YAHWEH when Jesus was born! Simeon *knew* that he would see The Messiah before he died. Simeon prophesied over the baby Jesus that He was the Messianic Deliverer, both a light to the Gentiles and the glory of Israel!

Andrew was excited about finding The Christ! John wrote that the Messiah was with God from the beginning and was God's creative force ~ that Messiah's LIFE is man's LIGHT! Messiah confirmed to the woman at the well that He was the ONE Who came to explain everything to us and that we have life in His Name! Jesus the Word is Christ in essence and totality, the WORD expressed as *God's mind.*

> **Marvin R. Vincent wrote in *Vincent's Word Studies of the Bible*:**
> WORD ~ As Logos has the double meaning of thought and speech, so CHRIST is related to God as the word to the idea, the word being not merely a name for the idea, but the idea itself expressed. The thought is the inward word. The Logos of John is the real, personal God [1:1], the Word, Who was originally before creation with God, and was God, One in essence and nature, yet personally distinct [1:1, 18]; the revealer and the interpreter of the hidden being of God; the reflection and visible image of God, and the organ of all His manifestation to the world.[8]
>
> He was ever in perfect harmony with the mind of heaven, engrossed and enthralled by the Father's will . . . girded with glorious strength, anointed by almighty authority, robed in resolute righteousness and went into battle against the foe fully armed with the accouterments of moral valor and spiritual virtue . . . His armor was impenetrable. He triumphed gloriously . . .[9]

Christ is the Mind of God ~ *God's creative thought ~ the Heartbeat of Heaven ~ the Mind of Heaven shared with us . . . to be reflected by us.* Pondering Christ's awesome role as our Teacher and Enabler inspires, refreshes, and excites our spirits as we grasp God's heavenly vision.

Lord Messiah, HEARTBEAT OF HEAVEN, please illuminate our hearts with the knowledge of You so that we will not be dismayed or deceived! The Consecrated Anointed title of Deity is Your birthright ~ You are *The Messiah* ~ our hope of glory!

Lord, teach us to love You, serve You, revere You, know You, and be a blessing to You.

Lord, take us through Your Holy Word and help us absorb some highlights of Your Truth.

Lord, give us a Panorama of Heaven ~ the PANORAMA OF MESSIAH!

**SHOW US HOW TO PRESS ON
TOWARD CHRIST, OUR HOPE OF GLORY
THE SON OF MAN, THE SON OF GOD
THE MESSIAH!**

IN THE BEGINNING GOD CREATED the Heavens, the earth, the light, and life. *HIS SPIRIT* hovered over creation [Gen. 1; Heb. 1: 1-3]

In the beginning was the Word.[10] [John 1a]

And the WORD was with GOD.[11] [John 1:1b]

And the Word was GOD![12] [John 1:1c]

He was in the beginning with GOD. [John 1:2]

All things came into being through HIM.[13] [John 1:3]

IN HIM WAS LIFE, AND THE LIFE WAS THE LIGHT OF MEN [John 1:4; Rev. 19:13]. The Word became flesh, and dwelt among us. We beheld His glory as of the only begotten from the Father, full of grace and truth [Son of Man, John 1:14 ~ Son of God, Mark 1:1]. The Law was given through Moses; grace and truth were realized through Yeshua the Messiah [John 1:17].

NO MAN HAS SEEN GOD AT ANY TIME; the only begotten Who is in the bosom of the Father, He has explained Him [John 1:17, 18].

Historically we know that the LORD Jesus Christ lived, died, and rose again according to multitudes of witnesses ~ *HE LIVES TODAY!*

THE ANGELS PROCLAIMED, " . . . today in the city of David there has been born for you a Savior [Yeshua], Who is Messiah [Christ] the LORD [Yahweh]" [Luke 1:11].

Isaiah said *THAT MESSIAH IS ALMIGHTY GOD WITH US* ~ Immanuel! People in darkness will see His great LIGHT. He brings justice and is our Eternal Father, Wonderful Counselor, and Prince of Peace [Isa. 7:14; 9:2,7].

Messiah, LIGHT to the nations ~ Righteous Covenant ~ high and lifted up [Isa. 52:13].

Messiah, the Suffering Servant, bore our grief and healed us [Isa. 53:4, 5]. Messiah our Intercessor ~ is the Arm of Yahweh Who reconciles, delivers, and liberates His People [Isa. 53:1-12].

Messiah gave us the oil of joy and the mantle of praise [Isa. 61:1-3].

Messiah ~ *The EXALTED ONE!* [Isa. 52:13]

Jeremiah **said** Messiah, the Hope of Israel, is the Righteous Branch and the One Who will act wisely, do justice and righteousness in the land ~ Messiah heals and saves us [Jer. 17:12, 13, 14; 23:5].

Daniel **called** Him the Son of Man Who was given authority, glory, and sovereign power. All peoples, nations, and men of every language will worship and serve Messiah. His everlasting dominion will never pass away or be destroyed. He is the Anointed One, the Ruler, Messiah the Prince [Dan. 7:13, 14; Dan. 9:24-26].

Micah **said** Messiah would rule over Israel and is of Ancient Origin! Messiah's peace, strength, majesty, and greatness reaches to the ends of the earth [Mic. 5:2; 5:4; 5:5].

Habakkuk **said** Messiah is the Everlasting Holy One and that He goes forth for His people [Hab. 1:12; 3:13].

Zechariah **called** Messiah the Servant and Branch of the LORD of Hosts ~ Who will build the temple of the LORD [Zech. 3:8-12].

Malachi **said** Messiah is the Messenger of the Covenant [Mal. 3:1].

Who is this Messiah Who was born of Mary? The One angels announced and proclaimed upon His birth in Bethlehem? Wise men traveled to see? Herod feared and sought to kill? [Matt. 2:9-13]

Simeon **was promised** that He would live to see the birth of His Messiah, the Savior, the Light and Revelation to the Gentiles [Luke 2:25-32].

The Son of David, the Son of Abraham and the son of Joseph, the husband of Mary of whom Jesus was born, is called The Messiah! John the Baptist, His messenger, said that Messiah would baptize with the Holy Spirit [Matt. 1:1-25; Mark 1:8].

Following Jesus' baptism by John, a voice from heaven said, "Thou art My Beloved Son, in Thee I am well pleased" [Mark 1:11]. The Bible teaches us that there is One God ~ One Mediator between man and God; the *man* called Messiah Yeshua [1 Tim. 2:5].

Andrew excitedly told his brother, we found The Messiah ~ which means The Anointed One. Jesus told those who believed that He is The Messiah . . . *to follow Him!* [Matt. 16:24]

The woman at the well said to Him, "I know that Messiah is coming (He Who is called THE CHRIST). When *that ONE* comes, He will declare all things to us" [John 4:25].

Jesus replied, *"I, Who speak to you, am HE."* [Matt. 1:25; John 4:26]

WHAT DID ANDREW AND THE WOMAN AT THE WELL UNDERSTAND? Why were they excited about Messiah? Who and what were they looking for? Why did some not know Him? The Rabbinic commentaries listed many Messianic Scriptures, some shared above, that prophesied about and described The Messiah as the Son of the Living God. Yet, if they acknowledged Jesus as Messiah, it constituted excommunication from the synagogue. They could safely say that Jesus was a prophet, a teacher, or a worker of signs and miracles. Any title was acceptable except that Jesus was the SON of GOD ~ *THE MESSIAH!*

Jesus asked Peter, "Who do you say that I am?"

Peter answered, "You are MESSIAH, the SON of the LIVING GOD!" [Matt. 16:16]

Jesus answered, "Blessed art thou, Simon Bar-jona: for flesh and blood [intellect and lineage] hath not revealed this unto thee, but My Father in heaven. And I say unto thee, thou art Peter, and upon this rock [the revelation that Jesus was the promised Messiah], I will build My church, and the gates of hell shall not prevail against it." [Matt. 16:18; 1 Cor. 10:4]

(Once again, the normal inclusion of [Scripture references] is suspended, in hopes that you will be blessed by the medley of our Messiah in the Word. Scripture references are in the Scripture Sequences at the end of the lesson.)

Matthew wrote that the Spirit of Christ, our Teacher and Leader, is sitting at the right hand of total power. All Authority has been given to Messiah in Heaven and on the earth. Messiah was crucified and arose as our victorious Savior. The LORD Jesus Christ lives today!

Jesus told His disciples (those closest to Him) that false christs and false prophets will arise and show great signs and wonders to mislead even the elect, if possible! But the *sign* of the Son of Man will be *seen* by *all* ~ *at once* ~ when He comes on clouds in the sky, with power and great glory, and sends forth His angels with a great trumpet to gather His elect.

Mark revealed that The Messiah's Words will not pass away! He said that the Son of the Blessed One, the One Who is sitting at the right hand of Power, *IS COMING SOON!* Jesus warned us not to neglect the Commandments of God or to hold to the traditions of men.

"Hear, O Israel! The LORD our God is One LORD. You shall love the LORD your God with all your heart, with all your soul, with all your mind, and with all your strength. You shall love your neighbor as yourself. There is no greater commandment

. . . go into all of the world and preach the gospel to all of creation."

The disciples went out and preached everywhere. The LORD worked with them and confirmed His Word by signs (miracles) that followed because the disciples believed in His Name!

Luke wrote that the angels proclaimed Messiah is Yahweh, the Chosen One. Messiah Yeshua is LORD of the Sabbath and calls us to repent so that we will not perish. Heaven and earth will pass away but Messiah's Words will not! Messiah opens the minds of mankind to understand Scripture and establishes Himself in our hearts as Yeshua The Messiah ~ the King, the Son of Man, the Chief Cornerstone. Yet, He said that He had nowhere to lay His head. Messiah said that *His house* is to be called a *House of Prayer*.

***Matthew, Mark and Luke* wrote** about Messiah's death tearing the veil of the temple in two. The Son of Man conquered flesh, death, returned in the flesh, and ascended in the flesh. Messiah walked through locked doors and was seen by many. His resurrected flesh was touched before He ascended in His glorified flesh to Father God!

***John* wrote** so that we may believe Yeshua is The Christ ~ the Son of God. And by believing we may have life in His Name, Messiah, the Word of Creation Who is One with the Father!

His Words are Spirit, life, justice, grace, and Truth. He is the LAMB OF GOD Who took away the sin of the world. Messiah is our resurrection and life Who gave us power to be His children!

John also wrote that Nathaniel said, "Rabbi, You are the Son of God, the King of Israel!" Jesus said that He could do nothing of Himself, unless it is something He sees the Father doing ~ then He does it in like manner. Jesus came to glorify the Father Who gave Him authority over all mankind. Yeshua Messiah prayed that the Father's love within Him will be in us ~ MESSIAH in us ~ that we may be one.

Messiah the Word is Spirit and Life. His Truth makes us free! Christ is the Good Shepherd Who speaks the Word of God which cannot be broken. Yeshua Messiah commanded us to love one another, to tend and shepherd His lambs, to feed His sheep, and said, "Follow Me!"

Luke wrote in Acts that Paul taught believers that Yeshua is Yahweh and Messiah. We are to be baptized in Messiah's Name. God verified Yeshua the Nazarene by miracles, signs, and wonders. Messiah Yeshua was raised up from the grave ~ it was impossible to hold Him in the agony and grip of death.

JESUS CHRIST, THE HEALER, causes the sick to arise and make their bed! Messiah's resurrection purchased His Church for God through the power of His Blood. Messiah was the first Who proclaimed to be the TRUE LIGHT to the Jews and Gentiles!

Paul wrote in Romans that in Messiah the Law of the Spirit of Life set us free from sin and death that we may be enslaved to God. Messiah is the Son of God with absolute power, according to the Spirit of Holiness, by His resurrection from the dead as promised by the prophets.

The Spirit of Christ makes our spirit alive in Him, because of His righteousness that bears witness that we are children of God and fellow heirs with Christ. Messiah is ever in intercession for us at the right hand of Father God. The LORD Jesus died for the ungodly. Christ is our reconciliation with God and His gift goes on ~ with no condemnation for those who are in Him.

Messiah, the revelation of God's mystery glorifies the only wise God! His overflowing gift of Grace provides for our baptism into His death, then into new life in Messiah, so that we can live for God through Him, and bear fruit with Him and by Him.

Paul wrote in Corinthians that Messiah is the very revelation of Father God's heart and is The One that empowers His Word within our thoughts.

Messiah *removed the veil* then entrusted God's mystery of the resurrection to us. Messiah calls us to be holy and tells us that His mind is within us. We have the mind of Christ Who is our Spiritual Rock! Messiah is our foundation in Jesus, the Truth! Christ cannot lie! Messiah speaks to us, through us, and is Mighty in us. Messiah the Passover Lamb is the power and wisdom of God Who brings the light out of darkness. Messiah's Blood is our thankfulness ~ His body is our Bread and all things are under His feet. His light shines out of darkness. We behold the LORD and are transformed into His image from Glory to glory.

Paul wrote in Galatians that we are called by Messiah's Grace. Messiah gave us freedom when He redeemed us from the curse. Our sinful nature, passions and desires were crucified with Christ. Christ is the seed of God's promise to Abraham and is the uncompromising boast in the Cross. Messiah Yeshua lives in us. We are one through faith in the Son of Man.

Paul wrote to Ephesians and they must have rejoiced to learn that Messiah came down from Heaven to dwell in our hearts. Christ is Love's provision for us to be adopted as God's sons.

ALL THINGS ARE SUMMED UP IN CHRIST. We were brought near by His Blood. He is our access in One Spirit to the Father. Messiah is the Church's profound mystery revealed ~ Christ is the hope, mark, and seal of the Holy Spirit ~ *our pledge of inheritance.*

By God's mighty strength, which was exerted through Christ, we are raised up to sit with Christ at the right hand of God. We are created in Christ Jesus to do good works. He brought us near through the Blood of Christ ~ He is our peace that breaks down barriers. The unfathomable love of Messiah gave us His Word to wash us and make us holy and blameless before Father God.

LORD Yeshua is the mystery of Christ within us; as fellow heirs, members and partakers of the promises in Messiah ~ *God's eternal accomplishment is through Jesus!* We are forgiven in Messiah and we are to forgive others in Messiah!

Paul wrote in Philippians, "Discern until His day comes." We are to have Messiah's attitude, be worthy of His Gospel and watch out for His interests. We are to know the power of His resurrection through the fellowship of His suffering on the Cross, live, work and believe in His Promises. Christ is the Peace that guards our hearts and glorifies Father God. We are in chains for Christ. There is no loss compared to gaining Messiah. Overflowing joy reveals and preaches *The Messiah!*

Paul wrote in Colossians that he wanted their hearts to be encouraged and knit together in love in the true knowledge of God's mystery. Christ is our reality and circumcision. His enriched Word is to be taught wisely. We're hidden with Messiah in God so that Deity's fullness and headship of power and authority can reside within our hearts. His Peace rules in our hearts when we sing psalms, hymns, and Spiritual songs that Messiah is all and in all!

Paul wrote in Thessalonians that they were to spread the Gospel of Messiah and encourage faith. They were taught to thank Messiah *in* all circumstances, knowing that those who die in Messiah will rise first! Christ's love gives us eternal encouragement and hope.

Paul wrote to Timothy about Messiah's eternal grace, faith, and love that came to save sinners. The LORD was revealed in Messiah's flesh, vindicated in the Spirit, beheld by angels, proclaimed among the nations, believed on in the world, and taken up in Glory for our ransom. Christ is our mediator and our strength. He defeated death! He is the blessed and only Sovereign KING of kings and LORD of lords. LORD God the Messiah is the sole possessor of immortality and He dwells in unapproachable light. To Him be honor and dominion forever and ever!

Paul also wrote to Timothy that the Messiah's church of the Living God will be pillars and the foundation of truth. By His grace His soldiers endure hardship when they are persecuted because they understand and rejoice in His reconciling glorious eternal salvation!

Paul wrote to Titus to encourage believers that Messiah redeemed us and is our Blessed Hope!

Paul and Timothy wrote to Philemon and fellow soldiers for them to pray that their fellowship would be effective in faith. They were exhorted to promote knowledge of all of the good that is ours in Messiah Yeshua, and that Messiah's confidence within enables His followers to do what is proper. They prayed for the Grace of the LORD Jesus Christ to be with believers' spirits!

Paul wrote in Hebrews that *God's final word is in Messiah Yeshua*, the Heir Who has ownership of all things, through Whom He made the world. Messiah is the radiance of God's Glory and exact representation of His nature.

Christ upholds all things and they exist by His powerful Word! Everything is in subjection under His feet. His character and intentions are unchangeable. Messiah's Blood was offered to cleanse our consciences so that we may serve the Living God.

Yeshua is the High Priest of our eternal redemption and our sure hope and safe anchor. Messiah, the King of Righteousness holds the Scepter of Peace, is the Mediator of the New Covenant, and is our Foundation for repentance and faith in God. He is the same yesterday, today, and tomorrow by virtue of the power of His indestructible life.

Messiah is alive forever and able to deliver and intercede on our behalf. He is coming again for those who eagerly wait for Him. Messiah is Holy, set apart, higher than the heavens. Christ is ever in intercession for us and serves us in the Holy Place. Messiah is a Consuming Fire, our Helper, and we are to offer Him a sacrifice of praise continually.

James wrote, as a bond-servant and slave of Messiah, blessed is the man who perseveres under trial . . . when approved he will receive the crown of life. He said we are not to hold our faith in the LORD with an attitude of personal favoritism. Only Christ the Judge and Lawgiver can save and destroy.

Peter wrote, (unto whom God revealed the office of Messiah Jesus as Son of God), that Messiah is our Living Hope. His revelation to us of His grace inspires us to praise His glory and honor Him as we rejoice during our trials. Messiah spoke through the prophets. The Eternal Living and Abiding Word came to be our enablement to be born again. The Messiah Yeshua is the Shepherd and the Guardian of our souls. Christ is the Cornerstone of our acceptance, Who called us out of darkness into His Light to proclaim God's excellencies.

Peter also wrote that Messiah is our Example and that we are to deal righteously with our flesh. Christ's wounds healed us by His body on the Cross. Yeshua Messiah died once for *all* and gave us life in His Spirit through participation in His sufferings. Messiah is the Unblemished Lamb Who redeemed us with His spotless Blood of Eternal Glory. Messiah wants none to perish but wants all to come to repentance. Angels, authorities and all powers have been put under His subjection. Witnesses saw Messiah's majesty, honor, and His glory! Peace to all who are in Christ Who sits at the right hand of God.

John wrote that the Messiah is our Defender and the Righteous One. Messiah lived for us and we are to live for others "in Messiah," believe in His Name, and love one another! Jesus proved that He is the True God of Eternal Life that came in the flesh by water and blood. We are to abide in Messiah's teachings!

Jude wrote to explain that Messiah is our Keeper, the Merciful Sovereign Master and LORD of eternal life, then ended with a proclamation of God's authority, "Unto Messiah, the only God and Savior through Yeshua our LORD, be glory, majesty, dominion and authority forever and ever!"

JESUS TOLD HIS DISCIPLES THAT SOME OF THEM would not die before they saw the kingdom of God after it has come with power. Six days later He led Peter, James, and John up a high mountain to be alone. He was transfigured before them. Surely they witnessed heaven's power when Father God said, "This is My Son, Whom I love, listen to Him."

Paul experienced Heavenly power on the road to Damascus! Matthew, Mark, Luke and John recorded Jesus' teachings about His divine power and Heaven. Peter viewed Heaven as a place of inheritance to be sought for and a possession that awaits us. Jesus went to prepare a place for us in Heaven. The disciples and Paul kept their hearts looking upward toward the place Messiah came from and returned to ~ *HEAVEN!*

DR. MARVIN VINCENT WROTE IN THE WORD STUDIES IN THE NEW TESTAMENT, VOLUME IV:

Christ attained messianic lordship through incarnation. Something was acquired as the result of His incarnation which He did not possess before it, and could not have possessed without it. Equality with God was His birthright; but out of His human life, death and resurrection came a type of sovereignty which could pertain to Him only through His triumph over human sin in the flesh, through His identification with men as their brother [Heb. 1:3]. Messianic Lordship could not pertain to His preincarnate state: it is a matter of function, not of inherent power and majesty. He was essentially Son of God; He must become Son of Man.[14]

Paul wrote in Ephesians::

". . . His incomparably great power for us who believe. That power is like the working of His mighty strength, which He exerted in Christ when He raised Him from the dead and seated Him at His right hand in the heavenly realms, far above all rule and authority, power and dominion, and every title that can be given, not only in the present age but also in the one to come.

"And God placed all things under His feet and appointed Him to be head over everything for the church, which is His body, the fullness of Him Who fills everything in every way" [Eph. 1:19-23].

John wrote in Revelation that he saw the "new Jerusalem coming down from God out of heaven prepared as a bride for her groom." Messiah will make everything new because He is the Beginning and the End and has given us the Fountain of Life. He saw that the LORD God Almighty ~ the LAMB is the temple ~ "for the glory of God did lighten it, and THE LAMB is the Light thereof."

REVEREND CHARLES ROLLS WROTE:

The Christ of God is the hope of glory, for He is the glory of our hope. The title means Anointed One, appointed of God to guard and guide the redeemed host. The rare qualities of The Christ ravish the heart, renew the mind and refresh the soul to the utmost repleteness of satisfaction, until we become complete in Him. The Messiah is eminently gracious, extremely precious and exceptionally glorious . . .

The Supreme One in a special sense: He is indivisible in purpose, irresistible in integrity and invincible in strength.

This is Christ our Conqueror, valiant in victory. His eternal triumph is attended with resurrection mastery, ascension glory and coronation majesty.[15]

LET US SEE MESSIAH YESHUA
THE LAMB OF GOD
AS JOHN DID
ON THE ISLE OF PATMOS . . .

HE IS COMING WITH CLOUDS OF GLORY

EVERY EYE SHALL SEE HIM
Even those who pierced Him
ALL the tribes of earth will mourn because of HIM

All will see MESSIAH YESHUA the YAHWEH
With the Name FAITHFUL and TRUE WRITTEN UPON Him

Riding a white horse in Righteousness
Judging and waging war with eyes of flaming fire
Wearing many crowns
Clothed in a robe dipped in blood

SOVEREIGN WORD OF GOD

THE ALMIGHTY

Using The Sharp Sword From His Mouth
On His Robe and His Thigh is Written

KING of kings and LORD of lords

HE WHO SITS ON THE THRONE DECLARES

"The Tabernacle of God Is Among Men

BEHOLD I AM COMING QUICKLY

My Reward Is With Me to Render to ALL What They Have Done!"

"I AM the ALPHA and the OMEGA!"

LORD YESHUA MESSIAH

MASTER and SAVIOR ~ ETERNAL CHRISTOS
Who Anoints and Leads His People to Walk in Victory
In His Absolute Sovereignty
From Eternity Throughout Eternity

COME LORD YESHUA MESSIAH IN ALL OF YOUR GLORY!

THE DISCIPLES KNEW THE GLORY AND POWER OF MESSIAH. Peter said "We must obey God, not man. The God of our fathers raised Yeshua up . . . God exalted this man at His right hand as Ruler and Savior, in order to enable Israel to repent and turn from their sins and have her sins forgiven. We are witnesses to these things; so is the Holy Spirit, Whom God has given to those who obey Him" [Acts 5:29-32 JNT]. Soon after this the disciples chose Stephen, a man full of faith and the Spirit of Christ, as one of the seven men to oversee the community of believers. Stephen was full of grace and power, and he performed great miracles and signs among the people. Opposition arose from members of the Synagogue . . . Everyone sitting in the Sanhedrin stared at Stephen and saw that his face looked like the face of an angel . . . They argued with Stephen, but when he spoke they could not stand up against his wisdom given by the Holy Spirit.

STEPHEN'S TESTIMONY ANGERED THE PRIESTS AND PEOPLE WHEN HE SAID, "Our fathers had the tabernacle of testimony in the wilderness . . . David found favor in God's sight and asked to find a dwelling place for the God of Jacob . . . But it was Solomon who built a tabernacle for Him.

"However, the MOST HIGH does not dwell in houses made by human hands," Stephen responded to the Council [Acts 7:44-48]. Then he quoted from Isaiah [66:1, 2]:

> "As the prophet says: Heaven is My Throne,
> And earth is the footstool of My feet;
> What kind of house will you build for Me?" says the LORD;
> "Or what place is there for My repose?
> "Was it not My hand which made all these things?

STEPHEN ACCUSED THEM, "STIFF-NECKED PEOPLE, with uncircumcised hearts and ears! You continually oppose the Holy Spirit! You do the same things your fathers did! Which of the prophets did your fathers not persecute? They killed those who told in advance about the coming of the Righteous One, and now you have become His betrayers and murderers! You! Who receive the Torah as having been delivered by angels ~ but do not keep it!" Now when the Council heard this they were cut to the quick and they began gnashing their teeth at him. [Excerpts from Acts 6:8-7:56 JNT.]

Indwelt by the Spirit of Christ, Stephen gazed intently into heaven, saw the glory of God and Jesus standing at the right hand of God. Stephen said, "Behold I see the heavens opened up and the Son of Man standing at the right hand of God."

When they rushed to kill Stephen and were stoning him, he called upon the Messiah, "LORD Jesus, receive my spirit . . . hold not this sin against them." Then Stephen's spirit rose to join Jesus in Heaven [Acts 7:54-60].

Stephen knew the power and wisdom of God. He had walked and talked with the Messiah! He did not look to the left or to the right when they stoned him, but looked into heaven and saw the *YESHUA and **THE GLORY OF GOD***.

He saw heavens opened and the Son of Man standing at the right hand of God.

EVERY EYE SHALL SEE HIM
EVEN THOSE WHO PIERCED HIM
ALL TRIBES OF EARTH WILL MOURN BECAUSE OF HIM

"THE LORD GOD, THE ALMIGHTY, AND THE LAMB ARE ITS TEMPLE.
THE GLORY OF GOD HAS ILLUMINED IT, ITS LAMP IS THE LAMB."

STEPHEN LOOKED UP AND SAW CHRIST'S GLORY, WISDOM, AND POWER standing as the Lamb of God. He caught a glimpse of the Panorama of Heaven, an infusion of heaven revealed in reality that had been made known through faith and hope during his walk on earth. We, too, need a glimpse of heaven to take us through persecutions that come in our lifetime.

E.M. BOUNDS, MIGHTY INTERCESSOR, TEACHER, OVERCOMER, WROTE PROFOUND THOUGHTS IN HIS FINAL BOOK, *CATCHING A GLIMPSE OF HEAVEN*.[16]

> The glory of God, brighter than the light of a thousand suns, will be our light. The mild sweet rays from the Lamb will cast their radiance over all of the land, scattering darkness, gloom, and sorrow. "For there shall be no night there" [Rev. 21:25].[17]

> The light of God's Presence hides and disperses all the feeble lights of earth.[18]

> No truth is more necessary to man and more in accordance with God's character, none more necessary to His glory, than the *doctrine of heaven*.[19]

> Heaven is a state as well as a place . . . a state of enthronement, elevation, and freedom . . . it will be a state of perfected knowledge.[20]

> As Jesus drew near to the end, important things engaged His attention. He must commit to His disciples the interests of His Kingdom. Heaven was all important. Heaven was to be kept in eye and heart at all time. Their deep spiritual

life, their personal holiness, and their conscious abiding in Christ were all important. Christ spoke of the necessity of Christ-life and Christ-likeness in His sacred words.[21]

If we meditated on the joys of heaven, we could not dispense with the deepest conviction, the most ardent faith, and the firmest loyalty. These heavenly thoughts strengthen our weakness, disperse our depression, and brighten our darkness. They call us to purity and nobleness and awaken us to righteousness. The thoughts of heaven quicken our faith. Our only sure and solid foundation is the hope of heaven . . . we need an infusion of heaven into our faith and hope that will create a homesickness for that blessed place.[22]

It is the thought, hope, and fact of heaven that forms Christian character and matures it into unearthly beauty and perfection.[23]

If we do not get back to peeps into Heaven, consciousness of the higher glory and the larger life, we shall lose our religion (faith); our altar will become a bare stone, unblessed by visitant from Heaven. Here is the world's need today . . . men who have seen their Lord.[24]

True faith brings a spiritual and moral transformation and an inward witness that cannot be mistaken. These come when we stop believing in belief and start believing in the Lord Jesus Christ indeed. True faith is not passive but active. It requires that we meet certain conditions, (that) we allow the teachings of Christ to dominate our total lives from the moment we believe. The man of saving faith must be willing to be different from others.[25]

SAVING FAITH COMES FROM HEARING THE WORD OF GOD [Rom. 10:17]. Have we received an infusion of Heaven for our faith? Do we need the gift of faith? [1 Cor. 12:9] Do we need a biblical faith that trusts in God's Character and the unsearchable riches of His Son, our LORD Jesus Christ? All that a believer needs to do is ask the Messiah for the gift of faith to live ardently for Him in firm loyalty.

PAUL WROTE ABOUT THE MYSTERY OF CHRIST [Eph. 3:4]. He exhorted believers to walk in Messiah's unfathomable riches to let everyone see the administration of Messiah's mystery which was kept *hidden by God* through the ages . . . *that through the church,* the manifold wisdom of God [that forms and executes His counsels] *should be made known to rulers and authorities in heavenly realms,* according to His purpose, that He accomplished in The Messiah Yeshua our LORD [Eph. 3:8b-11].

REVEREND TOZER WROTE, MAN, THE DWELLING PLACE OF GOD:
In Our Knowledge Of Divine Things three degrees may be distinguished: The knowledge furnished by reason, by faith, and by spiritual experience respectively. But there is knowledge beyond and above that furnished by observation; it is knowledge received by faith. . . . Divine revelation through the inspired Scriptures offers data which lie altogether outside of and above the power of the mind to discover.[26]

PAUL EXHORTED US, as believers, to pray that the eyes of our hearts may be enlightened to know the hope to which Christ Jesus our LORD has called us, and to know the riches of His glorious inheritance in the saints [Eph. 1:18-23]. We need to keep Paul's words about the mystery of Christ tucked into our hearts and praise the LORD that Christ is God's wisdom and power that has been revealed to our hearts.

Jesus taught us that HE is LORD *and* Messiah ~ the Hope of Glory!

IN A.W. TOZER'S ARTICLE, THE LORDSHIP OF THE MAN JESUS IS BASIC, he wrote marvelous quotes about The Christ of the New Testament ~ The Messiah Who was set forth clearly and plainly in the Scripture of Truth:

> This was the mighty, revolutionary message of the Early Church: A *man* named Jesus, Who had been crucified, was now raised from the dead and exalted to the right hand of God. Therefore let all the house of Israel know assuredly, that God hath made that same Jesus, Whom ye have crucified, both LORD and Christ [Acts 4:10].
> Christ is God of the substance of His Father, begotten before all ages . . . equal to His Father, as touching His Godhead; less than the Father, as touching His manhood. Who, although He be God and man, yet He is not two, but one Christ, by taking the manhood into God.
> When Christ walked the earth, He was God with men, but the equal truth is that where He sits now on His mediatorial throne He is Man with God . . . this exalted position He attained as a man. The apostles were declaring the preeminence of Christ as man, which was necessary . . . And the proof of this was the presence of the Holy Spirit among them.[27]

REVEREND TOZER'S EXHORTATION TO BELIEVERS:
> One cause of our moral weakness today is an inadequate Christology. We think of Christ as God but fail to conceive of Him as **a man glorified**. To recapture the power of the Early Church we must believe what they believed. And they believed they had a **God-approved man** representing them in heaven.[28]

WHEN WE SAY "THE LORD JESUS CHRIST" we are representing the fullness of the Godhead ~ the Son of Man glorified and standing in the Holy Place with God ~ the very essence of **man** that is "hidden with Christ in God."

FATHER GOD, like Stephen, help us to gaze upward toward Heaven to see the Messiah's glorious triumph. Enable us to refuse to look to the left or the right at the stones and flaming missiles hurled at us from every side.

May our thoughts be raised and elevated upward to fuse with Yours as one heartbeat ~ One in our thoughts, One in our heavenly prayers, One in Your triumph, One in administrating Your business on earth, One in proclamation of Your Almighty Kingdom.

May we lift holy hands with pure hearts and see our redemption draweth nigh! [Luke 21:28]

Let Us Praise The Lord
Heaven and Earth are filled with His Glory!

After this I heard what sounded like the roar of a great multitude in heaven shouting: "Hallelujah, Salvation and glory and power belong to our God, for true and just are His judgments ...

And again they shouted: "Hallelujah! The smoke from her goes up for ever and ever." The twenty-four elders and the four living creatures fell down and worshiped God, Who was seated on the throne. And they cried: "Amen, Hallelujah!" Then a voice came from the throne, saying: "Praise our God, all you His servants, you who fear Him, both small and great!"

Then I heard what sounded like a great multitude, like the roar of rushing waters, like loud peals of thunder, shouting: "Hallelujah! For our LORD God Almighty reigns.

"Let us rejoice and be glad and give Him glory! For the wedding of the Lamb has come, and His bride has made herself ready."

Then the angel said to me, "Write: 'Blessed are those who are invited to the wedding supper of the Lamb!'" And the angel added, "These are the true words of God."

"Come, gather together for the great supper of God."
[Rev. 19:1-9]

THE LAMB OF GOD IS COMING SOON

COME,
LORD JESUS, OUR MESSIAH!

AMEN and HALLELUJAH!

LIFE APPLICATION

1. When Jesus met God's supreme sacrifice, it provided for the Holy Spirit to _____, _____, and _____ believers. (P. 1)

2. A. What is one cause of our moral weakness today? B. What power did the early church share that most believer's are deficient in today? C. What did A.W. Tozer say that we must do to recapture the power of the early church? D. Who did the early church believe was representing them in heaven. (P. 1)

3. A. What did the early Christians talk about when they gathered together? B. What did they discover? C. What were they commissioned? (P. 1)

4. A. It is the _____ Himself Who teaches and enlightens. B. The Truth itself, the preaching of the Gospel, and the reading of the Scriptures has not inherent power to bring knowledge into the soul ~ they are only the instruments. The Spirit is the _____, they are only the sword, the Spirit is the _____, the hand that wields it. C. God causes the light of the _____ to shine into our hearts. (P. 2)

5. How were the New Testament believers focused on the LORD Yeshua their Messiah? (P. 2)

6. A. How have many lost the quest for communion with Christ? B. What are believers to seek? C. Why? D. When are we strengthened? E. What do we need to understand about the Holy Spirit? (P. 2)

7. There is one Mediator between ____ and God, the ____ called Messiah Yeshua! (P. 6)

8. What happened to Jews who acknowledged Jesus as Messiah? (P. 7)

9. A. Jesus told His disciples that false _____ and false _____ would do what? B. How will we know He's gathering the elect? C. What did Jesus warn us not to neglect? (P. 7)

10. What did Jesus say are the two greatest commandments? (P. 7)

11. How did the LORD confirm His Word to the disciples and why did He do it? (P. 8)

12. Rev. Rolls wrote that Christ is the Supreme One and that He is _____ in purpose, irresistible in _____ and _____ in strength. (P. 13)

13. A. What was Stephan's response to those stoning him? B. Who did he see? C. What was his dying request? (PP. 15, 16)

14. A. Why did E. M. Bounds say we should meditate on the joys of Heaven and what does it strengthen? B. What do we need in our faith and hope to create a homesickness for heaven? (P. 17)

15. What did E. M. Bounds say that forms Christian character and matures it into unearthly beauty and perfection? (P. 17)

16. What did Bounds say is the world's need today? (P. 17)

17. A. What did Bounds say that true faith brings believers? B. Is it passive or active? C. What does it require? (P. 17)

18. A. According to Tozer, what three degrees may be distinguished in our knowledge of Divine things? B. Knowledge beyond and above that furnished by observation is received by _____ . C. What will Divine revelation received through inspired Scripture reveal? (P. 17)

19. A. What did Tozer say was the mighty, revolutionary message of the Early Church? B. Who, although He is God and man, yet is not two, but One, takes what into God? (P. 18)

20. A. What did Tozer write that the apostles declared? B. What was the proof? (P. 18)

21. Who do you personally say the Messiah is after reading from the writings of men about God?

22. A. When we say "LORD JESUS CHRIST," what are we representing? B. Are you hidden with Christ in God (personal response)? C. Can you rejoice and be glad? (personal response) (P. 18)

23. A. Who did the voice from the throne tell to praise our God? B. Are you ready for the wedding? (personal response) (P. 19)

24. Please go back to page 13. Starting at the bottom, jointly read:

HE IS COMING WITH CLOUDS OF GLORY

… then continue together to read the Poster on the next page.

The amazing grace of the Master Jesus Christ,
the extravagant love of God,
the intimate friendship of the Holy Spirit
be with all of you.

2 Corinthians 13
THE MESSAGE

CHRIST the PANORAMA of HEAVEN SCRIPTURE SEQUENCES

Page 1
1 Cor. 1:24   [Christ the wisdom and power of God]

Page 2
John 7:38   ["He who believes in Me, as the Scripture said, 'From his innermost being shall flow rivers of living water."]
Gen. 2:1-26   [The Spirit of God created the heavens, earth, light and life]
John 1:1   [In the beginning was the Word, and the Word was with God, and the Word was God]

Page 3
Matt. 7:29   [Jesus taught them as one in authority, not as their scribes taught.]

Page 4
John 1:12   [Yet to all who received him, to those who believed in His name, He gave the right to become children of God]
John 1:1, 18   [In the beginning was the Word, and the Word was with God, and the Word was God. . . (18) No one has ever seen God, but God the One and Only, who is at the Father's side, has made Him known.]

Page 5
Gen. 1; Heb. 1:1-3 [God created the heavens, earth, light, life; His Spirit hovered over creation]
John 1:1a   [In the beginning was the WORD]
John 1:1b   [And the WORD was with God]
John 1:1c   [And the WORD was God!]
John 1:2   [The WORD was in the beginning with God]
John 1:3   [All things came into being through the WORD]
John 1:4   [In the WORD was life, and the life was the Light of Men]
Rev. 19:13   [Christ is the WORD of God]
John 1:14   [The WORD became flesh and dwelt among us ~ The WORD became the son of man]
Mark 1:1   [The WORD is the Son of God]
John 1:17   [The Law was given through Moses; grace and truth came through Jesus]
John 1:17, 18   [No man has seen God ~ The WORD has explained Him]
Luke 1:11   [Angels proclaimed a Savior, Messiah the LORD was born]
Isa. 7:14   [Messiah is Almighty God With us (Immanuel)]
Isa. 9:2, 7   [People in darkness will see His great Light]
Isa. 52:13   [Messiah, Light to the nations, Righteous]
Isa. 53:4, 5   [Messiah the Suffering Servant bore our grief and healed us]
Isa. 53:1-12   [Intercedes for transgressors]
Isa. 61:1, 3   [Messiah gives the oil of joy and the mantle of praise]

Page 6
Isa. 52:13   [My Servant will be high and lifted up and greatly exhalted.]Exalted]
Jer. 17:13   [The Hope of Israel]
Jer. 17:12   [Messiah the WORD is our glorious Sanctuary]
Jer. 17:14   [Messiah heals and saves us]
Jer. 23:5   [Messiah the Righteous Branch]
Dan. 7:13   [Son of Man with authority, and glory and sovereign power]
Dan. 7:14   [The kingdom of Messiah will never be destroyed; men of every nation will serve Him]
Dan. 9:24-2   [The Anointed One, the Ruler, Messiah the Prince]
Mic. 5:2   [Messiah rules over Israel and is of Ancient Origin]
Mic. 5:4   [He is our peace]
Mic. 5:5   [Messiah's, strength, Majesty and Greatness reaches to the ends of the earth]

Page 6 (continued)

Hab. 1:12	[Messiah is the Everlasting Holy One]
Hab. 3:13	[He goes forth for His people]
Zech. 3:8-12	[The Servant and Branch of the LORD of Hosts will build the temple of God]
Mal. 3:1	[Messiah is the Messenger of the Covenant]
Matt. 1:29	[Messiah conceived in Mary by the Holy Spirit]
Luke 2:25-32	[Simeon prophesied Messiah is Salvation/Light to the Gentiles.]
Mark 1:8	[John the Baptist said, "… He will baptize you with the Holy Spirit."]
Matt. 1:23	[Messiah to be called Immanuel which means God With Us]
Matt. 3:11	[John the Baptist said Messiah would baptize with the Holy Spirit and fire]
Mark 1:11	[God said from heaven "Thou art My Beloved Son, in Thee I am well pleased."]
1 Tim. 2:5	[Messiah Jesus is Mediator between God and man]
Matt. 16:24	[Jesus builds His church upon understanding the revelation that He is Messiah and tells His believers to follow Him]
John 4:25	[The woman at the well told Jesus that when Christ comes He will declare all things to us]
Matt. 1:25	[… and she called His Name Jesus]
John 4:26	[Jesus said, I Who speak to you am HE!]

Page 7

Matt. 16:16	["You are Messiah, the Son of the Living God."]
Matt. 16:18	[The gates of hell shall not prevail against Messiah's church]
1 Cor. 10:4	[Jews in wilderness drank from the spiritual rock which was Christ Who followed them]
Matt. 23:8	[Christ our Teacher and Master]
Matt. 23:10	[Messiah our Leader]
Matt. 26:63, 64	[Messiah sits at the right hand of power]
Matt. 28:18	[Messiah has all authority in heaven and earth]
Matt. 27	[Messiah Crucified, Risen, Victorious today!]
Matt. 28:6	[Christ is not in the tomb ... HE IS RISEN ... alive today]
Matt. 24:24	[False Christ's/false prophets will show many signs and wonders and mislead the elect]
Matt. 24:30, 31	[ALL will see the Son of Man come in power & great glory when He gathers His elect]
Mark 13:31	[Messiah's Words will not pass away]
Mark 14:61	[Messiah is the Son of the Blessed One and is sitting at the right hand of power.]
Mark 12:36	[Messiah is coming soon!]
Mark 7:8	Messiah warns us not to neglect God's commandments or hold to men's traditions]
Mark 12:30-31	[Jesus commands us to love God with all of our heart, soul, mind ~ preach Gospel to all]

Page 8

Mark 16:14-20	[Messiah works with disciples ~ confirms Word by signs as they believed in His Name]
Luke 2:11	[Angels proclaimed Messiah is Yahweh (LORD)]
Luke 23:35	[The Chosen One]
Luke 6:5	[Messiah Jesus is LORD of the Sabbath]
Luke 13:5	[We're called to repent so that we will not perish]
Luke 21:33	[Heaven and earth will pass away ~ but Messiah's words will not]
Luke 24:31, 32	[Messiah opens eyes (heart) to understand Scripture]
Luke 22:66-23:3	[Messiah establishes He is Yeshua the King and the Son of Man]
Matt. 21:13	[Jesus said, "It is written that My house will be called a house of prayer."]
Luke 20:17	[He is our Chief Cornerstone]
Luke 9:58	[Messiah Jesus had no where on earth to lay His head]
Matt. 27:51	[Messiah's death tore the veil of the temple in two]
Mark 15, 16	[The Son of Man conquered flesh, arose, appeared to many in His flesh, walked through locked doors, arose to sit at God's right hand]
Luke 24	[The Son of Man was beheld, touched and believed in; they touched His resurrected flesh (v.7) before He was taken up into Heaven (v.51) in His glorified flesh.]
Matt. 27:51	[Messiah's death tore the veil of the temple in two]
Mark 15:38	[Messiah conquered flesh, arose, then walked in His resurrected flesh through locked doors]

Page 8 (continued)

Luke 23:45	[Beheld, believed in, when they touched His resurrected flesh ~ then He ascended to the Father in His glorified flesh]
John 1:34	[Jesus is Messiah the Son of God]
John 20:31	[Believing in Messiah we have life in His Name]
John 6:63	[Christ is One with the Father ~ His Words are Spirit and Life]
John 1:17	[His Word is Grace and Truth]
John 1:29	[Messiah the LAMB OF GOD took away the sin of the world]
John 11:25	[Christ is <u>our</u> Resurrection and life]
John 1:12	[Jesus our Messiah gave us the right to be His children]
John 1:49	[Rabbi, the Son of God ~ the King of Israel]
John 8:28, 29	[Jesus did nothing of Himself ~ He did as He saw the Father do]
John 17:1, 2	[Jesus glorifies the Father Who gave Him authority over all mankind]
John 17:26	[Jesus made the Father's Name known to us and prayed that His love may be in us]
1 John 8:32	[Messiah's Words are spirit and life ~ His Truth sets us free]
John 10:35	[Messiah the Good Shepherd speaks the Word of God which cannot be broken]
John 21:15-17	[Yeshua Messiah commands us to love, tend, shepherd, feed His sheep and said "Follow Me."]
Acts 2:36	[Jesus is LORD and Christ]
Acts 2:22	[God verified Jesus the Nazarene by miracles, signs and wonders]
Acts 2:38	[We are to be baptized in Jesus Christ's Name for forgiveness of sin; receive gift of the Holy Spirit]
Acts 2:24	[God raised Messiah Yeshua up from the grave ~ He could not be held in the grip of agony & death]

Page 9

Acts 9:34	[Yeshua Christ is our healer Who causes the sick to rise and make their bed!]
Acts 20:28	[He purchased the church with His own blood]
Acts 26:23	[Messiah was the first to proclaim LIGHT to the Jews and Gentiles]
Rom. 6:22 NASB	[Messiah, the Law of the Spirit of Life set us free from sin & death to be enslaved to God]
Rom. 1:4	[Son of God with absolute power, according to the Spirit of Holiness, as prophesied and promised by His resurrection from death]
Rom. 8:16, 17	[The Holy Spirit bears witness with our spirit we are His children and co-equal heirs with Christ]
Rom. 8:34	[Christ is at the Father's right hand ever interceding for us]
Rom. 6:22-23	[Christ is our reconciliation and His gift goes on]
Rom. 4:6-10	[Messiah died for the ungodly and He is our reconciliation with God]
Rom. 5:16-18	[There is no condemnation for those in Christ Jesus]
Rom. 24:27	[Messiah, the revelation of God's mystery glorifies the only wise God]
Rom. 6:3	[His overflowing Grace provided our baptism into His death]
Rom. 6:4	[From death into new life in Messiah]
Rom. 7:4	[We are to live for God *through Messiah* ~ that we may bear fruit]
2 Cor. 4:6	[His LIGHT gives light in hearts of the knowledge of God's glory in the face of Messiah]
2 Cor. 4:7	[The surpassing greatness of His power within (our thoughts) is from God, not ourselves]
2 Cor. 3:14	[God removes the veil 'in Christ'.]
1 Cor. 15:50-58	[Entrusted with God's mystery of resurrection ~ victory in the LORD Jesus Christ]
1 Cor. 1:2	[Messiah calls His sanctified to be holy]
1 Cor. 2:6-16	[We have the mind of Christ within us]
1 Cor. 10:4	[We have the mind of Christ our Spiritual Rock]
1 Cor. 3:11	[Jesus Christ is our foundation]
2 Cor. 6:15	[Christ cannot lie]
2 Cor. 13:3, 4	[Messiah speaks through us and is mighty in us]
1 Cor. 1:24	[Christ the power of God and the wisdom of God]
1 Cor. 5:7	[Christ our Passover also has been sacrificed]
1 Cor. 10:16, 17	[The blood of Christ is our blessing (thanksgiving), His body our bread]
1 Cor. 15:25	[For He <u>has</u> (present tense) put all things in subjection under His feet]
2 Cor. 4:6	[Messiah is the LIGHT that shines out of darkness]
2 Cor. 4:4	[Unbelievers cannot see the Gospel Light ~ the glory of Christ Who is the image of God]
Gal. 1:6	[We are called by Messiah's grace]
Gal. 3:13	[Messiah gave us freedom when He redeemed us from the curse of the Law]

IX ~ THE PANORAMA OF HEAVEN

Page 9 (continued)

Gal. 2:20	[Crucified with Christ ~ we no longer live in the flesh, Christ lives in us through faith]
Gal. 5:24	[Those belonging to Christ Jesus have crucified the flesh with its passions and desires]
Gal. 3:29	[Belonging to Christ makes us Abraham's offspring, heirs according to promise]
Gal. 6:14	[Boast in the cross of our LORD Jesus Christ]
Gal. 2:20	[Christ lives in us]
Gal. 3:26, 28	[We are sons of God through faith in Christ Jesus; we are one through faith in the Son of Man]
Matt. 1:1-17	[Jesus Christ is the Son of Man]
Eph. 1:3	[Messiah is our spiritual blessing in the heavenly places]
Eph. 1:5	[Christ is Love's provision for our adoption as sons of God]

Page 10

Eph. 1:10	[All things are summed up in Messiah]
Eph. 2:13	[We have been brought near by the blood of Christ]
Eph. 2:18	[Christ is our access in one Spirit to the Father]
Eph. 3:1-10	[Messiah is the church's profound mystery revealed]
Eph. 1:10-14	[We are sealed in Messiah our hope ~ sealed in Him with the Holy Spirit of promise]
Eph. 1:14	[Messiah is given as the pledge of our inheritance as God's own possession ~ praise His glory]
Eph. 1:19	[Surpassing greatness of His power ~ who believe ~ according to His work and strength of Might]
Eph. 1:20	[His strength through Christ resurrected Him and sat Him at God's right hand]
Eph. 1:21	[Christ above all rule, authority, power, dominion, every name, now and in the ages to come]
Eph. 1:21	[All things are in subjection under Messiah's feet ~ He is head over all things to the church]
Eph. 1:22	[The church is His body ~ the fullness of Him Who fills all in all]
Eph. 2:10	[We are created in Christ Jesus for the good works that God prepared for us to walk in]
Eph. 2:13, 14	[Messiah's blood brings unity ~ His peace breaks down barriers]
Eph. 3:16-20	[The Spirit of Christ ~ the power working in us that reveals Messiah's unfathomable love]
Eph. 5:26, 27	[Christ sanctifies, cleanses us that He might present to Himself the church, holy and blameless]
Eph. 5:30-32	[The Mystery is great ~ Christ's love is revealed for His church ... the members of His body]
Eph. 4:32	[Forgive each other, just as God in Christ also has forgiven you]
Phil. 1:27	[Be worthy of Messiah's Gospel ~ stand firm, one spirit, mind, striving for faith of Gospel]
Phil. 3:10	[Know the power of His resurrection and fellowship of His sufferings through the Cross]
Phil. 4:7	[Messiah is the Peace that guards our hearts and glorifies our Father]
Phil. 3:7	[There is no loss compared to gaining Christ]
Col. 2:2	[Hearts knit in love & true knowledge of God's mystery ~ Christ within the hope of glory]
Col. 2:9	[In Messiah all the fullness of Deity dwells in bodily form]
Col. 2:10	[In Messiah we are made complete; He is the head over all rule and authority]
Col. 3:3	[We are hidden with Christ in God]
Col. 2:9-11	[Messiah is Deity's fullness and headship of power and authority in our hearts]
Col. 3:16a	[Let His enriched Word dwell within ~ with all wisdom teach and admonish others]
Col. 3:15-16b	[Peace rules in hearts that sing psalms, hymns, Spiritual songs: Messiah is all & in all]
1 Thess. 3:2	[Fellow workers are sent out to spread the Gospel of Messiah and encourage faith]
1 Thess. 5:18	[In everything give thanks ~ that is God's will for us in Christ Jesus]
1 Thess. 4:16	[The dead in Christ will rise first]
2 Thess. 2:16-17	[Messiah loves us and gives eternal encouragement and hope]
1 Tim. 1:14	[His eternal Grace, Faith and Love came to save sinners]
1 Tim. 3:16	[The mystery of godliness revealed in Messiah, vindicated in the Spirit, beheld by angels, proclaimed among nations, believed on in the world and taken up in Glory as our ransom]
1 Tim. 2:5	[Messiah Jesus is the one mediator between God and man]
2 Tim. 4:17	[Christ strengthens our proclamations and sees that they are accomplished]
2 Tim. 1:10	[Messiah abolished death]
1 Tim. 6:15, 16	[Blessed Sovereign King of kings and LORD of lords possesses immortality and dwells in unapproachable light ~ to Him be honor and dominion forever and ever]
1 Tim. 3:15	[The church of the Living God is the pillar of support and truth]
2 Tim. 2:10	[Soldiers endure when persecuted due to the knowledge of His glorious eternal Salvation]

Page 11

Reference	Description
Titus 2:13	[Believers are to be encouraged and reminded that Messiah redeemed us and is our Blessed Hope]
Philem. 2	[Believers are fellow soldiers]
Philem. 6a	[Prayer for believers' fellowship to be effective in faith]
Philem. 6b	[Promote the knowledge of all of the good that is ours in Messiah Yeshua]
Philem. 8	[We are enabled to do proper things because of Messiah's confidence in us]
Philem. 25	[The grace of the LORD Jesus Christ be with your spirit]
Heb. 1:2	[God's final Word is in Messiah Yeshua, appointed heir of all things ~ Whom made the world]
Heb. 1:3a, b	[Messiah is the radiance of God's glory; Messiah is the exact representation of God's nature]
Heb. 1:3c	[Messiah upholds all things by the Word of His power]
Heb. 2:8	[All things are under His feet]
Heb. 6:17	[His character and intentions are unchangeable]
Heb. 9:14	[Messiah's blood was offered to cleanse our conscience; that we might serve the Living God]
Heb. 9:11	[Messiah is the High Priest of our eternal redemption]
Heb. 1:8	[Messiah is the Righteous Scepter]
Heb. 6:19	[Our sure hope and safe anchor]
Heb. 7:2	[...His name means "King of Righteousness"; also, king of Salem means "King of Peace"]
Heb. 8:6	[Christ is the Mediator of the New Covenant]
Heb. 6:1	[Messiah is our foundation of repentance and faith in God]
Heb. 13:8	[Yeshua Christ is the same yesterday, today and tomorrow]
Heb. 7:16	[His life is indestructible]
Heb. 7:25	[Christ is alive forever and able to deliver and intercede for us]
Heb. 9:28	[He is coming for those who eagerly await Him]
Heb. 7:26	[Messiah is holy, set apart, and higher than the heavens]
Heb. 12:28	[Messiah is a consuming fire]
Heb. 13:6	[Christ is our Helper]
Heb. 13:15	[We are to continually offer to Christ a sacrifice of praise]
James 1:1	[Bondservant of God and the LORD Jesus Christ]
James 1:12a, b	[Blessed is the man who perseveres under trial; The approved will receive the crown of life]
James 2:1	[Hold not your faith in the LORD with an attitude of personal favoritism]
James 4:12	[The only One, Christ Jesus the LORD, is Judge and Lawgiver Who can save and destroy]
Matt. 16:16-18	[God reveals to Peter the office of Messiah Jesus, as the Son of God]
1 Pet. 1:3, 6	[Messiah is our Living Hope; rejoicing in trials brings Messiah into them]
1 Pet. 1:7	[Faith tested by fire brings praise, glory and honor at the revelation of Yeshua Christ]
1 Pet. 1:9-11	[The Spirit of Christ spoke through the prophets about salvation of our souls]
1 Pet. 1:23	[Messiah is our enablement to be born again through His eternal living and abiding Word]

Page 12

Reference	Description
1 Pet. 2:25	[Messiah is the Shepherd and Guardian of our souls]
1 Pet. 2:6, 7	[The Choice Stone, the precious Corner Stone of our belief]
1 Pet. 2:9	[God calls His Own in Christ out of darkness into His light to proclaim God's excellencies]
1 Pet. 2:21	[Messiah our Example]
1 Pet. 2:24, 25	[His wounds healed us through His body on the Cross]
1 Pet. 3:17, 18	[He gave us life through participation in His sufferings]
1 Pet. 1:19-21	[We were redeemed by Messiah's unblemished, spotless blood of eternal glory]
2 Pet. 3:9	[He wants none to perish but for all to come to repentance]
1 Pet. 3:22	[All angels, authorities, and powers are under Messiah's subjection]
2 Pet. 1:16-17JNT	[Witnesses saw Messiah's majesty, honor, and power. God said "This is My beloved Son Whom I love, with Whom I am well pleased."]
1 Pet. 5:14	[Peace be to you all who are in Messiah]
1 Pet. 3:22	[Messiah sits at the right hand of God]
1 John 2:1	[Messiah our Defender and Righteous One]
1 John 3:16	[Messiah lives for us so we must live for others]
1 John 3:23	[Believe in Messiah's name and love one another]
1 John 5:6	[Messiah came in the flesh by water and blood]

IX ~ THE PANORAMA OF HEAVEN   PAGE 27

Page 12 (continued)
1 John 5:20	[Messiah proved He is the True God of Eternal Life]
2 John 1:9	[We are to abide in Messiah's teachings]
Jude 1	[Messiah is our Keeper]
Jude 21	[Christ is our merciful Sovereign Master and LORD of eternal life]
Jude 25	[Messiah is the only God & Savior. Through Jesus our LORD, be Glory, Majesty, Dominion and Authority forever & ever]
Mark 9:1	[Some disciples will not die before seeing the kingdom of God in all of its power]
Mark 9:2-8	[Christ Jesus was transfigured before them]
Acts 7:54-60	[Stephen forgave them ~ He saw the Son of Man in the flesh standing at God's right hand]
1 Pet. 1:3-5	[Heaven is a place of inheritance to be sought and a possession awaiting us]
John 14:1-3	[Jesus went to prepare a place for overcomers]
Heb. 1:3	[As purification for our sins, Messiah the radiance of God, sits at His right hand]

Page 13
Eph. 1:19-23	[The blessings of redemption]
Rev. 21:2-5 KJV	[The New Jerusalem coming from God out of heaven, prepared as a bride for her groom]
Rev. 21:5	[Messiah makes all things new]
Rev. 21:6	[Messiah is the Beginning and the End ~ Messiah gives us the Fountain of Life]
Rev. 21:22, 23	[The God Almighty and the LAMB are the temple ~ "... for the glory of God illumined it, and its lamp is the Lamb."]

Page 14
Poster Page	**HE IS COMING WITH CLOUDS OF GLORY**
Rev. 1:7	[Behold, He is coming with the clouds and every eye shall see Him even those who pierced Him; all the tribes of the earth will mourn because of Him]
Rev. 19:11	[All will see Maschiach Yeshua the Yahweh with the Name Faithful and True written upon Him]
Rev. 19:11	[Messiah riding a white horse in Righteousness]
Rev. 19:11	[Messiah judging and waging war with eyes of flaming fire, wearing many crowns]
Rev. 19:13	[The Sovereign Word of God]
Rev. 19:6	[THE ALMIGHTY!]
Rev. 19:15	[Messiah using the sharp sword from His mouth while on His robe and on His thigh is written King of kings and LORD of LORDS]
Rev. 21:3	[The tabernacle of God among men ~ His people ~ is coming quickly to render His reward]
Rev. 21:6	[The beginning and the end ~ the Alpha and the Omega]

Page 15
Acts 5:29-32 JNT	[Messiah's glory and power; obey God not man; God raised Yeshua and exalted Him at His right hand as Ruler and Savior; Yeshua enabled Israel to repent and turn from their sins and were forgiven; Peter & disciples witnessed these things; the Holy Spirit Whom God gives to those who obey Him]
Acts 7:44-48	[Stephen's response to the Council]
Isa. 66:1, 2	[Heaven is His throne, the earth His footstool]
Acts 6:8-7:55	[excerpts ... Stephen gazed intently into Heaven and said, "Behold I see the glory of God and Jesus standing at the right hand of God."]

Page 16
Acts 7:56-60	[Stephen called upon the LORD, "receive my spirit ... hold not this sin against them." ~ His spirit rose to join Jesus in Heaven]
Rev. 21:6	[LORD Jesus the Messiah is the Alpha and Omega]
Rev. 21:22	[The LORD Jesus Messiah Almighty, and the Lamb are its temple]
Rev. 21:23	[The Glory of God has illumined it and its lamp is the Lamb]
Rev. 21:25	[For there shall be no night there]

PAGE 28   IX ~ THE PANORAMA OF HEAVEN

Page 17
Rom. 10:17   [Faith comes from hearing the message, and the message is heard through the word of Christ]
1 Cor. 12:9   [The gift of faith by the same Spirit]
Eph. 3:4   [Paul writes of the insight into the mystery of Christ]
Eph. 3:8   [Bringing to light administration of the mystery which for ages has been hidden in God, Who created all things]
Eph. 3:10   [Through the church (His body), the manifold wisdom of God (which forms and executes His counsels) is made known to the rulers and authorities in the heavenly realms]
Eph. 3:11   [... in accordance with His eternal purposes that He accomplished in Christ Jesus our LORD]

Page 18
Eph. 1:18-23   [The eyes of our hearts are enlightened to know the Hope of Glory & the riches of His inheritance]
Acts 4:10   [God made the man Jesus both LORD and Christ]
Luke 21:28   [Straighten up, lift up your heads, because your redemption is drawing nigh]

Page 19
Rev. 19:1-9   [The four-fold Hallelujah! The bride is ready ~ These are the true words of God]

AMEN AND HALLELUJAH!

CHRIST the PANORAMA of HEAVEN ENDNOTES

1. A.W. Tozer (1897-1973), *The Knowledge Of The Holy*, (New York, NY: Harper & Row), P.59.

2. W.E. Vine, *The Expanded Vines Expository Dictionary of New Testament Words,* (Minneapolis, MN: Bethany House Publishers, 1940).

   P.182 CHRIST, CHRISTOS, anointed, Messiah, the anointed of God (Ps. 105:15) . . . "It is distinctly a proper name in many passages . . . The single title Christos is sometimes used without the article to signify the ONE Who by His Holy Spirit and power indwells believers and molds their character in conformity to His likeness. The title with the article specifies the Lord Jesus as 'the Christ'; the title without the article stresses His Character and His relationship with believers."

3. Compiled by Anita M. Bailey, A.W. Tozer, *Man The Dwelling Place Of God*, (Camp Hill, PA: Christian Publications, 1966), p. 143.

4. Andrew Murray, *The Spirit of Christ*, (Fort Washington, PA: Christian Literature Crusade, unabridged 1974), p. 256.

5. Ibid. P.271

6. Ibid. P.257

7. Ibid. P.146

8. Marvin R. Vincent, D.D., *Vincent's Word Studies Of The New Testament*, (Peabody, MA: Henderson Publishers, Volume II), p. 32.

9. Charles J. Rolls, *The Indescribable Christ, Names and Titles of Jesus Christ, A-G*, (Neptune, NJ: Loizeaux Brothers, Inc., 1953, revised 1984), pp. 77-78.

10. Vincent, Ibid. Volume II, *The Gospel of John*.

    P.32 As Logos has the double meaning of thought and speech, so Christ is related to God as the word to the idea, the word being not merely a name for the idea, but the idea itself expressed. The thought is the inward word (Dr. Sclaff compares Hebrew expression "I speak in my heart: for 'I think.'")...The Logos of John is the real, personal God (v.1), the Word, who was originally before the creation with God, and was God, one in essence and nature, yet personally distinct (v.1,18); the reader and interpreter of the hidden being of God; the reflection and visible image of God and the organ of all His manifestations to the world. Compare Hebrews 1:3, He made all things, proceeding personally from God for the accomplishment of the act of creation (v.3) and became man in the person of Jesus Christ, accomplishing the redemption of the world.

11. Ibid. P.34
    . . . is often used in the New Testament in the sense of **with**; and that not merely **being near** or **beside**, but as a living union and communion; implying the active notion of intercourse . . . Thus John's statement is that the Divine Word not only abode with the Father from all eternity, but was in the living, active relation of communion with Him.

12. Ibid. PP.33, 35
    The word **God**, used attributively, maintains the personal distinction between God and the Word, but makes the unity of essence and nature to follow the distinction of person, and ascribes to the Word all the attributes of the divine essence. "There is something majestic in the way in which the description of the Logos, in the three brief but great propositions of verse 1, is unfolded with **increasing** fullness" (Meyer).

13. Ibid. P.37
    . . . use of the term **came into being** . . . as distinguished from **were created**, suggests that thought that creation is to be regarded as a manifestation of a divine law of love. Thus creation (all things came into being through Him) answers to the Incarnation (the Word became flesh). All the unfolding and infolding of finite being to the last issue lies in the fulfillment of His will who is love [Westcott, 1 John 2:17].

14. Vincent, Volume. IV, p. 380.

15. Rolls, Ibid. pp.77, 78

16. E. M. Bounds, Edited by David. L. Young, *Catching A Glimpse Of Heaven*, (Springdale, PA: Whitaker House, 1985).

17. Ibid. P.28

18. Ibid. P.43

19. Ibid. P.29

20. Ibid. P.69

21. Ibid. P.13

22. Ibid. P.50

23. Ibid. P.67

24. Mrs. Charles E. Cowman, *Streams In The Desert*, (Grand Rapids, MI: Zondervan Publishing House, 1925).

    P.343 Nov. 8, acknowledging quote from Dr. Charles Parker, in *The Lost Art Of Meditation*.

25. A.W. Tozer, *Man: The Dwelling Place of God*, p. 61.

26. Ibid. PP.49, 51

27. Ibid. P.141

28. Ibid. P.143

ETERNAL FATHER ... STRONG TO SAVE

*"Defend my cause and redeem me;
Preserve my life according to Your promise." Psalm 119:154*

The LORD answers our cries for help. He defends our cause and redeems us according to His promise [Ps. 119:154]. I know. I vividly remember when He redeemed us and preserved Rusty and me from a tragedy. He saved our lives ~ physically and spiritually.

I was sitting in the United States Naval Academy Chapel waiting for my beloved sister Rusty's memorial service, and was deeply moved when I saw above the altar the beautiful Tiffany stained glass of Jesus with His arms outstretched and ETERNAL FATHER STRONG TO SAVE written above Him. That was the confirmation I needed.

The night before, I awoke with the distinct thought that I should share our near tragedy experience during Rusty's Memorial Service. When asked if anyone had anything to share, I went to the pulpit and shared that the last time I had been to the United States Naval Academy Chapel was when I was Maid of Honor at Larry and Rusty Vogt's wedding at his graduation in 1959. Then I shared how just two days before Rusty died we had marveled over our near death experience, the outcome, and how our Father God had saved us. I believed she wanted me to share it.

Our near tragedy happened during the summer of 1948 between my seventh and eighth grade. The day began like a wonderful dream. Our mother took us to the bay area to seine for little shrimp to use as bait. I will never forget the water was smooth as a mirror as we motored several miles out into the Gulf of Mexico in our rowboat with kicker (outboard motor). Mom liked to catch a certain kind of snapper and was convinced that we had to go out far enough to catch them.

I was an unhappy camper. Mother had caught a lot of snappers with her rod and reel while I had not caught anything. Marion (Rusty she is known by) and I were getting hot and bored while I pouted inwardly that I'd never catch a fish with just a bamboo pole. My pole received a terrific yank! I jerked it back and saw an enormous fish erupt from the water and sail over my head then heard Mother shriek in pain! It was petrifying to turn and see a huge catfish thrashing wildly with its fin imbedded in her arm!

The boat rocked wildly back and forth as we struggled for what seemed like eternity to grasp it and pull the slippery catfish's fin out of her right arm. Mother suffered immense pain. Her pitiful groans filled my heart with guilt and grief as the fin's poison spread beyond her rapidly swelling arm before she went into shock . . . in the blink of an eye tranquility changed to chaos!

We were scared to death! (so to speak). We did not know how to start the motor. I tried and tried, but it would not start. Our boat began to rock and Rusty pointed to the white caps that had appeared on the water. Fear of the unknown, combined with the memory of nearly drowning when I was seven years old, added to my terror. I kept trying and trying to start the motor sobbing, "God! Please help us! Save us!"

That weeks' Sunday school memory verse popped into my mind ~ especially the last part of the promise, ". . . that whosoever believeth in Him should not perish, but have everlasting life." Jesus' words pierced to the very depths of my soul and took on a whole new meaning. *I wanted life! I did not want to perish!* [John 3:16 KJV]

"I believeth in You!" I cried out, desperately wanting to live. "Please help us! Save us!"

Calm surrounded the boat and embraced my mind [Ps. 55:16]. I retried the motor ~ *it started!* We shed buckets of tears in awed relief and thanksgiving to God that the motor had started. God had intervened in answer to our cries for help.

As day turned to dusk, I wished that I were at my church revival that night instead of in the Gulf of Mexico. Fear intensified as our boat crept slowly toward the wide and distant shoreline. Evening changed into a moonless night. I couldn't figure out which light was our harbor! Rusty cried out "Barbara, look a storm is coming!" It fast approached and we could see lightening. We were terribly frightened as waves rocked our little boat and it got darker.

"Father God," I cried out desperately, "Please show me where to go ~ I can't tell where to go or which light to head toward! Help me get Mama to shore in time to save her! "I'll go forward tomorrow night and give my life to You!"

A light began to grow brighter and brighter ~ it soon eclipsed all of the other lights and we headed for it. Amazingly, His Light guided us directly to our dock! Providentially, the LORD had people there to take our mother to the hospital where she was normalized and released without complications. God proved that He watches over His Word to perform it! We had prayed His Word and He had preserved us.

As I ended my sharing, I turned to point to the wonderful picture of Jesus with *ETERNAL FATHER STRONG TO SAVE* written above it, and declared, "His Light still guides us Home ~ He will always be our *Eternal Father Strong To Save!"*

God mercifully preserved our lives *according to His promise!* He is incredibly wonderful!

As a post note, the LORD not only saved me physically, *but He saved me spiritually!* I cannot help but chuckle remembering that earlier that day we had seined for bay shrimp for our bait. I did not dream that *The Fisher of Men* was going to use one of those tiny shrimp for "bait" to "catch" this child! Rusty had gone forward the night before and dedicated her life to Christ. I had planned to go to the revival service at our church that night. The very next night I joyfully went to the altar at Palmetto Baptist Church in Florida and dedicated my twelve-year-old heart to God.

That was a turning point in my spiritual journey. Although I did not understand it at the time, the LORD had transplanted His love, mercy, and grace into my heart and began the (ongoing) process of curing my attitudes and actions through the teachings in His Word [Ps. 119:71].

I will always praise God for our neighbors who took me to Sunday School. Christ became a part of my life when I was just a child. I have loved Him ever since I was taught by a Sunday school teacher, when I was three years old, that He had loved me before I was born and would always love me ~ *even if I needed a spanking!* I wanted to please Him, trust Him, and obey Him.

As far back as I can remember my life has been filled with ups and downs, but I always knew that my Father was with me and would help me. It continues to be a pilgrimage of surrendering my heart with thanksgiving for God's love and provisions, versus battling wrong attitudes and actions, then asking for forgiveness. I have long loved the verse that says, "If we confess our sins, that He is faithful and just and will forgive our sins and cleanse us from *all* unrighteousness" [1 John 1:9, emphasis added].

Many years later, I learned that it was up to me to work out my salvation and that I needed to seek God first to learn His revealed will for *all* of the areas of my life ~ then I need to trust Him to show me my part in His ever expanding purposes [Phil. 2:12, 13].

Many can point to a specific time when Jesus saved them and radically changed their lives. I have grown closer to Christ over the years ~ through good times and bad times, illness and health. I cannot remember when I have not prayed and talked to Him since childhood. There is so much to learn about our exhilarating God and so many blessings when we walk and talk in His will.

There are many challenges and occasions in our lives that are opportunities to trust Jesus to defend us, redeem us, and preserve our lives according to His many promises. [Ps. 119:154] Let us grow closer to Him and trust in Him to keep His promises and plans for our lives. Only THE LORD knows what is for our best.

May our LORD bless you and always keep you in the palm of His hand!

Barbara Waddell

BIOGRAPHY OF BARBARA S. WADDELL

Barbara was blessed to be married for 49 ½ years to her late husband, David E. "Gene" Waddell. They have two children, Diane and David, and three precious granddaughters. She resides in Akron, Ohio, winters in La Quinta, California, is a long time member of The Chapel (Akron, Ohio), and affiliate member of the Palm Desert Community Presbyterian Church in the winter.

Barbara currently serves on the Ronald Reagan Ranch Board of Governors and Heartbeat at 22 Board of Directors (Mama's House). She served on the Board of Trustees as Secretary for the American Lung Association of Northern Ohio, the University of Akron's Advisory Board to the School of Education, the Ohio Ballet Board, Summit County Bar Association Auxiliary, and various Christian endeavors, volunteer, civic, and social groups.

She taught *KNOWING GOD IN YOUR HEART* in Silver Lake, Ohio, THE CHAPEL, Akron, Ohio, Palm Desert Community Presbyterian Church in Palm Desert, CA, and Coachella Valley Rescue Mission in Indio, CA. Over the years she has spoken at conferences, taught Bible study groups, given seminars on intercession, the "how to's" for a balanced Christian walk, scriptural meditation, praising God's Hallowed Names, etc.; counseled for 700 Club's Stow, Ohio branch, co-founded Lydia of Ohio (an international prayer fellowship recently renamed A.S.K.), founded Prayer Warriors (a six-state prayer group that prayed for our states and state leaders). In 1990 founded and led the Ohio National Day of Prayer (ONDP) for nine years, taught at National Day of Prayer Conferences and in 1993, along with Valerie Harper, organized Bible Reading Marathons with concurrent Prayer Vigils in 86 of Ohio's 88 counties to proclaim and pray God's Word for local, state, and national spiritual and political leaders. She contributed articles about prayer directives for the International Bible Reading Association, founded by Dr. John Hash, President of Bible Pathway Ministries, and is a graduate of CLASSeminars.

Barbara attended Joe Aldrich's *Call to North American Christian Leaders Prayer Summit* in 1993 to repent and intercede for America, founded Let Us Pray Ministries, Inc., and was a member of the Christian Women Leader's AD 2000 Track (led by Evelyn Christenson, Kay Arthur, and Vonette Bright). In 1994 and 1995, attended Bill and Vonette Bright's (founders of Campus Crusade International) Christian Leadership Fasting and Prayer for America in Orlando, Florida, was one of 21 women delegates for AD2000 North America Women's Track to the Global Consultation On World Evangelization (GCOWE) at Seoul, Korea; was MinWin International Board Prayer Chair (ministry to pastors' wives founded and led by Lynne Dugan); Akron Bar Association Auxiliary Chairman for New Citizens Teas, Meals on Wheels, Bath Volunteers for Service, and Akron Pregnancy Services counselor; among other ministries.

ENDORSEMENTS

"In a word, this volume is superb. The author has managed to touch the heart devotionally, challenge and encourage the daily life motivationally, and stir the mind intellectually and theologically. Her efforts have achieved a wonderful mix and balance making this particular book valuable to everyone from the individual to the teacher, lecturer and pastor. There is a wonderful series of well-organized and beautifully outlined Bible lessons in this book. It is easy to follow, comprehend and teach. I would certainly recommend it to all who want to learn more about the God they love."

~ *Pastor Lynn Warner,* The Chapel, Akron, Ohio

"Having known Barbara Waddell for many years it is a joy and privilege to add my own endorsement for her book. This book and conference textbook is so rich in its spiritual depth. It is permeated with Scripture, which is the source of the wisdom of God. It magnifies our gracious God, Father, Son and Holy Spirit. The person who is so blessed as to obtain a copy will find keys to the Spirit filled life like few books provide. Barbara speaks from her own personal experience of walking an intimate walk with our Lord. When we know certain people who demonstrate the love and loveliness of the Lord Jesus, we know that a book like this one will lead us to a level of spirituality that we can only know by personally putting into practice the things taught in this precious book. The Bible is God's masterpiece of spiritual excellence. Barbara has drawn from it principles and applications that every Christian needs to know and experience. I highly commend this book for your own spiritual good."

~ *Dr. John A. Hash,*
Founder and President Bible Pathway and
International Bible Reading Association.

"I loved reviewing and working on *Knowing God In Your Heart*. The first time it lifted my prayer life and deepened my relationship with God. This time I realized how comprehensive it is. It is jam packed with praise, worship, and warfare tools. The citations from classic authors provide a depth of insight into the explanations. The conversational tone and personal experiences helped me relate to and better understand what the Bible directs us to do. I was blessed listening to the discussion of spiritually mature ladies in our pilot Bible Study and seeing how things impacted them. We had a lot of 'Ah Ha' moments as we discovered things we hadn't known, forgotten or realized before."

~ *Judy Wilfong,* Leader of Pilot Study Group

"I have reviewed the content of the *Knowing God In Your Heart* Bible Study and know it is a biblically based, scripturally sound study. There is a great need for deep sound biblical teaching which this study will provide." ~ *Art McMahon,* Retired History teacher,
Abundant Living 55+ Program Director at The Chapel, Akron, Ohio

"Have you ever wished you could know God better, not just intellectually, but down deep in the recesses of your heart? Barbara Waddell did, and she devised a way to know Him better. Now you can share her insights, and grow in your relationship to Him through her Bible Study. Her depth of knowledge shared in *Knowing God In Your Heart* and years of study have combined to make this a resource you will use over and over again. I know it has for me." ~ *Betty Southard,*
CLASS teaching faculty, Spiritual Director,
Author 3 books, Bible Study teacher for 35 years.

"Working through *Knowing God In Your Heart* has been a learning experience . . . the dedication and perseverance it took to complete this book is remarkable. Thank you for the opportunity to study with such a great group of people. The true life experiences that you have interwoven in these pages made them come alive!
~ *Joan Foor,* Author two books

"WOW! Just when I needed a touch from Him, I would set aside everything to read your manuscript. The beautiful teachings and words gave me knowledge and weaponry and confidence and encouragement. It got so bright in here. I praise God for you and your servanthood in HIM."
~ *Danna Testa*

Knowing God In Your Heart is an anointed, comprehensive Bible Seminar (study) that takes you where you never thought you would go ~ into the very heart of God Himself."   ~ *Lynne Dugan,*
Author of *Heart To Heart With Pastors' Wives*

"My good friend Barbara Waddell has written a marvelous book, *Knowing God In Your Heart.* It is one thing to understand God intellectually but to feel him deep within the recesses of our soul is the goal of all believers. Barbara's book will help move you toward this possibility. In addition to your own study the book is also excellent for small group discussions."   ~ *Ron Glosser,*
CEO Hershey Trust (retired),
Former board member of Guideposts,
Lloyd Ogilvie and Robert Schuller boards.

"I just need to thank you for *Knowing God In Your Heart* study. It was the best study I have ever participated in . . . Somehow we have to be able to get this study in the hands of other Bible studies, it is just too good not to be shared . . . It was life changing."   ~ *Paula Land,* Pilot Study Group

"I am completely overwhelmed. Your work is excellent, most comprehensive, detailed, and directed to one's heart. You've put together a wonderful work . . . A fabulous endeavor. Applause and congratulations!"
~ *Penny Wrobel*

"After reading the manuscript for your study, I was simply overwhelmed and blown away with the thoroughness and comprehensiveness of the text. This copy will make an excellent book and study. The thoroughness in which you cover the various biblical subjects is impressive. Your writing style is easy to comprehend, informative, and entertaining. I would recommend this book to any Christian looking for a more mature understanding of God's love and word."   ~ *Russell D. Sibert,*
Ronald Reagan Ranch Board of Governors
(Journalism background)

Knowing the many names of our God and what they mean has dramatically changed the way I pray and has given me a deep awareness of the vastness of God. Whether I pray to the Lord, Abba the Great Physician, the Messiah. El Shaddai, the Lamb of God or the Holy Spirit, they have all come to have a different meaning to me that I had not deeply considered before studying Knowing God In Your Heart. This study deeply enriched my prayer life.   ~ *Kathy Englhard,*
Palm Desert, California

"I thoroughly enjoyed reviewing the book. The emphasis on the importance of Scripture in our lives (rather than only interpretations of men) in enabling us to have an intimacy with God is made so clear. The book is presented at a level that most could easily understand, yet plumbs the depths and ascends the heights of how to experience God, to know Him in our hearts and have a meaningful prayer life. I thought the teaching and insight's about our thoughts and attitudes is so needful, and how to apply the armor for our inner protection in our spiritual warfare. Your own experiences are helpful in enabling anyone to be able to relate at the human level, they shed light on how to apply scripture for any difficult circumstances in our lives.

"Every lesson is filled with scripture and quotations from solid bible teachers and writers, reinforcing the excellent way that you have presented the Spirit filled life that is available to any who choose to submit to Him, and allow Christ to have first place in our hearts and lives.

"The teaching about the meaning of the many peerless names of God is so good, unfolding God's Old Testament names and those of our Lord Jesus Christ in the New. Christ is exalted throughout the study.

"No one participating in this study should leave without being challenged to have a deeper, more intimate relationship with Christ and to love Him more. I would not hesitate in recommending it to anyone."
~ *William Snyder,* Bible Scholar

"Thank you for your lovely gift, *Knowing God In Your Heart*. I am so impressed as I am moved. I will take the gift home with me and use it in my daily time of worship. I may want to use it in my ministry as well."
~ *Dr. Reverend Dennis Denning,*
Palm Desert Community Presbyterian Church,
Palm Desert, CA

Additional endorsements may be found in www.knowinggodinyourheart.com